D1520964

THE LOEB CLASSICAL LIBRARY

FOUNDED BY JAMES LOEB

EDITED BY

G. P. GOOLD

PREVIOUS EDITORS

T. E. PAGE	E. CAPPS
W. H. D. ROUSE	L. A. POST
E. H. WARMINGTON	

THE GREEK ANTHOLOGY

II

LCL 68

THE GREEK ANTHOLOGY

BOOKS VII–VIII

WITH AN ENGLISH TRANSLATION BY

W. R. PATON

HARVARD UNIVERSITY PRESS
CAMBRIDGE, MASSACHUSETTS
LONDON, ENGLAND

First published 1917
Reprinted 1919, 1925, 1939, 1953, 1960, 1970, 1993

ISBN 0-674-99075-7

Printed in Great Britain by St Edmundsbury Press Ltd,
Bury St Edmunds, Suffolk, on acid-free paper.
Bound by Hunter & Foulis Ltd, Edinburgh, Scotland.

CONTENTS

GREEK ANTHOLOGY

BOOK VII

SEPULCHRAL EPIGRAMS

THE genuine epitaphs (those actually engraved on tomb-stones) in this collection are comparatively few in number. It would be easy to draw up a list of them, but I refrain from this, as there are too many doubtful cases. Those on celebrities are of course all poetical exercises in the form of epitaphs, but a considerable number of those on unknown persons are doubtless the same. In order to appreciate the Greek sepulchral epigram as it was, we should have a selection of those actually preserved on stones. Cephalas has introduced a few copied from stones (330-335, 340, 346), but Meleager, Philippus, and Agathias drew, of course, from literary and not epigraphical sources in forming their anthologies.

Nothing can be less certain than the attributions to the elder poets (Anacreon, Simonides, etc.) in this book : we may be sure that, while they published their lyrics, they did not publish collections of occasional epigrams ; so that the latter are attributed to them merely by hearsay and guess-work. The authorship of the few epigrams (some very beautiful) attributed to Plato is now a matter of dispute, but I think we have no right to deny it, as they are very short and would have survived in memory. The attributions to later writers are doubtless in the main correct—the epigrams of Theocritus being included in MSS. of his works, and derived from such a MS. and not from Meleager, who does not, curiously enough, mention him in his Proem.

Here, as in Book VI, continuous portions of the three chief sources are the exception. Nos. 1-150, epigrams on famous men (chiefly poets and philosophers), could not of course comprise any such. Overlooking shorter fragments, Nos. 194-203,[1] 207-212, 246-273, 296-303, 314-318, 406-529, 535-541, 646-655, 707-740 are from Meleager's Wreath, 183-188, 233-240, 364-405, 622-645, 699-703 are from that of Philippus, and 551-614 from the Cycle of Agathias. Nos. 681-688 are by Palladas.

[1] All on animals, but in the alphabetical order of the first letters, like the fragments of Philippus' Wreath.

ΑΝΘΟΛΟΓΙΑ

Z

ΕΠΙΓΡΑΜΜΑΤΑ ΕΠΙΤΥΜΒΙΑ

1.—ΑΛΚΑΙΟΥ ΜΕΣΣΗΝΙΟΥ

Ἡρώων τὸν ἀοιδὸν Ἴῳ ἔνι παῖδες Ὅμηρον
  ἤκαχον, ἐκ Μουσέων γρῖφον ὑφηνάμενοι·
νέκταρι δ' εἰνάλιαι Νηρηΐδες ἐχρίσαντο,
  καὶ νέκυν ἀκταίῃ θῆκαν ὑπὸ σπιλάδι,
ὅττι Θέτιν κύδηνε καὶ υἱέα, καὶ μόθον ἄλλων   5
  ἡρώων, Ἰθακοῦ τ' ἔργματα Λαρτιάδεω.
ὀλβίστη νήσων πόντῳ Ἴος, ὅττι κέκευθε
  βαιὴ Μουσάων ἀστέρα καὶ Χαρίτων.

2.—ΑΝΤΙΠΑΤΡΟΥ ΣΙΔΩΝΙΟΥ

Τὰν μερόπων Πειθώ, τὸ μέγα στόμα, τὰν ἴσα Μούσαις
  φθεγξαμέναν κεφαλάν, ὦ ξένε, Μαιονίδεω
ἅδ' ἔλαχον νασῖτις Ἴου σπιλάς· οὐ γὰρ ἐν ἄλλᾳ
  ἱερόν, ἀλλ' ἐν ἐμοί, πνεῦμα θανὼν ἔλιπεν,

---

[1] The riddle which Homer, according to the story, could

2

GREEK ANTHOLOGY

BOOK VII

SEPULCHRAL EPIGRAMS

1.—ALCAEUS OF MESSENE

On Homer

In Ios the boys, weaving a riddle[1] at the bidding of
the Muses, vexed to death Homer the singer of the
heroes.   And the Nereids of the sea anointed him
with nectar and laid him dead under the rock on
the shore; because he glorified Thetis and her son
and the battle-din of the other heroes and the deeds
of Odysseus of Ithaca.   Blessed among the islands
in the sea is Ios, for small though she be, she covers
the star of the Muses and Graces.

2.—ANTIPATER OF SIDON

On the Same

O stranger, it is granted to me, this island rock
of Ios, to hold Maeonides, the Persuader of men, the
mighty-voiced, who sang even as the Muses.   For in
no other island but in me did he leave, when he died,
the holy breath with which he told of the almighty

not guess was: "What we caught we left, what we did not
catch we bring," *i.e.* lice.

3

ᾧ νεῦμα Κρονίδαο τὸ παγκρατές, ᾧ καὶ Ὄλυμπον   5
καὶ τὰν Αἴαντος ναύμαχον εἶπε βίαν,
καὶ τὸν Ἀχιλλείοις Φαρσαλίσιν Ἕκτορα πώλοις
ὀστέα Δαρδανικῷ δρυπτόμενον πεδίῳ.
εἰ δ᾽ ὀλίγα κρύπτω τὸν ταλίκον, ἴσθ᾽ ὅτι κεύθει
καὶ Θέτιδος γαμέταν ἁ βραχύβωλος Ἴκος.   10

2 B.—ΑΛΛΟ

Εἰ καὶ βαιὸς ὁ τύμβος, ὁδοιπόρε, μή με παρέλθῃς,
ἀλλὰ κατασπείσας, ἴσα θεοῖσι σέβου·
τὸν γὰρ Πιερίδεσσι τετιμένον ἔξοχα Μούσαις
ποιητὴν ἐπέων θεῖον Ὅμηρον ἔχω.

3.—ΑΔΗΛΟΝ

Ἐνθάδε τὴν ἱερὴν κεφαλὴν κατὰ γαῖα καλύπτει,
ἀνδρῶν ἡρώων κοσμήτορα, θεῖον Ὅμηρον.

4.—ΠΑΥΛΟΥ ΣΙΛΕΝΤΙΑΡΙΟΥ

Ἐνθάδε Πιερίδων τὸ σοφὸν στόμα, θεῖον Ὅμηρον,
κλεινὸς ἐπ᾽ ἀγχιάλῳ τύμβος ἔχει σκοπέλῳ.
εἰ δ᾽ ὀλίγη γεγαυῖα τόσον χάδεν ἀνέρα νῆσος,
μὴ τόδε θαμβήσῃς, ὦ ξένε, δερκόμενος·
καὶ γὰρ ἀλητεύουσα κασιγνήτη ποτὲ Δῆλος   5
μητρὸς ἀπ᾽ ὠδίνων δέξατο Λητοΐδην.

4

nod of Zeus, and of Olympus, and of the strength
of Ajax fighting for the ships, and of Hector his
flesh stripped from his bones by the Thessalian horses
of Achilles that dragged him over the plain of Troy.
If thou marvellest that I who am so small cover so
great a man, know that the spouse of Thetis like-
wise lies in Ikos that hath but a few clods of
earth.

2 B.—Anonymous

On the Same

Wayfarer, though the tomb be small, pass me not
by, but pour on me a libation, and venerate me as
thou dost the gods. For I hold divine Homer the
poet of the epic, honoured exceedingly by the Pierian
Muses.

3.—Anonymous

On the Same

Here the earth covereth the sacred man, divine
Homer, the marshaller of the heroes.

4.—PAULUS SILENTIARIUS

On the Same

Here the famous tomb on the rock by the sea
holdeth divine Homer, the skilled mouth by which
the Muses spoke. Wonder not, O stranger, as thou
lookest, if so little an island can contain so great a
man. For my sister Delos, while she wandered yet
on the waves, received Apollo from his mother's
womb.

5

5.—ΑΔΗΛΟΝ, οἱ δὲ φασὶν ΑΛΚΑΙΟΥ

Οὐδ' εἴ με χρύσειον ἀπὸ ῥαιστῆρος Ὅμηρον
  στήσητε φλογέαις ἐν Διὸς ἀστεροπαῖς,
οὐκ εἴμ' οὐδ' ἔσομαι Σαλαμίνιος, οὐδ' ὁ Μέλητος
  Δμησαγόρου· μὴ ταῦτ' ὄμμασιν Ἑλλὰς ἴδοι.
ἄλλον ποιητὴν βασανίζετε· τἀμὰ δέ, Μοῦσαι   5
  καὶ Χίος, Ἑλλήνων παισὶν ἀείσετ' ἔπη.

6.—ΑΝΤΙΠΑΤΡΟΥ ΣΙΔΩΝΙΟΥ

Ἡρώων κάρυκ' ἀρετᾶς, μακάρων δὲ προφήταν,
  Ἑλλάνων βιοτᾷ δεύτερον ἀέλιον,
Μουσῶν φέγγος Ὅμηρον, ἀγήραντον στόμα κόσμου
  παντός, ἁλιρροθία, ξεῖνε, κέκευθε κόνις.

7.—ΑΛΛΟ

Ἐνθάδε θεῖος Ὅμηρος, ὃς Ἑλλάδα πᾶσαν ἄεισε,
  Θήβης ἐκγεγαὼς τῆς ἑκατονταπύλου.

8.—ΑΝΤΙΠΑΤΡΟΥ ΣΙΔΩΝΙΟΥ

Οὐκέτι θελγομένας, Ὀρφεῦ, δρύας, οὐκέτι πέτρας
  ἄξεις, οὐ θηρῶν αὐτονόμους ἀγέλας·
οὐκέτι κοιμάσεις ἀνέμων βρόμον, οὐχὶ χάλαζαν,
  οὐ νιφετῶν συρμούς, οὐ παταγεῦσαν ἅλα.

---

[1] To call himself yours.
[2] This epigram is not meant to be sepulchral, but refers to

5.—Uncertain, by Some Attributed to ALCAEUS
On the Same

No, not even if ye set me, Homer, up all of beaten gold in the burning lightning of Zeus, I am not and will not be a Salaminian, I the son of Meles will not be the son of Dmesagoras ; let not Greece look on that. Tempt some other poet,[1] but it is thou, Chios, who with the Muses shalt sing my verses to the sons of Hellas.[2]

6.—ANTIPATER OF SIDON
On the Same

O stranger, the sea-beat earth covers Homer, the herald of the heroes' valour, the spokesman of the gods, a second sun to the life of the Greeks, the light of the Muses, the mouth that groweth not old of the whole world.

7.—Anonymous
On the Same

Here is divine Homer, who sang of all Hellas, born in Thebes of the hundred gates.[3]

8.—ANTIPATER OF SIDON
On the poet Orpheus, son of Oeagrus and Calliope

No more, Orpheus, shalt thou lead the charmed oaks and rocks and the shepherdless herds of wild beasts. No more shalt thou lull to sleep the howling winds and the hail, and the drifting snow, and

a statue of Homer at Salamis in Cyprus, one of the towns which claimed his parentage.

[3] *i.e.* Egyptian Thebes, which also claimed to be his birth-place.

ὤλεο γάρ· σὲ δὲ πολλὰ κατωδύραντο θύγατρες   5
  Μναμοσύνας, μάτηρ δ' ἔξοχα Καλλιόπα.
τί φθιμένοις στοναχεῦμεν ἐφ' υἱάσιν, ἁνίκ' ἀλαλκεῖν
  τῶν παίδων Ἀΐδην οὐδὲ θεοῖς δύναμις ;

9.—ΔΑΜΑΓΗΤΟΥ

Ὀρφέα Θρηϊκίῃσι παρὰ προμολῇσιν Ὀλύμπου
  τύμβος ἔχει, Μούσης υἱέα Καλλιόπης,
ᾧ δρύες οὐκ ἀπίθησαν, ὅτῳ σὺν ἅμ' ἕσπετο πέτρη
  ἄψυχος, θηρῶν θ' ὑλονόμων ἀγέλα,
ὅς ποτε καὶ τελετὰς μυστηρίδας εὕρετο Βάκχου,   5
  καὶ στίχον ἡρῴῳ ζευκτὸν ἔτευξε ποδί,
ὃς καὶ ἀμειλίκτοιο βαρὺ Κλυμένοιο νόημα
  καὶ τὸν ἀκήλητον θυμὸν ἔθελξε λύρᾳ.

10.—ΑΔΗΛΟΝ

Καλλιόπης Ὀρφῆα καὶ Οἰάγροιο θανόντα
  ἔκλαυσαν ξανθαὶ μυρία Βιστονίδες·
στικτοὺς δ' ἡμάξαντο βραχίονας, ἀμφιμελαίνῃ
  δευόμεναι σποδιῇ Θρηΐκιον πλόκαμον·
καὶ δ' αὐταὶ στοναχεῦντι σὺν εὐφόρμιγγι Λυκείῳ   5
  ἔρρηξαν Μοῦσαι δάκρυα Πιερίδες,
μυρόμεναι τὸν ἀοιδόν· ἐπωδύραντο δὲ πέτραι
  καὶ δρύες, ἃς ἐρατῇ τὸ πρὶν ἔθελγε λύρῃ.

11.—ΑΣΚΛΗΠΙΑΔΟΥ

Ὁ γλυκὺς Ἠρίννης οὗτος πόνος, οὐχὶ πολὺς μέν,
  ὡς ἂν παρθενικᾶς ἐννεακαιδεκέτευς,

the roaring sea. For dead thou art; and the
daughters of Mnemosyne bewailed thee much, and
before all thy mother Calliope.   Why sigh we for
our dead sons, when not even the gods have power
to protect their children from death?

9.—DAMAGETUS

On the Same

THE tomb on the Thracian skirts of Olympus holds
Orpheus, son of the Muse Calliope; whom the trees
disobeyed not and the lifeless rocks followed, and
the herds of the forest beasts; who discovered the
mystic rites of Bacchus, and first linked verse in
heroic feet; who charmed with his lyre even the
heavy sense of the implacable Lord of Hell, and his
unyielding wrath.

10.—ANONYMOUS

On the Same

THE fair-haired daughters of Bistonia shed a thou-
sand tears for Orpheus dead, the son of Calliope and
Oeagrus; they stained their tattooed arms with blood,
and dyed their Thracian locks with black ashes.
The very Muses of Pieria, with Apollo, the master
of the lute, burst into tears mourning for the singer,
and the rocks moaned, and the trees, that erst he
charmed with his lovely lyre.

11.—ASCLEPIADES

On Erinna (inscribed on a Volume of her Poems)

THIS is the sweet work of Erinna, not great indeed
in volume, as being that of a maiden of nineteen,

ἀλλ' ἑτέρων πολλῶν δυνατώτερος· εἰ δ' Ἀΐδας μοι
μὴ ταχὺς ἦλθε, τίς ἂν ταλίκον ἔσχ' ὄνομα;

J. H. Merivale, in *Collections from the Greek Anthology*,
1833, p. 205 ; J. A. Symonds the younger, in *Studies of the
Greek Poets*, ii. p. 305.

12.—ΑΔΗΛΟΝ

Ἄρτι λοχευομένην σε μελισσοτόκων ἔαρ ὕμνων,
  ἄρτι δὲ κυκνείῳ φθεγγομένην στόματι,
ἤλασεν εἰς Ἀχέροντα διὰ πλατὺ κῦμα καμόντων
  Μοῖρα, λινοκλώστου δεσπότις ἠλακάτης·
σὸς δ' ἐπέων, Ἤριννα, καλὸς πόνος οὔ σε γεγωνεῖ   5
  φθίσθαι, ἔχειν δὲ χοροὺς ἄμμιγα Πιερίσιν.

13.—ΛΕΩΝΙΔΟΥ, οἱ δὲ ΜΕΛΕΑΓΡΟΥ

Παρθενικὰν νεάοιδον ἐν ὑμνοπόλοισι μέλισσαν
  Ἤριναν, Μουσῶν ἄνθεα δρεπτομέναν,
Ἄδας εἰς ὑμέναιον ἀνάρπασεν. ἦ ῥα τόδ' ἔμφρων
  εἶπ' ἐτύμως ἁ παῖς· "Βάσκανος ἔσσ', Ἀΐδα."

14.—ΑΝΤΙΠΑΤΡΟΥ ΣΙΔΩΝΙΟΥ

Σαπφώ τοι κεύθεις, χθὼν Αἰολί, τὰν μετὰ Μούσαις
  ἀθανάταις θνατὰν Μοῦσαν ἀειδομέναν,
ἂν Κύπρις καὶ Ἔρως συνάμ' ἔτραφον, ἇς μέτα Πειθὼ
  ἔπλεκ' ἀείζωον Πιερίδων στέφανον,
Ἑλλάδι μὲν τέρψιν, σοὶ δὲ κλέος. ὦ τριέλικτον   5
  Μοῖραι δινεῦσαι νῆμα κατ' ἠλακάτας,
πῶς οὐκ ἐκλώσασθε πανάφθιτον ἦμαρ ἀοιδῷ
  ἄφθιτα μησαμένα δῶρ' Ἑλικωνιάδων ;

A. Lang, *Grass of Parnassus*, ed 2, p 173.

but greater in power than that of many others. If
Death had not come early to me, who would have
had such a name?

12.—Anonymous
On the Same

Just as thou wast giving birth to the spring of thy
honeyed hymns, and beginning to sing with thy
swan-like voice, Fate, mistress of the distaff that
spins the thread, bore thee over the wide lake of
the dead to Acheron. But the beautiful work,
Erinna, of thy verse cries aloud that thou art not
dead, but joinest in the dance of the Muses.

13.—LEONIDAS or MELEAGER
On the Same

As Erinna, the maiden honey-bee, the new singer
in the poets' quire, was gathering the flowers of the
Muses, Hades carried her off to wed her. That was
a true word, indeed, the girl spoke when she lived:
"Hades, thou art an envious god."

14.—ANTIPATER OF SIDON
On Sappho

O Aeolian land, thou coverest Sappho, who with
the immortal Muses is celebrated as the mortal Muse;
whom Cypris and Eros together reared, with whom
Peitho wove the undying wreath of song, a joy to
Hellas and a glory to thee. O ye Fates twirling the
triple thread on the spindle, why spun ye not an
everlasting life for the singer who devised the
deathless gifts of the Muses of Helicon?

15.—ΑΝΤΙΠΑΤΡΟΥ

Οὔνομά μευ Σαπφώ. τόσσον δ' ὑπερέσχον ἀοιδὰν
θηλειᾶν, ἀνδρῶν ὅσσον ὁ Μαιονίδας.

16.—ΠΙΝΥΤΟΥ

Ὀστέα μὲν καὶ κωφὸν ἔχει τάφος οὔνομα Σαπφοῦς·
αἱ δὲ σοφαὶ κείνης ῥήσιες ἀθάνατοι.

17.—ΤΥΛΛΙΟΥ ΛΑΤΡΕΑ

Αἰολικὸν παρὰ τύμβον ἰών, ξένε, μή με θανοῦσαν
τὰν Μυτιληναίαν ἔννεπ' ἀοιδοπόλον·
τόνδε γὰρ ἀνθρώπων ἔκαμον χέρες· ἔργα δὲ φωτῶν
ἐς ταχινὴν ἔρρει τοιάδε ληθεδόνα.
ἢν δέ με Μουσάων ἐτάσῃς χάριν, ὧν ἀφ' ἑκάστης   5
δαίμονος ἄνθος ἐμῇ θῆκα παρ' ἐννεάδι,
γνώσεαι ὡς Ἀΐδεω σκότον ἔκφυγον· οὐδέ τις ἔσται
τῆς λυρικῆς Σαπφοῦς νώνυμος ἠέλιος.

18.—ΑΝΤΙΠΑΤΡΟΥ ΘΕΣΣΑΛΟΝΙΚΕΩΣ

Ἀνέρα μὴ πέτρῃ τεκμαίρεο. λιτὸς ὁ τύμβος
ὀφθῆναι, μεγάλου δ' ὀστέα φωτὸς ἔχει.
εἰδήσεις Ἀλκμᾶνα, λύρης ἐλατῆρα Λακαίνης
ἔξοχον, ὃν Μουσέων ἐννέ' ἀριθμὸς ἔχει·
κεῖται δ' ἠπείροις διδύμοις ἔρις, εἴθ' ὅγε Λυδός,   5
εἴτε Λάκων· πολλαὶ μητέρες ὑμνοπόλων.

15.—ANTIPATER

On the Same

MY name is Sappho, and I excelled all women in song as much as Maeonides excelled men.

16.—PINYTUS

On the Same

THE tomb holds the bones and the dumb name of Sappho, but her skilled words are immortal.

17.—TULLIUS LAUREAS

On the Same

WHEN thou passest, O stranger, by the Aeolian tomb, say not that I, the Lesbian poetess, am dead. This tomb was built by the hands of men, and such works of mortals are lost in swift oblivion. But if thou enquirest about me for the sake of the Muses, from each of whom I took a flower to lay beside my nine flowers of song,[1] thou shalt find that I escaped the darkness of death, and that no sun shall dawn and set without memory of lyric Sappho.

18.—ANTIPATER OF THESSALONICA

On Alcman

Do not judge the man by the stone. Simple is the tomb to look on, but holds the bones of a great man. Thou shalt know Alcman the supreme striker of the Laconian lyre, possessed by the nine Muses. Here resteth he, a cause of dispute to two continents, if he be a Lydian or a Spartan. Minstrels have many mothers.

---

[1] *i.e.* books of verse.

19.—ΛΕΩΝΙΔΟΥ

Τὸν χαρίεντ' Ἀλκμᾶνα, τὸν ὑμνητῆρ' ὑμεναίων
κύκνον, τὸν Μουσῶν ἄξια μελψάμενον,
τύμβος ἔχει, Σπάρτας μεγάλαν χάριν, †εἴθ' ὅ γε λοῖσθος
ἄχθος ἀπορρίψας οἴχεται εἰς Ἀΐδαν.

20.—ΑΔΕΣΠΟΤΟΝ

Ἐσβέσθης, γηραιὲ Σοφόκλεες, ἄνθος ἀοιδῶν,
οἰνωπὸν Βάκχου βότρυν ἐρεπτόμενος.

21.—ΣΙΜΙΟΥ

Τὸν σὲ χοροῖς μέλψαντα Σοφοκλέα, παῖδα Σοφίλλου,
τὸν τραγικῆς Μούσης ἀστέρα Κεκρόπιον,
πολλάκις ὃν θυμέλῃσι καὶ ἐν σκηνῇσι τεθηλὼς
βλαισὸς Ἀχαρνίτης κισσὸς ἔρεψε κόμην,
τύμβος ἔχει καὶ γῆς ὀλίγον μέρος· ἀλλ' ὁ περισσὸς   5
αἰὼν ἀθανάτοις δέρκεται ἐν σελίσιν.

22.—ΤΟΥ ΑΥΤΟΥ

Ἠρέμ' ὑπὲρ τύμβοιο Σοφοκλέος, ἠρέμα, κισσέ,
ἑρπύζοις, χλοεροὺς ἐκπροχέων πλοκάμους,
καὶ πέταλον πάντη θάλλοι ῥόδου, ἥ τε φιλορρὼξ
ἄμπελος, ὑγρὰ πέριξ κλήματα χευαμένη,
εἵνεκεν εὐεπίης πινυτόφρονος, ἣν ὁ μελιχρὸς   5
ἤσκησ' ἐκ Μουσέων ἄμμιγα καὶ Χαρίτων.

19.—LEONIDAS (OF ALEXANDRIA ?)
On the Same

ALCMAN the graceful, the swan-singer of wedding hymns, who made music worthy of the Muses, lieth in this tomb, a great ornament to Sparta, or perhaps at the last he threw off his burden and went to Hades.

(*The last couplet is quite obscure as it stands.*)

20.—ANONYMOUS
On Sophocles

THY light is out, aged Sophocles, flower of poets, crowned with the purple clusters of Bacchus.

21.—SIMIAS
On the Same

O SOPHOCLES, son of Sophillus, singer of choral odes, Attic star of the tragic Muse, whose locks the curving ivy of Acharnae often crowned in the orchestra and on the stage, a tomb and a little portion of earth hold thee; but thy exquisite life shines yet in thy immortal pages.

22.—BY THE SAME
On the Same

GENTLY over the tomb of Sophocles, gently creep, O ivy, flinging forth thy green curls, and all about let the petals of the rose bloom, and the vine that loves her fruit shed her pliant tendrils around, for the sake of that wise-hearted beauty of diction that the Muses and Graces in common bestowed on the sweet singer.

23.—ΑΝΤΙΠΑΤΡΟΥ ΣΙΔΩΝΙΟΥ

Θάλλοι τετρακόρυμβος, Ἀνάκρεον, ἀμφὶ σὲ κισσός,
    ἁβρά τε λειμώνων πορφυρέων πέταλα·
πηγαὶ δ' ἀργινόεντος ἀναθλίβοιντο γάλακτος,
    εὐῶδες δ' ἀπὸ γῆς ἡδὺ χέοιτο μέθυ,
ὄφρα κέ τοι σποδιή τε καὶ ὀστέα τέρψιν ἄρηται,   5
    εἰ δή τις φθιμένοις χρίμπτεται εὐφροσύνα.

23 B.—ΕΙΣ ΤΟΝ ΑΥΤΟΝ

Ὦ τὸ φίλον στέρξας, φίλε, βάρβιτον, ὦ σὺν ἀοιδᾷ
    πάντα διαπλώσας καὶ σὺν ἔρωτι βίον.

24.—ΣΙΜΩΝΙΔΟΥ

Ἡμερὶ πανθέλκτειρα, μεθυτρόφε, μῆτερ ὀπώρας,
    οὔλης ἣ σκολιὸν πλέγμα φύεις ἕλικος,
Τηΐου ἡβήσειας Ἀνακρείοντος ἐπ' ἄκρῃ
    στήλῃ καὶ λεπτῷ χώματι τοῦδε τάφου,
ὡς ὁ φιλάκρητός τε καὶ οἰνοβαρὴς φιλοκώμοις   5
    παννυχίσιν κρούων τὴν φιλόπαιδα χέλυν,
κἠν χθονὶ πεπτηώς, κεφαλῆς ἐφύπερθε φέροιτο
    ἀγλαὸν ὡραίων βότρυν ἀπ' ἀκρεμόνων,
καί μιν ἀεὶ τέγγοι νοτερὴ δρόσος, ἧς ὁ γεραιὸς
    λαρότερον μαλακῶν ἔπνεεν ἐκ στομάτων.   10

25.—ΤΟΥ ΑΥΤΟΥ

Οὗτος Ἀνακρείοντα, τὸν ἄφθιτον εἵνεκα Μουσέων
    ὑμνοπόλον, πάτρης τύμβος ἔδεκτο Τέω,

23.—ANTIPATER OF SIDON

On Anacreon

LET the four-clustered ivy, Anacreon, flourish around thee, and the tender flowers of the purple meadows, and let fountains of white milk bubble up, and sweet-smelling wine gush from the earth, so that thy ashes and bones may have joy, if indeed any delight toucheth the dead.

23 B.—ANONYMOUS

On the Same

O BELOVED who didst love the clear lute, O thou who didst sail through thy whole life with song and with love.

24.—SIMONIDES (?)

On the Same

O VINE who soothest all, nurse of wine, mother of the grape, thou who dost put forth thy web of curling tendrils, flourish green in the fine soil and climb up the pillar of the grave of Teian Anacreon ; that he, the reveller heavy with wine, playing all through the night on his lad-loving lyre, may even as he lies low in earth have the glorious ripe clusters hanging from the branches over his head, and that he may be ever steeped in the dew that scented the old man's tender lips so sweetly.

25.—BY THE SAME (?)

On the Same

IN this tomb of Teos, his home, was Anacreon laid, the singer whom the Muses made deathless, who

17

ὃς Χαρίτων πνείοντα μέλη, πνείοντα δ' Ἐρώτων,
τὸν γλυκὺν ἐς παίδων ἵμερον ἡρμόσατο.
μοῦνος δ' εἰν Ἀχέροντι βαρύνεται, οὐχ ὅτι λείπων   5
ἠέλιον, Λήθης ἐνθάδ' ἔκυρσε δόμων·
ἀλλ' ὅτι τὸν χαρίεντα μετ' ἠϊθέοισι Μεγιστέα,
καὶ τὸν Σμερδίεω Θρῆκα λέλοιπε πόθον.
μολπῆς δ' οὐ λήγει μελιτερπέος, ἀλλ' ἔτ' ἐκεῖνον
βάρβιτον οὐδὲ θανὼν εὔνασεν εἰν Ἀΐδῃ.   10

26.—ΑΝΤΙΠΑΤΡΟΥ ΣΙΔΩΝΙΟΥ

Ξεῖνε, τάφον παρὰ λιτὸν Ἀνακρείοντος ἀμείβων,
εἴ τί τοι ἐκ βίβλων ἦλθεν ἐμῶν ὄφελος,
σπεῖσον ἐμῇ σποδιῇ σπεῖσον γάνος, ὄφρα κεν οἴνῳ
ὀστέα γηθήσῃ τἀμὰ νοτιζόμενα,
ὡς ὁ Διωνύσου μεμελημένος εὐάσι κώμοις,   5
ὡς ὁ φιλακρήτου σύντροφος ἁρμονίης
μηδὲ καταφθίμενος Βάκχου δίχα τοῦτον ὑποίσω
τὸν γενεῇ μερόπων χῶρον ὀφειλόμενον.

27.—ΤΟΥ ΑΥΤΟΥ

Εἴης ἐν μακάρεσσιν, Ἀνάκρεον, εὖχος Ἰώνων,
μήτ' ἐρατῶν κώμων ἄνδιχα, μήτε λύρης·
ὑγρὰ δὲ δερκομένοισιν ἐν ὄμμασιν οὖλον ἀείδοις,
αἰθύσσων λιπαρῆς ἄνθος ὕπερθε κόμης,
ἠὲ πρὸς Εὐρυπύλην τετραμμένος, ἠὲ Μεγιστῆ,   5
ἢ Κίκονα Θρηκὸς Σμερδίεω πλόκαμον,
ἡδὺ μέθυ βλύζων, ἀμφίβροχος εἵματα Βάκχῳ,
ἄκρητον λείβων νέκταρ ἀπὸ στολίδων.
τρισσοῖς γάρ, Μούσαισι, Διωνύσῳ καὶ Ἔρωτι,
πρέσβυ, κατεσπείσθη πᾶς ὁ τεὸς βίοτος.   10

set to the sweet love of lads measures breathing of
the Graces, breathing of Love. Alone in Acheron he
grieves not that he has left the sun and dwelleth
there in the house of Lethe, but that he has left
Megisteus, graceful above all the youth, and his
passion for Thracian Smerdies. Yet never doth he
desist from song delightful as honey, and even in
Hades he hath not laid that lute to rest.

26.—ANTIPATER OF SIDON

On the Same

STRANGER who passest by the simple tomb of Ana-
creon, if any profit came to thee from my books,
pour on my ashes, pour some drops, that my bones
may rejoice refreshed with wine, that I who de-
lighted in the loud-voiced revels of Dionysus, I who
dwelt amid such music as loveth wine, even in death
may not suffer without Bacchus my sojourn in this
land to which all the sons of men must come.

27.—BY THE SAME

On the Same

ANACREON, glory of Ionia, mayest thou among the
dead be not without thy beloved revels, or without
thy lyre, and still mayest thou sing with swimming
eyes, shaking the entwined flowers that rest on thy
essenced hair, turned towards Eurypyle, or Megisteus,
or the locks of Thracian Smerdies, spouting sweet
wine, thy robe drenched with the juice of the grape,
wringing untempered nectar from its folds. For all
thy life, O old man, was poured out as an offering to
these three, the Muses, Bacchus, and Love.

28.—ΑΔΕΣΠΟΤΟΝ

Ὦ ξένε, τόνδε τάφον τὸν Ἀνακρείοντος ἀμείβων,
  σπεῖσόν μοι παριών· εἰμὶ γὰρ οἰνοπότης.

29.—ΑΝΤΙΠΑΤΡΟΥ ΣΙΔΩΝΙΟΥ

Εὕδεις ἐν φθιμένοισιν, Ἀνάκρεον, ἐσθλὰ πονήσας,
  εὕδει δ᾽ ἡ γλυκερὴ νυκτιλάλος κιθάρη·
εὕδει καὶ Σμέρδις, τὸ Πόθων ἔαρ, ᾧ σὺ μελίσδων
  βάρβιτ᾽ ἀνεκρούου νέκταρ ἐναρμόνιον.
ἠίθέων γὰρ Ἔρωτος ἔφυς σκοπός· εἰς δὲ σὲ μοῦνον   5
  τόξα τε καὶ σκολιὰς εἶχεν ἐκηβολίας.

30.—ΤΟΥ ΑΥΤΟΥ

Τύμβος Ἀνακρείοντος· ὁ Τήιος ἐνθάδε κύκνος
  εὕδει, χἠ παίδων ζωροτάτη μανίη.
ἀκμὴν οἱ λυρόεν τι μελίζεται ἀμφὶ Βαθύλλῳ
  ἵμερα, καὶ κισσοῦ λευκὸς ὄδωδε λίθος.
οὐδ᾽ Ἀΐδης σοι ἔρωτας ἀπέσβεσεν, ἐν δ᾽ Ἀχέροντος   5
  ὢν ὅλος ὠδίνεις Κύπριδι θερμοτέρῃ.

31.—ΔΙΟΣΚΟΡΙΔΟΥ

Σμερδίη ὦ ἐπὶ Θρηκὶ τακεὶς καὶ ἐπ᾽ ἔσχατον ὀστεῦν,
  κώμου καὶ πάσης κοίρανε παννυχίδος,

28.—ANONYMOUS

On the Same

O STRANGER, who passest this tomb of Anacreon, pour a libation to me in going by, for I am a wine-bibber.

29.—ANTIPATER OF SIDON

On the Same

THOU sleepest among the dead, Anacreon, thy good day's labour done; thy sweet lyre that talked all through the night sleepeth too. And Smerdies sleeps, the spring-tide of the Loves, to whom, striking the lyre, thou madest music like unto nectar. For thou wast the target of Love, the Love of lads, and to shoot thee alone he had a bow and subtle archer craft.

30.—BY THE SAME

On the Same

THIS is Anacreon's tomb; here sleeps the Teian swan and the untempered madness of his passion for lads. Still singeth he some song of longing to the lyre about Bathyllus, and the white marble is perfumed with ivy. Not even death has quenched thy loves, and in the house of Acheron thou sufferest all through thee the pangs of the fever of Cypris.

31.—DIOSCORIDES

On the Same

O ANACREON, delight of the Muses, lord of all revels of the night, thou who wast melted to the

τερπνότατε Μούσῃσιν Ἀνάκρεον, ὦ ’πὶ Βαθύλλῳ
  χλωρὸν ὑπὲρ κυλίκων πολλάκι δάκρυ χέας,
αὐτόματαί τοι κρῆναι ἀναβλύζοιεν ἀκρήτου,   5
  κἠκ μακάρων προχοαὶ νέκταρος ἀμβροσίου·
αὐτόματοι δὲ φέροιεν ἴον, τὸ φιλέσπερον ἄνθος,
  κῆποι, καὶ μαλακῇ μύρτα τρέφοιτο δρόσῳ·
ὄφρα καὶ ἐν Δηοῦς οἰνωμένος ἁβρὰ χορεύσῃς,
  βεβληκὼς χρυσέην χεῖρας ἐπ’ Εὐρυπύλην.   10

32.—ΙΟΥΛΙΑΝΟΥ ΑΠΟ ΥΠΑΡΧΩΝ ΑΙΓΥΠΤΟΥ

Πολλάκι μὲν τόδ’ ἄεισα, καὶ ἐκ τύμβου δὲ βοήσω·
  “ Πίνετε, πρὶν ταύτην ἀμφιβάλησθε κόνιν.”

33.—ΤΟΥ ΑΥΤΟΥ

α. Πολλὰ πιὼν τέθνηκας, Ἀνάκρεον.   β. Ἀλλὰ
    τρυφήσας·
καὶ σὺ δὲ μὴ πίνων ἵξεαι εἰς Ἀΐδην.

34.—ΑΝΤΙΠΑΤΡΟΥ ΣΙΔΩΝΙΟΥ

Πιερικὰν σάλπιγγα, τὸν εὐαγέων βαρὺν ὕμνων
  χαλκευτάν, κατέχει Πίνδαρον ἅδε κόνις,
οὗ μέλος εἰσαΐων φθέγξαιό κεν, ὡς ἀπὸ Μουσῶν
  ἐν Κάδμου θαλάμοις σμῆνος ἀπεπλάσατο.

marrow of thy bones for Thracian Smerdies, O thou
who often bending o'er the cup didst shed warm tears
for Bathyllus, may founts of wine bubble up for thee
unbidden, and streams of ambrosial nectar from the
gods; unbidden may the gardens bring thee violets,
the flowers that love the evening, and myrtles grow
for thee nourished by tender dew, so that even in
the house of Demeter thou mayest dance deli-
cately in thy cups, holding golden Eurypyle in
thy arms.

32.—JULIANUS, PREFECT OF EGYPT
On the Same

OFTEN I sung this, and I will cry it from the tomb,
" Drink ere ye put on this garment of the dust."

33.—BY THE SAME
On the Same

A. "You died of drinking too much, Anacreon."
B. "Yes, but I enjoyed it, and you who do not drink
will come to Hades too."

34.—ANTIPATER OF SIDON
On Pindar

THIS earth holds Pindar, the Pierian trumpet, the
heavily smiting smith of well-outlined hymns, whose
melody when thou hearest thou wouldst exclaim that
a swarm of bees from the Muses fashioned it in the
bridal chamber of Cadmus.

35.—ΛΕΩΝΙΔΟΤ

Ἄρμενος ἦν ξείνοισιν ἀνὴρ ὅδε καὶ φίλος ἀστοῖς,
Πίνδαρος, εὐφώνων Πιερίδων πρόπολος.

36.—ΕΡΤΚΙΟΤ

Αἰεί τοι λιπαρῷ ἐπὶ σήματι, δῖε Σοφόκλεις,
    σκηνίτης μαλακοὺς κισσὸς ἅλοιτο πόδας,
αἰεί τοι βούπαισι περιστάζοιτο μελίσσαις
    τύμβος, Ὑμηττείῳ λειβόμενος μέλιτι,
ὡς ἄν τοι ῥείη μὲν ἀεὶ γάνος Ἀτθίδι δέλτῳ   5
    κηρός, ὑπὸ στεφάνοις δ' αἰὲν ἔχῃς πλοκάμους.

37.—ΔΙΟΣΚΟΡΙΔΟΤ

a. Τύμβος ὅδ' ἐστ', ὤνθρωπε, Σοφοκλέος, ὃν παρὰ
        Μουσέων
    ἱρὴν παρθεσίην, ἱερὸς ὤν, ἔλαχον·
ὅς με τὸν ἐκ Φλιοῦντος, ἔτι τρίβολον πατέοντα,
    πρίνινον, ἐς χρύσεον σχῆμα μεθηρμόσατο,
καὶ λεπτὴν ἐνέδυσεν ἁλουργίδα· τοῦ δὲ θανόντος 5
    εὔθετον ὀρχηστὴν τῇδ' ἀνέπαυσα πόδα.

---

¹ A machine for threshing, like a harrow.

24

35.—LEONIDAS

On the Same

CONGENIAL to strangers and dear to his countrymen was this man, Pindar, the servant of the sweet-voiced Muses.

36.—ERYCIAS

On Sophocles

EVER, O divine Sophocles, may the ivy that adorns the stage dance with soft feet over thy polished monument. Ever may the tomb be encompassed by bees that bedew it, the children of the ox, and drip with honey of Hymettus, that there be ever store of wax flowing for thee to spread on thy Attic writing tablets, and that thy locks may never want a wreath.

37.—DIOSCORIDES

On the Same

(A statue of a Satyr is supposed to speak)

A. "THIS is the tomb of Sophocles which I, his holy servant, received from the Muses as a holy trust to guard. It was he who, taking me from Phlius where I was carved of holly-oak and still trod the tribulum,[1] wrought me into a creature of gold and clothed me in fine purple.[2] On his death I ceased from the dance and rested my light foot here."

---

[2] *i.e.* from the rude Satyric drama he evolved Attic tragedy—a very exaggerated statement.

β. Ὄλβιος, ὡς ἁγνὴν ἔλαχες στάσιν· ἡ δ᾽ ἐνὶ χερσὶν
   κούριμος, ἐκ ποίης ἥδε διδασκαλίης;
α. Εἴτε σοι Ἀντιγόνην εἰπεῖν φίλον, οὐκ ἂν ἁμάρτοις,
   εἴτε καὶ Ἡλέκτραν· ἀμφότεραι γὰρ ἄκρον.   10

38.—ΔΙΟΔΩΡΟΥ

Θεῖος Ἀριστοφάνευς ὑπ᾽ ἐμοὶ νέκυς· εἰ τίνα πεύθῃ,
κωμικός, ἀρχαίης μνᾶμα χοροστασίης.

39.—ΑΝΤΙΠΑΤΡΟΥ ΘΕΣΣΑΛΟΝΙΚΕΩΣ

Ὁ τραγικὸν φώνημα καὶ ὀφρυόεσσαν ἀοιδὴν
   πυργώσας στιβαρῇ πρῶτος ἐν εὐεπίῃ,
Αἰσχύλος Εὐφορίωνος, Ἐλευσινίης ἑκὰς αἴης
   κεῖται, κυδαίνων σήματι Τρινακρίην.

40.—ΔΙΟΔΩΡΟΥ

Αἰσχύλον ἥδε λέγει ταφίη λίθος ἐνθάδε κεῖσθαι
   τὸν μέγαν, οἰκείης τῆλ᾽ ἀπὸ Κεκροπίης,
λευκὰ Γέλα Σικελοῖο παρ᾽ ὕδατα· τίς φθόνος, αἰαῖ,
   Θησείδας ἀγαθῶν ἔγκοτος αἰὲν ἔχει;

41.—ΑΔΕΣΠΟΤΟΝ

Ἀ μάκαρ ἀμβροσίῃσι συνέστιε φίλτατε Μούσαις,
   χαῖρε καὶ εἰν Ἀΐδεω δώμασι, Καλλίμαχε.

B. " Blessed art thou, how excellent thy post! And the mask of a girl in thy hand with shaven hair as of a mourner, from what play is she?" *A.* "Say Antigone if thou wilt, or say Electra; in either case thou art not wrong, for both are supreme." [1]

38.—DIODORUS
On Aristophanes

DIVINE Aristophanes lies dead beneath me. If thou askest which, it is the comic poet who keeps the memory of the old stage alive.

39.—ANTIPATER OF THESSALONICA
On Aeschylus

HERE, far from the Attic land, making Sicily glorious by his tomb, lies Aeschylus, son of Euphorion, who first built high with massive eloquence the diction of tragedy and its beetling song.

40.—DIODORUS
On the Same

THIS tombstone says that Aeschylus the great lies here, far from his own Attica, by the white waters of Sicilian Gelas. What spiteful grudge against the good is this, alas, that ever besets the sons of Theseus?

41.—ANONYMOUS
On Callimachus

HAIL blessed one, even in the house of Hades, Callimachus, dearest companion of the divine Muses.

[1] The Satyr would have carried the mask of Sophocles' best creation.

42.—ΑΛΛΟ

Ἀ μέγα Βαττιάδαο σοφοῦ περίπυστον ὄνειαρ,
  ἦ ῥ' ἐτεὸν κεράων, οὐδ' ἐλέφαντος ἔης.
τοῖα γὰρ ἄμμιν ἔφηνας, ἅτ' οὐ πάρος ἀνέρες ἴδμεν,
  ἀμφί τε ἀθανάτους, ἀμφί τε ἡμιθέους,
εὖτέ μιν ἐκ Λιβύης ἀναείρας εἰς Ἑλικῶνα   5
  ἤγαγες ἐν μέσσαις Πιερίδεσσι φέρων·
αἱ δέ οἱ εἰρομένῳ ἀμφ' ὠγυγίων ἡρώων
  Αἴτια καὶ μακάρων εἶρον ἀμειβόμεναι.

43.—ΙΩΝΟΣ

Χαῖρε μελαμπετάλοις, Εὐριπίδη, ἐν γυάλοισι
  Πιερίας τὸν ἀεὶ νυκτὸς ἔχων θάλαμον·
ἴσθι δ' ὑπὸ χθονὸς ὤν, ὅτι σοι κλέος ἄφθιτον ἔσται
  ἴσον Ὁμηρείαις ἀενάοις χάρισιν.

J. A. Symonds, the younger, *Studies of the Greek Poets*, ii. 302.

44.—ΙΩΝΟΣ

Εἰ καὶ δακρυόεις, Εὐριπίδη, εἷλέ σε πότμος,
  καί σε λυκορραῖσται δεῖπνον ἔθεντο κύνες,
τὸν σκηνῇ μελίγηρυν ἀηδόνα, κόσμον Ἀθηνῶν,
  τὸν σοφίῃ Μουσέων μιξάμενον χάριτα,
ἀλλ' ἔμολες Πελλαῖον ὑπ' ἠρίον, ὡς ἂν ὁ λάτρις   5
  Πιερίδων ναίῃς ἀγχόθι Πιερίδων.

42.—ANONYMOUS

On the Aetia (Origins) of the Same

AH! great and renowned dream of the skilled son of Battus,[1] verily thou wast of horn, not of ivory; for thou didst reveal things to us touching the gods and demigods which never man knew before, then when catching him up thou didst bear him from Libya to Helicon, and didst set him down in the midst of the Muses. And there as he wove the Origins of primeval heroes they in turn wove for him the Origins also of the gods.

43.—ION

On Euripides

HAIL, Euripides, dwelling in the chamber of eternal night in the dark-robed valleys of Pieria! Know, though thou art under earth, that thy renown shall be everlasting, equal to the perennial charm of Homer.

44.—BY THE SAME

On the Same

THOUGH a tearful fate befel thee, O Euripides, devoured by wolf-hounds, thou, the honey-voiced nightingale of the stage, the ornament of Athens, who didst mingle the grace of the Muses with wisdom, yet thou wast laid in the tomb at Pella, that the servant of the Pierian Muses should dwell near the home of his mistresses.

[1] Callimachus claimed that the Muses revealed the matter of the poem to him in a dream.

45.—ΘΟΤΚΤΔΙΔΟΤ

Μνῆμα μὲν Ἑλλὰς ἅπασ' Εὐριπίδου· ὀστέα δ' ἴσχει
  γῆ Μακεδών· ἦ γὰρ δέξατο τέρμα βίου.
πατρὶς δ' Ἑλλάδος Ἑλλάς, Ἀθῆναι· πλεῖστα δε
  Μούσαις
τέρψας, ἐκ πολλῶν καὶ τὸν ἔπαινον ἔχει.

46.—ΑΔΗΛΟΝ

Οὐ σὸν μνῆμα τόδ' ἔστ', Εὐριπίδη, ἀλλὰ σὺ τοῦδε·
  τῇ σῇ γὰρ δόξῃ μνῆμα τόδ' ἀμπέχεται.

47.—ΑΛΛΟ

Ἀπασ' Ἀχαιῒς μνῆμα σόν, Εὐριπίδη·
οὔκουν ἄφωνος, ἀλλὰ καὶ λαλητέος.

48.—ΑΛΛΟ

Αἰθαλέοιο πυρὸς σάρκες ῥιπῇσι τρυφηλαὶ
  ληφθεῖσαι, νοτίην ὦσαν ἅπ' αἰθόμεναι·
μοῦνα δ' ἔνεστι τάφῳ πολυδακρύῳ ὀστέα κωφά,
  καὶ πόνος εἰνοδίοις τῇδε παρερχομένοις.

49.—ΒΙΑΝΟΡΟΣ

Ἁ Μακέτις σε κέκευθε τάφου κόνις· ἀλλὰ πυρωθεὶς
  Ζανὶ κεραυνείῳ, γαῖαν ἀπημφίασας.
τρὶς γὰρ ἐπαστράψας, Εὐριπίδη, ἐκ Διὸς αἰθὴρ
  ἥγνισε τὰν θνατὰν σώματος †ἱστορίαν.[1]

[1] Bury suggests ἁρμονίαν in v. 4, and I render so.

45.—THUCYDIDES THE HISTORIAN
On the Same

ALL Hellas is the monument of Euripides, but the Macedonian land holds his bones, for it sheltered the end of his life. His country was Athens, the Hellas of Hellas, and as by his verse he gave exceeding delight, so from many he receiveth praise.

46.—ANONYMOUS
On the Same

THIS is not thy monument, Euripides, but thou art the memorial of it, for by thy glory is this monument encompassed.

47.—ANONYMOUS
On the Same

ALL Greece is thy tomb, O Euripides; so thou art not dumb, but even vocal.

48.—ANONYMOUS
On the Same

THY delicate flesh encompassed by the blast of glowing fire yielded up its moisture and burnt away. In the much-wept tomb is naught but dumb bones, and sorrow for the wayfarers who pass this way.

49.—BIANOR OF BITHYNIA
On the Same

THE Macedonian dust of the tomb covers thee, Euripides, but ere thou didst put on this cloak of earth thou wast scorched by the bolts of Zeus. For thrice the heaven lightened at his word and purified thy mortal frame.

50.—ΑΡΧΙΜΗΔΟΥΣ

Τὴν Εὐριπίδεω μήτ' ἔρχεο, μήτ' ἐπιβάλλου,
  δύσβατον ἀνθρώποις οἶμον, ἀοιδοθέτα.
λείη μὲν γὰρ ἰδεῖν καὶ ἐπίρροθος·[1] ἢν δέ τις αὐτὴν
  εἰσβαίνῃ, χαλεποῦ τρηχυτέρη σκόλοπος·
ἢν δὲ τὰ Μηδείης Αἰητίδος ἄκρα χαράξῃς,   5
  ἀμνήμων κείσῃ νέρθεν. ἔα στεφάνους.

51.—ΑΔΑΙΟΥ

Οὔ σε κυνῶν γένος εἷλ', Εὐριπίδη, οὐδὲ γυναικὸς
  οἶστρος, τὸν σκοτίης Κύπριδος ἀλλότριον,
ἀλλ' Ἀΐδης καὶ γῆρας· ὑπαὶ Μακέτῃ δ' Ἀρεθούσῃ
  κεῖσαι, ἑταιρείῃ τίμιος Ἀρχέλεω.
σὸν δ' οὐ τοῦτον ἐγὼ τίθεμαι τάφον, ἀλλὰ τὰ
      Βάκχου   5
  βήματα καὶ σκηνὰς ἐμβάδ'[2] ἐρειδομένας.

52.—ΔΗΜΙΟΥΡΓΟΥ

Ἑλλάδος εὐρυχόρου στέφανον καὶ κόσμον ἀοιδῆς,
  Ἀσκραῖον γενεὴν Ἡσίοδον κατέχω.

53.—ΑΔΗΛΟΝ

Ἡσίοδος Μούσαις Ἑλικωνίσι τόνδ' ἀνέθηκα,
  ὕμνῳ νικήσας ἐν Χαλκίδι θεῖον Ὅμηρον.

---

[1] I suggest ἐπίκροτος and render so.
[2] v. 4 ἔμβαλε MS.: I correct (ἐμβάδι πειθομ. Hermann).

50.—ARCHIMEDES

On the Same

TREAD not, O poet, the path of Euripides, neither essay it, for it is hard for man to walk therein. Smooth it is to look on, and well beaten, but if one sets his foot on it it is rougher than if set with cruel stakes. Scratch but the surface of *Medea*,[1] Aeetes' daughter, and thou shalt lie below forgotten. Hands off his crowns.

51.—ADAEUS

On the Same

NEITHER dogs slew thee, Euripides, nor the rage of women, thou enemy of the secrets of Cypris, but Death and old age, and under Macedonian Arethusa thou liest, honoured by the friendship of Archelaus. Yet it is not this that I account thy tomb, but the altar of Bacchus and the buskin-trodden stage.

52.—DEMIURGUS

On Hesiod

I HOLD Hesiod of Ascra the glory of spacious Hellas and the ornament of Poesy.

53.—ANONYMOUS

On an ex-voto dedicated by Hesiod

HESIOD dedicated this to the Heliconian Muses, having conquered divine Homer in the hymn contest at Chalcis.

[1] By retouching.

54.—ΜΝΑΣΑΛΚΟΥ

Ἄσκρη μὲν πατρὶς πολυλήϊος, ἀλλὰ θανόντος
ὀστέα πληξίππων γῆ Μινυῶν κατέχει
Ἡσιόδου, τοῦ πλεῖστον ἐν ἀνθρώποις κλέος ἐστὶν
ἀνδρῶν κρινομένων ἐν βασάνῳ σοφίης.

55.—ΑΛΚΑΙΟΥ

Λοκρίδος ἐν νέμεϊ σκιερῷ νέκυν Ἡσιόδοιο
  Νύμφαι κρηνίδων λοῦσαν ἀπὸ σφετέρων,
καὶ τάφον ὑψώσαντο· γάλακτι δὲ ποιμένες αἰγῶν
  ἔρραναν, ξανθῷ μιξάμενοι μέλιτι·
τοίην γὰρ καὶ γῆρυν ἀπέπνεεν ἐννέα Μουσέων   5
  ὁ πρέσβυς καθαρῶν γευσάμενος λιβάδων.

56.—ΑΔΗΛΟΝ

Ἦν ἄρα Δημοκρίτοιο γέλως τόδε, καὶ τάχα λέξει·
  "Οὐκ ἔλεγον γελόων, Πάντα πέλουσι γέλως;
καὶ γὰρ ἐγὼ σοφίην μετ' ἀπείρονα, καὶ στίχα βίβλων
  τοσσατίων, κεῖμαι νέρθε τάφοιο γέλως."

57.—ΑΛΛΟ

Καὶ τίς ἔφυ σοφὸς ὧδε; τίς ἔργον ἔρεξε τοσοῦτον,
  ὅσσον ὁ παντοδαὴς ἤνυσε Δημόκριτος;

54.—MNASALCAS
On the Same

Ascra, the land of broad corn-fields, was my country, but the land of the charioteer Minyae[1] holds my bones now I am dead. I am Hesiod, the most glorious in the eyes of the world of men who are judged by the test of wisdom.

55.—ALCAEUS (OF MYTILENE OR MESSENE)
On the Same

In a shady grove of Locris the Nymphs washed the body of Hesiod with water from their springs and raised a tomb to him. And on it the goat-herds poured libations of milk mixed with golden honey. For even such was the song the old man breathed who had tasted the pure fountains of the nine Muses.

56.—Anonymous
On Democritus of Abdera

So this was the cause of Democritus' laughter, and perchance he will say, "Did I not say, laughing, that all is laughter? For even I, after my limitless wisdom and the long series of my works, lie beneath the tomb a laughing-stock."

57.—DIOGENES LAERTIUS[2]
On the Same

Who was ever so wise, who wrought such a deed as omniscient Democritus, who had Death for three

[1] Orchomenus.
[2] For these epigrams of Diogenes see note to No. 83.

ὃς Θάνατον παρεόντα τρὶ ἤματα δώμασιν ἔσχεν,
καὶ θερμοῖς ἄρτων ἄσθμασιν ἐξένισεν.

58.—ΙΟΥΛΙΑΝΟΥ ΑΠΟ ΥΠΑΡΧΩΝ ΑΙΓΥΠΤΟΥ

Εἰ καὶ ἀμειδήτων νεκύων ὑπὸ γαῖαν ἀνάσσεις,
Φερσεφόνη, ψυχὴν δέχνυσο Δημοκρίτου
εὐμενέως γελόωσαν, ἐπεὶ καὶ σεῖο τεκοῦσαν
ἀχνυμένην ἐπὶ σοὶ μοῦνος ἔκαμψε γέλως.

59.—ΤΟΥ ΑΥΤΟΥ

Πλούτων δέξο μάκαρ Δημόκριτον, ὥς κεν ἀνάσσων
αἰὲν ἀμειδήτων καὶ γελόωντα λάχοις.

60.—ΣΙΜΙΟΥ

Σωφροσύνῃ προφέρων θνητῶν ἤθει τε δικαίῳ
ἐνθάδε κεῖται ἀνὴρ θεῖος Ἀριστοκλέης·
εἰ δέ τις ἐκ πάντων σοφίης μέγαν ἔσχεν ἔπαινον,
οὗτος ἔχει πλεῖστον, καὶ φθόνον οὐ φέρεται.

61.—ΑΔΕΣΠΟΤΟΝ

Γαῖα μὲν ἐν κόλποις κρύπτει τόδε σῶμα Πλάτωνος,
ψυχὴ δ᾽ ἀθάνατον τάξιν ἔχει μακάρων

---

¹ Democritus, on the point of death but wishing for his sister's sake to live out the three days of the feast of Demeter, which it was her duty to attend, ordered her to

days in his house and entertained him with the hot steam of bread ?[1]

58.—JULIANUS, PREFECT OF EGYPT
On the Same

THOUGH, Persephone, thou rulest over the unsmiling dead beneath the earth, receive the shade of Democritus with his kindly laugh; for only laughter turned away from sorrow thy mother when she was sore-hearted for thy loss.

59.—BY THE SAME
On the Same

RECEIVE Democritus, O blessed Pluto, so that thou, the ruler of the laughterless people, mayest have one subject who laughs.

60.—SIMIAS
On Plato

HERE lieth the divine Aristocles,[2] who excelled all mortals in temperance and the ways of justice.   If any one gained from all men much praise for wisdom it was he, and no envy therewith.

61.—ANONYMOUS
On the Same

THE earth in her bosom hides here the body of Plato, but his soul has its immortal station among the

supply him every day with hot loaves, and by putting the steaming bread to his nose kept himself alive until the feast was over.   [2] Plato's original name.

υἱοῦ ᾿Αρίστωνος, τόν τις καὶ τηλόθι ναίων
τιμᾷ ἀνὴρ ἀγαθός, θεῖον ἰδόντα βίον.

62.—ΑΛΛΟ

a. Αἰετέ, τίπτε βέβηκας ὑπὲρ τάφον; ἢ τίνος, εἰπέ,
ἀστερόεντα θεῶν οἶκον ἀποσκοπέεις;
β. Ψυχῆς εἰμὶ Πλάτωνος ἀποπταμένης ἐς Ὄλυμπον
εἰκών· σῶμα δὲ γῆ γηγενὲς ᾿Ατθὶς ἔχει.

P. B. Shelley, "Eagle, why soarest thou?. . .", *Works*
(Oxford ed.), p. 712.

63.—ΑΔΕΣΠΟΤΟΝ

Τὸν κύνα Διογένη, νεκυοστόλε, δέξο με, πορθμεῦ,
γυμνώσαντα βίου παντὸς ἐπισκύνιον.

64.—ΑΔΗΛΟΝ

a. Εἰπέ, κύον, τίνος ἀνδρὸς ἐφεστὼς σῆμα φυλάσ-
σεις;
β. Τοῦ Κυνός. a. ᾿Αλλὰ τίς ἦν οὗτος ἀνὴρ ὁ
Κύων;
β. Διογένης. a. Γένος εἰπέ. β. Σινωπεύς. a. Ὃς
πίθον ᾤκει;
β. Καὶ μάλα· νῦν δὲ θανὼν ἀστέρας οἶκον ἔχει.

J. A. Symonds, M.D., in his son's *Studies of the Greek
Poets*, ii. p. 304.

65.—ΑΝΤΙΠΑΤΡΟΥ

Διογένευς τόδε σῆμα, σοφοῦ κυνός, ὅς ποτε θυμῷ
ἄρσενι γυμνήτην ἐξεπόνει βίοτον,

blest, the soul of Ariston's son, whom every good man, even if he dwell in a far land, honours in that he saw the divine life.

62.—ANONYMOUS
On the Same

A. "EAGLE, why standest thou on the tomb, and on whose, tell me, and why gazest thou at the starry home of the gods?" *B.* "I am the image of the soul of Plato that hath flown away to Olympus, but his earth-born body rests here in Attic earth."

63.—ANONYMOUS
On Diogenes

O FERRYMAN of the dead, receive the Dog Diogenes, who laid bare the whole pretentiousness[1] of life.

64.—ANONYMOUS
On the Same

A. "TELL me, dog, who was the man on whose tomb thou standest keeping guard?" *B.* "The Dog." *A.* "But what man was that, the Dog?" *B.* "Diogenes." *A.* "Of what country?" *B.* "Of Sinope." *A.* "He who lived in a jar?" *B.* "Yes, and now he is dead, the stars are his home."

65.—ANTIPATER
On the Same

THIS is the tomb of Diogenes, the wise Dog who of old, with manly spirit, endured a life of self-denial.

---

[1] Literally "eye-brow" used like the Latin *supercilium* for "affectation."

ᾧ μία τις πήρα, μία διπλοΐς, εἷς ἄμ' ἐφοίτα
σκίπων, αὐτάρκους ὅπλα σαοφροσύνας.
ἀλλὰ τάφου τοῦδ' ἐκτὸς ἴτ', ἄφρονες, ὡς ὁ Σινωπεὺς 5
ἐχθαίρει φαῦλον πάντα καὶ εἰν Ἀίδῃ.

66.—ΟΝΕΣΤΟΥ

Βάκτρον καὶ πήρη καὶ διπλόον εἷμα σοφοῖο
Διογένευς βιότου φόρτος ὁ κουφότατος.
πάντα φέρω πορθμῆϊ· λέλοιπα γὰρ οὐδὲν ὑπὲρ γῆς·
ἀλλὰ κύον σαίνοις Κέρβερε τόν με κύνα.

67.—ΛΕΩΝΙΔΟΥ

Ἀίδεω λυπηρὲ διηκόνε, τοῦτ' Ἀχέροντος
ὕδωρ ὃς πλώεις πορθμίδι κυανέῃ,
δέξαι μ', εἰ καί σοι μέγα βρίθεται ὀκρυόεσσα
βᾶρις ἀποφθιμένων, τὸν κύνα Διογένην.
ὄλπη μοι καὶ πήρη ἐφόλκια, καὶ τὸ παλαιὸν 5
ἔσθος, χὠ φθιμένους ναυστολέων ὀβολός.
πάνθ' ὅσα κἠν ζωοῖς ἐπεπάμεθα, ταῦτα παρ' Ἅιδαν
ἔρχομ' ἔχων· λείπω δ' οὐδὲν ὑπ' ἠελίῳ.

68.—ΑΡΧΙΟΥ

Ἀίδος ὦ νεκυηγέ, κεχαρμένε δάκρυσι πάντων,
ὃς βαθὺ πορθμεύεις τοῦτ' Ἀχέροντος ὕδωρ,
εἰ καί σοι βέβριθεν ὑπ' εἰδώλοισι καμόντων
ὁλκάς, μὴ προλίπῃς Διογένη με κύνα.

One wallet he carried with him, one cloak, one staff, the weapons of self-sufficient sobriety. But turn aside from this tomb, all ye fools; for he of Sinope, even in Hades, hates every mean man.

66.—HONESTUS

On the Same

THE staff, and wallet, and thick cloak, were the very light burden of wise Diogenes in life. I bring all to the ferryman, for I left nothing on earth. But you, Cerberus dog, fawn on me, the Dog.

67.—LEONIDAS

On the Same

MOURNFUL minister of Hades, who dost traverse in thy dark boat this water of Acheron, receive me, Diogenes the Dog, even though thy gruesome bark is overloaded with spirits of the dead. My luggage is but a flask, and a wallet, and my old cloak, and the obol that pays the passage of the departed. All that was mine in life I bring with me to Hades, and have left nothing beneath the sun.

68.—ARCHIAS

On the Same

O BOATMAN of Hades, conveyor of the dead, delighting in the tears of all, who dost ply the ferry o'er this deep water of Acheron, though thy boat be heavy beneath its load of shades, leave me not behind, Diogenes the Dog. I have with me but a flask, and

ὄλπην καὶ σκίπωνα φέρω, καὶ διπλόον εἷμα,   5
καὶ πήρην, καὶ σοὶ ναυτιλίης ὀβολόν.
καὶ ζωὸς τάδε μοῦνον, ἃ καὶ νέκυς ὧδε κομίζω,
εἶχον· ὑπ' ἠελίου δ' οὔ τι λέλοιπα φάει.

69.—ΙΟΥΛΙΑΝΟΥ ΑΠΟ ΥΠΑΡΧΩΝ ΑΙΓΥΠΤΟΥ

Κέρβερε δειμαλέην ὑλακὴν νεκύεσσιν ἰάλλων,
ἤδη φρικαλέον δείδιθι καὶ σὺ νέκυν·
Ἀρχίλοχος τέθνηκε· φυλάσσεο θυμὸν ἰάμβων
δριμύν, πικροχόλου τικτόμενον στόματος.
οἶσθα βοῆς κείνοιο μέγα σθένος, εὖτε Λυκάμβεω   5
νηῦς μία σοὶ δισσὰς ἤγαγε θυγατέρας.

70.—ΤΟΥ ΑΥΤΟΥ

Νῦν πλέον ἢ τὸ πάροιθε πύλας κρατεροῖο βερέθρου
ὄμμασιν ἀγρύπνοις τρισσὲ φύλασσε κύον.
εἰ γὰρ φέγγος ἔλειπον ἀλυσκάζουσαι ἰάμβων
ἄγριον Ἀρχιλόχου φλέγμα Λυκαμβιάδες,
πῶς οὐκ ἂν προλίποι σκοτίων πυλεῶνας ἐναύλων   5
νεκρὸς ἅπας, φεύγων τάρβος ἐπεσβολίης;

71.—ΓΑΙΤΟΥΛΙΚΟΥ

Σῆμα τόδ' Ἀρχιλόχου παραπόντιον, ὅς ποτε πικρὴν
Μοῦσαν ἐχιδναίῳ πρῶτος ἔβαψε χόλῳ,

a staff, and a cloak, and a wallet, and the obol thy
fare. These things that I carry with me now I am
dead are all I had when alive, and I left nothing in
the daylight.

69.—JULIANUS, PREFECT OF EGYPT

On Archilochus

CERBERUS, whose bark strikes terror into the dead,
there comes a terrible shade before whom even thou
must tremble. Archilochus is dead. Beware the
acrid iambic wrath engendered by his bitter mouth.
Thou knowest the might of his words ever since one
boat brought thee the two daughters of Lycambes.[1]

70.—BY THE SAME

On the Same

Now, three-headed dog, better than ever with thy
sleepless eyes guard the gate of thy fortress, the pit.
For if the daughters of Lycambes to avoid the
savage bile of Archilochus' iambics left the light,
will not every soul leave the portals of this dusky
dwelling, flying from the terror of his slanderous
tongue?

71.—GAETULICUS

On the Same

THIS tomb by the sea is that of Archilochus, who
first made the Muse bitter dipping her in vipers'

---

[1] They hanged themselves owing to Archilochus' bitter
verses on them.

αἱμάξας Ἑλικῶνα τὸν ἥμερον.   οἶδε Λυκάμβης,
μυρόμενος τρισσῶν ἄμματα θυγατέρων.
ἠρέμα δὴ παράμειψον, ὁδοιπόρε, μή ποτε τοῦδε   5
κινήσῃς τύμβῳ σφῆκας ἐφεζομένους.

72.—ΜΕΝΑΝΔΡΟΥ ΚΩΜΙΚΟΥ

Χαῖρε, Νεοκλείδα, δίδυμον γένος, ὧν ὁ μὲν ὑμῶν
πατρίδα δουλοσύνας ῥύσαθ', ὁ δ' ἀφροσύνας.

73.—ΓΕΜΙΝΟΥ

Ἀντὶ τάφου λιτοῖο θὲς Ἑλλάδα, θὲς δ' ἐπὶ ταύταν
δούρατα, βαρβαρικᾶς σύμβολα ναυφθορίας,
καὶ τύμβῳ κρηπῖδα περίγραφε Περσικὸν Ἄρη
καὶ Ξέρξην· τούτοις θάπτε Θεμιστοκλέα.
στάλα δ' ἁ Σαλαμὶς ἐπικείσεται, ἔργα λέγουσα   5
τἀμά· τί με σμικροῖς τὸν μέγαν ἐντίθετε;

A. J. Butler, *Amaranth and Asphodel*, p. 58.

74.—ΔΙΟΔΩΡΟΥ

Τοῦτο Θεμιστοκλεῖ ξένον ἠρίον εἵσατο Μάγνης
λαός, ὅτ' ἐκ Μήδων πατρίδα ῥυσάμενος
ὀθνείην ὑπέδυ χθόνα καὶ λίθον.   ἦ θέλεν οὕτως
ὁ φθόνος· αἱ δ' ἀρεταὶ μεῖον ἔχουσι γέρας.

gall, staining mild Helicon with blood. Lycambes knows it, mourning for his three daughters hanged. Pass quietly by, O way-farer, lest haply thou arouse the wasps that are settled on his tomb.

72.—MENANDER

On Epicurus and Themistocles

HAIL, ye twin-born sons of Neocles, of whom the one saved his country from slavery the other from folly.

73.—GEMINUS

On Themistocles

IN place of a simple tomb put Hellas, and on her put ships significant of the destroyed barbaric fleets, and round the frieze of the tomb paint the Persian host and Xerxes—thus bury Themistocles. And Salamis shall stand thereon, a pillar telling of my deeds. Why lay you so great a man in a little space?

74.—DIODORUS

On the Same

THE people of Magnesia raised to Themistocles this monument in a land not his own, when after saving his country from the Medes, he was laid in foreign earth under a foreign stone. Verily Envy so willed, and deeds of valour have less privilege than she.

45

75.—ΑΝΤΙΠΑΤΡΟΥ

Στασίχορον, ζαπληθὲς ἀμέτρητον στόμα Μούσης,
  ἐκτέρισεν Κατάνας αἰθαλόεν δάπεδον,
οὗ, κατὰ Πυθαγόρου φυσικὰν φάτιν, ἁ πρὶν Ὁμήρου
  ψυχὰ ἐνὶ στέρνοις δεύτερον ᾠκίσατο.

76.—ΔΙΟΣΚΟΡΙΔΟΥ

Ἐμπορίης λήξαντα Φιλόκριτον, ἄρτι δ᾽ ἀρότρου
  γευόμενον, ξείνῳ Μέμφις ἔκρυψε τάφῳ,
ἔνθα δραμὼν Νείλοιο πολὺς ῥόος ὕδατι λάβρῳ
  τἀνδρὸς τὴν ὀλίγην βῶλον ἀπημφίασε.
καὶ ζωὸς μὲν ἔφευγε πικρὴν ἅλα· νῦν δὲ καλυφθεὶς   5
  κύμασι ναυηγὸν σχέτλιος ἔσχε τάφον.

77.—ΣΙΜΩΝΙΔΟΥ

Οὗτος ὁ τοῦ Κείοιο Σιμωνίδεω ἐστὶ σαωτήρ,
  ὃς καὶ τεθνηὼς ζῶντ᾽ ἀπέδωκε χάριν.

78.—ΔΙΟΝΥΣΙΟΥ ΚΥΖΙΚΗΝΟΥ

Πρηΰτερον γῆράς σε, καὶ οὐ κατὰ νοῦσος ἀμαυρὴ
  ἔσβεσεν· εὐνήθης δ᾽ ὕπνον ὀφειλόμενον,
ἄκρα μεριμνήσας, Ἐρατόσθενες· οὐδὲ Κυρήνη
  μαῖά σε πατρῴων ἐντὸς ἔδεκτο τάφων,

---

[1] This epigram is out of place here, as Philocritus is a
person unknown to history.

[2] This lemma is wrong. The couplet is said to have been

46

75.—ANTIPATER (OF SIDON?)
On Stesichorus

STESICHORUS, the vast immeasurable voice of the Muse, was buried in Catana's fiery land, he in whose breast, as telleth the philosopher Pythagoras, Homer's soul lodged again.

76.—DIOSCORIDES [1]

PHILOCRITUS, his trading over and yet a novice at the plough, lay buried at Memphis in a foreign land. And there the Nile running in high flood stripped him of the scanty earth that covered him. So in his life he escaped from the salt sea, but now covered by the waves hath, poor wretch, a shipwrecked mariner's tomb.

77.—SIMONIDES
On Simonides (?) [2]

THE saviour of the Ceian Simonides is this man, who even in death requited him who lived.

78.—DIONYSIUS OF CYZICUS
On Eratosthenes

A MILD old age, no darkening disease, put out thy light, Eratosthenes son of Aglaus, and, thy high studies over, thou sleepest the appointed sleep. Cyrene thy mother did not receive thee into the

written by Simonides on the tomb of a man whose corpse he found on the shore and buried, and whose ghost appeared and forbade him to sail in a ship which was wrecked on her voyage.

Ἀγλαοῦ υἱέ· φίλος δὲ καὶ ἐν ξείνῃ κεκάλυψαι   5
πὰρ τόδε Πρωτῆος κράσπεδον αἰγιαλοῦ.

79.—ΜΕΛΕΑΓΡΟΥ

a. Ὤνθρωπ', Ἡράκλειτος ἐγὼ σοφὰ μοῦνος ἀνευρεῖν
   φαμί· τὰ δ' ἐς πάτραν κρέσσονα καὶ σοφίης·
   λὰξ γὰρ καὶ τοκέωνας, ἰὼ ξένε, δύσφρονας ἄνδρας
   ὑλάκτευν. β. Λαμπρὰ θρεψαμένοισι χάρις.
a. Οὐκ ἀπ' ἐμεῦ; β. Μὴ τρηχύς. a. Ἐπεὶ τάχα   5
   καὶ σύ τι πεύσῃ
   τρηχύτερον πάτρας. β. Χαῖρε. a. Σὺ δ' ἐξ
   Ἐφέσου.

80.—ΚΑΛΛΙΜΑΧΟΥ

Εἶπέ τις, Ἡράκλειτε, τεὸν μόρον, ἐς δέ με δάκρυ
   ἤγαγεν, ἐμνήσθην δ' ὁσσάκις ἀμφότεροι
ἥλιον ἐν λέσχῃ κατεδύσαμεν· ἀλλὰ σὺ μέν που,
   ξεῖν' Ἁλικαρνησεῦ, τετράπαλαι σποδιή·
αἱ δὲ τεαὶ ζώουσιν ἀηδόνες, ᾗσιν ὁ πάντων   5
   ἁρπακτὴς Ἀΐδης οὐκ ἐπὶ χεῖρα βαλεῖ.

W. Johnson Cory, *Ionica*, ed. 1905, p. 7.

81.—ΑΝΤΙΠΑΤΡΟΥ ΣΙΔΩΝΙΟΥ

Ἑπτὰ σοφῶν, Κλεόβουλε, σὲ μὲν τεκνώσατο Λίνδος·
   φατὶ δὲ Σισυφία χθὼν Περίανδρον ἔχειν·

---

[1] i.e. at Alexandria.

tombs of thy fathers, but thou art buried on this fringe of Proteus' shore,[1] beloved even in a strange land.

79.—MELEAGER

On Heraclitus of Ephesus

A. "Sir, I am Heraclitus, and assert that I alone discovered wisdom, and my services to my country were better than wisdom. Ay Sir; for I assailed even my own parents, evil-minded folks, with contumely." *B.* "A fine return for thy bringing up!" *A.* "Be off!" *B.* "Don't be rough." *A.* "Because you may soon hear something rougher than my people heard from me." *B.* "Farewell." *A.* "And you get out of Ephesus." [2]

80.—CALLIMACHUS

On Heraclitus of Halicarnassus, the Elegiac Poet

One told me of thy death, Heraclitus, and it moved me to tears, when I remembered how often the sun set on our talking. And thou, my Halicarnassian friend, liest somewhere, gone long long ago to dust; but they live, thy Nightingales,[3] on which Hades who seizeth all shall not lay his hand.

81.—ANTIPATER OF SIDON

On the Seven Sages

Of the seven sages Lindus bore thee, O Cleobulus, and the land of Sisyphus [4] says that Periander is

[2] The epigram is obscure and the arrangement of the dialogue doubtful. I follow Headlam (*Class. Rev.* xv. p. 401).
[3] The title of a book of poems. [4] Corinth.

49

Πιττακὸν ἁ Μιτυλᾶνα· Βίαντα δὲ δῖα Πριήνη·
Μίλητος δὲ Θαλῆν, ἄκρον ἔρεισμα Δίκας·
ἁ Σπάρτα Χίλωνα· Σόλωνα δὲ Κεκροπὶς αἶα,   5
πάντας ἀριζάλου σωφροσύνας φύλακας.

82.—ΑΔΗΛΟΝ

Δωρίδος ἐκ Μούσης κεκορυθμένον ἀνέρα Βάκχῳ
καὶ Σατύροις Σικελὸν τῇδ' Ἐπίχαρμον ἔχω.

83.—ΑΛΛΟ

Τόνδε Θαλῆν Μίλητος Ἰὰς θρέψασ' ἀνέδειξεν,
ἀστρολόγων πάντων πρεσβύτατον σοφίῃ.

84.—ΑΛΛΟ

Ἦ ὀλίγον τόδε σᾶμα, τὸ δὲ κλέος οὐρανόμηκες
τοῦ πολυφροντίστου τοῦτο Θάλητος ὅρη.

85. <ΔΙΟΓΕΝΟΥΣ ΛΑΕΡΤΙΟΥ>

Γυμνικὸν αὖ ποτ' ἀγῶνα θεώμενον, ἠέλιε Ζεῦ,
τὸν σοφὸν ἄνδρα Θαλῆν ἥρπασας ἐκ σταδίου.
αἰνέω ὅττι μιν ἐγγὺς ἀπήγαγες· ἦ γὰρ ὁ πρέσβυς
οὐκέθ' ὁρᾶν ἀπὸ γῆς ἀστέρας ἠδύνατο.

---

[1] Nos. 83–133 are all derived from Diogenes Laertius'
Lives of the Philosophers. Those of his own composition
are not only very poor work (perhaps the worst verses ever
published), but are often unintelligible apart from the silly

hers. Mytilene bore Pittacus and fair Priene Bias, and Miletus Thales, best support of Justice, Sparta Chilon, and Attica Solon—all guardians of admirable Prudence.

82.—ANONYMOUS

On Epicharmus

I HOLD Sicilian Epicharmus, a man armed by the Doric Muse for the service of Bacchus and the Satyrs.

83.[1]—ANONYMOUS

On Thales

IONIAN Miletus nourished and revealed this Thales, first in wisdom of all astronomers.

84.—ANONYMOUS

On the Same

SMALL is the tomb, but see how the fame of the deep thinker Thales reaches to the heavens.

85.—DIOGENES LAERTIUS

On the Same

ONCE, Zeus the Sun, didst thou carry off from the stadion, as he was viewing the games, Thales the sage. I praise thee for taking him away to be near thee, for in truth the old man could no longer see the stars from earth.[2]

anecdotes to which they refer. These I give in such cases in the briefest possible form.

[2] Thales died from the effect of heat and thirst while watching the games.

GREEK ANTHOLOGY

86.—ΑΔΗΛΟΝ

Ἡ Μήδων ἄδικον παύσασ' ὕβριν ἥδε Σόλωνα
τόνδε τεκνοῖ Σαλαμὶς θεσμοθέτην ἱερόν.

87. <ΔΙΟΓΕΝΟΥΣ ΛΑΕΡΤΙΟΥ>

Σῶμα μὲν ἦρε Σόλωνος ἐν ἀλλοδαπῇ Κύπριον πῦρ,
ὀστὰ δ' ἔχει Σαλαμίς, ὧν κόνις ἀστάχυες·
ψυχὴν δ' ἄξονες εὐθὺς ἐς οὐρανὸν ἤγαγον· εὖ γὰρ
θῆκε νόμοις ἀστοῖς ἄχθεα κουφότατα.

88. <ΤΟΥ ΑΥΤΟΥ>

Φωσφόρε σοὶ Πολύδευκες ἔχω χάριν, οὕνεκεν υἱὸς
Χίλωνος πυγμῇ χλωρὸν ἕλεν κότινον·
εἰ δ' ὁ πατὴρ στεφανοῦχον ἰδὼν <τέκνον> ἤμυσεν
ἠσθείς,
οὐ νεμεσητόν· ἐμοὶ τοῖος ἴτω θάνατος.

89. <ΚΑΛΛΙΜΑΧΟΥ>

Ξεῖνος Ἀταρνείτης τις ἀνείρετο Πιττακὸν οὕτω
τὸν Μυτιληναῖον, παῖδα τὸν Ὑρράδιον·
"Ἄττα γέρον, δοιός με καλεῖ γάμος· ἡ μία μὲν δὴ
νύμφη καὶ πλούτῳ καὶ γενεῇ κατ' ἐμέ·

86.—Anonymous

On Solon

THIS island of Salamis which once put an end to the unrighteous insolence of the Medes, gave birth to this Solon the holy law-giver.

87.—DIOGENES LAERTIUS

On the Same

IN a strange land, a Cyprian fire consumed the body of Solon, but Salamis holds his bones, whose dust becomes corn. But his tables of the law carried his soul at once to heaven, for by his good laws he lightened the burdens of his countrymen.

88.— By the Same

On Chilon

O POLLUX, giver of light, I give thee thanks in that the son of Chilon gained by boxing the green olive-crown. And if his father seeing his son crowned, died of joy, why should we complain? May such a death be mine.[1]

89.—CALLIMACHUS

On Pittacus (not Sepulchral)

A GUEST from Atarne thus questioned Pittacus of Mytilene, the son of Hyrrha. "Daddy grey-beard! a two-fold marriage invites me. The one bride is suitable to me in fortune and family, but

---

[1] This explains itself. Castor and Pollux were the patrons of boxing and were also stars.

ἡ δ' ἑτέρη προβέβηκε. τί λώϊον; εἰ δ' ἄγε σύν μοι   5
  βούλευσον, ποτέρην εἰς ὑμέναιον ἄγω."
εἶπεν· ὁ δὲ σκίπωνα, γεροντικὸν ὅπλον, ἀείρας,
  "῾Ηνιδ', ἐκεῖνοί σοι πᾶν ἐρέουσιν ἔπος"
(οἱ δ' ἄρ' ὑπὸ πληγῇσι θοὰς βέμβικας ἔχοντες
  ἔστρεφον εὐρείη παῖδες ἐνὶ τριόδῳ·)   10
"κείνων ἔρχεο," φησί, "μετ' ἴχνια." χὠ μὲν ἐπέστη
  πλησίον· οἱ δ' ἔλεγον· "Τὴν κατὰ σαυτὸν ἔλα."
ταῦτ' ἀΐων ὁ ξεῖνος ἐφείσατο μείζονος οἴκου
  δράξασθαι, παίδων κληδόνα συνθέμενος.
τὴν δ' ὀλίγην ὡς κεῖνος ἐς οἶκον ἐπήγετο νύμφην,   15
  οὕτω καὶ σύ γ' ἰὼν τὴν κατὰ σαυτὸν ἔλα.

90.—ΑΛΛΟ

Κλεινοῖς ἐν δαπέδοισι Πριήνης φύντα καλύπτει
  ἥδε Βίαντα πέτρη, κόσμον ῎Ιωσι μέγαν.

91. <ΔΙΟΓΕΝΟΥΣ ΛΑΕΡΤΙΟΥ>

Τῇδε Βίαντα κέκευθα, τὸν ἀτρέμας ἤγαγεν ῾Ερμῆς
  εἰς ᾿Αΐδην, πολιῷ γήραϊ νιφόμενον·
εἶπε γάρ, εἶπε δίκην ἑτάρου τινός· εἶτ' ἀποκλινθεὶς
  παιδὸς ἐς ἀγκαλίδας μακρὸν ἔτεινεν ὕπνον.

---

[1] The boys were saying, each to his own top, "Drive the way that suits you" ("Go the way you like"). The same phrase means "Drive her that suits you." "Drive" in Greek often has a coarse meaning.

the other is my better. Which is best? Come,
advise me which to take to wife." So spoke he and
Pittacus raising his staff, the weapon of his old age,
said " Look! they will tell you all you need know "—
The boys at the broad cross-roads were whipping
their swift tops—" Go after them," he said, and the
man went and stood close to them, and they were
saying, " Drive the way that suits you." The
stranger, hearing this, refrained from catching at a
match with a greater home, understanding the oracle
of the boys' words. Therefore as he brought home
the bride of low estate, so do thou, go and " drive
her that suits you." [1]

90.—ANONYMOUS

On Bias

THIS stone covers Bias the great ornament of Ionia
born on the famous soil of Priene.

91.—DIOGENES LAERTIUS

On the Same

HERE I cover Bias, whom Hermes led gently to
Hades, his head white with the snows of age.
He spoke for a friend in court and then sinking
into the boy's arms he continued to sleep a long
sleep. [2]

[2] Bias, after having made a speech in court on behalf of
some one, was fatigued and rested his head on his nephew's
breast. His client won the case, but at its close Bias was
found to be dead.

92. <ΤΟΥ ΑΥΤΟΥ>

'Ες Σκυθίην 'Ανάχαρσις ὅτ' ἤλυθε πολλὰ μογήσας,
πάντας ἔπειθε βιοῦν ἤθεσιν ἑλλαδικοῖς·
τὸν δ' ἔτι μῦθον ἄκραντον ἐνὶ στομάτεσσιν ἔχοντα
πτηνὸς ἐς ἀθανάτους ἥρπασεν ὦκα δόναξ.

93.—ΑΛΛΟ

Εἰς Φερεκύδην

Τῆς σοφίης πάσης ἐν ἐμοὶ τέλος· ἢν δέ τι πάσχω,
Πυθαγόρη τῷ 'μῷ λέγε ταῦθ', ὅτι πρῶτος ἁπάντων
ἐστὶν ἀν' Ἑλλάδα γῆν. οὐ ψεύδομαι ὧδ' ἀγορεύων.

94.—ΑΔΗΛΟΝ

'Ενθάδε, πλεῖστον ἀληθείας ἐπὶ τέρμα περήσας
οὐρανίου κόσμου, κεῖται 'Αναξαγόρας.

95.—ΔΙΟΓΕΝΟΥΣ ΛΑΕΡΤΙΟΥ

Ἥλιον πυρόεντα μύδρον ποτὲ φάσκεν ὑπάρχειν,
καὶ διὰ τοῦτο θανεῖν μέλλεν 'Αναξαγόρας·
ἀλλ' ὁ φίλος Περικλῆς μὲν ἐρύσατο τοῦτον· ὁ δ' αὐτὸν
ἐξάγαγεν βιότου μαλθακίῃ σοφίης.

92.—By the Same

On Anacharsis

When Anacharsis went to Scythia after many toils he was persuading them all to live in the Greek manner. His unfinished speech was still on his lips, when a winged reed carried him off swiftly to the immortals.[1]

93.—Anonymous

On Pherecydes

The end of all wisdom is in me. If aught befall me, tell my Pythagoras that he is the first of all in the land of Hellas. In speaking thus I do not lie.

94.—Anonymous

On Anaxagoras

Here lies Anaxagoras who advanced furthest towards the goal of truth concerning the heavenly universe.

95.—DIOGENES LAERTIUS

On the Same

Anaxagoras once said that the sun was a red-hot mass, and for this was about to be killed. His friend Pericles saved him, but he ended his own life owing to the sensitiveness of his wise mind.

[1] Anacharsis was shot by his brother for trying to introduce Greek religious rites.

96. <ΤΟΥ ΑΥΤΟΥ>

Πῖνέ νυν ἐν Διὸς ὤν, ὦ Σώκρατες· ἦ σε γὰρ ὄντως
    καὶ σοφὸν εἶπε θεός, καὶ θεὸς ἡ σοφία.
πρὸς γὰρ Ἀθηναίων κώνειον ἁπλῶς σὺ ἐδέξω,
    αὐτοὶ δ' ἐξέπιον τοῦτο τεῷ στόματι.

97. <ΤΟΥ ΑΥΤΟΥ>

Οὐ μόνον ἐς Πέρσας ἀνέβη Ξενοφῶν διὰ Κῦρον,
    ἀλλ' ἄνοδον ζητῶν ἐς Διὸς ἥτις ἄγοι·
παιδείης γὰρ ἑῆς Ἑλληνικὰ πράγματα δείξας,
    ὡς καλὸν ἡ σοφίη μνήσατο Σωκράτεος.

98. <ΤΟΥ ΑΥΤΟΥ>

Εἰ καὶ σέ, Ξενοφῶν, Κραναοῦ Κέκροπός τε πολῖται
    φεύγειν κατέγνων τοῦ φίλου χάριν Κύρου,
ἀλλὰ Κόρινθος ἔδεκτο φιλόξενος, ᾗ σὺ φιληδῶν
    οὕτως ἀρέσκῃ κεῖθι καὶ μένειν ἔγνως.

99.—ΠΛΑΤΩΝΟΣ ΦΙΛΟΣΟΦΟΥ

Δάκρυα μὲν Ἑκάβῃ τε καὶ Ἰλιάδεσσι γυναιξὶ
    Μοῖραι ἐπέκλωσαν δή ποτε γεινομέναις·
σοὶ δέ, Δίων, ῥέξαντι καλῶν ἐπινίκιον ἔργων
    δαίμονες εὐρείας ἐλπίδας ἐξέχεαν.

96.—By the Same

On Socrates

DRINK now, O Socrates, in the house of Zeus. Of a truth a god called thee wise and Wisdom is a goddess. From the Athenians thou didst receive simply hemlock, but they themselves drank it by thy mouth.

97.—By the Same

On Xenophon

XENOPHON not only went up country to the Persians for Cyrus' sake, but seeking a way up to the house of Zeus. For after showing that the affairs of Greece belonged to his education, he recorded how beautiful was the wisdom of Socrates.[1]

98.—By the Same

IF the citizens of Cranaus and Cecrops[2] condemned you, Xenophon, to exile because of your friend Cyrus, yet hospitable Corinth received you, with which you were so pleased and content, and decided to remain there.

99.—PLATO

On Dio

THE Fates decreed tears for Hecuba and the Trojan women even at the hour of their birth; and after thou, Dio, hadst triumphed in the accomplishment of noble deeds, the gods spilt all thy far-

---

[1] Little sense can be made of line 3. I think there is an attempt to allude to both the *Cyropaedia* and the *Hellenica*.
[2] Both legendary kings of Athens.

κεῖσαι δ᾽ εὐρυχόρῳ ἐν πατρίδι τίμιος ἀστοῖς,　5
ὦ ἐμὸν ἐκμήνας θυμὸν ἔρωτι Δίων.

100.—ΠΛΑΤΩΝΟΣ

Νῦν ὅτε μηδέν, Ἄλεξις, ὅσον μόνον εἶφ᾽, ὅτι καλός,
ὦπται, καὶ πάντη πᾶσι περιβλέπεται.
θυμέ, τί μηνύεις κυσὶν ὀστέον, εἶτ᾽ ἀνιήσει
ὕστερον; οὐχ οὕτω Φαῖδρον ἀπωλέσαμεν;

101. <ΔΙΟΓΕΝΟΥΣ ΛΑΕΡΤΙΟΥ>

Ἀλλ᾽ εἰ μὴ Σπεύσιππον ἐμάνθανον ὧδε θανεῖσθαι,
οὐκ ἂν ἔπεισέ μέ τις τόδε λέξαι,
ὡς ἦν οὐχὶ Πλάτωνι πρὸς αἵματος· οὐ γὰρ ἀθυμῶν
κάτθανεν ἂν διά τι σφόδρα μικρόν.

102. <ΤΟΥ ΑΥΤΟΥ>

Χαλκῇ προσκόψας λεκάνῃ ποτέ, καὶ τὸ μέτωπον
πλήξας, ἴαχεν Ὦ σύντονον, εἶτ᾽ ἔθανεν,
ὁ πάντα πάντη Ξενοκράτης ἀνὴρ γεγώς.

---

[1] Speusippus was Plato's nephew. Diogenes Laertius does not as a fact deny this. He committed suicide, according to

reaching hopes.   But thou liest in thy spacious city,
honoured by thy countrymen, Dio, who didst madden
my soul with love.

100.—By the Same

On Alexis and Phaedrus (not an epitaph)

Now when I said nothing except just that Alexis is
fair, he is looked at everywhere and by everyone
when he appears.   Why, my heart, dost thou point
out bones to dogs and have to sorrow for it after-
wards ?   Was it not thus that I lost Phaedrus ?

101.—DIOGENES LAERTIUS

On Speusippus

If I had not heard that Speusippus would die so,
no one would have persuaded me to say this, that he
was not akin to Plato ; for then he would not have
died disheartened by reason of a matter exceeding
small.[1]

102.—By the Same

On Xenocrates

Stumbling once over a brazen cauldron and hitting
his forehead Xenocrates, who in all matters and
everywhere had shown himself to be a man, called
out Oh ! sharply and died.

the story referred to, owing to being insulted by the cynic
Diogenes.

103. <ΑΝΤΑΓΟΡΟΥ>

<Μνήματι τῷδε Κράτητα θεουδέα καὶ Πολέμωνα
  ἔννεπε κρύπτεσθαι, ξεῖνε, παρερχόμενος,>
ἄνδρας ὁμοφροσύνῃ μεγαλήτορας, ὧν ἀπὸ μῦθος
  ἱερὸς ἤισσεν δαιμονίου στόματος,
καὶ βίοτος καθαρὸς σοφίας ἐπὶ θεῖον ἐκόσμει   5
  αἰὼν ἀστρέπτοις δόγμασι πειθόμενος.

104. <ΔΙΟΓΕΝΟΥΣ ΛΑΕΡΤΙΟΥ>

Ἀρκεσίλαε, τί μοι τί τοσοῦτον ἄκρητον ἀφειδῶς
  ἔσπασας, ὥστε φρενῶν ἐκτὸς ὄλισθες ἐών;
οἰκτείρω σ᾽ οὐ τόσσον ἐπεὶ θάνες, ἀλλ᾽ ὅτι Μούσας
  ὕβρισας, οὐ μετρίῃ χρησάμενος κύλικι.

105.—ΤΟΥ ΑΥΤΟΥ

Καὶ σέο, Λακύδη, φάτιν ἔκλυον, ὡς ἄρα καί σε
  Βάκχος ἑλὼν ἀΐδην ποσσὶν ἔσυρεν ἄκροις.
ἦ σαφὲς ἦν· Διόνυσος ὅτ᾽ ἂν πολὺς ἐς δέμας ἔλθῃ,
  λῦσε μέλη· διὸ δὴ μήτι Λυαῖος ἔφυ;

106.—ΤΟΥ ΑΥΤΟΥ

"Χαίρετε καὶ μέμνησθε τὰ δόγματα" τοῦτ᾽ Ἐπίκουρος
  ὕστατον εἶπε φίλοις οἷσιν ἀποφθίμενος·
θερμὴν ἐς πύελον γὰρ ἐσήλυθε, καὶ τὸν ἄκρητον
  ἔσπασεν, εἶτ᾽ ἀΐδην ψυχρὸν ἐπεσπάσατο.

---

[1] "Life" in the Greek, but English will not bear the repetition.

103.—ANTAGORAS
On Polemo and Crates

STRANGER, as thou passest by, tell that this tomb holds god-like Crates and Polemo, great-hearted kindred spirits, from whose inspired mouths the holy word rushed. A pure pursuit[1] of wisdom, obedient to their unswerving doctrines, adorned their divine lives.

104.—DIOGENES LAERTIUS[2]
On Arcesilaus

ARCESILAUS, why did you drink so much wine, and so unsparingly as to slip out of your senses? I am not so sorry for you because you died as because you did violence to the Muses by using immoderate cups.[3]

105.—*On Lacydes*

AND about you too, Lacydes, I heard that Bacchus took hold of you by the toes and dragged you to Hades. It is clear; when Bacchus enters the body in force he paralyses the limbs. Is that not why he is called Lyaeus?[4]

106.—*On Epicurus*

"ADIEU, and remember my doctrines," were Epicurus' last words to his friends when dying. For after entering a warm bath, he drank wine and then on the top of it he drank cold death.

[2] 104–116 are all by him.
[3] Lacydes died of paralysis caused by intemperance.
[4] *i.e.* Loosener.

107.—ΤΟΥ ΑΥΤΟΥ

Μέλλων Εὐρυμέδων ποτ' Ἀριστοτέλην ἀσεβείας
   γράψασθαι, Δηοῦς μύστιδος ὢν πρόπολος,
ἀλλὰ πιὼν ἀκόνιτον ὑπέκφυγε· τοῦτ' ἀκονιτὶ
   ἦν ἄρα νικῆσαι συκοφάσεις ἀδίκους.

108.—ΤΟΥ ΑΥΤΟΥ

Καὶ πῶς εἰ μὴ Φοῖβος ἂν' Ἑλλάδα φῦσε Πλάτωνα,
   ψυχὰς ἀνθρώπων γράμμασιν ἠκέσατο;
καὶ γὰρ ὁ τοῦδε γεγὼς Ἀσκληπιός ἐστιν ἰητὴρ
   σώματος, ὡς ψυχῆς ἀθανάτοιο Πλάτων.

109.—ΤΟΥ ΑΥΤΟΥ

Φοῖβος ἔφυσε βροτοῖς Ἀσκληπιὸν ἠδὲ Πλάτωνα,
   τὸν μὲν ἵνα ψυχήν, τὸν δ' ἵνα σῶμα σάοι·
δαισάμενος δὲ γάμον, πόλιν ἤλυθεν ἥν ποθ' ἑαυτῷ
   ἔκτισε, καὶ δαπέδῳ Ζηνὸς ἐνιδρύσατο.

110.—ΤΟΥ ΑΥΤΟΥ

Οὐκ ἄρα τοῦτο μάταιον ἔπος μερόπων τινὶ λέχθη,
   ῥήγνυσθαι σοφίης τόξον ἀνιέμενον·
δὴ γὰρ καὶ Θεόφραστος ἕως ἐπόνει μὲν ἄπηρος
   ἦν δέμας, εἶτ' ἀνεθεὶς κάτθανε πηρομελής.

---

[1] There is a bad pun which cannot be rendered.
[2] The first couplet is not Diogenes' own, but is stated by
Olympiodorus to have actually been inscribed on Plato's

107.—*On Aristotle*

EURYMEDON, the priest of Demeter, was once about to prosecute Aristotle for impiety, but he escaped by drinking hemlock. This was then, it seems, to overcome unjust slander without trouble.[1]

108.—*On Plato*

How, if Phoebus had not produced Plato in Greece, could he cure men's souls by letters? For his son Asclepius is the healer of the body, as Plato is of the immortal soul.

109.—*On the Same*

PHOEBUS generated for mortals both Asclepius and Plato, the one to save the body, the other the soul. After celebrating a marriage he went to the city which he had founded for himself and was established in the house of Zeus.[2]

110.—*On Theophrastus*

THIS, then, was no idle word that some man spoke, that the bow of wisdom breaks when relaxed. As long as Theophrastus worked he was sound of limb, but when he grew slack he died infirm.

tomb. Plato is said to have died after attending a wedding feast. By the "city he had founded for himself" Diogenes means the Republic.

111.—ΤΟΥ ΑΥΤΟΥ

Λεπτὸς ἀνὴρ δέμας ἦν—εἰ μὴ προσέχῃς, ἀποχρῆ μοι·
  Στράτωνα τοῦτ᾽ οὖν φημί γε,
Λαμψακὸς ὅν ποτ᾽ ἔφυσεν· ἀεὶ δὲ νόσοισι παλαίων
  θνήσκει λαθών, οὐδ᾽ ᾔσθετο.

112.—ΤΟΥ ΑΥΤΟΥ

Οὐ μὰ τόν, οὐδὲ Λύκωνα παρήσομεν, ὅττι ποδαλγὴς
  κάτθανε· θαυμάζω τοῦτο μάλιστα δ᾽ ἐγώ,
τὴν οὕτως ἀίδαο μακρὴν ὁδὸν εἰ πρὶν ὁ ποσσὶν
  ἀλλοτρίοις βαδίσας ἔδραμε νυκτὶ μιῇ.

113.—ΤΟΥ ΑΥΤΟΥ

Ἀνεῖλεν ἀσπὶς τὸν σοφὸν Δημήτριον
  ἰὸν ἔχουσα πολὺν
ἄσμηκτον, οὐ στίλβουσα φῶς ἀπ᾽ ὀμμάτων,
  ἀλλ᾽ ἀίδην μέλανα.

114.—ΤΟΥ ΑΥΤΟΥ

Ἤθελες ἀνθρώποισι λιπεῖν φάτιν, Ἡρακλείδη,
  ὥς ῥα θανὼν ἐγένου ζωὸς ἅπασι δράκων·
ἀλλὰ διεψεύσθης σεσοφισμένε· δὴ γὰρ ὁ μὲν θὴρ
  ἦε δράκων, σὺ δὲ θήρ, οὐ σοφὸς ὤν, ἔάλως.

---

¹ Strato grew so thin that he died without feeling it.
² Heraclides begged his friends to hide his body when he

111.—*On Strato*

THIS Strato to whom Lampsacus gave birth was a thin man (I don't mind if you don't attend. I assert this at least). He ever fought with disease and died without feeling it.[1]

112.—*On Lyco*

No by— neither shall we neglect to tell how Lyco died of the gout. The thing that surprises me most is that he who formerly walked with other people's feet managed in one night to run all the way to Hades.

113.—*On Demetrius Phalereus*

AN asp that had much poison, not to be wiped off, darting no light but black death from its eyes, slew wise Demetrius.

114.—*On Heraclides Ponticus*

HERACLIDES, you wished to leave a report among men that when you died you became a live serpent in the eyes of all. But you were taken in, cunning wise man, for the beast was indeed a serpent, but you, being no wise man, were shown to be a beast.[2]

died and put a serpent on his bed that it might be supposed to be his spirit. The stratagem however was discovered.

GREEK ANTHOLOGY

115.—ΤΟΥ ΑΥΤΟΥ

Τὸν βίον ἦσθα Κύων, ᾿Αντίσθενες, ὧδε πεφυκώς,
   ὥστε δακεῖν κραδίην ῥήμασιν, οὐ στόμασιν.
ἀλλ᾿ ἔθανες φθισικός, τάχ᾿ ἐρεῖ τις ἴσως· τί δὲ τοῦτο;
   πάντως εἰς ἀΐδην δεῖ τιν᾿ ὁδηγὸν ἔχειν.

116.—ΤΟΥ ΑΥΤΟΥ

Διόγενες, ἄγε λέγε, τίς ἔλαβέ σε μόρος
ἐς ᾿Αΐδος; ἔλαβέ με κυνὸς ἄγριον ὀδάξ.

117. <ΖΗΝΟΔΟΤΟΥ>

Ἔκτισας αὐτάρκειαν, ἀφεὶς κενεαυχέα πλοῦτον,
   Ζήνων, σὺν πολιῷ σεμνὸς ἐπισκυνίῳ·
ἄρσενα γὰρ λόγον εὗρες, ἐνηθλήσω δὲ προνοίᾳ,
   αἵρεσιν ἀτρέστου μητέρ᾿ ἐλευθερίης.
εἰ δὲ πάτρα Φοίνισσα, τίς ὁ φθόνος; ἦν καὶ ὁ Κάδμος 5
   κεῖνος, ἀφ᾿ οὗ γραπτὰν Ἑλλὰς ἔχει σελίδα.

118.—ΔΙΟΓΕΝΟΥΣ ΛΑΕΡΤΙΟΥ

Τὸν Κιτιέα Ζήνωνα θανεῖν λόγος ὡς ὑπὸ γήρως
   πολλὰ καμὼν ἐλύθη μένων ἄσιτος·
<οἱ δ᾿ ὅτι προσκόψας ποτ᾿ ἔφη χερὶ γᾶν ἀλοήσας,
   "Ἔρχομαι αὐτόματος· τί δὴ καλεῖς με;">

---

[1] i.e. Cynic.
[2] Zeno stumbled and broke his finger : striking his hand

68

115.—*On Antisthenes*

You were in your lifetime a Dog,[1] Antisthenes, of such a nature that you bit the heart with words, not with your mouth. But someone perchance will say you died of consumption. What does that matter? One must have someone to guide one to Hades.

116.—*On Diogenes*

"Diogenes, tell what fate took you to Hades?' "A dog's fierce bite."

117.—ZENODOTUS
On Zeno

Zeno, reverend grey-browed sage, thou didst found the self-sufficient life, abandoning the pursuit of vainglorious wealth; for virile (and thou didst train thyself to foresight) was the school of thought thou didst institute, the mother of dauntless freedom. If thy country were Phoenicia what reproach is that? Cadmus too, from whom Greece learnt writing, was a Phoenician.

118.—DIOGENES LAERTIUS
On the Same

Some say that Zeno of Citium, suffering much from old age, remained without food, and others that striking the earth with his hand he said, " I come of my own accord. Why dost thou call me?"[2]

on the ground, he cried, " I come; why callest thou me?" and at once strangled himself.

119.—ΑΔΗΛΟΝ

Ἡνίκα Πυθαγόρης τὸ περικλεὲς εὕρετο γράμμα
κεῖν', ἐφ' ὅτῳ κλεινὴν ἤγαγε βουθυσίην.

120.—ΞΕΝΟΦΑΝΟΥΣ

Καί ποτέ μιν στυφελιζομένου σκύλακος παριόντα
φασὶν ἐποικτεῖραι, καὶ τόδε φάσθαι ἔπος·
"Παῦσαι, μηδὲ ῥάπιζ', ἐπεὶ φίλου ἀνέρος ἐστὶ
ψυχή, τὴν ἔγνων, φθεγξαμένης ἀΐων."

121.—ΔΙΟΓΕΝΟΥΣ ΛΑΕΡΤΙΟΥ

Οὐ μόνος ἐμψύχων ἄπεχες χέρας, ἀλλὰ καὶ ἡμεῖς·
τίς γὰρ ὃς ἐμψύχων ἥψατο, Πυθαγόρη;
ἀλλ' ὅταν ἑψηθῇ τι καὶ ὀπτηθῇ καὶ ἁλισθῇ
δὴ τότε καὶ ψυχὴν οὐκ ἔχον ἐσθίομεν.

122.—ΤΟΥ ΑΥΤΟΥ

Αἰαῖ, Πυθαγόρης τί τόσον κυάμους ἐσεβάσθη,
καὶ θάνε φοιτηταῖς ἄμμιγα τοῖς ἰδίοις;
χωρίον ἦν κυάμων· ἵνα μὴ τούτους δὲ πατήσῃ
ἐξ Ἀκραγαντίνων κάτθαν' ἐνὶ τριόδῳ.

119.—ANONYMOUS

On Pythagoras

DEDICATED when Pythagoras discovered that famous figure [1] to celebrate which he made a grand sacrifice of an ox.

120.—XENOPHANES

On the Same

THEY say that once he passed by as a dog was being beaten, and pitying it spoke as follows, "Stop, and beat it not; for the soul is that of a friend; I know it, for I heard it speak."

121.—DIOGENES LAERTIUS

On the Same

NOT you alone, Pythagoras, abstained from living things, but we do so likewise; who ever touched living things? But when they are boiled and roasted and salted, then they have no life in them and we eat them.

122.—BY THE SAME

On the Same

ALAS! why did Pythagoras reverence beans so much and die together with his pupils? There was a field of beans, and in order to avoid trampling them he let himself be killed on the road by the Agrigentines.

[1] *i.e.* what is now called the Forty-seventh Proposition of Euclid, Book I.

71

123.—ΤΟΥ ΑΥΤΟΥ

Καὶ σύ ποτ', Ἐμπεδόκλεις, διερῇ φλογὶ σῶμα
  καθήρας
πῦρ ἀπὸ κρητήρων ἔκπιες ἀθάνατον·
οὐκ ἐρέω δ' ὅτι σαυτὸν ἑκὼν βάλες ἐς ῥόον Αἴτνης,
  ἀλλὰ λαθεῖν ἐθέλων ἔμπεσες οὐκ ἐθέλων.

124.—ΤΟΥ ΑΥΤΟΥ

Ναὶ μὴν Ἐμπεδοκλῆα θανεῖν λόγος ὥς ποτ' ἀμάξης
  ἔκπεσε, καὶ μηρὸν κλάσσατο δεξιτερόν·
εἰ δὲ πυρὸς κρητῆρας ἐσήλατο καὶ πίε τὸ ζῆν,
  πῶς ἂν ἔτ' ἐν Μεγάροις δείκνυτο τοῦδε τάφος;

125.—ΑΔΗΛΟΝ

Εἴ τι παραλλάσσει φαέθων μέγας ἄλιος ἄστρων,
  καὶ πόντος ποταμῶν μείζον' ἔχει δύναμιν,
φαμὶ τοσοῦτον ἐγὼ σοφίᾳ προέχειν Ἐπίχαρμον,
  ὃν πατρὶς ἐστεφάνωσ' ἅδε Συρακοσίων.

126. <ΔΙΟΓΕΝΟΥΣ ΛΑΕΡΤΙΟΥ>

Τὴν ὑπόνοιαν πᾶσι μάλιστα λέγω θεραπεύειν·
  εἰ γὰρ καὶ μὴ δρᾷς, ἀλλὰ δοκεῖς, ἀτυχεῖς.
οὕτω καὶ Φιλόλαον ἀνεῖλε Κρότων ποτὲ πάτρη,
  ὥς μιν ἔδοξε θέλειν δῶμα τύραννον ἔχειν.

123.—By the Same

On Empedocles

And you too, Empedocles, purifying your body by
liquid flame, drank immortal fire from the crater.[1] I
will not say that you threw yourself on purpose into
Etna's stream, but wishing to hide you fell in
against your will.

124.—By the Same

On the Same

They say Empedocles died by a fall from a carriage,
breaking his right thigh. But if he jumped into the
fiery bowl and drank life, how is it his tomb is shown
still in Megara?

125.—Anonymous

On Epicharmus

Even as the great burning sun surpasseth the stars
and the sea is stronger than the rivers, so I say that
Epicharmus, whom this his city Syracuse crowned,
excelleth all in wisdom.

126.—DIOGENES LAERTIUS

On Philolaus

I advise all men to cure suspicion, for even if you
don't do a thing, but people think you do, it is ill for
you. So Croton, his country, once slew Philolaus
because they thought he wished to have a house like
a tyrant's.

---

[1] With a play on the other meaning "bowl."

73

GREEK ANTHOLOGY

127.—ΤΟΥ ΑΥΤΟΥ

Πολλάκις Ἡράκλειτον ἐθαύμασα, πῶς ποτὲ τὸ ζῆν
ὧδε διαντλήσας δύσμορος, εἶτ' ἔθανεν·
σῶμα γὰρ ἀρδεύουσα κακὴ νόσος ὕδατι, φέγγος
ἔσβεσεν ἐκ βλεφάρων καὶ σκότον ἠγάγετο.

128.—ΑΔΗΛΟΝ

Ἡράκλειτος ἐγώ· τί μ' ἄνω κάτω ἕλκετ' ἄμουσοι;
οὐχ ὑμῖν ἐπόνουν, τοῖς δ' ἔμ' ἐπισταμένοις.
εἷς ἐμοὶ ἄνθρωπος τρισμύριοι, οἱ δ' ἀνάριθμοι
οὐδείς.   ταῦτ' αὐδῶ καὶ παρὰ Περσεφόνῃ.

129. <ΔΙΟΓΕΝΟΥΣ ΛΑΕΡΤΙΟΥ>

Ἤθελες, ὦ Ζήνων, καλὸν ἤθελες, ἄνδρα τύραννον
κτείνας ἐκλῦσαι δουλοσύνης Ἐλέαν·
ἀλλ' ἐδάμης· δὴ γάρ σε λαβὼν ὁ τύραννος ἐν ὅλμῳ
κόψε· τί τοῦτο λέγω; σῶμα γάρ, οὐχὶ δὲ σέ.

130.—ΤΟΥ ΑΥΤΟΥ

Καὶ σεῦ, Πρωταγόρη, φάτιν ἔκλυον, ὡς ἄρ' Ἀθηνῶν
ἔκ ποτ' ἰὼν καθ' ὁδὸν πρέσβυς ἐὼν ἔθανες·
εἵλετο γάρ σε φυγεῖν Κέκροπος πόλις· ἀλλὰ σὺ
    μέν που
Παλλάδος ἄστυ φύγες, Πλουτέα δ' οὐκ ἔφυγες.

127.—By the Same
On Heraclitus

I often wondered about Heraclitus, how after leading such an unhappy life, he finally died. For an evil disease, watering his body, put out the light in his eyes and brought on darkness.

128.—Anonymous
On the Same

I am Heraclitus. Why do you pull me this way and that, ye illiterate? I did not work for you, but for those who understand me. One man for me is equivalent to thirty thousand and countless men are but as nobody. This I proclaim even in the house of Persephone.[1]

129.—DIOGENES LAERTIUS
On Zeno the Eleatic

You wished, Zeno—'twas a goodly wish—to kill the tyrant and free Elea, but you were slain, for the tyrant caught you and pounded you in a mortar. Why do I speak thus? It was your body, not you.

130.—By the Same
On Protagoras

About you, too, Protagoras, I heard that once leaving Athens in your old age you died on the road; for the city of Cecrops decreed your exile. So you escaped from Athens but not from Pluto.

[1] The same saying is attributed to Democritus by Seneca, and both philosophers no doubt shared this contempt for the many.

131.—ΑΛΛΟ

Πρωταγόρην λόγος ὧδε θανεῖν φέρει· ἀλλὰ γὰρ †οὗτι
ἤκατο σῶμα γαῖαν, ψυχὰ δ᾽ ἆλτο σοφοῖς.

132.—ΑΛΛΟ

Καὶ σέο, Πρωταγόρη, σοφίης ἴδμεν βέλος ὀξύ,
ἀλλ᾽ οὐ τιτρῶσκον, †ὧν δὲ γλυκὺ †κρῆμα.[1]

133. <ΔΙΟΓΕΝΟΥΣ ΛΑΕΡΤΙΟΥ>

Πτίσσετε, Νικοκρέων, ἔτι καὶ μάλα, θύλακός ἐστι·
πτίσσετ᾽, Ἀνάξαρχος δ᾽ ἐν Διός ἐστι πάλαι·
καὶ σὲ διαστείλασα γνάφοις ὀλίγον τάδε λέξει
ῥήματα Περσεφόνη· "Ἔρρε μυλωθρὲ κακέ."

134.—ΑΔΗΛΟΝ

Ἐνθάδε Γοργίου ἡ κεφαλὴ κυνικοῦ κατάκειμαι,
οὐκέτι χρεμπτομένη, οὔτ᾽ ἀπομυσσομένη.

135.—ΑΛΛΟ

Θεσσαλὸς Ἱπποκράτης, Κῷος γένος, ἐνθάδε κεῖται,
Φοίβου ἀπὸ ῥίζης ἀθανάτου γεγαώς,

χρῖμα has been suggested by Boissonade and I render so.

76

131.—ANONYMOUS

On the Same

PROTAGORAS is said to have died here; but ... his body alone reached the earth, his soul leapt up to the wise.

132.—ANONYMOUS

On the Same

WE know too, Protagoras, the sharp arrow of thy wisdom. Yet it wounds not, but is a sweet unguent.

133.—DIOGENES LAERTIUS

On Anaxarchus

BRAY it in the mortar still more, Nicocreon, it is a bag, bray it, but Anaxarchus is already in the house of Zeus, and Persephone soon, carding you, will say, "Out on thee, evil miller." [1]

134.—ANONYMOUS

On Gorgias

HERE I lie, the head of Cynic Gorgias, no longer clearing my throat nor blowing my nose.

135.—ANONYMOUS

On Hippocrates of Cos, the Physician

HERE lieth Thessalian Hippocrates, by descent a Coan, sprung from the immortal stock of Phoebus.

---

[1] Nicocreon, the Cyprian tyrant, is said to have pounded Anaxarchus to death. Anaxarchus exclaimed, "Pound this bag (my body), but you do not pound Anaxarchus himself." This is a well-attested story.

πλεῖστα τρόπαια νοσων στήσας ὅπλοις Ὑγιείης,
δόξαν ἑλὼν πολλῶν οὐ τύχᾳ, ἀλλὰ τέχνᾳ.

136.—ΑΝΤΙΠΑΤΡΟΥ

Ἥρωος Πριάμου βαιὸς τάφος· οὐχ ὅτι τοίου
ἄξιος, ἀλλ᾽ ἐχθρῶν χερσὶν ἐχωννύμεθα.

137.—ΑΔΕΣΠΟΤΟΝ

Μή με τάφῳ σύγκρινε τὸν Ἕκτορα, μηδ᾽ ἐπὶ τύμβῳ
μέτρει τὸν πάσης Ἑλλάδος ἀντίπαλον.
Ἰλιάς, αὐτὸς Ὅμηρος ἐμοὶ τάφος, Ἑλλάς, Ἀχαιοὶ
φεύγοντες—τούτοις πᾶσιν ἐχωννύμεθα·
[εἰ δ᾽ ὀλίγην ἀθρεῖς ἐπ᾽ ἐμοὶ κόνιν, οὐκ ἐμοὶ αἶσχος·   5
Ἑλλήνων ἐχθραῖς χερσὶν ἐχωννύμεθα.]

138.—ΑΚΗΡΑΤΟΥ ΓΡΑΜΜΑΤΙΚΟΥ

Ἕκτορ Ὁμηρείῃσιν ἀεὶ βεβοημένε βίβλοις,
θειοδόμου τείχευς ἕρκος ἐρυμνότατον,
ἐν σοὶ Μαιονίδης ἀνεπαύσατο· σοῦ δὲ θανόντος,
Ἕκτορ, ἐσιγήθη καὶ σελὶς Ἰλιάδος.

139.—ΑΛΛΟ

Ἕκτορι μὲν Τροίη συγκάτθανεν, οὐδ᾽ ἔτι χεῖρας
ἀντῆρεν Δαναῶν παισὶν ἐπερχομένοις·
Πέλλα δ᾽ Ἀλεξάνδρῳ συναπώλετο. πατρίδες ἄρα
ἀνδράσιν, οὐ πάτραις ἄνδρες ἀγαλλόμεθα.

Armed by Health he gained many victories over Disease, and won great glory not by chance, but by science.

136.—ANTIPATER

On Priam

SMALL am I, the barrow of Priam the hero, not that I am worthy of such a man, but because I was built by the hands of his foes.

137.—ANONYMOUS

On Hector

Do not judge Hector by his tomb or measure by his barrow the adversary of all Hellas. The Iliad, Homer himself, Greece, the Achaeans in flight— these are my tomb—by these all was my barrow built. (If the earth you see above me is little, it is no disgrace to me, I was entombed by the hands of my foes the Greeks.)

138.—ACERATUS GRAMMATICUS

On the Same

HECTOR, constant theme of Homer's books, strongest bulwark of the god-built wall, Homer rested at thy death and with that the pages of the Iliad were silenced.

139.—ANONYMOUS

On the Same and on Alexander of Macedon

WITH Hector perished Troy and no longer raised her hand to resist the attack of the Danai. And Pella, too, perished with Alexander. So fatherlands glory in men, their sons, not men in their fatherlands.

140.—ΑΡΧΙΟΥ ΜΑΚΕΔΟΝΟΣ

Καὶ γενέταν τοῦ νέρθε καὶ οὔνομα καὶ χθόνα φώνει,
στάλα, καὶ ποία κηρὶ δαμεὶς ἔθανε.—
πατὴρ μὲν Πρίαμος, γᾶ δ' Ἴλιον, οὔνομα δ' Ἕκτωρ,
ὦνερ, ὑπὲρ πάτρας δ' ὤλετο μαρνάμενος.

141.—ΑΝΤΙΦΙΛΟΥ ΒΥΖΑΝΤΙΟΥ

Θεσσαλὲ Πρωτεσίλαε, σὲ μὲν πολὺς ᾄσεται αἰών,
Τροίᾳ ὀφειλομένου πτώματος ἀρξάμενον·
σῆμα δέ τοι πτελέῃσι συνηρεφὲς ἀμφικομεῦσι
Νύμφαι, ἀπεχθομένης Ἰλίου ἀντιπέρας·
δένδρα δὲ δυσμήνιτα, καὶ ἢν ποτὶ τεῖχος ἴδωσι   5
Τρώϊον, αὐαλέαν φυλλοχοεῦντι κόμην,
ὅσσος ἐν ἡρώεσσι τότ' ἦν χόλος, εἰ μέρος ἀκμὴν
ἐχθρὸν ἐν ἀψύχοις σώζεται ἀκρεμόσιν;

142.—ΑΔΗΛΟΝ

Τύμβος Ἀχιλλῆος ῥηξήνορος, ὅν ποτ' Ἀχαιοὶ
δώμησαν, Τρώων δεῖμα καὶ ἐσσομένων·
αἰγιαλῷ δὲ νένευκεν, ἵνα στοναχῇσι θαλάσσης
κυδαίνοιτο πάϊς τῆς ἁλίας Θέτιδος.

W. M. Hardinge, in *The Nineteenth Century*, Nov. 1878,
p. 873.

143.—ΑΔΗΛΟΝ

Ἄνδρε δύω φιλότητι καὶ ἐν τεύχεσσιν ἀρίστω,
χαίρετον, Αἰακίδη, καὶ σύ, Μενοιτιάδη.

BOOK VII. EPIGRAMS 140–143

140.—ARCHIAS OF MACEDON
On Hector

TELL, O column, the parentage of him beneath thee and his name and country and by what death he died. "His father was Priam, his country Ilion, his name Hector, and he perished fighting for his native land."

141.—ANTIPHILUS OF BYZANTIUM.
On Protesilaus

O THESSALIAN Protesilaus, long ages shall sing of thee, how thou didst strike the first blow in Troy's predestined fall. The Nymphs tend and encircle with overshadowing elms thy tomb opposite hated Ilion. Wrathful are the trees, and if they chance to see the walls of Troy, they shed their withered leaves. How bitter was the hatred of the heroes if a part of their enmity lives yet in soulless branches.

142.—ANONYMOUS
On Achilles

THIS is the tomb of Achilles the man-breaker, which the Achaeans built to be a terror to the Trojans even in after generations, and it slopes to the beach, that the son of Thetis the sea-goddess may be saluted by the moan of the waves.

143.—ANONYMOUS
On Achilles and Patroclus

HAIL Aeacides and Menoetiades, ye twain supreme in Love and Arms.

81

144.—ΑΔΕΣΠΟΤΟΝ

Ἡδυεπὴς Νέστωρ Πύλιος Νηλήϊος ἥρως
ἐν Πύλῳ ἠγαθέῃ τύμβον ἔχει τριγέρων.

145.—ΑΣΚΛΗΠΙΑΔΟΥ

Ἅδ᾽ ἐγὼ ἁ τλάμων Ἀρετὰ παρὰ τῷδε κάθημαι
Αἴαντος τύμβῳ κειραμένα πλοκάμους,
θυμὸν ἄχει μεγάλῳ βεβολημένα, εἰ παρ᾽ Ἀχαιοῖς
ἁ δολόφρων Ἀπάτα κρέσσον ἐμεῦ δύναται.

146.—ΑΝΤΙΠΑΤΡΟΥ ΣΙΔΩΝΙΟΥ

Σῆμα παρ᾽ Αἰάντειον ἐπὶ Ῥοιτηῗσιν ἀκταῖς
θυμοβαρὴς Ἀρετὰ μύρομαι ἑζομένα,
ἀπλόκαμος, πινόεσσα, διὰ κρίσιν ὅττι Πελασγῶν
οὐκ ἀρετὰ νικᾶν ἔλλαχεν, ἀλλὰ δόλος.
τεύχεα δ᾽ ἂν λέξειεν Ἀχιλλέος· "᾽Ἄρσενος ἀκμᾶς,   5
οὐ σκολιῶν μύθων ἄμμες ἐφιέμεθα."

147.—ΑΡΧΙΟΥ

Μοῦνος ἐναιρομένοισιν ὑπέρμαχος ἀσπίδα τείνας,
νηυσὶ βαρὺν Τρώων, Αἶαν, ἔμεινας ἄρην·
οὐδέ σε χερμαδίων ὦσεν κτύπος, οὐ νέφος ἰών,
οὐ πῦρ, οὐ δοράτων, οὐ ξιφέων πάταγος·
ἀλλ᾽ αὕτως προβλής τε καὶ ἔμπεδος, ὥς τις ἐρίπνα   5
ἱδρυθείς, ἔτλης λαίλαπα δυσμενέων.

144.—ANONYMOUS

On Nestor

SWEET-SPOKEN Nestor of Pylus, the hero-son of Neleus, the old, old man, has his tomb in pleasant Pylus.

145.—ASCLEPIADES

On Ajax

HERE sit I, miserable Virtue, by this tomb of Ajax, with shorn hair, smitten with heavy sorrow that cunning Fraud hath more power with the Greeks than I.

146.—ANTIPATER OF SIDON

On the Same

BY the tomb of Ajax on the Rhoetean shore, I, Virtue, sit and mourn, heavy at heart, with shorn locks, in soiled raiment, because that in the judgment court of the Greeks not Virtue but Fraud triumphed. Achilles' arms would fain cry, " We want no crooked words, but manly valour."

147.—ARCHIAS

On the Same

ALONE in defence of the routed host, with extended shield didst thou, Ajax, await the Trojan host that threatened the ships. Neither the crashing stones moved thee, nor the cloud of arrows, nor the clash of spears and swords; but even so, like some crag, standing out and firmly planted thou didst face the hurricane of the foes. If Hellas did

εἰ δέ σε μὴ τεύχεσσιν Ἀχιλλέος ὥπλισεν Ἑλλάς,
ἄξιον ἀντ' ἀρετᾶς ὅπλα πορούσα γέρας,
Μοιράων βουλῆσι τάδ' ἤμπλακεν, ὡς ἂν ὑπ' ἐχθρῶν
μή τινος, ἀλλὰ σὺ σῇ πότμον ἕλῃς παλάμῃ.   10

148.—ΑΔΕΣΠΟΤΟΝ

Σῆμα τόδ' Αἴαντος Τελαμωνίου, ὃν κτάνε Μοῖρα,
αὐτοῦ χρησαμένα καὶ χερὶ καὶ ξίφεϊ.
οὐδὲ γὰρ ἐν θνητοῖσι δυνήσατο καὶ μεμαυῖα
εὑρέμεναι Κλωθὼ τῷδ' ἕτερον φονέα.

149.—ΛΕΟΝΤΙΟΥ ΣΧΟΛΑΣΤΙΚΟΥ

Κεῖται ἐνὶ Τροίῃ Τελαμώνιος, οὔ τινι δ' ἔμπης
ἀντιβίων ὀπάσας εὖχος ἑοῦ θανάτου·
τόσσης γὰρ χρόνος ἄλλον ἐπάξιον ἀνέρα τόλμης
οὐχ εὑρών, παλάμῃ θῆκεν ὑπ' αὐτοφόνῳ.

150.—ΤΟΥ ΑΥΤΟΥ

Αἴας ἐν Τροίῃ μετὰ μυρίον εὖχος ἀέθλων
μέμφεται οὐκ ἐχθροῖς κείμενος, ἀλλὰ φίλοις.

151.—ΑΛΛΟ

Εκτωρ Αἴαντι ξίφος ὥπασεν, Ἕκτορι δ' Αἴας
ζωστῆρ'· ἀμφοτέρων ἡ χάρις εἰς θάνατος.

not give thee the arms of Achilles to wear, a worthy
reward of thy valour, it was by the counsel of the
Fates that she erred, in order that thou shouldst
meet with doom from no foe, but at thine own
hand.

148.—ANONYMOUS
On the Same

THIS is the tomb of Telamonian Ajax whom Fate
slew by means of his own hand and sword.   For
Clotho, even had she wished it, could not find
among mortals another able to kill him.

149.—LEONTIUS SCHOLASTICUS
On the Same

THE Telamonian lies low in Troy, but he gave no
foeman cause to boast of his death.   For Time
finding no other man worthy of such a deed en-
trusted it to his own self-slaying hand.

150.—BY THE SAME
On the Same

AJAX lieth in Troy after a thousand vaunted deeds
of prowess, blaming not his foes but his friends.

151.—ANONYMOUS
On Ajax and Hector

HECTOR gave his sword to Ajax and Ajax his
girdle to Hector, and the gifts of both are alike
instruments of death.

152.—ΑΛΛΟ

Πικρὴν ἀλλήλοις Ἕκτωρ χάριν ἠδὲ φέρασπις
  Αἴας ἐκ πολέμου μνῆμ᾽ ἔπορον φιλίης·
Ἕκτωρ γὰρ ζωστῆρα λαβὼν ξίφος ἔμπαλι δῶκε·
  τὴν δὲ χάριν δώρων πείρασαν ἐν θανάτῳ·
τὸ ξίφος εἷλ᾽ Αἴαντα μεμηνότα, καὶ πάλι ζωστὴρ   5
  εἵλκυσε Πριαμίδην δίφρια συρόμενον.
οὕτως ἐξ ἐχθρῶν αὐτοκτόνα πέμπετο δῶρα,
  ἐν χάριτος προφάσει μοῖραν ἔχοντα μόρου.

153.—ΟΜΗΡΟΤ, οἱ δὲ ΚΛΕΟΒΟΤΛΟΤ ΤΟΤ ΛΙΝΔΙΟΤ

Χαλκῆ παρθένος εἰμί, Μίδα δ᾽ ἐπὶ σήματι κεῖμαι.
ἔστ᾽ ἂν ὕδωρ τε νάῃ, καὶ δένδρεα μακρὰ τεθήλῃ,
αὐτοῦ τῇδε μένουσα πολυκλαύτῳ ἐπὶ τύμβῳ,
ἀγγελέω παριοῦσι, Μίδας ὅτι τῇδε τέθαπται.

R. G. McGregor, *Greek Anthology*, p. 422.

154.—ΑΔΗΛΟΝ

Εἰς Κόροιβον

Κοινὸν ἐγὼ Μεγαρεῦσι καὶ Ἰναχίδαισιν ἄθυρμα
  ἵδρυμαι, Ψαμάθης ἔκδικον οὐλομένης·
εἰμὶ δὲ Κὴρ τυμβοῦχος· ὁ δὲ κτείνας με Κόροιβος·
  κεῖται δ᾽ ὧδ᾽ ὑπ᾽ ἐμοῖς ποσσὶ διὰ τρίποδα·
Δελφὶς γὰρ φάμα τόδ᾽ ἐθέσπισεν, ὄφρα γενοίμαν   5
  τᾶς κείνου νύμφας σῆμα καὶ ἱστορίης.

---

[1] Apollo, to avenge the death of the child which Psamathe
the Argive princess bore him, sent a female demon (Ποινή)
which carried off babies. This demon was killed by Coroebus.

152.—Anonymous
On the Same

BITTER favours did Hector and Ajax of the great shield give each other after the fight in memory of their friendship. For Hector received a girdle and gave a sword in return, and they proved in death the favour that was in the gifts. The sword slew Ajax in his madness, and the girdle dragged Hector behind the chariot. Thus the adversaries gave each other the self-destroying gifts, which held death in them under pretence of kindness.

153.—HOMER or CLEOBULUS OF LINDUS
On Midas

I AM a maiden of brass, and rest on Midas' tomb. As long as water flows, and tall trees put forth their leaves, abiding here upon the tearful tomb, I tell the passers-by that Midas is buried here.

Here ends the collection of fictitious epitaphs on celebrities, but a few more will be found scattered in other parts of the book.

154.—Anonymous
On Coroebus

I AM set here, an image common to the Megarians and the Argives, the avenger of unhappy Psamathe. A ghoul, a denizen of the tomb am I, and he who slew me was Coroebus; here under my feet he lies, all for the tripod. For even so did the voice of Delphi decree, that I should be the monument of Apollo's bride and tell her story.[1]

He was pardoned by Apollo and ordered to settle wherever a tripod he carried fell. This was near Megara, and on his tomb at Megara he was represented killing the Ποινή.

155.—ΑΔΕΣΠΟΤΟΝ

Εἰς Φιλιστίωνα τὸν Νικαέα γελωτοποιόν

Ὁ τὸν πολυστένακτον ἀνθρώπων βίον
γέλωτι κεράσας Νικαεὺς Φιλιστίων
ἐνταῦθα κεῖμαι, λείψανον παντὸς βίου,
πολλάκις ἀποθανών, ὧδε δ' οὐδεπώποτε.

156.—ΙΣΙΔΩΡΟΤ ΑΙΓΕΑΤΟΤ

Ἰξῷ καὶ καλάμοισιν ἀπ' ἠέρος αὐτὸν ἔφερβεν
    Εὔμηλος, λιτῶς, ἀλλ' ἐν ἐλευθερίῃ.
οὔποτε δ' ὀθνείην ἔκυσεν χέρα γαστρὸς ἕκητι·
    τοῦτο τρυφὴν κείνῳ, τοῦτ' ἔφερ' εὐφροσύνην.
τρὶς δὲ τριηκοστὸν ζήσας ἔτος ἐνθάδ' ἰαύει,
    παισὶ λιπὼν ἰξὸν καὶ πτερὰ καὶ καλάμους.

157.—ΑΔΗΛΟΝ

Τρεῖς ἐτέων δεκάδας, τριάδας δύο, μέτρον ἔθηκαν
    ἡμετέρης βιοτῆς μάντιες αἰθέριοι.
ἀρκοῦμαι τούτοισιν· ὁ γὰρ χρόνος ἄνθος ἄριστον
    ἡλικίης· ἔθανεν χὠ τριγέρων Πύλιος.

158.—ΑΔΗΛΟΝ

Εἰς Μάρκελλον τὸν Σιδίτην ἰατρόν

Μαρκέλλου τόδε σῆμα περικλυτοῦ ἰητῆρος,
φωτὸς κυδίστοιο τετιμένου ἀθανάτοισιν,
οὗ βίβλους ἀνέθηκεν ἐϋκτιμένη ἐνὶ Ῥώμῃ
Ἀδριανὸς προτέρων προφερέστερος ἡγεμονήων,
καὶ πάϊς Ἀδριανοῖο μέγ' ἔξοχος Ἀντωνῖνος,

155.—Anonymous

On Philistion the Actor of Nicaea

I, PHILISTION of Nicaea, who tempered with laughter the miserable life of men, lie here, the remains of all life [1]; I often died, but never yet just in this way.

156.—ISIDORUS OF AEGAE

BY his bird-lime and canes Eumelus lived on the creatures of the air, simply but in freedom. Never did he kiss a strange hand for his belly's sake. This his craft supplied him with luxury and delight. Ninety years he lived, and now sleeps here, having left to his children his bird-lime, nets and canes.

157.—Anonymous

THREE decades and twice three years did the heavenly augurs fix as the measure of my life. I am content therewith, for that age is the finest flower of life. Even ancient Nestor died.

158.—Anonymous

On Marcellus the Physician of Side

THIS is the tomb of Marcellus the renowned physician, a most celebrated man, honoured by the gods, whose books were presented (to the public library) in fair-built Rome by Hadrian the best of our former emperors, and by admirable Antoninus,

[1] i.e. he had represented all kinds of life on the stage.

ὄφρα καὶ ἐσσομένοισι μετ' ἀνδράσι κῦδος ἄροιτο
εἵνεκεν εὐεπίης, τήν οἱ πόρε Φοῖβος Ἀπόλλων,
ἡρῴῳ μέλψαντι μέτρῳ θεραπήϊα νούσων
βίβλοις ἐν πινυταῖς Χειρωνίσι τεσσαράκοντα.

159.—ΝΙΚΑΡΧΟΥ

Ὀρφεὺς μὲν κιθάρᾳ πλεῖστον γέρας εἵλετο θνητῶν,
Νέστωρ δὲ γλώσσης ἡδυλόγου σοφίῃ,
τεκτοσύνῃ δ' ἐπέων πολυΐστωρ θεῖος Ὅμηρος,
Τηλεφάνης δ' αὐλοῖς, οὗ τάφος ἐστὶν ὅδε.

160.—ΑΝΑΚΡΕΟΝΤΟΣ

Καρτερὸς ἐν πολέμοις Τιμόκριτος, οὗ τόδε σᾶμα·
Ἄρης δ' οὐκ ἀγαθῶν φείδεται, ἀλλὰ κακῶν.

161.—ΑΝΤΙΠΑΤΡΟΥ ΣΙΔΩΝΙΟΥ

α. Ὄρνι, Διὸς Κρονίδαο διάκτορε, τεῦ χάριν ἔστας
γοργὸς ὑπὲρ μεγάλου τύμβον Ἀριστομένους;
β. Ἀγγέλλω μερόπεσσιν ὅθ' οὕνεκεν ὅσσον ἄριστος
οἰωνῶν γενόμαν, τόσσον ὅδ' ἠϊθέων.
δειλαί τοι δειλοῖσιν ἐφεδρήσσουσι πέλειαι·   5
ἄμμες δ' ἀτρέστοις ἀνδράσι τερπόμεθα.

162.—ΔΙΟΣΚΟΡΙΔΟΥ

Εὐφράτην μὴ καῖε, Φιλώνυμε, μηδὲ μιήνῃς
πῦρ ἐπ' ἐμοί· Πέρσης εἰμὶ καὶ ἐκ πατέρων,
Πέρσης αὐθιγενής, ναὶ δέσποτα· πῦρ δὲ μιῆναι
ἡμῖν τοῦ χαλεποῦ πικρότερον θανάτου.
ἀλλὰ περιστείλας με δίδου χθονί· μηδ' ἐπὶ νεκρῷ   5
λουτρὰ χέῃς· σέβομαι, δέσποτα, καὶ ποταμούς.

Hadrian's son; so that among men in after years he might win renown for his eloquence, the gift of Phoebus Apollo. He sung of the treatment of diseases in forty skilled books of heroic verse called the Chironides.

159.—NICARCHUS

ORPHEUS won the highest prize among mortals by his harp, Nestor by the skill of his sweet-phrased tongue, divine Homer, the learned in lore, by the art of his verse, but Telephanes, whose tomb this is, by the flute.

160.—ANACREON

VALIANT in war was Timocritus, whose tomb this is. War is not sparing of the brave, but of cowards.

161.—ANTIPATER OF SIDON

On Aristomenes, on whose Tomb stood an Eagle

"FLEET-WINGED bird of Zeus, why dost thou stand in splendour on the tomb of great Aristomenes?" "I tell unto men that as I am chief among the birds, so was he among the youth. Timid doves watch over cowards, but we delight in dauntless men."

162.—DIOSCORIDES

BURN not Euphrates,[1] Philonymus, nor defile Fire for me. I am a Persian as my fathers were, a Persian of pure stock, yea, master: to defile Fire is for us bitterer than cruel death. But wrap me up and lay me in the ground, washing not my corpse; I worship rivers also, master.

[1] The slave's name.

163.—ΛΕΩΝΙΔΟΥ

α. Τίς τίνος εὖσα, γύναι, Παρίην ὑπὸ κίονα κεῖσαι;
  β. Πρηξὼ Καλλιτέλευς.   α. Καὶ ποδαπή;
  β. Σαμίη.
α. Τίς δέ σε καὶ κτερέϊξε; β. Θεόκριτος, ᾧ με γονῆες
  ἐξέδοσαν.   α. Θνήσκεις δ᾽ ἐκ τίνος ; β. Ἐκ
  τοκετοῦ.
α. Εὖσα πόσων ἐτέων ; β. Δύο κεἴκοσιν. α. Ἦ
  ῥά γ᾽ ἄτεκνος ;   5
  β. Οὔκ, ἀλλὰ τριετῆ Καλλιτέλην ἔλιπον.
α. Ζώοι σοί κεῖνός γε, καὶ ἐς βαθὺ γῆρας ἵκοιτο.
  β. Καὶ σοί, ξεῖνε, πόροι πάντα Τύχη τὰ καλά.

164.—ΑΝΤΙΠΑΤΡΟΥ ΣΙΔΩΝΙΟΥ

α. Φράζε, γύναι, γενεήν, ὄνομα, χθόνα. β. Καλλι-
  τέλης μὲν
  ὁ σπείρας, Πρηξὼ δ᾽ οὔνομα, γῆ δὲ Σάμος.
α. Σῆμα δὲ τίς τόδ᾽ ἔχωσε ; β. Θεόκριτος, ὁ πρὶν
  ἄθικτα
  ἡμετέρας λύσας ἄμματα παρθενίης.
α. Πῶς δ᾽ ἔθανες; β. Λοχίοισιν ἐν ἄλγεσιν· α. Εἰπὲ
  δὲ ποίην   5
  ἦλθες ἐς ἡλικίην. β. Δισσάκις ἑνδεκέτις.
α. Ἦ καὶ ἄπαις; β. Οὔ, ξεῖνε· λέλοιπα γὰρ ἐν νεότητι
  Καλλιτέλη, τριετῆ παῖδ᾽ ἔτι νηπίαχον.
α. Ἔλθοι ἐς ὀλβιστὴν πολιὴν τρίχα. β. Καὶ σόν,
  ὁδῖτα,
  οὔριον ἰθύνοι πάντα Τύχη βίοτον.   10

163.—LEONIDAS

A. " Who art thou, who thy father, lady lying under the column of Parian marble ? " *B.* " Praxo, daughter of Calliteles." *A.* " And thy country ? " *B.* " Samos." *A.* " Who laid thee to rest ? " *B.* " Theocritus to whom my parents gave me in marriage." *A.* " And how didst thou die ? " *B.* " In childbirth." *A.* " How old ? " *B.* " Twenty-two." *A.* " Childless then ? " *B.* " No ! I left behind my three year old Calliteles." *A.* " May he live and reach a ripe old age." *B.* " And to thee, stranger, may Fortune give all good things."

164.—ANTIPATER OF SIDON

A Variant of the Last

A. " Tell me, lady, thy parentage, name and country." *B.* " Calliteles begat me, Praxo was my name, and my land Samos." *A.* " And who erected this monument ? " *B.* " Theocritus who loosed my maiden zone, untouched as yet." *A.* " How didst thou die ? " *B.* " In the pains of labour." *A.* " And tell me what age thou hadst reached." *B.* " Twice eleven years." *A.* " Childless ? " *B.* " No, stranger, I left Calliteles behind me, my baby boy." *A.* " May he reach a grey and blessed old age." *B.* " And may Fortune, O stranger, steer the course of all thy life before a fair breeze."

165.—ΤΟΥ ΑΥΤΟΥ, οἱ δὲ ΑΡΧΙΟΥ

α. Εἰπὲ γύναι τίς ἔφυς. β. Πρηξώ. α. Τίνος ἔπλεο
   πατρός ;
   β. Καλλιτέλευς. α. Πάτρας δ᾽ ἐκ τίνος ἐσσί;
   β. Σάμου.
α. Μνᾶμα δέ σου τίς ἔτευξε; β. Θεόκριτος, ὅς με
   σύνευνον
   ἤγετο. α. Πῶς δ᾽ ἐδάμης; β. Ἄλγεσιν ἐν λο-
   χίοις.
α. Εἰν ἔτεσιν τίσιν εὖσα; β. Δὶς ἔνδεκα. α. Παῖδα
   δὲ λείπεις ;   5
   β. Νηπίαχον τρισσῶν Καλλιτέλην ἐτέων.
α. Ζωῆς τέρμαθ᾽ ἵκοιτο μετ᾽ ἀνδράσι. β. Καὶ σέο δοίη
   παντὶ Τύχη βιότῳ τερπνόν, ὁδῖτα, τέλος.

166.—ΔΙΟΣΚΟΡΙΔΟΥ, οἱ δὲ ΝΙΚΑΡΧΟΥ

Τὴν γοεραῖς πνεύσασαν ἐν ὠδίνεσσι Λαμίσκην
   ὕστατα, Νικαρέτης παῖδα καὶ Εὐπόλιδος,
σὺν βρέφεσιν διδύμοις, Σαμίην γένος, αἱ παρὰ Νείλῳ
   κρύπτουσιν Λιβύης ἠόνες εἰκοσέτιν.
ἀλλά, κόραι, τῇ παιδὶ λεχώϊα δῶρα φέρουσαι,   5
   θερμὰ κατὰ ψυχροῦ δάκρυα χεῖτε τάφου.

167.—ΤΟΥ ΑΥΤΟΥ, οἱ δὲ ΕΚΑΤΑΙΟΥ ΘΑΣΙΟΥ

Ἀρχέλεώ με δάμαρτα Πολυξείνην, Θεοδέκτου
   παῖδα καὶ αἰνοπαθοῦς ἔννεπε Δημαρέτης,
ὅσσον ἐπ᾽ ὠδῖσιν καὶ μητέρα· παῖδα δὲ δαίμων
   ἔφθασεν οὐδ᾽ αὐτῶν εἴκοσιν ἠελίων.
ὀκτωκαιδεκέτις δ᾽ αὐτὴ θάνον, ἄρτι τεκοῦσα,   5
   ἄρτι δὲ καὶ νύμφη, πάντ᾽ ὀλιγοχρόνιος.

165.—By the Same, or by ARCHIAS

Another Variant

A. "Tell me, lady, who thou wast?" *B.*
"Praxo." *A.* "Who thy father?" *B.* "Calli-
teles." *A.* "And from what country art thou?"
B. "Samos." *A.* "Who made thy tomb?" *B.*
"Theocritus who took me to wife." *A.* "How
didst thou die?" *B.* "In labour pangs." *A.* "At
what age?" *B.* "Twenty-two." *A.* "Hast thou
left a child?" *B.* "Calliteles, a baby of three."
A. "May he grow to manhood." *B.* "And may
Fortune, O wayfarer, end thy life happily."

166.—DIOSCORIDES or NICARCHUS

In Africa on the banks of the Nile resteth with
her twin babes Lamisca of Samos the twenty year
old daughter of Nicarete and Eupolis, who breathed
her last in the bitter pangs of labour. Bring to the
girl, ye maidens, such gifts as ye give to one newly
delivered, and shed warm tears upon her cold tomb.

167.—By the Same, or by HECATAEUS OF THASOS

Call me Polyxena the wife of Archelaus, daughter
of Theodectes and ill-fated Demarete, a mother too
in so far at least as I bore a child; for Fate over-
took my babe ere it was twenty days old, and I died
at eighteen, for a brief time a mother, for a brief
time a bride—in all short-lived.

168.—ΑΝΤΙΠΑΤΡΟΥ ΘΕΣΣΑΛΟΝΙΚΟΥ

" Εὐχέσθω τις ἔπειτα γυνὴ τόκον," εἶπε Πολυξώ,
γαστέρ' ὑπὸ τρισσῶν ῥηγνυμένη τεκέων·
μαίης δ' ἐν παλάμῃσι χύθη νέκυς· οἱ δ' ἐπὶ γαῖαν
ὤλισθον κοίλων ἄρρενες ἐκ λαγόνων,
μητέρος ἐκ νεκρῆς ζωὸς γόνος· εἷς ἄρα δαίμων   5
τῆς μὲν ἀπὸ ζωὴν εἵλετο, τοῖς δ' ἔπορεν.

169.—ΑΔΕΣΠΟΤΟΝ

Εἰς τὴν δάμαλιν τὴν ἱσταμένην πέραν Βυζαντίου ἐν
Χρυσοπόλει

Ἰναχίης οὐκ εἰμὶ βοὸς τύπος, οὐδ' ἀπ' ἐμεῖο
κλήζεται ἀντωπὸν Βοσπόριον πέλαγος.
κείνην γὰρ τὸ πάροιθε βαρὺς χόλος ἤλασεν Ἥρης
ἐς Φάρον· ἥδε δ' ἐγὼ Κεκροπίς εἰμι νέκυς.
εὐνέτις ἦν δὲ Χάρητος· ἔπλων δ' ὅτ' ἔπλωεν ἐκεῖνος   5
τῇδε, Φιλιππείων ἀντίπαλος σκαφέων.
Βοΐδιον δὲ καλεῦμαι ἐγὼ τότε· νῦν δὲ Χάρητος
εὐνέτις ἠπείροις τέρπομαι ἀμφοτέραις.

170.—ΠΟΣΕΙΔΙΠΠΟΥ, ἢ ΚΑΛΛΙΜΑΧΟΥ

Τὸν τριετῆ παίζοντα περὶ φρέαρ Ἀρχιάνακτα
εἴδωλον μορφᾶς κωφὸν ἐπεσπάσατο·
ἐκ δ' ὕδατος τὸν παῖδα διάβροχον ἥρπασε μάτηρ
σκεπτομένα ζωᾶς εἴ τινα μοῖραν ἔχει·
Νύμφας δ' οὐκ ἐμίηνεν ὁ νήπιος, ἀλλ' ἐπὶ γούνων   5
ματρὸς κοιμαθεὶς τὸν βαθὺν ὕπνον ἔχει.

168.—ANTIPATER OF THESSALONICA

"Let women after this pray for children," cried Polyxo, her belly torn by three babes; and in the midwife's hands she fell dead, while the boys slid from her hollow flanks to the ground, a live birth from a dead mother.   So one god took life from her and gave it to them.

169.—ANONYMOUS

On the statue of a heifer that stands opposite Byzantium in Chrysopolis.   Inscribed on the column.

I AM not the image of the Argive heifer, nor is the sea that faces me, the Bosporus, called after me.   She of old was driven to Pharos by the heavy wrath of Hera; but I here am a dead Athenian woman, I was the bed-fellow of Chares, and sailed with him when he sailed here to meet Philip's ships in battle.[1]   I was called Boeidion (little cow) then, and now I, bed-fellow of Chares, enjoy a view of two continents.

170.—POSEIDIPPUS OR CALLIMACHUS

THE dumb image of himself attracted Archianax the three year old boy, as he was playing by the well.   His mother dragged him all dripping from the water, asking herself if any life was left in him.   The child defiled not with death the dwelling of the Nymphs, but fell asleep on his mother's knees, and slumbers sound.

[1] B.C. 340.

171.—ΜΝΑΣΑΛΚΟΤ ΣΙΚΤΩΝΙΟΤ

Ἀμπαύσει καὶ τῇδε θοὸν πτερὸν ἱερὸς ὄρνις,
    τᾶσδ᾿ ὑπὲρ ἀδείας ἑζόμενος πλατάνου·
ὤλετο γὰρ Ποίμανδρος ὁ Μάλιος, οὐδ᾿ ἔτι νεῖται
    ἰξὸν ἐπ᾿ ἀγρευταῖς χευάμενος καλάμοις.

172.—ΑΝΤΙΠΑΤΡΟΤ ΣΙΔΩΝΙΟΤ

Ὁ πρὶν ἐγὼ καὶ ψῆρα καὶ ἁρπάκτειραν ἐρύκων
    σπέρματος, ὑψιπετῆ Βιστονίαν γέρανον,
ῥινοῦ χερμαστῆρος ἐΰστροφα κῶλα τιταίνων,
    Ἀλκιμένης, πτανῶν εἶργον ἄπωθε νέφος·
καί μέ τις οὐτήτειρα παρὰ σφυρὰ διψὰς ἔχιδνα   5
    σαρκὶ τὸν ἐκ γενύων πικρὸν ἐνεῖσα χόλον
ἠελίου χήρωσεν· ἴδ᾿ ὡς τὰ κατ᾿ αἰθέρα λεύσσων
    τοὐμ ποσὶν οὐκ ἐδάην πῆμα κυλινδόμενον.

173.—ΔΙΟΤΙΜΟΤ, οἱ δὲ ΛΕΩΝΙΔΟΤ

Αὐτόμαται δείλῃ ποτὶ ταύλιον αἱ βόες ἦλθον
    ἐξ ὄρεος, πολλῇ νιφόμεναι χιόνι·
αἰαῖ, Θηρίμαχος δὲ παρὰ δρυῒ τὸν μακρὸν εὕδει
    ὕπνον· ἐκοιμήθη δ᾿ ἐκ πυρὸς οὐρανίου.

A. Lang, *Grass of Parnassus*, ed. 2, p. 160.

174.—ΕΡΤΚΙΟΤ

Οὐκέτι συρίγγων νόμιον μέλος ἀγχόθι ταύτας
    ἁρμόζῃ βλωθρᾶς, Θηρίμαχε, πλατάνου·
οὐδέ σευ ἐκ καλάμων κερααὶ βόες ἁδὺ μέλισμα
    δέξονται, σκιερᾷ πὰρ δρυῒ κεκλιμένου.
ὤλεσε γὰρ πρηστήρ σε κεραύνιος· αἱ δ᾿ ἐπὶ μάνδραν   5
    ὀψὲ βόες νιφετῷ σπερχόμεναι κατέβαν.

98

171.—MNASALCAS OF SICYON.

HERE, too, the birds of heaven shall rest their swift wings, alighting on this sweet plane-tree. For Poemander of Melos is dead, and cometh here no longer, his fowling canes smeared with lime.

172.—ANTIPATER OF SIDON

I, ALCIMENES, who used to protect the crops from the starlings and that high-flying robber the Bistonian crane, was swinging the pliant arms of my leathern sling to keep the crowd of birds away, when a dipsas viper wounded me about the ankles, and injecting into my flesh the bitter bile from her jaws robbed me of the sunlight. Look ye how gazing at what was in the air I noticed not the evil that was creeping at my feet.

173.—DIOTIMUS OR LEONIDAS

OF themselves in the evening the kine came home to byre from the hill through the heavy snow. But Therimachus, alas! sleeps the long sleep under the oak. The fire of heaven laid him to rest.

174.—ERYCIAS

On the Same

No longer, Therimachus, dost thou play thy shepherds' tunes on the pipes near this crooked-leaved plane. Nor shall the horned kine listen again to the sweet music thou didst make, reclining by the shady oak. The burning bolt of heaven slew thee, and they at nightfall came down the hill to their byre driven by the snow.

99

175.—ΑΝΤΙΦΙΛΟΥ

Ὀύτω πᾶσ' ἀπόλωλε, γεωπόνε, βῶλος ἀρότροις,
  ἤδη καὶ τύμβους νωτοβατοῦσι βόες,
ἡ δ' ὕνις ἐν νεκύεσσι; τί τοι πλέον; ἢ πόσος οὗτος
  πυρός, ὃν ἐκ τέφρης, κοὐ χθονὸς ἁρπάσετε;
οὐκ αἰεὶ ζήσεσθε, καὶ ὑμέας ἄλλος ἀρώσει,   5
  τοίης ἀρξαμένους πᾶσι κακοσπορίης.

176.—ΤΟΥ ΑΥΤΟΥ

Οὐχ ὅτι με φθίμενον κῆδος λίπεν, ἐνθάδε κεῖμαι
  γυμνὸς ὑπὲρ γαίης πυροφόροιο νέκυς·
ταρχύθην γὰρ ἐγὼ τὸ πρίν ποτε, νῦν δ' ἀροτῆρος
  χερσὶ σιδηρείη μ' ἐξεκύλισεν ὕνις.
ἦ ῥα κακῶν θάνατόν τις ἐρεῖ λύσιν, ὁππότ' ἐμεῖο,   5
  ξεῖνε, πέλει παθέων ὕστατον οὐδὲ τάφος;

177.—ΣΙΜΩΝΙΔΟΥ

Σᾶμα τόδε Σπίνθηρι πατὴρ ἐπέθηκε θανόντι.

178.—ΔΙΟΣΚΟΡΙΔΟΥ ΝΙΚΟΠΟΛΙΤΟΥ

Λυδὸς ἐγώ, ναὶ Λυδός, ἐλευθερίῳ δέ με τύμβῳ,
  δέσποτα, Τιμάνθη τὸν σὸν ἔθευ τροφέα.
εὐαίων ἀσινῆ τείνοις βίον· ἢν δ' ὑπὸ γήρως
  πρός με μόλῃς, σὸς ἐγώ, δέσποτα, κἠν 'Αΐδῃ.

J. A. Pott, *Greek Love Songs and Epigrams*, p. 48.

175.—ANTIPHILUS

So there is no more turf, husbandman, left for thee to break up, and thy oxen tread on the backs of tombs, and the share is among the dead! What doth it profit thee? How much is this wheat ye shall snatch from ashes, not from earth? Ye shall not live for ever, and another shall plough you up, you who set to all the example of this evil husbandry.[1]

176.—By the Same

Not because I lacked funeral when I died, do I lie here, a naked corpse on wheat-bearing land. Duly was I buried once on a time, but now by the ploughman's hand the iron share hath rolled me out of my tomb. Who said that death was deliverance from evil, when not even the tomb, stranger, is the end of my sufferings?

177.—SIMONIDES

This monument his father erected above Spinther on his death (*the rest is missing*).

178.—DIOSCORIDES OF NICOPOLIS

I am a Lydian, yea a Lydian, but thou, master, didst lay me, thy foster-father Timanthes, in a freeman's grave. Live long and prosper free from calamity, and if stricken in years thou comest to me, I am thine, O master, in Hades too.

---

[1] The verses are supposed to be spoken by the dead man whose grave the ploughman has disturbed.

179.—ΑΔΗΛΟΝ

Σοὶ καὶ νῦν ὑπὸ γῆν, ναί, δέσποτα, πιστὸς ὑπάρχω,
   ὡς πάρος, εὐνοίης οὐκ ἐπιληθόμενος,
ὥς με τότ' ἐκ νούσου τρὶς ἐπ' ἀσφαλὲς ἤγαγες ἴχνος,
   καὶ νῦν ἀρκούσῃ τῇδ' ὑπέθου καλύβῃ,
Μάνην ἀγγείλας, Πέρσην γένος. εὖ δέ με ῥέξας   5
   ἕξεις ἐν χρείῃ δμῶας ἑτοιμοτέρους.

180.—ΑΠΟΛΛΩΝΙΔΟΤ

Ἠλάχθη θανάτοιο τεὸς μόρος, ἀντὶ δὲ σεῖο,
   δέσποτα, δοῦλος ἐγὼ στυγνὸν ἔπλησα τάφον·
ἡνίκα σεῦ δακρυτὰ κατὰ χθονὸς ἠρία τεῦχον,
   ὡς ἂν ἀποφθιμένου κεῖθι δέμας κτερίσω·
ἀμφὶς[1] ἔμ' ὤλισθεν γυρὴ κόνις. οὐ βαρὺς ἡμῖν   5
   ἔστ' Ἀΐδης· ζήσω τὸν σὸν ὑπ' ἠέλιον.

181.—ΑΝΔΡΟΝΙΚΟΤ

Οἰκτρὰ δὴ δνοφερὸν δόμον ἤλυθες εἰς Ἀχέροντος,
   Δαμοκράτεια φίλα, ματρὶ λιποῦσα γόους.
ἁ δέ, σέθεν φθιμένας, πολιοὺς νεοθῆγι σιδάρῳ
   κείρατο γηραλέας ἐκ κεφαλᾶς πλοκάμους.

182.—ΜΕΛΕΑΓΡΟΤ

Οὐ γάμον, ἀλλ' Ἀΐδαν ἐπινυμφίδιον Κλεαρίστα
   δέξατο, παρθενίας ἅμματα λυομένα.
ἄρτι γὰρ ἑσπέριοι νύμφας ἐπὶ δικλίσιν ἄχευν
   λωτοί, καὶ θαλάμων ἐπλαταγεῦντο θύραι·

---

[1] I write so : ἀμφὶ δ' MS.

179.—Anonymous

Now, too, underground I remain faithful to thee, master, as before, not forgetting thy kindness—how thrice when I was sick thou didst set me safe upon my feet, and hast laid me now under sufficient shelter, announcing on the stone my name, Manes, a Persian. Because thou hast been good to me thou shalt have slaves more ready to serve thee in the hour of need.

180.—APOLLONIDES

The doom of death hath been transferred, and in thy place, master, I, thy slave, fill the loathly grave. When I was building thy tearful chamber underground to lay thy body in after death, the earth around slid and covered me.   Hades is not grievous to me.   I shall dwell under thy sun.[1]

181.—ANDRONICUS

Sore pitied, dear Democrateia, didst thou go to the dark house of Acheron, leaving thy mother to lament.   And she, when thou wast dead, shore the grey hairs from her old head with the newly-sharpened steel.

182.—MELEAGER

No husband but Death did Clearista receive on her bridal night as she loosed her maiden zone. But now at eve the flutes were making music at the door of the bride, the portals of her chamber

---

[1] *i.e.* as long as you think kindly of me Hades will be sunlit to me.

ἠῷοι δ' ὀλολυγμὸν ἀνέκραγον, ἐκ δ' Ὑμέναιος   5
σιγαθεὶς γοερὸν φθέγμα μεθαρμόσατο·
αἱ δ' αὐταὶ καὶ φέγγος ἐδαδούχουν παρὰ παστῷ
πεῦκαι, καὶ φθιμένᾳ νέρθεν ἔφαινον ὁδόν.

H. C. Beeching, *In a Garden*, p. 100 ; A. Lang, *Grass of Parnassus*, ed. 2, p. 167.

183.—ΠΑΡΜΕΝΙΩΝΟΣ

. . . .
Ἄδης τὴν Κροκάλης ἔφθασε παρθενίην·
εἰς δὲ γόους Ὑμέναιος ἐπαύσατο· τὰς δὲ γαμούντων
ἐλπίδας οὐ θάλαμος κοίμισεν, ἀλλὰ τάφος.

184.—ΤΟΥ ΑΥΤΟΥ

Παρθενικῆς τάφος εἴμ' Ἑλένης, πένθει δ' ἔπ' ἀδελφοῦ
προφθιμένου διπλᾶ μητρὸς ἔχω δάκρυα·
μνηστῆρσιν δ' ἔλιπον κοίν' ἄλγεα· τὴν γὰρ ἔτ' οὔπω
οὐδενὸς ἡ πάντων ἐλπὶς ἔκλαυσεν ἴσως.

185.—ΑΝΤΙΠΑΤΡΟΥ ΘΕΣΣΑΛΟΝΙΚΕΩΣ

Αὐσονίη με Λίβυσσαν ἔχει κόνις, ἄγχι δὲ Ρώμης
κεῖμαι παρθενικὴ τῇδε παρὰ ψαμάθῳ·
ἡ δέ με θρεψαμένη Πομπηίη ἀντὶ θυγατρός,
κλαυσαμένη τύμβῳ θῆκεν ἐλευθερίῳ,
πῦρ ἕτερον σπεύδουσα· τὸ δ' ἔφθασεν, οὐδὲ κατ'
εὐχὴν   5
ἡμετέραν ἧψεν λαμπάδα Περσεφόνη.

echoed to knocking hands.   And at morn the death
wail was loud, the bridal song was hushed and
changed to a voice of wailing.   The same torches
that flamed round her marriage bed lighted her
dead on her downward way to Hades.

183.—PARMENION

(As she had just loosed her maiden zone) Death
came first and took the maidenhood of Crocale.
The bridal song ended in wailing, and the fond
anxiety of her parents was set to rest not by marriage
but by the tomb.

184.—By the Same

I am the tomb of the maiden Helen, and in mourn-
ing too for her brother who died before her I receive
double tears from their mother.   To her suitors I left
a common grief; for the hope of all mourned equally
for her who was yet no one's.

185.—ANTIPATER OF THESSALONICA

The Italian earth holds me an African, and near
to Rome I lie, a virgin yet, by these sands.   Pompeia
who reared me wept for me as for a daughter and
laid me in a freewoman's grave.   Another light[1] she
hoped for, but this came earlier, and the torch was
lit not as we prayed, but by Persephone.

[1] *i.e.* that of the bridal chamber, not of my funeral pyre.

186.—ΦΙΛΙΠΠΟΥ

Ἄρτι μὲν ἐν θαλάμοις Νικιππίδος ἡδὺς ἐπήχει
  λωτός, καὶ γαμικοῖς †ὕμνος[1] ἔχαιρε κρότοις·
θρῆνος δ᾽ εἰς ὑμέναιον ἐκώμασεν· ἡ δὲ τάλαινα,
  οὔπω πάντα γυνή, καὶ νέκυς ἐβλέπετο.
δακρυόεις Ἀΐδη, τί πόσιν νύμφης διέλυσας,   5
  αὐτὸς ἐφ᾽ ἁρπαγίμοις τερπόμενος λέχεσιν;

187.—ΤΟΥ ΑΥΤΟΥ

Ἡ γρῆϋς Νικὼ Μελίτης τάφον ἐστεφάνωσε
  παρθενικῆς. Ἀΐδη, τοῦθ᾽ ὁσίως κέκρικας;

188.—ΑΝΤΩΝΙΟΥ ΘΑΛΛΟΥ

Δύσδαιμον Κλεάνασσα, σὺ μὲν γάμῳ ἔπλεο, κούρη,
  ὥριος, ἀκμαίης οἷά τ᾽ ἐφ᾽ ἡλικίης·
ἀλλὰ τεοῖς θαλάμοισι γαμοστόλος οὐχ Ὑμέναιος,
  οὐδ᾽ Ἥρης ζυγίης λαμπάδες ἠντίασαν,
πένθιμος ἀλλ᾽ Ἀΐδης ἐπεκώμασεν, ἀμφὶ δ᾽ Ἐρινὺς   5
  φοίνιος ἐκ στομάτων μόρσιμον ἧκεν ὄπα·
ἤματι δ᾽ ᾧ νυμφεῖος ἀνήπτετο λαμπάδι παστάς,
  τούτῳ πυρκαϊῆς, οὐ θαλάμων ἔτυχες.

189.—ΑΡΙΣΤΟΔΙΚΟΥ ΡΟΔΙΟΥ

Οὐκέτι δή σε λίγεια κατ᾽ ἀφνεὸν Ἀλκίδος οἶκον
  ἀκρὶ μελιζομέναν ὄψεται ἀέλιος·
ἤδη γὰρ λειμῶνας ἐπὶ Κλυμένου πεπότησαι
  καὶ δροσερὰ χρυσέας ἄνθεα Περσεφόνας.

[1] Jacobs suggests οἶκος and I render so.

186.—PHILIPPUS

BUT now the sweet flute was echoing in the bridal chamber of Nikippis, and the house rejoiced in the clapping of hands at her wedding. But the voice of wailing burst in upon the bridal hymn, and we saw her dead, the poor child, not yet quite a wife. O tearful Hades, why didst thou divorce the bridegroom and bride, thou who thyself takest delight in ravishment?

187.—BY THE SAME

AGED Nico garlanded the tomb of maiden Melite. Hades, was thy judgement righteous?

188.—ANTONIUS THALLUS

UNHAPPY Cleanassa, thou wast ripe for marriage, being in the bloom of thine age. But at thy wedding attended not Hymenaeus to preside at the feast, nor did Hera who linketh man and wife come with her torches. Black-robed Hades burst in and by him the fell Erinys chanted the dirge of death. On the very day that the lights were lit around thy bridal bed thou camest to no wedding chamber, but to thy funeral pyre.

189.—ARISTODICUS OF RHODES

No longer, shrill-voiced locust, shall the sun look on thee, as thou singest in the wealthy house of Alkis, for now thou hast flown to the meadows of Hades and the dewy flowers of golden Persephone.

190.—ΑΝΥΤΗΣ, οἱ δὲ ΛΕΩΝΙΔΟΥ

Ἀκρίδι τᾷ κατ' ἄρουραν ἀηδόνι, καὶ δρυοκοίτᾳ
τέττιγι ξυνὸν τύμβον ἔτευξε Μυρώ,
παρθένιον στάξασα κόρα δάκρυ· δισσὰ γὰρ αὐτᾶς
παίγνι' ὁ δυσπειθὴς ᾤχετ' ἔχων Ἀΐδας.

191.—ΑΡΧΙΟΥ

Ἁ πάρος ἀντίφθογγον ἀποκλάγξασα νομεῦσι
πολλάκι καὶ δρυτόμοις κίσσα καὶ ἰχθυβόλοις,
πολλάκι δὲ κρέξασα πολύθροον, οἷά τις ἀχώ,
κέρτομον ἀντῳδοῖς χείλεσιν ἁρμονίαν,
νῦν εἰς γᾶν ἄγλωσσος ἀναύδητός τε πεσοῦσα   5
κεῖμαι, μιμητὰν ζᾶλον ἀνηναμένα.

192.—ΜΝΑΣΑΛΚΟΥ

Οὐκέτι δὴ πτερύγεσσι λιγυφθόγγοισιν ἀείσεις,
ἀκρί, κατ' εὐκάρπους αὔλακας ἑζομένα,
οὐδέ με κεκλιμένον σκιερὰν ὑπὸ φυλλάδα τέρψεις,
ξουθᾶν ἐκ πτερύγων ἁδὺ κρέκουσα μέλος.

193.—ΣΙΜΙΟΥ

Τάνδε κατ' εὔδενδρον στείβων δρίος εἴρυσα χειρὶ
πτώσσουσαν βρομίης οἰνάδος ἐν πετάλοις,
ὄφρα μοι εὐερκεῖ καναχὰν δόμῳ ἔνδοθι θείη,
τερπνὰ δι' ἀγλώσσου φθεγγομένα στόματος.

190.—ANYTE or LEONIDAS

For her locust, the nightingale of the fields, and her cicada that resteth on the trees one tomb hath little Myro made, shedding girlish tears ; for inexorable Hades hath carried off her two pets.

191.—ARCHIAS

A magpie I, that oft of old screeched in answer to the speech of the shepherds and woodcutters and fishermen. Often like some many-voiced Echo, with responsive lips I struck up a mocking strain. Now I lie on the ground, tongueless and speechless, having renounced my passion for mimicry.

192.—MNASALCAS

On a Locust

No longer, locust, sitting in the fruitful furrows shalt thou sing with thy shrill-toned wings, nor shalt thou delight me as I lie under the shade of the leaves, striking sweet music from thy tawny wings.

193.—SIMIAS

(Not an Epitaph)

This locust crouching in the leaves of a vine I caught as I was walking in this copse of fair trees, so that in a well-fenced home it may make noise for me, chirping pleasantly with its tongueless mouth.

194.—ΜΝΑΣΑΛΚΟΤ

Ἀκρίδα Δημοκρίτου μελεσίπτερον ἅδε θανοῦσαν
  ἄργιλος δολιχὰν ἀμφὶ κέλευθον ἔχει,
ἇς καί, ὅτ᾽ ἰθύσειε πανέσπερον ὕμνον ἀείδειν,
  πᾶν μέλαθρον μολπᾶς ἴαχ᾽ ὑπ᾽ εὐκελάδου.

195.—ΜΕΛΕΑΓΡΟΤ

Ἀκρίς, ἐμῶν ἀπάτημα πόθων, παραμύθιον ὕπνου,
  ἀκρίς, ἀρουραίη Μοῦσα, λιγυπτέρυγε,
αὐτοφυὲς μίμημα λύρας, κρέκε μοί τι ποθεινόν,
  ἐγκρούουσα φίλοις ποσσὶ λάλους πτέρυγας,
ὥς με πόνων ῥύσαιο παναγρύπνοιο μερίμνης,   5
  ἀκρί, μιτωσαμένη φθόγγον ἐρωτοπλάνον.
δῶρα δέ σοι γήτειον ἀειθαλὲς ὀρθρινὰ δώσω,
  καὶ δροσερὰς στόματι σχιζομένας ψακάδας.

196.—ΤΟΥ ΑΥΤΟΥ

Ἀχήεις τέττιξ, δροσεραῖς σταγόνεσσι μεθυσθείς,
  ἀγρονόμαν μέλπεις μοῦσαν ἐρημολάλον·
ἄκρα δ᾽ ἐφεζόμενος πετάλοις, πριονώδεσι κώλοις
  αἰθίοπι κλάζεις χρωτὶ μέλισμα λύρας.
ἀλλά, φίλος, φθέγγου τι νέον δενδρώδεσι Νύμφαις   5
  παίγνιον, ἀντῳδὸν Πανὶ κρέκων κέλαδον,
ὄφρα φυγὼν τὸν Ἔρωτα, μεσημβρινὸν ὕπνον ἀγρεύσω
  ἐνθάδ᾽ ὑπὸ σκιερᾷ κεκλιμένος πλατάνῳ.

---

[1] According to others, Argilos is a town.
[2] Literally "divided by my mouth." He means water

194.—MNASALCAS

THIS clay vessel[1] set beside the far-reaching road holds the body of Democritus' locust that made music with its wings. When it started to sing its long evening hymn, all the house rang with the melodious song.

195.—MELEAGER

(*This and 196 are not epitaphs but amatory poems*)

LOCUST, beguiler of my loves, persuader of sleep, locust, shrill-winged Muse of the corn fields, Nature's mimic lyre, play for me some tune I love, beating with thy dear feet thy talking wings, that so, locust, thou mayest deliver me from the pains of sleepless care, weaving a song that enticeth Love away. And in the morning I will give thee a fresh green leek, and drops of dew sprayed from my mouth.[2]

196.—BY THE SAME

On a Cicada

NOISY cicada, drunk with dew drops, thou singest thy rustic ditty that fills the wilderness with voice, and seated on the edge of the leaves, striking with saw-like legs thy sunburnt skin thou shrillest music like the lyre's. But sing, dear, some new tune to gladden the woodland nymphs, strike up some strain responsive to Pan's pipe, that I may escape from Love and snatch a little midday sleep, reclining here beneath the shady plane-tree.

blown out in a spray from the mouth, as I have often seen done to freshen tobacco that was dry.

197.—ΦΑΕΝΝΟΥ

Δαμοκρίτῳ μὲν ἐγώ, λιγυρὰν ὄκα μοῦσαν ἐνείην
ἀκρὶς ἀπὸ πτερύγων, τὸν βαθὺν ἆγον ὕπνον·
Δαμόκριτος δ᾽ ἐπ᾽ ἐμοὶ τὸν ἐοικότα τύμβον, ὁδῖτα,
ἐγγύθεν Ὠρωποῦ χεῦεν ἀποφθιμένᾳ.

198.—ΛΕΩΝΙΔΟΥ ΤΑΡΕΝΤΙΝΟΥ

Εἰ καὶ μικρὸς ἰδεῖν καὶ ἐπ᾽ οὔδεος, ὦ παροδῖτα,
λᾶας ὁ τυμβίτης ἄμμιν ἐπικρέμαται,
αἰνοίης, ὤνθρωπε, Φιλαινίδα· τὴν γὰρ ἀοιδὸν
ἀκρίδα, τὴν εὖσαν τὸ πρὶν ἀκανθοβάτιν,
διπλοῦς ἐς λυκάβαντας ἐφίλατο τὴν καλαμῖτιν,   5
κἀμφίεφ᾽ ὑμνιδίῳ χρησαμένην πατάγῳ·
καί μ᾽ οὐδὲ φθιμένην ἀπανήνατο· τοῦτο δ᾽ ἐφ᾽ ἡμῖν
τὠλίγον ὤρθωσεν σᾶμα πολυστροφίης.

199.—ΤΥΜΝΕΩ

Ὄρνεον ὦ Χάρισιν μεμελημένον, ὦ παρόμοιον
ἀλκυόσιν τὸν σὸν φθόγγον ἰσωσάμενον,
ἡρπάσθης, φίλ᾽ ἐλαιέ· σὰ δ᾽ ἤθεα καὶ τὸ σὸν ἡδὺ
πνεῦμα σιωπηραὶ νυκτὸς ἔχουσιν ὁδοί.

J. A. Pott, *Greek Love Songs and Epigrams*, ii. p. 58.

200.—ΝΙΚΙΟΥ

Οὐκέτι δὴ τανύφυλλον ὑπὸ †κλάκα κλωνὸς ἑλιχθεὶς
τέρψομ᾽ ἀπὸ ῥαδινῶν φθόγγον ἱεὶς πτερύγων·
χεῖρα γὰρ εἰς †ἀρετὰν παιδὸς πέσον, ὅς με λαθραίως
μάρψεν, ἐπὶ χλωρῶν ἑζόμενον πετάλων.

197.—PHAENNUS

I AM the locust who brought deep sleep to Democritus, when I started the shrill music of my wings. And Democritus, O wayfarer, raised for me when I died a seemly tomb near Oropus.

198.—LEONIDAS OF TARENTUM

WAYFARER, though the tombstone that surmounts my grave seems small and almost on the ground, blame not Philaenis. Me, her singing locust, that used to walk on thistles, a thing that looked like a straw, she loved and cherished for two years, because I made a melodious noise. And even when I was dead she cast me not away, but built this little monument of my varied talent.

199.—TYMNES

On an unknown bird called elaeus

BIRD, nursling of the Graces, who didst modulate thy voice till it was like unto a halcyon's, thou art gone, dear elaeus, and the silent ways of night possess thy gentleness and thy sweet breath.

200.—NICIAS

No longer curled under the leafy branch shall I delight in sending forth a voice from my tender wings. For I fell into the . . . . hand of a boy, who caught me stealthily as I was seated on the green leaves.

201.—ΠΑΜΦΙΛΟΥ

Οὐκέτι δὴ χλωροῖσιν ἐφεζόμενος πετάλοισιν
  ἀδεῖαν μέλπων ἐκπροχέεις ἰαχάν·
ἀλλά σε γηρύοντα κατήναρεν, ἠχέτα τέττιξ,
  παιδὸς ἀπ᾿ ἠλιθίου χεὶρ ἀναπεπταμένα.

202.—ΑΝΥΤΗΣ

Οὐκέτι μ᾿ ὡς τὸ πάρος πυκιναῖς πτερύγεσσιν ἐρέσσων
  ὄρσεις ἐξ εὐνῆς ὄρθριος ἐγρόμενος·
ἦ γάρ σ᾿ ὑπνώοντα σίνις λαθρηδὸν ἐπελθὼν
  ἔκτεινεν λαιμῷ ῥίμφα καθεὶς ὄνυχα.

203.—ΣΙΜΙΟΥ

Οὐκέτ᾿ ἀν᾿ ὑλῆεν δρίος εὔσκιον, ἀγρότα πέρδιξ,
  ἠχήεσσαν ἵης γῆρυν ἀπὸ στομάτων,
θηρεύων βαλίους συνομήλικας ἐν νομῷ ὕλης·
  ᾤχεο γὰρ πυμάταν εἰς Ἀχέροντος ὁδόν.

204.—ΑΓΑΘΙΟΥ ΣΧΟΛΑΣΤΙΚΟΥ

Οὐκέτι που, τλῆμον, σκοπέλων μετανάστρια πέρδιξ,
  πλεκτὸς λεπταλέαις οἶκος ἔχει σε λύγοις,
οὐδ᾿ ὑπὸ μαρμαρυγῇ θαλερώπιδος Ἠριγενείης
  ἄκρα παραιθύσσεις θαλπομένων πτερύγων.
σὴν κεφαλὴν αἴλουρος ἀπέθρισε, τἆλλα δὲ πάντα   5
  ἥρπασα, καὶ φθονερὴν οὐκ ἐκόρεσσε γένυν.
νῦν δέ σε μὴ κούφη κρύπτοι κόνις, ἀλλὰ βαρεῖα,
  μὴ τὸ τεὸν κείνη λείψανον ἐξερύσῃ.

201.—PAMPHILUS

No longer perched on the green leaves dost thou shed abroad thy sweet call, for as thou wast singing, noisy cicada, a foolish boy with outstretched hand slew thee.

202.—ANYTE

On a Cock

No longer, as of old, shalt thou awake early to rouse me from bed, flapping rapidly thy wings; for the spoiler[1] stole secretly upon thee, as thou didst sleep, and slew thee, nipping thy throat swiftly with his claws.

203.—SIMIAS

No longer, my decoy partridge, dost thou shed from thy throat thy resonant cry through the shady coppice, hunting thy pencilled fellows in their woodland feeding-ground; for thou art gone on thy last journey to the house of Acheron.

204.—AGATHIAS SCHOLASTICUS

No longer, my poor partridge, exiled from the rocks, does thy plaited house hold thee in its light withes; no longer in the shine of the bright-eyed Dawn dost thou shake the tips of thy sun-warmed wings. Thy head the cat bit off, but all the rest of thee I seized from her, nor did she satisfy her wicked jaws. Now may the dust lie not light on thee but heavy, lest she drag thy corpse from the tomb.

[1] Presumably a fox.

205.—ΤΟΥ ΑΥΤΟΥ

Οἰκογενὴς αἴλουρος ἐμὴν πέρδικα φαγοῦσα
  ζώειν ἡμετέροις ἔλπεται ἐν μεγάροις;
οὔ σε, φίλη πέρδιξ, φθιμένην ἀγέραστον ἐάσω,
  ἀλλ' ἐπὶ σοὶ κτείνω τὴν σέθεν ἀντιβίην.
ψυχὴ γὰρ σέο μᾶλλον ὀρίνεται, εἰσόκε ῥέξω   5
  ὅσσ' ἐπ' Ἀχιλλῆος Πύρρος ἔτευξε τάφῳ.

206.—ΔΑΜΟΧΑΡΙΔΟΣ ΓΡΑΜΜΑΤΙΚΟΥ
ΚΑΙ ΜΑΘΗΤΟΥ ΑΥΤΟΥ

Ἀνδροβόρων ὁμότεχνε κυνῶν, αἴλουρε κακίστη,
  τῶν Ἀκταιονίδων ἐσσὶ μία σκυλάκων.
κτήτορος Ἀγαθίαο τεοῦ πέρδικα φαγοῦσα,
  λυπεῖς, ὡς αὐτὸν κτήτορα δασσαμένη.
καὶ σὺ μὲν ἐν πέρδιξιν ἔχεις νόον· οἱ δὲ μύες νῦν   5
  ὀρχοῦνται, τῆς σῆς δραξάμενοι σπατάλης.

207.—ΜΕΛΕΑΓΡΟΥ

Τὸν ταχύπουν, ἔτι παῖδα συναρπασθέντα τεκούσης
  ἄρτι μ' ἀπὸ στέρνων, οὐατόεντα λαγὼν
ἐν κόλποις στέργουσα διέτρεφεν ἁ γλυκερόχρως
  Φανίον, εἰαρινοῖς ἄνθεσι βοσκόμενον.
οὐδέ με μητρὸς ἔτ' εἶχε πόθος· θνήσκω δ' ὑπὸ θοίνης   5
  ἀπλήστου, πολλῇ δαιτὶ παχυνόμενος.
καί μου πρὸς κλισίαις κρύψεν νέκυν, ὡς ἐν ὀνείροις
  αἰὲν ὁρᾶν κοίτης γειτονέοντα τάφον.

205.—By the Same

DOES the house-cat, after eating my partridge, expect to live in my halls? No! dear partridge, I will not leave thee unhonoured in death, but on thy body I will slay thy foe. For thy spirit grows ever more perturbed until I perform the rites that Pyrrhus executed on the tomb of Achilles.[1]

206.—DAMOCHARIS THE GRAMMARIAN, PUPIL OF AGATHIAS

WICKEDEST of cats, rival of the man-eating pack, thou art one of Actaeon's hounds. By eating the partridge of Agathias thy master, thou hurtest him no less than if thou hadst feasted on himself. Thy heart is set now on partridges, but the mice meanwhile are dancing, running off with thy dainties.

207.—MELEAGER

I WAS a swift-footed long-eared leveret, torn from my mother's breast while yet a baby, and sweet Phanion cherished and reared me in her bosom, feeding me on flowers of spring. No longer did I pine for my mother, but I died of surfeiting, fattened by too many banquets. Close to her couch she buried me so that ever in her dreams she might see my grave beside her bed.

---

[1] The sacrifice of Polyxena.

208.—ΑΝΥΤΗΣ ΛΥΡΙΚΗΣ

Μνᾶμα τόδε φθιμένου μενεδαΐου εἴσατο Δᾶμις
ἵππου, ἐπεὶ στέρνον τοῦδε δαφοινὸς Ἄρης
τύψε· μέλαν δέ οἱ αἷμα ταλαυρίνου διὰ χρωτὸς
ζέσσ', ἐπὶ δ' ἀργαλέᾳ βῶλον ἔδευσε φονᾷ.

209.—ΑΝΤΙΠΑΤΡΟΥ

Αὐτοῦ σοὶ παρ' ἅλωνι, δυηπαθὲς ἐργάτα μύρμηξ,
ἠρίον ἐκ βώλου διψάδος ἐκτισάμαν,
ὄφρα σε καὶ φθίμενον Δηοῦς σταχυητρόφος αὖλαξ
θέλγῃ, ἀροτραίῃ κείμενον ἐν θαλάμῃ.

210.—ΤΟΥ ΑΥΤΟΥ

Ἄρτι νεηγενέων σε, χελιδόνι, μητέρα τέκνων,
ἄρτι σε θάλπουσαν παῖδας ὑπὸ πτέρυγι,
ἀΐξας ἔντοσθε νεοσσοκόμοιο καλιῆς
νόσφισεν ὠδίνων τετραέλικτος ὄφις,
καὶ σὲ κινυρομέναν ὁπότ' ἀθρόος ἦλθε δαΐζων,
ἤριπεν ἐσχαρίου λαβρὸν ἐπ' ἆσθμα πυρός.
ὣς θάνεν ἠλιτοεργός· ἴδ' ὡς Ἥφαιστος ἀμύντωρ
τὰν ἀπ' Ἐριχθονίου παιδὸς ἔσωσε γονάν.

211.—ΤΥΜΝΕΩ

Τῇδε τὸν ἐκ Μελίτης ἀργὸν κύνα φησὶν ὁ πέτρος
ἴσχειν, Εὐμήλου πιστότατον φύλακα.
Ταῦρόν μιν καλέεσκον, ὅτ' ἦν ἔτι· νῦν δὲ τὸ κείνου
φθέγμα σιωπηραὶ νυκτὸς ἔχουσιν ὁδοί.

208.—ANYTE

THIS tomb Damis built for his steadfast war-horse pierced through the breast by gory Ares. The black blood bubbled through his stubborn hide, and he drenched the earth in his sore death-pangs.

209.—ANTIPATER OF SIDON

HERE by the threshing-floor, O ant, thou care-worn toiler, I built for thee a grave-mound of thirsty clod, so that in death too thou mayest delight in the corn-bearing furrow of Demeter, as thou liest chambered in the earth the plough upturned.

210.—BY THE SAME

JUST when thou hadst become the mother, swallow, of a new-born brood, just when thou first wast warming thy children under thy wings, a many-coiled serpent, darting into the nest where lay thy young, robbed thee of the fruit of thy womb. Then when with all his might he came to slay thee, too, as thou wast lamenting them, he fell into the greedy breath of the hearth-fire. So died he the deed undone. See how Hephaestus succoured and saved the race of his son Erichthonius.[1]

211.—TYMNES

THE stone tells that it contains here the white Maltese dog, Eumelus' faithful guardian. They called him Bull while he still lived, but now the silent paths of night possess his voice.

[1] Procne, who was changed into a swallow, was the daughter of Erichthonius.

212.—ΜΝΑΣΑΛΚΟΤ

Αἰθυίας, ξένε, τόνδε ποδηνέμου ἔννεπε τύμβον,
  τᾶς ποτ' ἐλαφρότατον χέρσος ἔθρεψε γόνυ·
πολλάκι¹ γὰρ νάεσσιν ἰσόδρομον ἄνυσε μᾶκος,
  ὄρνις ὅπως δολιχὰν ἐκπονέουσα τρίβον.

213.—ΑΡΧΙΟΤ

Πρὶν μὲν ἐπὶ χλωροῖς ἐριθηλέος ἔρνεσι πεύκας
  ἥμενος, ἢ σκιερᾶς ἀκροκόμου πίτυος,
ἔκρεκες εὐτάρσοιο δι' ἰξύος ἀχέτα μολπὰν
  τέττιξ, οἰονόμοις τερπνότερον χέλυος.
νῦν δέ σε, μυρμάκεσσιν ὑπ' εἰνοδίοισι δαμέντα,   5
  Ἄϊδος ἀπροϊδὴς ἀμφεκάλυψε μυχός.
εἰ δ' ἑάλως, συγγνωστόν, ἐπεὶ καὶ κοίρανος ὕμνων
  Μαιονίδας γρίφοις ἰχθυβόλων ἔθανεν.

214.—ΤΟΥ ΑΥΤΟΥ

Οὐκέτι παφλάζοντα διαΐσσων βυθὸν ἅλμης
  δελφίς, πτοιήσεις εἰναλίων ἀγέλας,
οὐδὲ πολυτρήτοιο μέλος καλάμοιο χορεύων
  ὑγρὸν ἀναρρίψεις ἄλμα παρὰ σκαφίσιν·
οὐδὲ σύ γ', ἀφρηστά, Νηρηΐδας ὡς πρὶν ἀείρων   5
  νώτοις πορθμεύσεις Τηθύος εἰς πέρατα.
ἦ γὰρ ἴσον πρηῶνι Μαλείης ὡς ἐκυκήθη,
  κῦμα πολυψάμμους ὦσέ σ' ἐπὶ ψαμάθους.

---

¹ I write so : πολλαῖς MS.

212.—MNASALCAS

On a Mare

STRANGER, say that this is the tomb of wind-footed Aethyia, a child of the dry land, lightest of limb; often toiling over the long course, she, like a bird,[1] travelled as far as do the ships.

213.—ARCHIAS

ONCE, shrilling cicada, perched on the green branches of the luxuriant pine,[2] or of the shady domed stone-pine, thou didst play with thy delicately-winged back a tune dearer to shepherds than the music of the lyre. But now the unforeseen pit of Hades hides thee vanquished by the wayside ants. If thou wert overcome it is pardonable; for Maeonides, the lord of song, perished by the riddle of the fishermen.[3]

214.—BY THE SAME

No longer, dolphin, darting through the bubbling brine, shalt thou startle the flocks of the deep, nor, dancing to the tune of the pierced reed, shalt thou throw up the sea beside the ships. No longer, foamer, shalt thou take the Nereids on thy back as of yore and carry them to the realms of Tethys; for the waves when they rose high as the headland of Malea drove thee on to the sandy beach.

[1] *i.e.* like the sea-bird (αἴθυια) whose name she bore.
[2] Pinus maritima.   [3] See note to No. 1.

215.—ΑΝΥΤΗΣ ΜΕΛΟΠΟΙΟΥ

Οὐκέτι δὴ πλωτοῖσιν ἀγαλλόμενος πελάγεσσιν
αὐχέν' ἀναρρίψω βυσσόθεν ὀρνύμενος,
οὐδὲ περὶ †σκαλάμοισι νεὼς περικαλλέα χείλη
ποιφύσσω, τἀμὰ τερπόμενος προτομᾷ·
ἀλλά με πορφυρέα πόντου νοτὶς ὧσ' ἐπὶ χέρσον,
κεῖμαι δὲ †ῥαδινὰν τάνδε παρ' ἠϊόνα.

216.—ΑΝΤΙΠΑΤΡΟΥ ΘΕΣΣΑΛΟΝΙΚΕΩΣ

Κύματα καὶ τρηχύς με κλύδων ἐπὶ χέρσον ἔσυρεν
δελφῖνα, ξείνοις κοινὸν ὅραμα τύχης.
ἀλλ' ἐπὶ μὲν γαίης ἐλέῳ τόπος· οἱ γὰρ ἰδόντες
εὐθύ με πρὸς τύμβους ἔστεφον εὐσεβέες·
νῦν δὲ τεκοῦσα θάλασσα διώλεσε. τίς παρὰ πόντῳ
πίστις, ὃς οὐδ' ἰδίης φείσατο συντροφίης;

217.—ΑΣΚΛΗΠΙΑΔΟΥ

Ἀρχεάνασσαν ἔχω, τὰν ἐκ Κολοφῶνος ἑταίραν,
ἇς καὶ ἐπὶ ῥυτίδων ὁ γλυκὺς ἕζετ' Ἔρως.
ἆ νέον ἥβης ἄνθος ἀποδρέψαντες ἐρασταὶ
πρωτοβόλου, δι' ὅσης ἤλθετε πυρκαϊῆς.

218.—ΑΝΤΙΠΑΤΡΟΥ ΣΙΔΩΝΙΟΥ

Τὴν καὶ ἅμα χρυσῷ καὶ ἁλουργίδι καὶ σὺν Ἔρωτι
θρυπτομένην, ἁπαλῆς Κύπριδος ἁβροτέραν
Λαΐδ' ἔχω, πολιῆτιν ἁλιζώνοιο Κορίνθου,
Πειρήνης λευκῶν φαιδροτέραν λιβάδων,

215.—ANYTE

No longer exulting in the sea that carries me, shall I lift up my neck as I rush from the depths; no longer shall I snort round the decorated bows of the ship, proud of her figure-head, my image.   But the dark sea-water threw me up on the land and here I lie by this narrow (?) beach.

216.—ANTIPATER OF THESSALONICA

The waves and rough surges drove me, the dolphin, on the land, a spectacle of misfortune for all strangers to look on.   Yet on earth pity finds a place, for the men who saw me straightway in reverence decked me for my grave.   But now the sea who bore me has destroyed me.   What faith is there in the sea, that spared not even her own nursling?

217.—ASCLEPIADES

(A slightly different version is attributed by Athenaeus to Plato)

I hold Archeanassa the courtesan from Colophon even on whose wrinkles sweet Love sat.   Ah, ye lovers, who plucked the fresh flowers of her youth in its first piercing brilliance, through what a fiery furnace did you pass!

218.—ANTIPATER OF SIDON

I contain her who in Love's company luxuriated in gold and purple, more delicate than tender Cypris, Lais the citizen of sea-girt Corinth, brighter than the white waters of Pirene; that mortal Cytherea

123

τὴν θνητὴν Κυθέρειαν, ἐφ' ᾗ μνηστῆρες ἀγαυοὶ   5
  πλείονες ἢ νύμφης εἵνεκα Τυνδαρίδος,
δρεπτόμενοι χάριτάς τε καὶ ὠνητὴν ἀφροδίτην·
  ἧς καὶ ὑπ' εὐώδει τύμβος ὄδωδε κρόκῳ,
ἧς ἔτι κηώεντι μύρῳ τὸ διάβροχον ὀστεῦν,
  καὶ λιπαραὶ θυόεν ἆσθμα πνέουσι κόμαι·   10
ᾗ ἔπι καλὸν ἄμυξε κατὰ ῥέθος Ἀφρογένεια,
  καὶ γοερὸν λύζων ἐστονάχησεν Ἔρως.
εἰ δ' οὐ πάγκοινον δούλην θέτο κέρδεος εὐνήν,
  Ἑλλὰς ἄν, ὡς Ἑλένης, τῆσδ' ὕπερ ἔσχε πόνον.

219.—ΠΟΜΠΗΙΟΤ ΝΕΩΤΕΡΟΤ

Ἡ τὸ καλὸν καὶ πᾶσιν ἐράσμιον ἀνθήσασα,
  ἡ μούνη Χαρίτων λείρια δρεψαμένη,
οὐκέτι χρυσοχάλινον ὁρᾷ δρόμον ἠελίοιο
  Λαΐς, ἐκοιμήθη δ' ὕπνον ὀφειλόμενον,
κώμους, καὶ τὰ νέων ζηλώματα, καὶ τὰ ποθεύντων   5
  κνίσματα, καὶ μύστην λύχνον ἀπειπαμένη.

220.—ΑΓΑΘΙΟΤ ΣΧΟΛΑΣΤΙΚΟΤ

Ἕρπων εἰς Ἐφύρην τάφον ἔδρακον ἀμφὶ κέλευθον
  Λαΐδος ἀρχαίης, ὡς τὸ χάραγμα λέγει.
δάκρυ δ' ἐπισπείσας, "Χαίροις, γύναι, ἐκ γὰρ ἀκουῆς
  οἰκτείρω σέ γ'," ἔφην, "ἣν πάρος οὐκ ἰδόμην.
ἆ πόσον ἠϊθέων νόον ἤκαχες· ἀλλ' ἴδε, Λήθην   5
  ναίεις, ἀγλαΐην ἐν χθονὶ κατθεμένη."

J. A. Pott, *Greek Love Songs and Epigrams*, i. p. 129.

who had more noble suitors than the daughter of Tyndareus, all plucking her mercenary favours. Her very tomb smells of sweet-scented saffron; her bones are still soaked with fragrant ointment, and her anointed locks still breathe a perfume as of frankincense. For her Aphrodite tore her lovely cheeks, and sobbing Love groaned and wailed. Had she not made her bed the public slave of gain, Greece would have battled for her as for Helen.

219.—POMPEIUS THE YOUNGER

Lais, whose bloom was so lovely and delightful in the eyes of all, she who alone culled the lilies of the Graces, no longer looks on the course of the Sun's golden-bitted steeds, but sleeps the appointed sleep, having bid farewell to revelling and young men's rivalries and lovers' torments and the lamp her confidant.

220.—AGATHIAS SCHOLASTICUS

On my way to Corinth I saw by the roadside the tomb of Lais of old time, so said the inscription; and shedding a tributary tear, I said " Hail, woman, for from report I pity thee whom I never saw. Ah, how didst thou vex the young men's minds! but look, thou dwellest in Lethe, having laid thy beauty in the earth."

221.—ΑΔΕΣΠΟΤΟΝ

Ἀκμαίη πρὸς ἔρωτα καὶ ἡδέα Κύπριδος ἔργα,
  Πατροφίλα, κανθοὺς τοὺς γλυκεροὺς ἔμυσας·
ἐσβέσθη δὲ τὰ φίλτρα τὰ κωτίλα, χὠ μετ᾽ ἀοιδῆς
  ψαλμός, καὶ κυλίκων αἱ λαμυραὶ προπόσεις.
Ἅδη δυσκίνητε, τί τὴν ἐπέραστον ἑταίρην   5
  ἥρπασας; ἢ καὶ σὴν Κύπρις ἔμηνε φρένα;

222.—ΦΙΛΟΔΗΜΟΥ

Ἐνθάδε τῆς τρυφερῆς μαλακὸν ῥέθος, ἐνθάδε κεῖται
  Τρυγόνιον, σαβακῶν ἄνθεμα σαλμακίδων·
ᾗ καλύβη καὶ δοῦπος ἐνέπρεπεν, ἢ φιλοπαίγμων
  στωμυλίη, Μητὴρ ἣν ἐφίλησε θεῶν·
ἡ μούνη στέρξασα τὰ Κύπριδος ἡμιγυναίκων[1]   5
  ὄργια, καὶ φίλτρων Λαΐδος ἁψαμένη.
φῦε κατὰ στήλης, ἱερὴ κόνι, τῇ φιλοβάκχῳ
  μὴ βάτον, ἀλλ᾽ ἁπαλὰς λευκοΐων κάλυκας.

223.—ΘΥΙΛΛΟΥ

Ἡ κροτάλοις ὀρχηστρὶς Ἀρίστιον, ἡ περὶ πεύκας
  τῇ Κυβέλῃ πλοκάμους ῥῖψαι ἐπισταμένη,
ἡ λωτῷ κερόεντι φορουμένη, ἡ τρὶς ἐφεξῆς
  εἰδυῖ᾽ ἀκρήτου χειλοποτεῖν κύλικας,
ἐνθάδ᾽ ὑπὸ πτελέαις ἀναπαύεται, οὐκέτ᾽ ἔρωτι,   5
  οὐκέτι παννυχίδων τερπομένη καμάτοις.
κῶμοι καὶ μανίαι, μέγα χαίρετε· κεῖθ᾽ <ἱερὰ θρίξ>[2]
  ἡ τὸ πρὶν στεφάνων ἄνθεσι κρυπτομένη.

---

[1] I write so : ἀμφὶ γυναικῶν MS. See *Class. Rev.* 1916, p. 48.
[2] I supply so. The verse is imperfect in the MS.

221.—ANONYMOUS

PATROPHILA, ripe for love and the sweet works of Cypris, thou hast closed thy gentle eyes; gone is the charm of thy prattle, gone thy singing and playing, and thy eager pledging of the cup. Inexorable Hades, why didst thou steal our loveable companion? Hath Cypris maddened thee too?

222.—PHILODEMUS

HERE lies the tender body of the tender being; here lies Trygonion[1] the ornament of the wanton band of the emasculated, he who was at home by the holy shrine of Rhea, amid the noise of music and the gay prattling throng, the darling of the Mother of the gods, he who alone among his effeminate fellows really loved the rites of Cypris, and whose charms came near those of Lais. Give birth, thou holy soil, round the grave-stone of the maenad not to brambles but to the soft petals of white violets.

223.—THYILLUS

THE castanet dancer Aristion, who used to toss her hair among the pines in honour of Cybele, carried away by the music of the horned flute; she who could empty one upon the other three cups of untempered wine, rests here beneath the poplars, no more taking delight in love and the fatigue of the night-festivals. A long farewell to revels and frenzy! It lies low, the holy head that was covered erst by garlands of flowers.

[1] Little dove.

GREEK ANTHOLOGY

224.—ΑΔΕΣΠΟΤΟΝ

Εἴκοσι Καλλικράτεια καὶ ἐννέα τέκνα τεκοῦσα,
οὐδ' ἑνὸς οὐδὲ μιῆς ἐδρακόμην θάνατον·
ἀλλ' ἑκατὸν καὶ πέντε διηνυσάμην ἐνιαυτούς,
σκίπωνι τρομερὰν οὐκ ἐπιθεῖσα χέρα.

225.—ΑΔΕΣΠΟΤΟΝ

Ψήχει καὶ πέτρην ὁ πολὺς χρόνος, οὐδὲ σιδήρου
φείδεται, ἀλλὰ μιῇ πάντ' ὀλέκει δρεπάνῃ·
ὡς καὶ Λαέρταο τόδ' ἠρίον, ὃ σχεδὸν ἀκτῆς
βαιὸν ἄπο, ψυχρῶν λείβεται ἐξ ὑετῶν.
οὔνομα μὴν ἥρωος ἀεὶ νέον· οὐ γὰρ ἀοιδὰς   5
ἀμβλύνειν αἰών, κἣν ἐθέλῃ, δύναται.

226.—ΑΝΑΚΡΕΟΝΤΟΣ ΤΗΙΟΥ

Ἀβδήρων προθανόντα τὸν αἰνοβίην Ἀγάθωνα
πᾶσ' ἐπὶ πυρκαϊῆς ἧδ' ἐβόησε πόλις.
οὔ τινα γὰρ τοιόνδε νέων ὁ φιλαίματος Ἄρης
ἠνάρισεν στυγερῆς ἐν στροφάλιγγι μάχης.

227.—ΔΙΟΤΙΜΟΥ

Οὐδὲ λέων ὣς δεινὸς ἐν οὔρεσιν, ὡς ὁ Μίκωνος
υἱὸς Κριναγόρης ἐν σακέων πατάγῳ.
εἰ δὲ κάλυμμ' ὀλίγον, μὴ μέμφεο· μικρὸς ὁ χῶρος,
ἀλλ' ἄνδρας πολέμου τλήμονας οἶδε φέρειν.

228.—ΑΔΕΣΠΟΤΟΝ

Αὐτῷ καὶ τεκέεσσι γυναικί τε τύμβον ἔδειμεν
Ἀνδροτίων· οὔπω δ' οὐδενός εἰμι τάφος.
οὕτω καὶ μείναιμι πολὺν χρόνον· εἰ δ' ἄρα καὶ δεῖ,
δεξαίμην ἐν ἐμοὶ τοὺς προτέρους προτέρους.

Rendered by Ausonius, Epit. 37.

128

224.—Anonymous

I, Callicratia, bore nine and twenty children and did not witness the death of one, boy or girl; I lived to the age of a hundred and five without ever resting my trembling hand on a staff.

225.—Anonymous

Time wears stone away and spares not iron, but with one sickle destroys all things that are. So this grave-mound of Laertes that is near the shore is being melted away by the cold rain. But the hero's name is ever young, for Time cannot, even if he will, make poesy dim.

226.—ANACREON OF TEOS

This whole city acclaimed Agathon, the doughty warrior, as he lay on the pyre after dying for Abdera; for Ares greedy of blood slew no other young man like to him in the whirlwind of the dreadful fight.

227.—DIOTIMUS

Not even a lion is as terrible in the mountains, as was Mico's son Crinagoras in the clash of the shields. If this his covering be little, find no fault thereat; little is this land, but it bears men brave in war.

228.—Anonymous

Androtion built me for himself, his children and his wife. As yet I am no one's grave and so may I remain for long; but if it must be so, may I give earlier welcome to the earlier born.

229.—ΔΙΟΣΚΟΡΙΔΟΤ

Τᾷ Πιτάνᾳ Θρασύβουλος ἐπ᾽ ἀσπίδος ἤλυθεν ἄπνους,
   ἑπτὰ πρὸς Ἀργείων τραύματα δεξάμενος,
δεικνὺς ἀντία πάντα· τὸν αἱματόεντα δ᾽ ὁ πρέσβυς
   παῖδ᾽ ἐπὶ πυρκαϊὴν Τύννιχος εἶπε τιθείς·
"Δειλοὶ κλαιέσθωσαν· ἐγὼ δὲ σέ, τέκνον, ἄδακρυς 5
   θάψω, τὸν καὶ ἐμὸν καὶ Λακεδαιμόνιον."

230.—ΕΡΤΚΙΟΤ ΚΤΖΙΚΗΝΟΤ

Ἁνίκ᾽ ἀπὸ πτολέμου τρέσσαντά σε δέξατο μάτηρ,
   πάντα τὸν ὁπλιστὰν κόσμον ὀλωλεκότα,
αὐτά τοι φονίαν, Δαμάτριε, αὐτίκα λόγχαν
   εἶπε διὰ πλατέων ὠσαμένα λαγόνων·
"Κάτθανε, μηδ᾽ ἐχέτω Σπάρτα ψόγον· οὐ γὰρ
    ἐκείνα 5
   ἤμπλακεν, εἰ δειλοὺς τοὐμὸν ἔθρεψε γάλα."

231.—ΔΑΜΑΓΗΤΟΤ

Ὧδ᾽ ὑπὲρ Ἀμβρακίας ὁ βοαδρόμος ἀσπίδ᾽ ἀείρας
   τεθνάμεν ἢ φεύγειν εἵλετ᾽ Ἀρισταγόρας,
υἱὸς ὁ Θευπόμπου. μὴ θαῦμ᾽ ἔχε· Δωρικὸς ἀνὴρ
   πατρίδος, οὐχ ἥβας ὀλλυμένας ἀλέγει.

232.—ΑΝΤΙΠΑΤΡΟΤ

Λύδιον οὖδας ἔχει τόδ᾽ Ἀμύντορα, παῖδα Φιλίππου,
   πολλὰ σιδηρείης χερσὶ θιγόντα μάχης·
οὐδέ μιν ἀλγινόεσσα νόσος δόμον ἄγαγε Νυκτός,
   ἀλλ᾽ ὄλετ᾽ ἀμφ᾽ ἑτάρῳ σχὼν κυκλόεσσαν ἴτυν.

229.—DIOSCORIDES

Dead on his shield to Pitana came Thrasybulus, having received seven wounds from the Argives, exposing his whole front to them; and old Tynnichus, as he laid his son's blood-stained body on the pyre, said "Let cowards weep, but I will bury thee, my son, without a tear, thee who art both mine and Sparta's."

230.—ERYCIUS OF CYZICUS

Demetrius, when thy mother received thee after thy flight from the battle, all thy fine arms lost, herself she straightway drove the death-dealing spear through thy sturdy side, and said "Die and let Sparta bear no blame; it was no fault of hers if my milk reared cowards."

231.—DAMAGETUS

Thus for Ambracia's sake the warrior Aristagoras, son of Theopompus, holding his shield on high, chose death rather than flight. Wonder not thereat: a Dorian cares for his country, not for the loss of his young life.

232.—ANTIPATER OF SIDON

This Lydian land holds Amyntor, Philip's son, whose hands were often busied with iron war. Him no painful disease led to the house of Night, but he perished holding his round shield over his comrade.

233.—ΑΠΟΛΛΩΝΙΔΟΤ

Αἴλιος, Αὐσονίης στρατιῆς πρόμος, ὁ χρυσέοισι
  στέμμασι σωρεύσας αὐχένας ὁπλοφόρους,
νοῦσον ὅτ᾽ εἰς ὑπάτην ὠλίσθανε τέρμα τ᾽ ἄφυκτον
  εἶδεν, ἀριστείην †ἐμφανὲς εἰς ἰδίην·
πῆξε δ᾽ ὑπὸ σπλάγχνοισιν ἑὸν ξίφος, εἰπέ τε
    θνήσκων·   5
"Αὐτὸς ἑκὼν ἐδάμην, μὴ νόσος εὖχος ἔχῃ."

234.—ΦΙΛΙΠΠΟΤ ΘΕΣΣΑΛΟΝΙΚΕΩΣ

Αἴλιος ὁ θρασύχειρ Ἄρεος πρόμος, ὁ ψελιώσας
  αὐχένα χρυσοδέτοις ἐκ πολέμου στεφάνοις,
τηξιμελεῖ νούσῳ κεκολουμένος, ἔδραμε θυμῷ
  ἐς προτέρην ἔργων ἄρσενα μαρτυρίην,
ὦσε δ᾽ ὑπὸ σπλάγχνοις πλατὺ φάσγανον, ἓν μόνον
    εἰπών·   5
"Ἄνδρας Ἄρης κτείνει, δειλοτέρους δὲ νόσος."

235.—ΔΙΟΔΩΡΟΤ ΤΑΡΣΕΩΣ

Μὴ μέτρει Μάγνητι τὸ πηλίκον οὔνομα τύμβῳ,
  μηδὲ Θεμιστοκλέους ἔργα σε λανθανέτω.
τεκμαίρου Σαλαμῖνι καὶ ὁλκάσι τὸν φιλόπατριν·
  γνώσῃ δ᾽ ἐκ τούτων μείζονα Κεκροπίης.

236.—ΑΝΤΙΠΑΤΡΟΤ ΘΕΣΣΑΛΟΝΙΚΕΩΣ

Οὐχὶ Θεμιστοκλέους Μάγνης τάφος· ἀλλὰ κέχωσμαι
  Ἑλλήνων φθονερῆς σῆμα κακοκρισίης.

---

[1] That this is the sense required is shown by the next
epigram.

233.—APOLLONIDES

AELIUS, the Roman captain, whose armed neck was loaded with golden torques, when he fell into his last illness and saw the end was inevitable, was minded of[1] his own valour and driving his sword into his vitals, said as he was dying "I am vanquished of my own will, lest Disease boast of the deed."

234.—PHILIPPUS OF THESSALONICA

AELIUS, the bold captain, whose neck was hung with the golden torques he had won in the wars, when crippled by wasting disease, ran back in his mind to the history of his past deeds of valour, and drove his sword into his vitals, saying but this : "Men perish by the sword, cowards by disease."

235.—DIODORUS OF TARSUS

MEASURE not by this Magnesian tomb the greatness of the name, nor forget the deeds of Themistocles. Judge of the patriot by Salamis and the ships, and thereby shalt thou find him greater than Athens herself.

236.—ANTIPATER OF THESSALONICA

I, THIS Magnesian tomb, am not that of Themistocles, but I was built as a record of the envious misjudgment of the Greeks.[2]

[2] The ashes of Themistocles were transferred from Magnesia to Athens. The lines are, however, somewhat obscure.

237.—ΑΛΦΕΙΟΥ ΜΙΤΤΛΗΝΑΙΟΥ

Οὐρεά μευ καὶ πόντον ὑπὲρ τύμβοιο χάρασσε,
    καὶ μέσον ἀμφοτέρων μάρτυρα Λητοΐδην,
ἀενάων τε βαθὺν ποταμῶν ῥόον, οἵ ποτε ῥείθροις
    Ξέρξου μυριόναυν οὐχ ὑπέμειναν Ἄρην.
ἔγγραφε καὶ Σαλαμῖνα, Θεμιστοκλέους ἵνα σῆμα   5
    κηρύσσει Μάγνης δῆμος ἀποφθιμένου.

238.—ΑΔΔΑΙΟΥ

Ἠμαθίην ὃς πρῶτος ἐς Ἄρεα βῆσα Φίλιππος,
    Αἰγαίην κεῖμαι βῶλον ἐφεσσάμενος,
ῥέξας οἷ' οὔπω βασιλεὺς τὸ πρίν· εἰ δέ τις αὐχεῖ
    μεῖζον ἐμεῦ, καὶ τοῦθ' αἵματος ἡμετέρου.

239.—ΠΑΡΜΕΝΙΩΝΟΣ

Φθῖσθαι Ἀλέξανδρον ψευδὴς φάτις, εἴπερ ἀληθὴς
    Φοῖβος. ἀνικήτων ἅπτεται οὐδ' Ἀΐδης.

240.—ΑΔΔΑΙΟΥ

Τύμβον Ἀλεξάνδροιο Μακηδόνος ἤν τις ἀείδῃ,
    ἠπείρους κείνου σῆμα λέγ' ἀμφοτέρας.

241.—ΑΝΤΙΠΑΤΡΟΥ ΣΙΔΩΝΙΟΥ

Μυρία σοι, Πτολεμαῖε, πατὴρ ἔπι, μυρία μάτηρ
    τειρομένα θαλεροὺς ἠκίσατο πλοκάμους·
πολλὰ τιθηνητὴρ ὀλοφύρατο, χερσὶν ἀμήσας
    ἀνδρομάχοις δνοφερὰν κρατὸς ὕπερθε κόνιν.

---

[1] The last line does not seem to me to have much meaning, if any, as it stands. We expect " that the Magnesians may duly honour the tomb."

237.—ALPHEIUS OF MITYLENE

CARVE on my tomb the mountains and the sea, and midmost of both the sun as witness; yea, and the deep currents of the ever-flowing rivers, whose streams sufficed not for Xerxes' host of the thousand ships. Carve Salamis too, here where the Magnesian people proclaim the tomb of dead Themistocles.[1]

238.—ADDAEUS

I, PHILIP, who first set the steps of Macedonia in the path of war, lie here clothed in the earth of Aegae. No king before me did such deeds, and if any have greater to boast of, it is because he is of my blood.[2]

239.—PARMENION

IT is a lying report that Alexander is dead if Phoebus be true. Not even Hades can lay hand on the invincible.[3]

240.—ADDAEUS

IF one would sing of the tomb of Alexander of Macedon, let him say that both continents are his monument.

241.—ANTIPATER OF SIDON

AGAIN and again did thy father and mother, Ptolemy,[4] defile their hair in their grief for thee: and long did thy tutor lament thee, gathering in his warlike hands the dark dust to scatter on his head

[2] This refers to Alexander.
[3] Phoebus had proclaimed him invincible.
[4] It is not certain which of the Egyptian princes this is.

ἁ μεγάλα δ᾽ Αἴγυπτος ἑὰν ὠλόψατο χαίταν,   5
  καὶ πλατὺς Εὐρώπας ἐστονάχησε δόμος.
καὶ δ᾽ αὐτὰ διὰ πένθος ἀμαυρωθεῖσα Σελάνα
  ἄστρα καὶ οὐρανίας ἀτραπιτοὺς ἔλιπεν.
ὤλεο γὰρ διὰ λοιμὸν ὅλας θοινήτορα χέρσου,
  πρὶν πατέρων νεαρᾷ σκᾶπτρον ἑλεῖν παλάμᾳ·   10
οὐ δέ σε νὺξ ἐκ νυκτὸς ἐδέξατο· δὴ γὰρ ἄνακτας
  τοίους οὐκ Ἀΐδας, Ζεὺς δ᾽ ἐς Ὄλυμπον ἄγει.

242.—ΜΝΑΣΑΛΚΟΥ

Οἵδε πάτραν, πολύδακρυν ἐπ᾽ αὐχένι δεσμὸν ἔχουσαν,
  ῥυόμενοι, δνοφερὰν ἀμφεβάλοντο κόνιν·
ἄρνυνται δ᾽ ἀρετᾶς αἶνον μέγαν. ἀλλά τις ἀστῶν
  τούσδ᾽ ἐσιδὼν θνάσκειν τλάτω ὑπὲρ πατρίδος.

243.—ΛΟΛΛΙΟΥ ΒΑΣΣΟΥ

Φωκίδι πὰρ πέτρῃ δέρκευ τάφον· εἰμὶ δ᾽ ἐκείνων
  τῶν ποτὲ Μηδοφόνων μνᾶμα τριηκοσίων,
οἳ Σπάρτας ἀπὸ γᾶς τηλοῦ πέσον, ἀμβλύναντες
  Ἄρεα καὶ Μῆδον καὶ Λακεδαιμόνιον.
ἢν δ᾽ ἐσορῇς ἐπ᾽ ἐμεῖο †βοόστρυχον εἰκόνα θηρός,   5
  ἔννεπε· "Τοῦ ταγοῦ μνᾶμα Λεωνίδεω."

244.—ΓΑΙΤΟΥΛΙΚΟΥ

Δισσὰ τριηκοσίων τάδε φάσγανα θούριος Ἄρης
  ἔσπασεν Ἀργείων καὶ Λακεδαιμονίων,
ἔνθα μάχην ἔτλημεν ἀνάγγελον, ἄλλος ἐπ᾽ ἄλλῳ
  πίπτοντες· Θυρέαι δ᾽ ἦσαν ἄεθλα δορός.

---

[1] Sidon.   [2] i.e. a lion.
[3] On the celebrated fight for Thyreae between three

Great Egypt tore her hair and the broad home of Europa[1] groaned aloud. The very moon was darkened by mourning and deserted the stars and her heavenly path. For thou didst perish by a pestilence that devastated all the land, before thou couldst grasp in thy young hand the sceptre of thy fathers. Yet night did not receive thee from night; for such princes are not led by Hades to his house, but by Zeus to Olympus.

242.—MNASALCAS

THESE men delivering their country from the tearful yoke that rested on her neck, clothed themselves in the dark dust. High praise win they by their valour, and let each citizen looking on them dare to die for his country.

243.—LOLLIUS BASSUS

LOOK on this tomb beside the Phocian rock. I am the monument of those three hundred who were slain by the Persians, who died far from Sparta, having dimmed the might of Media and Lacedaemon alike. As for the image of an ox-slaying (?) beast[2] say "It is the monument of the commander Leonidas."

244.—GAETULICUS

FIERCE Ares drew these our swords, the three hundred from Argos and as many from Sparta, there where we fought out the fight from which no messenger returned, falling dead one upon another. Thyreae was the prize of the battle.[3]

hundred Argives and as many Spartans. See Herod. i. 82, and Nos. 431, 432, below.

245.—ΤΟΥ ΑΥΤΟΥ

Ὦ Χρόνε, παντοίων θνητοῖς πανεπίσκοπε δαῖμον,
    ἄγγελος ἡμετέρων πᾶσι γενοῦ παθέων·
ὡς ἱερὰν σώζειν πειρώμενοι Ἑλλάδα χώρην,
    Βοιωτῶν κλεινοῖς θνήσκομεν ἐν δαπέδοις.

246.—ΑΝΤΙΠΑΤΡΟΥ ΣΙΔΩΝΙΟΥ

Ἰσσοῦ ἐπὶ προμολῇσιν ἁλὸς παρὰ κῦμα Κιλίσσης
    ἄγριον αἱ Περσῶν κείμεθα μυριάδες,
ἔργον Ἀλεξάνδροιο Μακηδόνος, οἵ ποτ᾽ ἄνακτι
    Δαρείῳ πυμάτην οἶμον ἐφεσπόμεθα.

247.—ΑΛΚΑΙΟΥ

Ἄκλαυστοι καὶ ἄθαπτοι, ὁδοιπόρε, τῷδ᾽ ἐπὶ τύμβῳ
    Θεσσαλίας τρισσαὶ κείμεθα μυριάδες,
Ἡμαθίῃ μέγα πῆμα· τὸ δὲ θρασὺ κεῖνο Φιλίππου
    πνεῦμα θοῶν ἐλάφων ᾤχετ᾽ ἐλαφρότερον.

248.—ΣΙΜΩΝΙΔΟΥ

Μυριάσιν ποτὲ τῇδε τριηκοσίαις ἐμάχοντο
    ἐκ Πελοποννάσου χιλιάδες τέτορες.

249.—ΤΟΥ ΑΥΤΟΥ

Ὦ ξεῖν᾽, ἄγγειλον Λακεδαιμονίοις ὅτι τῇδε
    κείμεθα, τοῖς κείνων ῥήμασι πειθόμενοι.

W. Lisle Bowles, in *The Greek Anthology* (Bohn), p. 14.

---

[1] Probably on the Greeks who fell at the battle of
Chaeronea (B.C. 338).
[2] On the Macedonians slain at the battle of Cynoscephalae

245.—By the Same (?)

O Time, god who lookest upon all that befalls mortals, announce our fate to all, how striving to save the holy land of Hellas, we fell in the glorious Boeotian field.[1]

246.—ANTIPATER OF SIDON

On the promontory of Issus by the wild waves of the Cilician sea we lie, the many myriads of Persians who followed our King Darius on our last journey. Alexander's the Macedonian is the deed.

247.—ALCAEUS

Unwept, O wayfarer, unburied we lie on this Thessalian hillock, the thirty thousand, a great woe to Macedonia ; and nimbler than fleet-footed deer, fled that dauntless spirit of Philip.[2]

248.—SIMONIDES

Four thousand from Peloponnesus once fought here with three millions.[3]

249.—By the Same

Stranger, bear this message to the Spartans, that we lie here obedient to their laws.

(B.C. 197), where Philip V. was defeated by Flamininus. For the king's bitter retort see Book XVI. No. 26**.
[3] On the general monument of all the Greeks who fell at Thermopylae, No. 249 being on that of the Spartans.

250.—ΤΟΥ ΑΥΤΟΥ

Ἀκμᾶς ἑστακυῖαν ἐπὶ ξυροῦ Ἑλλάδα πᾶσαν
ταῖς αὑτῶν ψυχαῖς κείμεθα ῥυσάμενοι.

251.—ΤΟΥ ΑΥΤΟΥ

Ἄσβεστον κλέος οἵδε φίλῃ περὶ πατρίδι θέντες
κυάνεον θανάτου ἀμφεβάλοντο νέφος.
οὐδὲ τεθνᾶσι θανόντες, ἐπεί σφ' ἀρετὴ καθύπερθε
κυδαίνουσ' ἀνάγει δώματος ἐξ Ἀΐδεω.

252.—ΑΝΤΙΠΑΤΡΟΥ

Οἵδ' Ἀΐδαν στέρξαντες ἐνόπλιον, οὐχ, ἅπερ ἄλλοι,
στάλαν, ἀλλ' ἀρετὰν ἀντ' ἀρετᾶς ἔλαχον.

253.—ΣΙΜΩΝΙΔΟΥ

Εἰ τὸ καλῶς θνῄσκειν ἀρετῆς μέρος ἐστὶ μέγιστον,
ἡμῖν ἐκ πάντων τοῦτ' ἀπένειμε Τύχη·
Ἑλλάδι γὰρ σπεύδοντες ἐλευθερίην περιθεῖναι
κείμεθ' ἀγηράτῳ χρώμενοι εὐλογίῃ.

254.—ΤΟΥ ΑΥΤΟΥ

Χαίρετ' ἀριστῆες πολέμου μέγα κῦδος ἔχοντες,
κοῦροι Ἀθηναίων, ἔξοχοι ἱπποσύνῃ,
οἵ ποτε καλλιχόρου περὶ πατρίδος ὠλέσαθ' ἥβην
πλείστοις Ἑλλήνων ἀντία μαρνάμενοι.

250.—By the Same

WE lie here, having given our lives to save all Hellas when she stood on a razor's edge.[1]

251.—By the Same

THESE men having clothed their dear country in inextinguishable glory, donned the dark cloud of death; and having died, yet they are not dead, for their valour's renown brings them up from the house of Hades.[2]

252.—ANTIPATER

THESE men who loved death in battle, got them no grave-stone like others, but valour for their valour.[3]

253.—SIMONIDES

IF to die well be the chief part of virtue, Fortune granted this to us above all others; for striving to endue Hellas with freedom, we lie here possessed of praise that groweth not old.

254.—By the Same

HAIL, ye champions who won great glory in war, ye sons of Athens, excellent horsemen; who once for your country of fair dancing-floors lost your young lives, fighting against a great part of the Greeks.

[1] On the tomb of the Corinthians who fell at Salamis. The stone has been found.
[2] This is probably on the Spartan dead at Plataea, No. 253 being on the Athenian dead.
[3] Possibly a statue of Virtue.

254A.—ΤΟΥ ΑΥΤΟΥ

Κρὴς γενεὰν Βρόταχος Γορτύνιος ἐνθάδε κεῖμαι,
οὐ κατὰ τοῦτ' ἐλθών, ἀλλὰ κατ' ἐμπορίην.

255.—ΑΙΣΧΥΛΟΥ

Κυανέη καὶ τούσδε μενέγχεας ὤλεσεν ἄνδρας
Μοῖρα, πολύρρηνον πατρίδα ῥυομένους.
ζωὸν δὲ φθιμένων πέλεται κλέος, οἵ ποτε γυίοις
τλήμονες Ὀσσαίαν ἀμφιέσαντο κόνιν.

C. Merivale, *Collections from the Greek Anthology*, 1833,
p. 94.

256.—ΠΛΑΤΩΝΟΣ

Οἵδε ποτ' Αἰγαίοιο βαρύβρομον οἶδμα λιπόντες
Ἐκβατάνων πεδίῳ κείμεθ' ἐνὶ μεσάτῳ.
χαῖρε, κλυτή ποτε πατρὶς Ἐρέτρια· χαίρετ', Ἀθῆναι
γείτονες Εὐβοίης· χαῖρε, θάλασσα φίλη.

J. A. Symonds, the younger, *Studies of the Greek Poets*,
vol. ii. p. 294.

257.—ΑΔΗΛΟΝ

Παῖδες Ἀθηναίων Περσῶν στρατὸν ἐξολέσαντες
ἤρκεσαν ἀργαλέην πατρίδι δουλοσύνην.

258.—ΣΙΜΩΝΙΔΟΥ

Οἵδε παρ' Εὐρυμέδοντά ποτ' ἀγλαὸν ὤλεσαν ἥβην
μαρνάμενοι Μήδων τοξοφόρων προμάχοις
αἰχμηταὶ πεζοί τε καὶ ὠκυπόρων ἐπὶ νηῶν·
κάλλιστον δ' ἀρετῆς μνῆμ' ἔλιπον φθίμενοι.

J. H. Merivale, in *Collections from the Greek Anthology*,
1833, p. 66.

BOOK VII. EPIGRAMS 254ᴀ–258

254ᴀ.—By the Same

I, Brotachos, a Gortynian of Crete, lie here, where I came not for this end, but to trade.

255.—AESCHYLUS

Dark Fate likewise slew these staunch spearmen, defending their country rich in flocks. Living is the fame of the dead, who steadfast to the last lie clothed in the earth of Ossa.

256.—PLATO

Leaving behind the sounding surge of the Aegean we lie on the midmost of the plains of Ecbatana. Farewell, Eretria, once our glorious country; farewell, Athens, the neighbour of Euboea; farewell, dear Sea.[1]

257.—Anonymous

The sons of Athens utterly destroying the army of the Persians repelled sore slavery from their country.

258.—SIMONIDES

These men once by the Eurymedon[2] lost their bright youth, fighting with the front ranks of the Median bowmen, both on foot and from the swift ships; and dying they left behind them the glorious record of their courage.

[1] On the Eretrians settled in Persia by Darius. See Herod. vi. 119.

[2] In this battle Cimon defeated the Persians, B.C. 466.

259.—ΠΛΑΤΩΝΟΣ

Εὐβοίης γένος ἐσμὲν Ἐρετρικόν, ἄγχι δὲ Σούσων
κείμεθα· φεῦ, γαίης ὅσσον ἀφ' ἡμετέρης.

L. Campbell, in G. R. Thomson's *Selections from the Greek
Anthology*, p. 231.

260.—ΚΑΡΦΥΛΛΙΔΟΥ

Μὴ μέμψῃ παριὼν τὰ μνήματά μου, παροδῖτα·
οὐδὲν ἔχω θρήνων ἄξιον οὐδὲ θανών.
τέκνων τέκνα λέλοιπα· μιῆς ἀπέλαυσα γυναικὸς
συγγήρου· τρισσοῖς παισὶν ἔδωκα γάμους,
ἐξ ὧν πολλάκι παῖδας ἐμοῖς ἐνεκοίμισα κόλποις,   5
οὐδενὸς οἰμώξας οὐ νόσον, οὐ θάνατον,
οἵ με κατασπείσαντες ἀπήμονα, τὸν γλυκὺν ὕπνον
κοιμᾶσθαι, χώρην πέμψαν ἐπ' εὐσεβέων.

261.—ΔΙΟΤΙΜΟΥ

Τί πλέον εἰς ὠδῖνα πονεῖν, τί δὲ τέκνα τεκέσθαι,
ἢ τέκοι εἰ μέλλει παιδὸς ὁρᾶν θάνατον;
ἠιθέῳ γὰρ σῆμα Βιάνορι χεύατο μήτηρ·
ἔπρεπε δ' ἐκ παιδὸς μητέρα τοῦδε τυχεῖν.

262.—ΘΕΟΚΡΙΤΟΥ ΒΟΥΚΟΛΙΚΟΥ

Αὐδήσει τὸ γράμμα τί σᾶμά τε καὶ τίς ὑπ' αὐτῷ.
Γλαύκης εἰμὶ τάφος τῆς ὀνομαζομένης.

263.—ΑΝΑΚΡΕΟΝΤΟΣ ΤΗΙΟΥ

Καὶ σέ, Κλεηνορίδη, πόθος ὤλεσε πατρίδος αἴης
θαρσήσαντα Νότου λαίλαπι χειμερίῃ.
ὥρη γάρ σε πέδησεν ἀνέγγυος· ὑγρὰ δὲ τὴν σὴν
κύματ' ἀφ' ἱμερτὴν ἔκλυσεν ἡλικίην.

259.—PLATO

WE are Eretrians from Euboea and we lie near Susa, alas! how far from our own land.[1]

260.—CARPHYLLIDES

FIND no fault with my fate, traveller, in passing my tomb; not even in death have I aught that calls for mourning. I left children's children, I enjoyed the company of one wife who grew old together with me. I married my three children, and many children sprung from these unions I lulled to sleep on my lap, never grieving for the illness or loss of one. They all, pouring their libations on my grave, sent me off on a painless journey to the home of the pious dead to sleep the sweet sleep.

261.—DIOTIMUS

WHAT profiteth it to labour in childbirth and bring forth children if she who bears them is to see them dead! So his mother built the tomb for her little Bianor, while he should have done this for his mother.

262.—THEOCRITUS

THE writing will tell what tomb-stone is this and who lies under it. I am the tomb of famous Glauca.

263.—ANACREON

AND thee too, Clenorides, homesickness drove to death when thou didst entrust thyself to the wintry blasts of the south wind. That faithless weather stayed thy journey and the wet seas washed out thy lovely youth.

---

[1] See No. 256.

GREEK ANTHOLOGY

264.—ΛΕΩΝΙΔΟΥ

Εἴη ποντοπόρῳ πλόος οὔριος· ὃν δ' ἄρ' ἀήτης,
ὡς ἐμέ, τοῖς Ἀίδεω προσπελάσῃ λιμέσιν,
μεμφέσθω μὴ λαῖτμα κακόξενον, ἀλλ' ἕο τόλμαν,
ὅστις ἀφ' ἡμετέρου πείσματ' ἔλυσε τάφου.

265.—ΠΛΑΤΩΝΟΣ

Ναυηγοῦ τάφος εἰμί· ὁ δ' ἀντίον ἐστὶ γεωργοῦ·
ὡς ἁλὶ καὶ γαίῃ ξυνὸς ὕπεστ' Ἀίδης.

A. Esdaile, *The Poetry Review*, Sept. 1913.

266.—ΛΕΩΝΙΔΟΥ

Ναυηγοῦ τάφος εἰμὶ Διοκλέος· οἱ δ' ἀνάγονται,
φεῦ τόλμης, ἀπ' ἐμοῦ πείσματα λυσάμενοι.

267.—ΠΟΣΕΙΔΙΠΠΟΥ

Ναυτίλοι, ἐγγὺς ἁλὸς τί με θάπτετε; πολλὸν ἄνευθε
χῶσαι ναυηγοῦ τλήμονα τύμβον ἔδει.
φρίσσω κύματος ἦχον, ἐμὸν μόρον. ἀλλὰ καὶ οὕτως
χαίρετε, Νικήτην οἵτινες οἰκτίρετε.

268.—ΠΛΑΤΩΝΟΣ

Ναυηγόν με δέδορκας. ὃν οἰκτείρασα θάλασσα
γυμνῶσαι πυμάτου φάρεος ᾐδέσατο,
ἄνθρωπος παλάμῃσιν ἀταρβήτοις μ' ἀπέδυσε,
τόσσον ἄγος τόσσου κέρδεος ἀράμενος.
κεῖνο καὶ ἐνδύσαιτο, καὶ εἰς Ἀίδαο φέροιτο,   5
καί μιν ἴδοι Μίνως τοὐμὸν ἔχοντα ῥάκος.

146

264.—LEONIDAS

A GOOD voyage to all who travel on the sea; but let him who looses his cable from my tomb, if the storm carries him like me to the haven of Hades, blame not the inhospitable deep, but his own daring.

265.—PLATO

I AM the tomb of a shipwrecked man, and that opposite is the tomb of a husbandman. So death lies in wait for us alike on sea and land.

266.—LEONIDAS

I AM the tomb of the shipwrecked Diocles. Out on the daring of those who start from here, loosing their cable from me!

267.—POSIDIPPUS

SAILORS, why do you bury me near the sea? Far away from it ye should have built the poor tomb of the shipwrecked man. I shudder at the noise of the waves my destroyers. Yet even so I wish you well for taking pity on Nicetas.

268.—PLATO

I WHOM ye look upon am a shipwrecked man. The sea pitied me, and was ashamed to bare me of my last vesture. It was a man who with fearless hands stripped me, burdening himself with so heavy a crime for so light a gain. Let him put it on and take it with him to Hades, and let Minos see him wearing my old coat.

147

269.—ΤΟΥ ΑΥΤΟΥ

Πλωτῆρες, σώζοισθε καὶ εἰν ἁλὶ καὶ κατὰ γαῖαν·
ἴστε δὲ ναυηγοῦ σῆμα παρερχόμενοι.

270.—ΣΙΜΩΝΙΔΟΤ

Τούσδε ποτ' ἐκ Σπάρτας ἀκροθίνια Φοίβῳ ἄγοντας
ἐν πέλαγος, μία νύξ, ἐν σκάφος ἐκτέρισεν.

A. Esdaile, *The Poetry Review*, Sept. 1913.

271.—ΚΑΛΛΙΜΑΧΟΤ

Ὤφελε μηδ' ἐγένοντο θοαὶ νέες· οὐ γὰρ ἂν ἡμεῖς
παῖδα Διοκλείδου Σώπολιν ἐστένομεν·
νῦν δ' ὁ μὲν εἰν ἁλί που φέρεται νέκυς· ἀντὶ δ' ἐκείνου
οὔνομα καὶ κενεὸν σῆμα παρερχόμεθα.

H. C. Beeching, *In a Garden*, p. 95.

272.—ΤΟΥ ΑΥΤΟΥ

Νάξιος οὐκ ἐπὶ γῆς ἔθανεν Λύκος, ἀλλ' ἐνὶ πόντῳ
ναῦν ἅμα καὶ ψυχὴν εἶδεν ἀπολλυμένην,
ἔμπορος Αἰγίνηθεν ὅτ' ἔπλεε· χὼ μὲν ἐν ὑγρῇ
νεκρός· ἐγὼ δ' ἄλλως οὔνομα τύμβος ἔχων,
κηρύσσω πανάληθες ἔπος τόδε· "Φεῦγε θαλάσσῃ   5
συμμίσγειν Ἐρίφων, ναυτίλε, δυομένων."

273.—ΛΕΩΝΙΔΟΤ

Εὔρου με τρηχεῖα καὶ αἰπήεσσα καταιγίς,
καὶ νύξ, καὶ δνοφερῆς κύματα πανδυσίης

148

269.—By the Same

Mariners, may ye be safe on sea and land ; but know that this tomb ye are passing is a shipwrecked man's.

270.—SIMONIDES

These men, when bringing the firstfruits from Sparta to Phoebus, one sea, one night, one ship brought to the grave.

271.—CALLIMACHUS

Would that swift ships had never been, for then we should not be lamenting Sopolis the son of Dioclides.   Now somewhere on the sea his corpse is tossing, and what we pass by here is not himself, but a name and an empty grave.

272.—By the Same

Lycus of Naxos died not on land, but in the sea he saw his ship and his life lost together, as he sailed from Aegina to trade.   Now he is somewhere in the sea, a corpse, and I his tomb, bearing his idle name, proclaim this word of truth " Sailor, foregather not with the sea when the Kids are setting." [1]

273.— LEONIDAS

The fierce and sudden squall of the south-east wind, and the night and the waves that Orion at his dark

[1] *i.e.* Middle of November.

ἔβλαψ᾽ Ὠρίωνος· ἀπώλισθον δὲ βίοιο
   Κάλλαισχρος, Λιβυκοῦ μέσσα θέων πελάγευς.
κἀγὼ μὲν πόντῳ δινεύμενος, ἰχθύσι κῦρμα,   5
   οἴχημαι· ψεύστης δ᾽ οὗτος ἔπεστι λίθος.

274.—ΟΝΕΣΤΟΥ ΒΥΖΑΝΤΙΟΥ

Οὔνομα κηρύσσω Τιμοκλέος, εἰς ἅλα πικρὴν
   πάντη σκεπτομένη ποῦ ποτ᾽ ἄρ᾽ ἐστὶ νέκυς.
αἰαῖ· τὸν δ᾽ ἤδη φάγον ἰχθύες· ἡ δὲ περισσὴ
   πέτρος ἐγὼ τὸ μάτην γράμμα τορευθὲν ἔχω.

275.—ΓΑΙΤΟΥΛΙΚΟΥ

Ἁ Πέλοπος νᾶσος καὶ δύσπλοος ὤλεσε Κρήτα,
   καὶ Μαλέου τυφλαὶ καμπτομένου σπιλάδες
Δάμιδος Ἀστυδάμαντα Κυδώνιον. ἀλλ᾽ ὁ μὲν ἤδη
   ἔπλησεν θηρῶν νηδύας εἰναλίων·
τὸν ψεύσταν δέ με τύμβον ἐπὶ χθονὶ θέντο. τί
     θαῦμα;   5
   Κρῆτες ὅπου ψεῦσται, καὶ Διός ἐστι τάφος.

276.—ΗΓΗΣΙΠΠΟΥ

Ἐξ ἁλὸς ἡμίβρωτον ἀνηνέγκαντο σαγηνεῖς
   ἄνδρα, πολύκλαυτον ναυτιλίης σκύβαλον·
κέρδεα δ᾽ οὐκ ἐδίωξαν ἃ μὴ θέμις· ἀλλὰ σὺν αὐτοῖς
   ἰχθύσι τῇδ᾽ ὀλίγη θῆκαν ὑπὸ ψαμάθῳ.
ὦ χθών, τὸν ναυηγὸν ἔχεις ὅλον· ἀντὶ δὲ λοιπῆς   5
   σαρκὸς τοὺς σαρκῶν γευσαμένους ἐπέχεις.

setting[1] arouses were my ruin, and I, Callaeschrus, glided out of life as I sailed the middle of the Libyan deep. I myself am lost, whirled hither and thither in the sea a prey to fishes, and it is a liar, this stone that rests on my grave.

274.—HONESTUS OF BYZANTIUM

I ANNOUNCE the name of Timocles and look round in every direction over the salt sea, wondering where his corpse may be. Alas! the fishes have devoured him ere this, and I, this useless stone, bear this idle writing carved on me.

275.—GAETULICUS

THE Peloponnesus and the perilous sea of Crete and the blind cliffs of Cape Malea when he was turning it were fatal to Astydamas son of Damis the Cydonian. Ere this he has gorged the bellies of sea monsters. But on the land they raised me his lying tomb. What wonder! since "Cretans are liars," and even Zeus has a tomb there.[2]

276.—HEGESIPPUS

THE fishermen brought up from the sea in their net a half eaten man, a most mournful relic of some sea-voyage. They sought not for unholy gain, but him and the fishes too they buried under this light coat of sand. Thou hast, O land, the whole of the ship-wrecked man, but instead of the rest of his flesh thou hast the fishes who fed on it.

---

[1] Early in November.
[2] He refers to some verses of Callimachus in his Hymn to Zeus (v. 8). "Cretans are always liars" was a proverb found also in the verse quoted by St. Paul (*Titus*, i. 12).

277.—ΚΑΛΛΙΜΑΧΟΥ

Τίς, ξένος ὦ ναυηγέ; Λεόντιχος ἐνθάδε νεκρὸν
εὗρέ σ᾽ ἐπ᾽ αἰγιαλοῦ, χῶσε δὲ τῷδε τάφῳ,
δακρύσας ἐπίκηρον ἐὸν βίον· οὐδὲ γὰρ αὐτὸς
ἥσυχος, αἰθυίῃ δ᾽ ἶσα θαλασσοπορεῖ.

278.—ΑΡΧΙΟΥ ΒΥΖΑΝΤΙΟΥ

Οὐδὲ νέκυς, ναυηγὸς ἐπὶ χθόνα Θῆρις ἐλασθεὶς
κύμασιν, ἀγρύπνων λήσομαι ἠϊόνων.
ἦ γὰρ ἁλιρρήκτοις ὑπὸ δειράσιν, ἀγχόθι πόντου
δυσμενέος, ξείνου χερσὶν ἔκυρσα τάφου·
αἰεὶ δὲ βρομέοντα καὶ ἐν νεκύεσσι θαλάσσης   5
ὁ τλήμων ἀΐω δοῦπον ἀπεχθόμενον·
μόχθων οὐδ᾽ Ἀΐδης με κατεύνασεν, ἡνίκα μοῦνος
οὐδὲ θανὼν λείῃ κέκλιμαι ἡσυχίῃ.

A. Lang, *Grass of Parnassus*, ed. 2, p. 155.

279.—ΑΔΗΛΟΝ

Παῦσαι νηὸς ἐρετμὰ καὶ ἔμβολα τῷδ᾽ ἐπὶ τύμβῳ
αἰὲν ἐπὶ ψυχρῇ ζωγραφέων σποδιῇ.
ναυηγοῦ τὸ μνῆμα. τί τῆς ἐνὶ κύμασι λώβης
αὖθις ἀναμνῆσαι τὸν κατὰ γῆς ἐθέλεις;

280.—ΙΣΙΔΩΡΟΥ ΑΙΓΕΑΤΟΥ

Τὸ χῶμα τύμβος ἐστίν· ἀλλὰ τὼ βόε
ἐπίσχες οὗτος, τὰν ὕνιν τ᾽ ἀνάσπασον·
κινεῖς σποδὸν γάρ. ἐς δὲ τοιαύταν κόνιν
μὴ σπέρμα πυρῶν, ἀλλὰ χεῦε δάκρυα.

277.—CALLIMACHUS

WHO art thou, shipwrecked stranger? Leontichus found thee here dead on the beach, and buried thee in this tomb, weeping for his own uncertain life; for he also rests not, but travels over the sea like a gull.

278.—ARCHIAS OF BYZANTIUM

NOT even now I am dead shall I, shipwrecked Theris, cast up on land by the waves, forget the sleepless surges. For here under the brine-beaten hill, near the sea my foe, a stranger made my grave; and, ever wretched that I am, even among the dead the hateful roar of the billows sounds in my ears. Not even Hades gave me rest from trouble, since I alone even in death cannot lie in unbroken repose.

279.—ANONYMOUS

CEASE to paint ever on this tomb oars and the beaks of ships over my cold ashes. The tomb is a shipwrecked man's. Why wouldst thou remind him who is under earth of his disfigurement by the waves.

280.—ISIDORUS OF AEGAE

THIS hummock is a tomb; you there! hold in your oxen and pull up the ploughshare, for you are disturbing ashes. On such earth shed no seed of corn, but tears.

GREEK ANTHOLOGY

281.—ΗΡΑΚΛΕΙΔΟΥ

Ἄπισχ᾽, ἄπισχε χεῖρας, ὦ γεωπόνε,
μηδ᾽ ἀμφίταμνε τὰν ἐν ἠρίῳ κόνιν.
αὐτὰ κέκλαυται βῶλος· ἐκ κεκλαυμένας δ᾽
οὔτοι κομάτας ἀναθαλήσεται στάχυς.

282.—ΘΕΟΔΩΡΙΔΟΥ

Ναυηγοῦ τάφος εἰμί· σὺ δὲ πλέε· καὶ γὰρ ὅθ᾽ ἡμεῖς
ὠλλύμεθ᾽, αἱ λοιπαὶ νῆες ἐποντοπόρουν.

H. Wellesley, in *Anthologia Polyglotta*, p. 300.

283.—ΛΕΩΝΙΔΟΥ

Τετρηχυῖα θάλασσα, τί μ᾽ οὐκ οἰζυρὰ παθόντα
τηλόσ᾽ ἀπὸ ψιλῆς ἔπτυσας ἠϊόνος;
ὡς σεῦ μηδ᾽ Ἀΐδαο κακὴν ἐπιειμένος ἀχλὺν
Φυλεὺς Ἀμφιμένευς ἆσσον ἐγειτόνεον.

284.—ΑΣΚΛΗΠΙΑΔΟΥ

Ὀκτώ μευ πήχεις ἄπεχε, τρηχεῖα θάλασσα,
καὶ κύμαινε, βόα θ᾽ ἡλίκα σοι δύναμις·
ἢν δὲ τὸν Εὐμάρεω καθέλῃς τάφον, ἄλλο μὲν οὐδὲν
κρήγυον, εὑρήσεις δ᾽ ὀστέα καὶ σποδιήν.

R. Garnett, *A Chaplet from the Greek Anthology*, cx.

285.—ΓΛΑΥΚΟΥ ΝΙΚΟΠΟΛΙΤΟΥ

Οὐ κόνις οὐδ᾽ ὀλίγον πέτρης βάρος, ἀλλ᾽ Ἐρασίππου
ἢν ἐσορᾷς αὕτη πᾶσα θάλασσα τάφος·
ὤλετο γὰρ σὺν νηΐ· τὰ δ᾽ ὀστέα ποῦ ποτ᾽ ἐκείνου
πύθεται, αἰθυίαις γνωστὰ μόναις ἐνέπειν.

154

281.—HERACLIDES

HANDS off, hands off, labourer! and cut not through this earth of the tomb. This clod is soaked with tears, and from earth thus soaked no bearded ear shall spring.

282.—THEODORIDAS

I AM the tomb of a shipwrecked man; but set sail, stranger; for when we were lost, the other ships voyaged on.

283.—LEONIDAS

WHY, roaring sea, didst thou not cast me up, Phyleus, son of Amphimenes, when I came to a sad end, far away from the bare beach, so that even wrapped in the evil mist of Hades I might not be near to thee?

284.—ASCLEPIADES

KEEP off from me, thou fierce sea, eight cubits' space and swell and roar with all thy might. But if thou dost destroy the tomb of Eumares, naught shall it profit thee, for naught shalt thou find but bones and ashes.

285.—GLAUCUS OF NICOPOLIS

NOT this earth or this light stone that rests thereon is the tomb of Erasippus, but all this sea whereon thou lookest. For he perished along with his ship, and his bones are rotting somewhere, but where only the gulls can tell.

286.—ΑΝΤΙΠΑΤΡΟΥ ΘΕΣΣΑΛΟΝΙΚΟΥ

Δύσμορε Νικάνωρ, πολιῷ μεμαραμμένε πόντῳ,
 κεῖσαι δὴ ξείνη γυμνὸς ἐπ᾽ ἠϊόνι,
ἢ σύ γε πρὸς πέτρῃσι· τὰ δ᾽ ὄλβια κεῖνα μέλαθρα
 φροῦδα <καὶ ἡ> πάσης ἐλπὶς ὄλωλε Τύρου.
οὐδέ τί σε κτεάνων ἐρρύσατο· φεῦ, ἐλεεινέ,   5
 ὤλεο μοχθήσας ἰχθύσι καὶ πελάγει.

287.—ΑΝΤΙΠΑΤΡΟΥ

Καὶ νέκυν ἀπρήϋντος ἀνιήσει με θάλασσα
 Λῦσιν, ἐρημαίη κρυπτὸν ὑπὸ σπιλάδι,
στρηνὲς ἀεὶ φωνεῦσα παρ᾽ οὔατι, καὶ παρὰ κωφὸν
 σῆμα. τί μ᾽, ὤνθρωποι, τῇδε παρῳκίσατε,
ἣ πνοιῆς χήρωσε τὸν οὐκ ἐπὶ φορτίδι νηῒ   5
 ἔμπορον, ἀλλ᾽ ὀλίγης ναυτίλον εἰρεσίης
θηκαμένη ναυηγόν; ὁ δ᾽ ἐκ πόντοιο ματεύων
 ζωήν, ἐκ πόντου καὶ μόρον εἱλκυσάμην.

288.—ΤΟΥ ΑΥΤΟΥ

Οὐδετέρης ὅλος εἰμὶ θανὼν νέκυς, ἀλλὰ θάλασσα
 καὶ χθὼν τὴν ἀπ᾽ ἐμεῦ μοῖραν ἔχουσιν ἴσην.
σάρκα γὰρ ἐν πόντῳ φάγον ἰχθύες· ὀστέα δ᾽ αὖτε
 βέβρασται ψυχρῇ τῇδε παρ᾽ ἠϊόνι.

289.—ΑΝΤΙΠΑΤΡΟΥ ΜΑΚΕΔΟΝΟΣ

Ἀνθέα τὸν ναυηγὸν ἐπὶ στόμα Πηνειοῖο
 νυκτὸς ὑπὲρ βαιῆς νηξάμενον σανίδος,
μούνιος ἐκ θάμνοιο θορὼν λύκος, ἄσκοπον ἄνδρα,
 ἔκτανεν. ὢ γαίης κύματα πιστότερα.

286.—ANTIPATER OF THESSALONICA

Unhappy Nicanor, wasted by the grey sea, thou liest naked on a strange beach or perchance near the rocks; gone from thee are thy rich halls, and the hope of all Tyre has perished. None of thy possessions saved thee; alas, poor wight, thou art dead and hast laboured but for the fishes and the sea.

287.—ANTIPATER

Even in death shall the unappeased sea vex me, Lysis, buried as I am beneath this desert rock, sounding ever harshly in my ears close to my deaf tomb. Why, O men, did ye lay me next to her who reft me of breath, who wrecked me not trading on a merchantman, but embarked on a little rowing-boat? From the sea I sought to gain my living, and from the sea I drew forth death.

288.—By the Same

I belong entirely to neither now I am dead, but sea and land possess an equal portion of me. My flesh the fishes ate in the sea, but my bones have been washed up on this cold beach.

289.—ANTIPATER OF MACEDONIA

When shipwrecked Antheus had swum ashore at night on a small plank to the mouth of the Peneus, a solitary wolf rushing from the thicket slew him off his guard. O waves less treacherous than the land!

290.—ΣΤΑΤΥΛΛΙΟΥ ΦΛΑΚΚΟΥ

Λαίλαπα καὶ μανίην ὀλοῆς προφυγόντα θαλάσσης
   ναυηγόν, Λιβυκαῖς κείμενον ἐν ψαμάθοις,
οὐχ ἑκὰς ἠιόνων, πυμάτῳ βεβαρημένον ὕπνῳ,
   γυμνόν, ἀπὸ στυγερῆς ὡς κάμε ναυφθορίης,
ἔκτανε λυγρὸς ἔχις. τί μάτην πρὸς κύματ' ἐμόχθει,   5
   τὴν ἐπὶ γῆς φεύγων μοῖραν ὀφειλομένην;

291.—ΞΕΝΟΚΡΙΤΟΥ ΡΟΔΙΟΥ

Χαῖταί σου στάζουσιν ἔθ' ἁλμυρά, δύσμορε κούρη,
   ναυηγέ, φθιμένης εἰν ἁλί, Λυσιδίκη.
ἦ γάρ, ὀρινομένου πόντου, δείσασα θαλάσσης
   ὕβριν ὑπὲρ κοίλου δούρατος ἐξέπεσες.
καὶ σὸν μὲν φωνεῖ τάφος οὔνομα, καὶ χθόνα Κύμην,   5
   ὀστέα δὲ ψυχρῷ κλύζετ' ἐπ' αἰγιαλῷ,
πικρὸν Ἀριστομάχῳ γενέτῃ κακόν, ὅς σε κομίζων
   ἐς γάμον, οὔτε κόρην ἤγαγεν οὔτε νέκυν.

292.—ΘΕΩΝΟΣ ΑΛΕΞΑΝΔΡΕΩΣ

Ἀλκυόσιν, Ληναῖε, μέλεις τάχα· κωφὰ δὲ μήτηρ
   μύρεθ' ὑπὲρ κρυεροῦ δυρομένη σε τάφου.

293.—ΙΣΙΔΩΡΟΥ ΑΙΓΕΑΤΟΥ

Οὐ χεῖμα Νικόφημον, οὐκ ἄστρων δύσις
ἁλὸς Λιβύσσης κύμασιν κατέκλυσεν·
ἀλλ' ἐν γαλήνῃ, φεῦ τάλας, ἀνηνέμῳ
πλόῳ πεδηθείς, ἐφρύγη δίψευς ὕπο.
καὶ τοῦτ' ἀήτεων ἔργον· ἃ πόσον κακὸν   5
ναύταισιν ἢ πνέοντες ἢ μεμυκότες.

290.—STATYLLIUS FLACCUS

THE shipwrecked mariner had escaped the whirl-wind and the fury of the deadly sea, and as he was lying on the Libyan sand not far from the beach, deep in his last sleep, naked and exhausted by the unhappy wreck, a baneful viper slew him. Why did he struggle with the waves in vain, escaping then the fate that was his lot on the land ?

291.—XENOCRITUS OF RHODES

THE salt sea still drips from thy locks, Lysidice, unhappy girl, shipwrecked and drowned. When the sea began to be disturbed, fearing its violence, thou didst fall from the hollow ship. The tomb proclaims thy name and that of thy land, Cyme, but thy bones are wave-washed on the cold beach. A bitter sorrow it was to thy father Aristomachus, who, escorting thee to thy marriage, brought there neither his daughter nor her corpse.

292.—THEON OF ALEXANDRIA

THE halcyons, perchance, care for thee, Lenaeus, but thy mother mourns for thee dumbly over thy cold tomb.

293.—ISIDORUS OF AEGAE

No tempest, no stormy setting of a constellation overwhelmed Nicophemus in the waters of the Libyan Sea. But alas, unhappy man ! stayed by a calm he was burnt up by thirst. This too was the work of the winds. Ah, what a curse are they to sailors, whether they blow or be silent !

294.—ΤΥΛΛΙΟΥ ΛΑΤΡΕΑ

Γρυνέα τὸν πρέσβυν, τὸν ἀλιτρύτου ἀπὸ κύμβης
  ζῶντα, τὸν ἀγκίστροις καὶ μογέοντα λίνοις,
ἐκ δεινοῦ τρηχεῖα Νότου κατέδυσε θάλασσα,
  ἔβρασε δ' ἐς κροκάλην πρώϊον ἠϊόνα,
χεῖρας ἀποβρωθέντα. τίς οὐ νόον ἰχθύσιν εἴποι
  ἔμμεναι, οἳ μούνας, αἷς ὀλέκοντο, φάγον;

295.—ΛΕΩΝΙΔΑ ΤΑΡΕΝΤΙΝΟΥ

Θῆριν τὸν τριγέροντα, τὸν εὐάγρων ἀπὸ κύρτων
  ζῶντα, τὸν αἰθυίης πλείονα νηξάμενον,
ἰχθυσιληϊστῆρα, σαγηνέα, χηραμοδύτην,
  οὐχὶ πολυσκάλμου πλώτορα ναυτιλίης,
ἔμπης οὔτ' Ἀρκτοῦρος ἀπώλεσεν, οὔτε καταιγὶς
  ἤλασε τὰς πολλὰς τῶν ἐτέων δεκάδας·
ἀλλ' ἔθαν' ἐν καλύβῃ σχοινίτιδι, λύχνος ὁποῖα,
  τῷ μακρῷ σβεσθεὶς ἐν χρόνῳ αὐτόματος.
σῆμα δὲ τοῦτ' οὐ παῖδες ἐφήρμοσαν, οὐδ' ὁμόλεκτρος,
  ἀλλὰ συνεργατίνης ἰχθυβόλων θίασος.

A. Lang, *Grass of Parnassus*, ed. 2, p. 168.

296.—ΣΙΜΩΝΙΔΟΥ ΤΟΥ ΚΗΙΟΥ

Ἐξ οὗ γ' Εὐρώπην Ἀσίας δίχα πόντος ἔνειμε,
  καὶ πόλεμον λαῶν θοῦρος Ἄρης ἐφέπει,
οὐδαμά πω κάλλιον ἐπιχθονίων γένετ' ἀνδρῶν
  ἔργον ἐν ἠπείρῳ καὶ κατὰ πόντον ἅμα.
οἵδε γὰρ ἐν Κύπρῳ Μήδων πολλοὺς ὀλέσαντες,
  Φοινίκων ἑκατὸν ναῦς ἕλον ἐν πελάγει
ἀνδρῶν πληθούσας· μέγα δ' ἔστενεν Ἀσὶς ὑπ' αὐτῶν
  πληγεῖσ' ἀμφοτέραις χερσὶ κράτει πολέμου.

---

[1] *i.e.* the season of Arcturus' setting, September.

294.—TULLIUS LAUREAS

GRYNEUS, the old man who got his living by his sea-worn wherry, busying himself with lines and hooks, the sea, roused to fury by a terrible southerly gale, swamped and washed up in the morning on the beach, his hands eaten off. Who would say that they had no sense, the fish who ate just those parts of him by which they used to perish?

295.—LEONIDAS OF TARENTUM

THERIS, the old man who got his living from his lucky weels, who rode on the sea more than a gull, the preyer on fishes, the seine-hauler, the prober of crevices in the rocks, who sailed on no many-oared ship, in spite of all owed not his end to Arcturus,[1] nor did any tempest drive to death his many decades, but he died in his reed hut, going out like a lamp of his own accord owing to his length of years. This tomb was not set up by his children or wife, but by the guild of his fellow fishermen.

296.—SIMONIDES

SINCE the sea parted Europe from Asia, since fierce Ares directs the battles of nations, never was a more splendid deed of arms performed by mortals on land and on the sea at once. For these men after slaying many Medes in Cyprus, took a hundred Phoenician ships at sea with their crews. Asia groaned aloud, smitten with both hands by their triumphant might.[2]

[2] This is the epitaph of those who fell in Cimon's last campaign in Cyprus (B.C. 449).

297.—ΠΟΛΥΣΤΡΑΤΟΥ

Τὸν μεγαν᾿ Ἀκροκορινθον Ἀχαιϊκόν, Ἑλλάδος ἄστρον
    καὶ διπλῆν Ἰσθμοῦ σύνδρομον ἠϊόνα
Λεύκιος ἐστυφέλιξε· δοριπτοίητα δὲ νεκρῶν
    ὀστέα σωρευθεὶς εἷς ἐπέχει σκόπελος.
τοὺς δὲ δόμον Πριάμοιο πυρὶ πρήσαντας Ἀχαιοὺς
    ἀκλαύστους κτερέων νόσφισαν Αἰνεάδαι.

298.—ΑΔΕΣΠΟΤΟΝ

Αἰαῖ, τοῦτο κάκιστον, ὅταν κλαίωσι θανόντα
    νυμφίον ἢ νύμφην· ἡνίκα δ᾿ ἀμφοτέρους,
Εὔπολιν ὡς ἀγαθήν τε Λυκαίνιον, ὧν ὑμέναιον
    ἔσβεσεν ἐν πρώτῃ νυκτὶ πεσὼν θάλαμος,
οὐκ ἄλλῳ τόδε κῆδος ἰσόρροπον, ᾧ σὺ μὲν υἱόν,
    Νῖκι, σὺ δ᾿ ἔκλαυσας, Θεύδικε, θυγατέρα.

299.—ΝΙΚΟΜΑΧΟΥ

"Αδ᾿ ἔσθ᾿—ἅδε Πλάταια τί τοι λέγω;—ἄν ποτε
    σεισμὸς
ἐλθὼν ἐξαπίνας κάββαλε πανσυδίῃ·
λείφθη δ᾿ αὖ μοῦνον τυτθὸν γένος· οἱ δὲ θανόντες
    σᾶμ᾿ ἐρατὰν πάτραν κείμεθ᾿ ἐφεσσάμενοι.

300.—ΣΙΜΩΝΙΔΟΥ

Ἐνθάδε Πυθώνακτα κασίγνητόν τε κέκευθεν
    γαῖ᾿, ἐρατῆς ἥβης πρὶν τέλος ἄκρον ἰδεῖν.
μνῆμα δ᾿ ἀποφθιμένοισι πατὴρ Μεγάριστος ἔθηκεν
    ἀθάνατον θνητοῖς παισὶ χαριζόμενος.

297.—POLYSTRATUS

Lucius [1] has smitten sore the great Achaean Acrocorinth, the star of Hellas, and the twin parallel shores of the Isthmus. One heap of stones covers the bones of those slain in the rout; and the sons of Aeneas left unwept and unhallowed by funeral rites the Achaeans who burnt the house of Priam.

298.—ANONYMOUS

WOE is me! this is the worst of all, when men weep for a bride or bridegroom dead; but worse when it is for both, as for Eupolis and good Lycaenion, whose chamber falling in on the first night extinguished their wedlock. There is no other mourning to equal this by which you, Nicis, bewailed your son, and you, Theodicus, your daughter.

299.—NICOMACHUS

THIS (why say I "this?") is that Plataea which a sudden earthquake tumbled down utterly: only a little remnant was left, and we, the dead, lie here with our beloved city laid on us for a monument.

300.—SIMONIDES

HERE the earth covers Pythonax and his brother, before they saw the prime of their lovely youth. Their father, Megaristus, set up this monument to them dead, an immortal gift to his mortal sons.

[1] Mummius, who sacked Corinth 146 B.C.

301.—ΤΟΥ ΑΥΤΟΥ

Εὐκλέας αἶα κέκευθε, Λεωνίδα, οἳ μετὰ σεῖο
    τῆδ᾽ ἔθανον, Σπάρτης εὐρυχόρου βασιλεῦ,
πλείστων δὴ τόξων τε καὶ ὠκυπόδων σθένος ἵππων
    Μηδείων ἀνδρῶν δεξάμενοι πολέμῳ.

302.—ΤΟΥ ΑΥΤΟΥ

Τῶν αὐτοῦ τις ἕκαστος ἀπολλυμένων ἀνιᾶται·
    Νικόδικον δὲ φίλοι καὶ πόλις ἥδε †πολή.

303.—ΑΝΤΙΠΑΤΡΟΥ ΣΙΔΩΝΙΟΥ

Τὸν μικρὸν Κλεόδημον ἔτι ζώοντα γάλακτι,
    ἴχνος ὑπὲρ τοίχων νηὸς ἐρεισάμενον,
ὁ Θρῆιξ ἐτύμως Βορέης βάλεν εἰς ἁλὸς οἶδμα,
    κῦμα δ᾽ ἀπὸ ψυχὴν ἔσβεσε νηπιάχου.
Ἰνοῖ, ἀνοικτίρμων τις ἔφυς θεός, ἢ Μελικέρτεω
    ἥλικος οὐκ Ἀΐδην πικρὸν ἀπηλάσαο.

304.—ΠΕΙΣΑΝΔΡΟΥ ΡΟΔΙΟΥ

Ἀνδρὶ μὲν Ἱππαίμων ὄνομ᾽ ἦν, ἵππῳ δὲ Πόδαργος,
    καὶ κυνὶ Λήθαργος, καὶ θεράποντι Βάβης,
Θεσσαλός, ἐκ Κρήτης, Μάγνης γένος, Αἵμονος υἱός·
    ὤλετο δ᾽ ἐν προμάχοις ὀξὺν Ἄρη συνάγων.

---

[1] This, on the Spartans who fell at Thermopylae, is doubtless not Simonides', but a later production.
[2] i.e. savage.
[3] A real epitaph, it seems to me, very naïvely expressed.

301.—By the Same[1]

Leonidas, King of spacious Sparta, illustrious are they who died with thee and are buried here. They faced in battle with the Medes the force of multitudinous bows and of steeds fleet of foot.

302.—By the Same

Every man grieves at the death of those near to him, but his friends and the city regret (?) Nicodicus.

303.—ANTIPATER OF SIDON

When little Cleodemus, still living on milk, set his foot outside the edge of the ship, the truly Thracian[2] Boreas cast him into the swelling sea, and the waves put out the light of the baby's life. Ino, thou art a goddess who knowest not pity, since thou didst not avert bitter death from this child of the same age as thy Melicertes.

304.—PISANDER OF RHODES

The man's name was Hippaemon, the horse's Podargos, the dog's Lethargos, and the serving-man's Babes, a Thessalian, from Crete, of Magnesian race, the son of Haemon. He perished fighting in the front ranks.[3]

Much fun was made of it in Antiquity, as the complicated description of the " état civil " of Hippaemon was maliciously interpreted as comprising the " état civil " of the animals.

GREEK ANTHOLOGY

305.—ΑΔΔΑΙΟΥ ΜJΤΥΛΗΝΑΙΟΥ

Ὁ γριπεὺς Διότιμος, ὁ κύμασιν ὁλκάδα πιστὴν
  κὴν χθονὶ τὴν αὐτὴν οἶκον ἔχων πενίης,
νήγρετον ὑπνώσας Ἀΐδαν τὸν ἀμείλιχον ἷκτο
  αὐτερέτης, ἰδίῃ νηΐ κομιζόμενος·
ἣν γὰρ ἔχε ζωῆς παραμύθιον, ἔσχεν ὁ πρέσβυς
  καὶ φθίμενος πύματον πυρκαϊῆς ὄφελος.

306.—ΑΔΕΣΠΟΤΟΝ

Ἀβρότονον Θρήϊσσα γυνὴ πέλον· ἀλλὰ τεκέσθαι
  τὸν μέγαν Ἕλλησιν φημὶ Θεμιστοκλέα.

307.—ΠΑΥΛΟΥ ΣΙΛΕΝΤΙΑΡΙΟΥ

α. Οὔνομά μοι. β. Τί δὲ τοῦτο; α. Πατρὶς δέ μοι.
  β. Ἐς τί δὲ τοῦτο;
  α. Κλεινοῦ δ᾽ εἰμὶ γένους. β. Εἰ γὰρ ἀφαυροτάτου;
α. Ζήσας δ᾽ ἐνδόξως ἔλιπον βίον. β. Εἰ γὰρ ἀδόξως;
  α. Κεῖμαι δ᾽ ἐνθάδε νῦν. β. Τίς τίνι ταῦτα λέγεις;

W. Cowper, *Works* (Globe ed.), p. 498 ; J. A. Pott, *Greek Love Songs and Epigrams*, i. p. 119.

308.—ΛΟΥΚΙΑΝΟΥ

Παῖδά με πενταέτηρον, ἀκηδέα θυμὸν ἔχοντα,
  νηλειὴς Ἀΐδης ἥρπασε Καλλίμαχον.
ἀλλά με μὴ κλαίοις· καὶ γὰρ βιότοιο μετέσχον
  παύρου, καὶ παύρων τῶν βιότοιο κακῶν.

W. Headlam, *A Book of Greek Verse*, p. 259.

305.—ADDAEUS OF MITYLENE

THE fisherman, Diotimus, whose boat, one and the same, was his faithful bearer at sea and on land the abode of his penury, fell into the sleep from which there is no awakening, and rowing himself, came to relentless Hades in his own ship; for the boat that had supported the old man in life paid him its last service in death too by being the wood for his pyre.

306.—ANONYMOUS

I WAS Abrotonon, a Thracian woman; but I say that I bare for Greece her great Themistocles.

307.—PAULUS SILENTIARIUS

A. "My name is ——" *B.* "What does it matter?" *A.* "My country is ——" *B.* "And what does that matter?" *A.* "I am of noble race." *B.* "And if you were of the very dregs?" *A.* "I quitted life with a good reputation." *B.* "And had it been a bad one?" *A.* "And I now lie here." *B.* "Who are you and to whom are you telling this?"

308.—LUCIANUS

MY name is Callimachus, and pitiless Hades carried me off when I was five years old and knew not care. Yet weep not for me; but a small share of life was mine and a small share of life's evil.

309.—ΑΔΕΣΠΟΤΟΝ

Ἑξηκοντούτης Διονύσιος ἐνθάδε κεῖμαι,
  Ταρσεύς, μὴ γήμας· αἴθε δὲ μηδ' ὁ πατήρ.

Alma Strettell, in G. R. Thomson, *Selections from the Greek Anthology*, p. 48.

310.—ΑΔΕΣΠΟΤΟΝ

Θάψεν ὅ με κτείνας κρύπτων φόνον· εἰ δέ με τύμβῳ
  δωρεῖται, τοίης ἀντιτύχοι χάριτος.

311.—ΑΓΑΘΙΟΥ ΣΧΟΛΑΣΤΙΚΟΥ

Εἰς τὴν γυναῖκα Λώτ

Ὁ τύμβος οὗτος ἔνδον οὐκ ἔχει νεκρόν·
ὁ νεκρὸς οὗτος ἐκτὸς οὐκ ἔχει τάφον,
ἀλλ' αὐτὸς αὑτοῦ νεκρός ἐστι καὶ τάφος.

312.—ΑΣΙΝΙΟΥ ΚΟΤΑΔΡΑΤΟΥ

Εἰς τοὺς ἀναιρεθέντας ὑπὸ τοῦ τῶν Ῥωμαίων ὑπάτου Σύλα

Οἱ πρὸς Ῥωμαίους δεινὸν στήσαντες Ἄρηα
  κεῖνται, ἀριστείης σύμβολα δεικνύμενοι·
οὐ γάρ τις μετὰ νῶτα τυπεὶς θάνεν, ἀλλ' ἅμα πάντες
  ὤλοντο κρυφίῳ καὶ δολερῷ θανάτῳ.

313.—ΑΔΕΣΠΟΤΟΝ

Εἰς Τίμωνα τὸν μισάνθρωπον

Ἐνθάδ' ἀπορρήξας ψυχὴν βαρυδαίμονα κεῖμαι·
  τοὔνομα δ' οὐ πεύσεσθε, κακοὶ δὲ κακῶς ἀπόλοισθε.

309.—ANONYMOUS

I, DIONYSIUS, lie here, sixty years old. I am of Tarsus; I never married and I wish my father never had.

310.—ANONYMOUS

MY murderer buried me, hiding his crime: since he gives me a tomb, may he meet with the same kindness as he shewed me.

311.—AGATHIAS SCHOLASTICUS

On Lot's Wife

THIS tomb has no corpse inside it; this corpse has no tomb outside it, but it is its own corpse and tomb.

312.—ASINIUS QUADRATUS

On those slain by Sulla

THEY who took up arms against the Romans lie exhibiting the tokens of their valour. Not one died wounded in the back, but all alike perished by a secret treacherous death.

313.—ANONYMOUS

On Timon the Misanthrope

HERE I lie, having broken away from my luckless soul. My name ye shall not learn, and may ye come, bad men, to a bad end.

314.—ΠΤΟΛΕΜΑΙΟΥ

Εἰς τὸν αὐτὸν Τίμωνα

Μὴ πόθεν εἰμὶ μάθῃς, μηδ᾽ οὔνομα· πλὴν ὅτι
   θνήσκειν
τοὺς παρ᾽ ἐμὴν στήλην ἐρχομένους ἐθέλω.

315.—ΖΗΝΟΔΟΤΟΥ, οἱ δὲ ΡΙΑΝΟΥ

Εἰς τὸν αὐτὸν Τίμωνα

Τρηχεῖαν κατ᾽ ἐμεῦ, ψαφαρὴ κόνι, ῥάμνον ἑλίσσοις
   πάντοθεν, ἢ σκολιῆς ἄγρια κῶλα βάτου,
ὡς ἐπ᾽ ἐμοὶ μηδ᾽ ὄρνις ἐν εἴαρι κοῦφον ἐρείδοι
   ἴχνος, ἐρημάζω δ᾽ ἥσυχα κεκλιμένος.
ἦ γὰρ ὁ μισάνθρωπος, ὁ μηδ᾽ ἀστοῖσι φιληθεὶς   5
   Τίμων οὐδ᾽ Ἀΐδῃ γνήσιός εἰμι νέκυς.

316.—ΛΕΩΝΙΔΑ ἢ ΑΝΤΙΠΑΤΡΟΥ

Εἰς τὸν αὐτὸν ὁμοίως

Τὴν ἐπ᾽ ἐμεῦ στήλην παραμείβεο, μήτε με χαίρειν
   εἰπών, μήθ᾽ ὅστις, μὴ τίνος ἐξετάσας·
ἢ μὴ τὴν ἀνύεις τελέσαις ὁδόν· ἢν δὲ παρέλθῃς
   σιγῇ, μηδ᾽ οὕτως ἢν ἀνύεις τελέσαις.

317.—ΚΑΛΛΙΜΑΧΟΥ

Εἰς τὸν αὐτὸν Τίμωνα

α. Τίμων (οὐ γὰρ ἔτ᾽ ἐσσί), τί τοι, σκότος ἢ φάος,
   ἐχθρόν;
β. Τὸ σκότος· ὑμέων γὰρ πλείονες εἰν Ἀΐδῃ.

(314—320 *are on the Same*)

314.—PTOLEMAEUS

Learn not whence I am nor my name; know only that I wish those who pass my monument to die.

315.—ZENODOTUS or RHIANUS

Dry earth, grow a prickly thorn to twine all round me, or the wild branches of a twisting bramble, that not even a bird in spring may rest its light foot on me, but that I may repose in peace and solitude. For I, the misanthrope, Timon, who was not even beloved by my countrymen, am no genuine dead man even in Hades.[1]

316.—LEONIDAS or ANTIPATER

Pass by my monument, neither greeting me, nor asking who I am and whose son. Otherwise mayst thou never reach the end of the journey thou art on, and if thou passest by in silence, not even then mayst thou reach the journey's end.

317.—CALLIMACHUS

"Timon—for thou art no more—which is most hateful to thee, darkness or light?"   "Darkness; there are more of you in Hades."

---

[1] I cannot be regarded as a real citizen of Hades, being the enemy of my fellow ghosts.

318.—ΤΟΥ ΑΥΤΟΥ

Εἰς τὸν αὐτὸν Τίμωνα

Μὴ χαίρειν εἴπῃς με, κακὸν κέαρ, ἀλλὰ πάρελθε·
ἶσον ἐμοὶ χαίρειν ἐστὶ τὸ μὴ σὲ πελᾶν.

319.—ΑΔΗΛΟΝ

Εἰς τὸν αὐτὸν Τίμωνα

Καὶ νέκυς ὢν Τίμων ἄγριος· σὺ δέ γ᾽, ὦ πυλαωρὲ
Πλούτωνος, τάρβει, Κέρβερε, μή σε δάκῃ.

320.—ΗΓΗΣΙΠΠΟΥ

Εἰς τὸν αὐτὸν Τίμωνα μισέλληνα

Ὀξεῖαι πάντῃ περὶ τὸν τάφον εἰσὶν ἄκανθαι
καὶ σκόλοπες· βλάψεις τοὺς πόδας, ἢν προσίῃς·
Τίμων μισάνθρωπος ἐνοικέω· ἀλλὰ πάρελθε,
οἰμώζειν εἴπας πολλά, πάρελθε μόνον.

321.—ΑΔΕΣΠΟΤΟΝ

Γαῖα φίλη, τὸν πρέσβυν Ἀμύντιχον ἔνθεο κόλποις,
πολλῶν μνησαμένη τῶν ἐπὶ σοὶ καμάτων.
καὶ γὰρ ἀειπέταλόν σοι ἐνεστήριξεν ἐλαίην
πολλάκι, καὶ Βρομίου κλήμασιν ἠγλάϊσεν,
καὶ Δηοῦς ἔπλησε, καὶ ὕδατος αὔλακας ἕλκων   5
θῆκε μὲν εὐλάχανον, θῆκε δ᾽ ὀπωροφόρον.
ἀνθ᾽ ὧν σὺ πρηεῖα κατὰ κροτάφου πολιοῖο
κεῖσο, καὶ εἰαρινὰς ἀνθοκόμει βοτάνας.

322.—ΑΔΕΣΠΟΤΟΝ

Κνωσίου Ἰδομενῆος ὅρα τάφον· αὐτὰρ ἐγώ τοι
πλησίον ἵδρυμαι Μηριόνης ὁ Μόλου.

318.—By the Same(?)

Wish me not well, thou evil-hearted, but pass on.
It is the same as if it were well with me if I get rid
of thy company.

319.—Anonymous

Timon is savage even now he is dead. Cerberus,
door-keeper of Pluto, take care he doesn't bite
you.

320.—HEGESIPPUS

All around the tomb are sharp thorns and stakes;
you will hurt your feet if you go near. I, Timon the
misanthrope, dwell in it. But pass on—wish me all
evil if you like, only pass on.

321.—Anonymous

Dear Earth, receive old Amyntichus in thy bosom,
mindful of all his toil for thee. Many an evergreen
olive he planted in thee and with the vines of
Bacchus he decked thee; he caused thee to abound
in corn, and guiding the water in channels he made
thee rich in pot-herbs and fruit. Therefore lie gently
on his grey temples and clothe thee with many
flowers in spring.

322.—Anonymous

Look on the tomb of Cnossian Idomeneus, and I,
Meriones the son of Molos, have mine hard by.

323.—ΑΔΕΣΠΟΤΟΝ

Εἷς δύ᾽ ἀδελφειοὺς ἐπέχει τάφος· ἓν γὰρ ἐπέσχον
ἦμαρ καὶ γενεῆς οἱ δύο καὶ θανάτου.

324.—ΑΔΕΣΠΟΤΟΝ

῍Αδ᾽ ἐγὼ ἁ περίβωτος ὑπὸ πλακὶ τῇδε τέθαμμαι,
μούνῳ ἑνὶ ζώναν ἀνέρι λυσαμένα.

325.—ΑΔΕΣΠΟΤΟΝ

Εἰς τὸν Σαρδανάπαλλον

Τόσσ᾽ ἔχω ὅσσ᾽ ἔφαγον καὶ ἔπιον, καὶ μετ᾽ ἐρώτων
τέρπν᾽ ἐδάην· τὰ δὲ πολλὰ καὶ ὄλβια πάντα
λέλειπται.

326.—ΚΡΑΤΗΤΟΣ ΘΗΒΑΙΟΥ

Ταῦτ᾽ ἔχω ὅσσ᾽ ἔμαθον καὶ ἐφρόντισα, καὶ μετὰ
    Μουσῶν
σέμν᾽ ἐδάην· τὰ δὲ πολλὰ καὶ ὄλβια τῦφος ἔμαρψεν.

J. A. Pott, *Greek Love Songs and Epigrams*, ii. p. 13.

327.—ΑΔΕΣΠΟΤΟΝ

Εἰς Κάσανδρον τὸν ὡραῖον ἐν Λαρίσσῃ κείμενον

Μὴ σύγε θνητὸς ἐὼν ὡς ἀθάνατός τι λογίζου·
    οὐδὲν γὰρ βιότου πιστὸν ἐφημερίοις,
εἰ καὶ τόνδε Κάσανδρον ἔχει σορὸς ἥδε θανόντα,
    ἄνθρωπον φύσεως ἄξιον ἀθανάτου.

323.—ANONYMOUS

ONE tomb holds two brothers, for both were born and died on the same day.

324.—ANONYMOUS

BENEATH this stone I lie, the celebrated woman who loosed my zone to one man alone.

325.—ANONYMOUS

On Sardanapallus

I HAVE all I ate and drank and the delightful things I learnt with the Loves, but all my many and rich possessions I left behind.

326.—CRATES OF THEBES

I HAVE all I got by study and by thought and the grave things I learnt with the Muses, but all my many and rich possessions Vanity seized on.

327.—ANONYMOUS

On Casandros the beautiful, buried at Larissa

Do not thou, being mortal, reckon on anything as if thou wert immortal, for nothing in life is certain for men, the children of a day.   See how this sarcophagus holds Casandros dead, a man worthy of an immortal nature.

328.—ΑΔΕΣΠΟΤΟΝ

Τίς λίθος οὐκ ἐδάκρυσε, σέθεν φθιμένοιο, Κάσανδρε;
τίς πέτρος, ὃς τῆς σῆς λήσεται ἀγλαΐης;
ἀλλά σε νηλειὴς καὶ βάσκανος ὤλεσε δαίμων
ἡλικίην ὀλίγην εἴκοσιν ἐξ ἐτέων,
ὃς χήρην ἄλοχον θῆκεν, μογερούς τε τοκῆας
γηραλέους, στυγερῷ πένθεϊ τειρομένους.

329.—ΑΛΛΟ

Μυρτάδα τὴν ἱεραῖς με Διωνύσου παρὰ ληνοῖς
ἄφθονον ἀκρήτου σπασσαμένην κύλικα,
οὐ κεύθει φθιμένην βαιὴ κόνις· ἀλλὰ πίθος μοι,
σύμβολον εὐφροσύνης, τερπνὸς ἔπεστι τάφος.

330.—ΑΛΛΟ

Ἐν τῷ Δορυλαίῳ

Τὴν σορόν, ἣν ἐσορᾷς, ζῶν Μάξιμος αὐτὸς ἑαυτῷ
θῆκεν, ὅπως ναίῃ παυσάμενος βιότου·
σύν τε, γυναικὶ Καληποδίῃ τεῦξεν τόδε σῆμα,
ὡς ἵνα τὴν στοργὴν κἠν φθιμένοισιν ἔχοι.

331.—ΑΛΛΟ

Εἰς Ὤρακα ἐν Φρυγίᾳ

Τύμβον ἐμοὶ τοῦτον γαμέτης δωρήσατο Φρούρης,
ἄξιον ἡμετέρης εὐσεβίης στέφανον·
λείπω δ᾽ ἐν θαλάμοις γαμέτου χορὸν εὐκλέα παίδων,
πιστὸν ἐμοῦ βιότου μάρτυρα σωφροσύνης.
μουνόγαμος θνήσκω, δέκα δ᾽ ἐν ζωοῖσιν ἔτι ζῶ,
νυμφικὸν εὐτεκνίης καρπὸν ἀειραμένη.

176

328.—Anonymous

On the Same

WHAT stone did not shed tears at thy death, Casandros, what rock shall forget thy beauty? But the merciless and envious demon slew thee aged only six and twenty, widowing thy wife and thy afflicted old parents, worn by hateful mourning.

329.—Anonymous

I AM Myrtas who quaffed many a generous cup of unwatered wine beside the holy vats of Dionysus, and no light layer of earth covers me, but a wine-jar, the token of my merrymaking, rests on me, a pleasant tomb.

330.—Anonymous

In Dorylaeum

THE sarcophagus that you see was set here by Maximus during his life for himself to inhabit after his death.   He made this monument too for his wife Calepodia, that thus among the dead too he might have her love.

331.—Anonymous

At Oraca in Phrygia

THIS tomb was given me by my husband Phroures, a reward worthy of my piety.   In my husband's house I leave a fair-famed company of children, to bear faithful testimony to my virtue.   I die the wife of one husband, and still live in ten living beings, having enjoyed the fruit of prolific wedlock.

332.—ΑΛΛΟ

Εἰς Ἀκμονίαν

Αἰνόμορον Βάκχῃ με κατέκτανε θηροτρόφον πρίν,
οὐ κρίσει ἐν σταδίοις, γυμνασίαις δὲ κλυταῖς.

333.—ΑΛΛΟ

Εἰς Ἀδριανοὺς ἐν Φρυγίᾳ

Μηδὲ καταχθονίοις μετὰ δαίμοσιν ἄμμορος εἴης
ἡμετέρων δώρων, ὧν σ' ἐπέοικε τυχεῖν,
ἀμμία, οὕνεκα Νικόμαχος θυγάτηρ τε Διώνη
τύμβον καὶ στήλην σὴν ἐθέμεσθα χάριν.

334.—ΑΛΛΟ

Εὑρέθη ἐν Κυζίκῳ

Νηλεὲς ὦ δαῖμον, τί δέ μοι καὶ φέγγος ἔδειξας
εἰς ὀλίγων ἐτέων μέτρα μινυνθάδια;
ἢ ἵνα λυπήσῃς δι' ἐμὴν βιότοιο τελευτὴν
μητέρα δειλαίην δάκρυσι καὶ στοναχαῖς,
ἤ μ' ἔτεχ', ἤ μ' ἀτίτηλε, καὶ ἢ πολὺ μείζονα πατρὸς   ε
φροντίδα παιδείης ἤνυσεν ἡμετέρης;
ὃς μὲν γὰρ τυτθόν τε καὶ ὀρφανὸν ἐν μεγάροισι
κάλλιπεν· ἡ δ' ἐπ' ἐμοὶ πάντας ἔτλη καμάτους.
ἦ μὲν ἐμοὶ φίλον ἦεν ἐφ' ἁγνῶν ἡγεμονήων
ἐμπρεπέμεν μύθοις ἀμφὶ δικασπολίας·   10
ἀλλά μοι οὐ γενύων ὑπεδέξατο κούριμον ἄνθος
ἡλικίης ἐρατῆς, οὐ γάμον, οὐ δαΐδας·

332.—ANONYMOUS

At Acmonia

I HAD an unhappy end, for I was a rearer of animals and Bacche slew me, not in a race on the course, but during the training for which I was renowned.[1]

333.—ANONYMOUS

At Hadriani in Phrygia

MOTHER, not even there with the infernal deities shouldest thou be without a share of the gifts it is meet we should give thee. Therefore have I, Nicomachus, and thy daughter Dione erected this tomb and pillar for thy sake.

334.—ANONYMOUS

Found at Cyzicus

CRUEL fate, why didst thou show me the light for the brief measure of a few years? Was it to vex my unhappy mother with tears and lamentations owing to my death? She it was who bore me and reared me and took much more pains than my father in my education. For he left me an orphan in his house when I was but a tiny child, but she toiled all she could for my sake. My desire was to distinguish myself in speaking in the courts before our righteous magistrates, but it did not fall to her to welcome the first down on my chin, herald of lovely prime, nor my marriage torches; she never sang the solemn bridal hymn for

---

[1] Bacche must have been a mare which somehow killed him while being trained.

οὐχ ὑμέναιον ἄεισε περικλυτόν, οὐ τέκος εἶδε,
δύσποτμος, ἐκ γενεῆς λείψανον ἡμετέρης,
τῆς πολυθρηνήτου· λυπεῖ δέ με καὶ τεθνεῶτα
μητρὸς Πωλίττης πένθος ἀεξόμενον,
Φρόντωνος γοεραῖς ἐπὶ φροντίσιν, ἣ τέκε παῖδα
ὠκύμορον, κενεὸν χάρμα φίλης πατρίδος.

335.—ΑΛΛΟ

α. Πώλιττα, τλῆθι πένθος, εὔνασον δάκρυ.
πολλαὶ θανόντας εἶδον υἱεῖς μητέρες.
β. Ἀλλ' οὐ τοιούτους τὸν τρόπον καὶ τὸν βίον,
οὐ μητέρων σέβοντας ἡδίστην θέαν.
α. Τί περισσὰ θρηνεῖς; τί δὲ μάτην ὀδύρεαι;
εἰς κοινὸν Ἅδην πάντες ἥξουσι βροτοί.

336.—ΑΛΛΟ

Γήραϊ καὶ πενίῃ τετρυμένος, οὐδ' ὀρέγοντος
οὐδενὸς ἀνθρώπου δυστυχίης ἔρανον,
τοῖς τρομεροῖς κώλοισιν ὑπήλυθον ἠρέμα τύμβον,
εὑρὼν οἰζυροῦ τέρμα μόλις βιότου.
ἠλλάχθη δ' ἐπ' ἐμοὶ νεκύων νόμος· οὐ γὰρ
ἔθνησκον
πρῶτον, ἔπειτ' ἐτάφην· ἀλλὰ ταφεὶς ἔθανον.

337.—ΑΔΗΛΟΝ

Μή με θοῶς, κύδιστε, παρέρχεο τύμβον, ὁδῖτα,
σοῖσιν ἀκοιμήτοις ποσσί, κελευθοπόρε·
δερκόμενος δ' ἐρέεινε, τίς ἢ πόθεν; Ἁρμονίαν γὰρ
γνώσεαι, ἧς γενεὴ λάμπεται ἐν Μεγάροις·

me, nor looked, poor woman, upon a child of mine who would keep the memory of our lamented race alive. Yea, even in death it grieves me sore, the ever-growing sorrow of my mother Politta as she mourns and thinks of her Fronto, she who bore him short-lived, an empty delight of our dear country.

335.—ANONYMOUS

A. "Politta, support thy grief and still thy tears; many mothers have seen their sons dead." *B.* "But not such as he was in character and life, not so reverencing their mother's dearest face." *A.* "Why mourn in vain, why this idle lamentation? All men shall come to Hades."

336.—ANONYMOUS

Worn by age and poverty, no one stretching out his hand to relieve my misery, on my tottering legs I went slowly to my grave, scarce able to reach the end of my wretched life. In my case the law of death was reversed, for I did not die first to be then buried, but I died after my burial.

337.—ANONYMOUS

Do not, most noble wayfarer, pass by the tomb hurrying on thy way with tireless feet, but look on it, and ask "Who art thou, and whence?" So shalt thou know Harmonia whose family is illustrious in Megara. For in her one could observe

πάντα γάρ, ὅσσα βροτοῖσι φέρει κλέος, ἦεν ἰδέσθαι, 5
  εὐγενίην ἐρατήν, ἤθεα, σωφροσύνην.
τοίης τυμβον ἄθρησον· ἐς οὐρανίας γὰρ ἀταρποὺς
  ψυχὴ παπταίνει σῶμ' ἀποδυσαμένη.

338.—ΑΔΗΛΟΝ

ᵈΑδε τοι, Ἀρχίου υἱὲ Περίκλεες, ἁ λιθίνα 'γὼ
  ἕστακα στάλα, μνᾶμα κυναγεσίας·
πάντα δέ τοι περὶ σᾶμα τετεύχαται, ἵπποι, ἄκοντες,
  αἱ κύνες, αἱ στάλικες, δίκτυ' ὑπὲρ σταλίκων,
αἰαῖ, λάινα πάντα· περιτροχάουσι δὲ θῆρες·
  αὐτὸς δ' εἰκοσέτας νήγρετον ὕπνον ἔχεις.

339.—ΑΔΗΛΟΝ

Οὐδὲν ἁμαρτήσας γενόμην παρὰ τῶν με τεκόντων·
  γεννηθεὶς δ' ὁ τάλας ἔρχομαι εἰς Ἀΐδην.
ὦ μῖξις γονέων θανατηφόρος· ὤ μοι ἀνάγκης,
  ἥ με προσπελάσει τῷ στυγερῷ θανάτῳ.
οὐδὲν ἐὼν γενόμην· πάλιν ἔσσομαι, ὡς πάρος,
    οὐδέν·
  οὐδὲν καὶ μηδὲν τῶν μερόπων τὸ γένος·
λοιπόν μοι τὸ κύπελλον ἀποστίλβωσον, ἑταῖρε,
  καὶ λύπης †ὀδύνην τὸν Βρόμιον πάρεχε.

340.—ΑΔΗΛΟΝ

Εὑρέθη ἐν Θεσσαλονίκῃ

Νικόπολιν Μαράθωνις ἐθήκατο τῇδ' ἐνὶ πέτρῃ,
  ὀμβρήσας δακρύοις λάρνακα μαρμαρέην.
ἀλλ' οὐδὲν πλέον ἔσχε· τί γὰρ πλέον ἀνέρι κήδευς
  μούνῳ ὑπὲρ γαίης, οἰχομένης ἀλόχου;

A. Esdaile, *Lux Juventutis*, p. 79.

all things which bring fame to men, a loveable nobility, a gentle character and virtue. Such was she whose tomb you look on; her soul putting off the body strives to gain the paths of heaven.

338.—ANONYMOUS

HERE stand I, O Pericles, son of Archias, the stone stele, a record of thy chase. All are carved about thy monument; thy horses, darts, dogs, stakes and the nets on them. Alas! they are all of stone; the wild creatures run about free, but thou aged only twenty sleepest the sleep from which there is no awakening.

339.—ANONYMOUS

(*Not Sepulchral*)

IT was not for any sin of mine that I was born of my parents. I was born, poor wretch, and I journey towards Hades. Oh death-dealing union of my parents! Oh for the necessity which will lead me to dismal death! From nothing I was born, and again I shall be nothing as at first. Nothing, nothing is the race of mortals. Therefore make the cup bright, my friend, and give me wine the consoler of sorrow.

340.—ANONYMOUS

Found in Thessalonica

MARATHONIS laid Nicopolis in this sarcophagus, bedewing the marble chest with tears. But it profited him naught. What is left but sorrow for a man alone in the world, his wife gone?

341.—ΠΡΟΚΛΟΥ

Πρόκλος ἐγὼ Λύκιος γενόμην γένος, ὃν Συριανὸς
ἐνθάδ᾽ ἀμοιβὸν ἑῆς θρέψε διδασκαλίης.
ξυνὸς δ᾽ ἀμφοτέρων ὅδε σώματα δέξατο τύμβος,
αἴθε δὲ καὶ ψυχὰς χῶρος ἕεις λελάχοι.

342.—ΑΔΗΛΟΝ

Κάτθανον, ἀλλὰ μένω σε· μενεῖς δέ τε καὶ σύ τιν᾽
ἄλλον·
πάντας ὁμῶς θνητοὺς εἰς ᾽Αίδης δέχεται.

W. H. D. Rouse, *An Echo of Greek Song*, p. 41.

343.—ΑΔΗΛΟΝ

Πατέριον λιγύμυθον, ἐπήρατον, ἔλλαχε τύμβος,
Μιλτιάδου φίλον υἷα καὶ ᾽Αττικίης βαρυτλήτου,
Κεκροπίης βλάστημα, κλυτὸν γένος Αἰακιδάων,
ἔμπλεον Αὐσονίων θεσμῶν σοφίης τ᾽ ἀναπάσης,
τῶν πισύρων ἀρετῶν ἀμαρύγματα πάντα φέροντα·   5
ἠίθεον χαρίεντα, τὸν ἥρπασε μόρσιμος αἶσα,
οἷά τε ἀγλαόμορφον ἀπὸ χθονὸς ἔρνος ἀήτης,
εἰκοσικαιτέτρατον βιότου λυκάβαντα περῶντα·
λεῖψε φίλοις δὲ τοκεῦσι γόον καὶ πένθος ἄλαστον.

344α.—ΣΙΜΩΝΙΔΟΥ

Θηρῶν μὲν κάρτιστος ἐγώ, θνατῶν δ᾽ ὃν ἐγὼ νῦν
φρουρῶ, τῷδε τάφῳ λαΐνῳ ἐμβεβαώς.

J. A. Pott, *Greek Love Songs and Epigrams*, ii. p. 6.

344β.—ΚΑΛΛΙΜΑΧΟΥ

᾽Αλλ᾽ εἰ μὴ θυμόν γε Λέων ἐμὸν οὔνομά τ᾽ εἶχεν,
οὐκ ἂν ἐγὼ τύμβῳ τῷδ᾽ ἐπέθηκα πόδας.

341.—PROCLUS

I am Proclus of Lycia, whom Syrianus educated here to be his successor in the school. This our common tomb received the bodies of both, and would that one place might receive our spirits too.

342.—Anonymous

I am dead, but await thee, and thou too shalt await another. One Hades receives all mortals alike.

343.—Anonymous

The tomb possesses Paterius, sweet-spoken and loveable, the dear son of Miltiades and sorrowing Atticia, a child of Athens of the noble race of the Aeacidae, full of knowledge of Roman law and of all wisdom, endowed with the brilliance of all the four virtues, a young man of charm, whom Fate carried off, even as the whirlwind uproots a beautiful sapling. He was in his twenty-fourth year and left to his dear parents undying lament and mourning.

344a.—SIMONIDES

I am the most valiant of beasts, and most valiant of men is he whom I guard standing on this stone tomb.[1]

344b.—CALLIMACHUS

Never, unless Leo had had my courage and strength would I have set foot on this tomb.[2]

[1] Probably on the tomb of Leonidas, on which stood a lion, alluding to his name.
[2] On the tomb of one Leo, on which stood a lion.

345.—ΑΔΕΣΠΟΤΟΝ

Ἐγὼ Φιλαινὶς ἡ 'πίβωτος ἀνθρώποις
ἐνταῦθα γήρᾳ τῷ μακρῷ κεκοίμημαι.
μή μ', ὦ μάταιε ναῦτα, τὴν ἄκραν κάμπτων,
χλεύην τε ποιεῦ καὶ γέλωτα καὶ λάσθην.
οὐ γάρ, μὰ τὸν Ζῆν' οὐδὲ τοὺς κάτω Κούρους,   5
οὐκ ἦν ἐς ἄνδρας μάχλος οὐδὲ δημώδης·
Πολυκράτης δὲ τὴν γονὴν Ἀθηναῖος,
λόγων τι παιπάλημα καὶ κακὴ γλῶσσα,
ἔγραψεν οἷ' ἔγραψ', ἐγὼ γὰρ οὐκ οἶδα.

346.—ΑΔΕΣΠΟΤΟΝ

Τοῦτό τοι ἡμετέρης μνημήϊον, ἐσθλὲ Σαβῖνε,
ἡ λίθος ἡ μικρή, τῆς μεγάλης φιλίης.
αἰεὶ ζητήσω σε· σὺ δ', εἰ θέμις, ἐν φθιμένοισι
τοῦ Λήθης ἐπ' ἐμοὶ μή τι πίῃς ὕδατος.

Goldwin Smith, in *The Greek Anthology* (Bohn), xliv.

347.—ΑΔΕΣΠΟΤΟΝ

Οὗτος Ἀδειμάντου κείνου τάφος, οὗ διὰ βουλὰς
Ἑλλὰς ἐλευθερίης ἀμφέθετο στέφανον.

A. Esdaile, *Lux Juventutis*, p. 80.

348.—ΣΙΜΩΝΙΔΟΤ

Πολλὰ πιὼν καὶ πολλὰ φαγών, καὶ πολλὰ κάκ'
εἰπὼν
ἀνθρώπους, κεῖμαι Τιμοκρέων Ῥόδιος.

W. Peter, in his *Specimens*, p. 53; W. H. D. Rouse, *An Echo of Greek Song*, p. 72.

345.—Anonymous

I Philaenis, celebrated among men, have been laid to rest here, by extreme old age. Thou silly sailor, as thou roundest the cape, make no sport and mockery of me; insult me not. For by Zeus I swear and the Infernal Lords I was not lascivious with men or a public woman; but Polycrates the Athenian, a cozener in speech and an evil tongue, wrote whatever he wrote; for I know not what it was.[1]

346.—Anonymous

In Corinth

This little stone, good Sabinus, is a memorial of our great friendship. I shall ever miss thee; and if so it may be, when with the dead thou drinkest of Lethe, drink not thou forgetfulness of me.

347.—Anonymous

This is the tomb of that Adeimantus through whose counsel Greece put on the crown of freedom.[2]

348.—SIMONIDES

Here I lie, Timocreon of Rhodes, after drinking much and eating much and speaking much ill of men.

[1] A certain obscene book was attributed to Philaenis.
[2] The Corinthian admiral at the battle of Salamis.

349.—ΑΔΗΛΟΝ

Βαιὰ φαγὼν καὶ βαιὰ πιὼν καὶ πολλὰ νοσήσας,
   ὀψὲ μέν, ἀλλ' ἔθανον. ἔρρετε πάντες ὁμοῦ.

350.—ΑΔΗΛΟΝ

Ναυτίλε, μὴ πεύθου τίνος ἐνθάδε τύμβος ὅδ' εἰμί,
   ἀλλ' αὐτὸς πόντου τύγχανε χρηστοτέρου.

351.—ΔΙΟΣΚΟΡΙΔΟΥ

Οὐ μὰ τόδε φθιμένων σέβας ὅρκιον, αἵδε Λυκάμβεω,
   αἳ λάχομεν στυγερὴν κληδόνα, θυγατέρες,
οὔτε τι παρθενίην ᾐσχύναμεν, οὔτε τοκῆας,
   οὔτε Πάρον νῆσον αἰπυτάτην ἱερῶν.
ἀλλὰ καθ' ἡμετέρης γενεῆς ῥιγηλὸν ὄνειδος
   φήμην τε στυγερὴν ἔβλυσεν Ἀρχίλοχος.
Ἀρχίλοχον, μὰ θεοὺς καὶ δαίμονας, οὔτ' ἐν ἀγυιαῖς
   εἴδομεν, οὔθ' Ἥρης ἐν μεγάλῳ τεμένει.
εἰ δ' ἦμεν μάχλοι καὶ ἀτάσθαλοι, οὐκ ἂν ἐκεῖνος
   ἤθελεν ἐξ ἡμέων γνήσια τέκνα τεκεῖν. [1]

352.—ΑΔΕΣΠΟΤΟΝ, οἱ δὲ ΜΕΛΕΑΓΡΟΥ

Δεξιτερὴν Ἀΐδαο θεοῦ χέρα καὶ τὰ κελαινὰ
   ὄμνυμεν ἀρρήτου δέμνια Περσεφόνης,
παρθένοι ὡς ἔτυμον καὶ ὑπὸ χθονί· πολλὰ δ' ὁ
      πικρὸς
   αἰσχρὰ καθ' ἡμετέρης ἔβλυσε παρθενίης

---

[1] i.e. this our tomb.
[2] Archilochus had accused them of disgraceful conduct in
these public places.

349.—Anonymous

After eating little and drinking little and suffering much sickness I lasted long, but at length I did die. A curse on you all!

350.—Anonymous

Ask not, sea-farer, whose tomb I am, but thyself chance upon a kinder sea.

351.—DIOSCORIDES

Not, by this,[1] the solemn oath of the dead, did we daughters of Lycambes, who have gotten such an evil name, ever disgrace our maidenhead or our parents or Paros, queen of the holy islands; but Archilochus poured on our family a flood of horrible reproach and evil report.   By the gods and demons we swear that we never set eyes on Archilochus, either in the streets or in Hera's great precinct.[2]   If we had been wanton and wicked, he would never have wished lawful children born to him by us.[3]

352

Anonymous, by some attributed to MELEAGER

We swear by the right hand of Hades and the dark couch of Persephone whom none may name,[4] that we are truly virgins even here under ground; but bitter Archilochus poured floods of abuse on

---

[3] Archilochus is only said to have married one of them.
[4] *i.e.* whose mystic name it was not allowed to utter.

Ἀρχίλοχος· ἐπέων δὲ καλὴν φάτιν οὐκ ἐπὶ καλὰ   5
ἔργα, γυναικεῖον δ᾽ ἔτραπεν ἐς πόλεμον.
Πιερίδες, τί κόρῃσιν ἔφ᾽ ὑβριστῆρας ἰάμβους
ἐτράπετ᾽, οὐχ ὁσίῳ φωτὶ χαριζόμεναι;

353.—ΑΝΤΙΠΑΤΡΟΥ ΣΙΔΩΝΙΟΥ

Τῆς πολιῆς τόδε σῆμα Μαρωνίδος, ἧς ἐπὶ τύμβῳ
γλυπτὴν ἐκ πέτρης αὐτὸς ὁρᾷς κύλικα.
ἡ δὲ φιλάκρητος καὶ ἀείλαλος οὐκ ἐπὶ τέκνοις
μύρεται, οὐ τεκέων ἀκτεάνῳ πατέρι·
ἓν δὲ τόδ᾽ αἰάζει καὶ ὑπ᾽ ἠρίον, ὅττι τὸ Βάκχου   5
ἄρμενον οὐ βάκχου πλῆρες ἔπεστι τάφῳ.

354.—ΓΑΙΤΟΥΛΙΚΟΥ

Παίδων Μηδείης οὗτος τάφος, οὓς ὁ πυρίπνους
ζᾶλος τῶν Γλαύκης θῦμ᾽ ἐποίησε γάμων,
οἷς αἰεὶ πέμπει μειλίγματα Σισυφὶς αἶα,
μητρὸς ἀμείλικτον θυμὸν ἱλασκομένα.

355.—ΔΑΜΑΓΗΤΟΥ

Τὴν ἱλαρὰν φωνὴν καὶ τίμιον, ὦ παριόντες,
τῷ χρηστῷ "χαίρειν" εἴπατε Πραξιτέλει·
ἦν δ᾽ ὡνὴρ Μουσέων ἱκανὴ μερίς, ἠδὲ παρ᾽ οἴνῳ
κρήγυος. ὦ χαίροις Ἄνδριε Πραξίτελες.

356.—ΑΔΗΛΟΝ

Εἴς τινα ὑπὸ λῃστοῦ ἀναιρεθέντα καὶ ὑπ᾽ αὐτοῦ πάλιν
θαπτόμενον

Ζωὴν συλήσας, δωρῇ τάφον· ἀλλά με κρύπτεις,
οὐ θάπτεις. τοίου καὐτὸς ὄναιο τάφου.

190

our maidenhood, directing to no noble end but to
war with women the noble language of his verse.
Ye Muses, why to do favour to an impious man, did
ye turn upon girls those scandalous iambics?

353.—ANTIPATER OF SIDON

This is the monument of grey-haired Maronis, on
whose tomb you see a wine cup carved in stone.
She the wine-bibber and chatterer, is not sorry for
her children or her children's destitute father, but
one thing she laments even in her grave, that the
device of the wine-god on the tomb is not full of
wine.

354.—GAETULICUS

This is the tomb of Medea's children, whom her
burning jealousy made the victims of Glauce's wed-
ding. To them the Corinthian land ever sends peace-
offerings, propitiating their mother's implacable soul.

355.—DAMAGETUS

Bid good Praxiteles "hail," ye passers-by, that
cheering and honouring word. He was well gifted
by the Muses and a jolly after-dinner companion.
Hail, Praxiteles of Andros!

356.—Anonymous

*On one who was killed by a robber and then buried
by him*

You robbed me of my life, and then you give me
a tomb. But you hide me, you don't bury me. May
you have the benefit of such a tomb yourself!

357.—ΑΛΛΟ

Εἰς τὸν αὐτόν

Κἄν με κατακρύπτῃς, ὡς οὐδενὸς ἀνδρὸς ὁρῶντος,
ὄμμα Δίκης καθορᾷ πάντα τὰ γινόμενα.

358.—ΑΛΛΟ

Εἰς τὸν αὐτόν

Ἔκτανες, εἶτά μ᾽ ἔθαπτες, ἀτάσθαλε, χερσὶν ἐκείναις.
αἷς με διεχρήσω· μή σε λάθοι Νέμεσις.

359.—ΑΛΛΟ

Εἰς τὸν αὐτόν

Εἴ με νέκυν κατέθαπτες ἰδὼν οἰκτίρμονι θυμῷ,
εἶχες ἂν ἐκ μακάρων μισθὸν ἐπ᾽ εὐσεβίῃ·
νῦν δ᾽ ὅτε δὴ τύμβῳ με κατακρύπτεις ὁ φονεύσας,
τῶν αὐτῶν μετέχοις ὧνπερ ἐμοὶ παρέχεις.

360.—ΑΛΛΟ

Εἰς τὸν αὐτόν

Χερσὶ κατακτείνας τάφον ἔκτισας, οὐχ ἵνα θάψῃς,
ἀλλ᾽ ἵνα με κρύψῃς· ταὐτὸ δὲ καὶ σὺ πάθοις.

361.—ΑΔΗΛΟΝ

Υἷι πατὴρ τόδε σῆμα· τὸ δ᾽ ἔμπαλιν ἦν τὸ δίκαιον·
ἦν δὲ δικαιοσύνης ὁ φθόνος ὀξύτερος.

362.—ΦΙΛΙΠΠΟΥ ΘΕΣΣΑΛΟΝΙΚΕΩΣ

Ἐνθάδε τὴν ἱερὴν κεφαλὴν σορὸς ἥδε κέκευθεν
Ἀετίου χρηστοῦ, ῥήτορος ἐκπρεπέος.

(357–360 are anonymous variants on the same theme)

357

THOUGH you hide me as if no one saw you, the eye of Justice sees all that happens.

358

WRETCH! you killed and then buried me with those hands that slew me. May you not escape Nemesis.

359

IF you had found me dead and buried me out of pity, the gods would have rewarded you for your piety. But now that you who slew me hide me in a tomb, may you meet with the same treatment that I met with at your hands.

360

HAVING killed me with your hands you build me a tomb, not to bury me, but to hide me. May you meet with the same fate!

361.—ANONYMOUS

THE father erects this tomb to his son. The reverse had been just, but Envy was quicker than Justice.

362.—PHILIPPUS OF THESSALONICA

HERE the sarcophagus holds the holy head of good Aetius, the distinguished orator. To the house of

ἦλθεν δ' εἰς Ἀΐδαο δέμας, ψυχὴ δ' ἐν Ὀλύμπῳ
τέρπεθ' ἅμα Ζηνὶ καὶ ἄλλοισιν μακάρεσσι
. . . . ἀθάνατον δὲ
οὔτε λόγος ποιεῖν οὔτε θεὸς δύναται.

363.—ΑΔΕΣΠΟΤΟΝ

†Τετμενάνης ὅδε τύμβος ἐϋγλύπτοιο μετάλλου
ἥρωος μεγάλου νέκυος κατὰ σῶμα καλύπτει
Ζηνοδότου· ψυχὴ δὲ κατ' οὐρανόν, ἧχί περ Ὀρφεύς,
ἧχι Πλάτων, ἱερὸν θεοδέγμονα θῶκον ἐφεῦρεν.
Ἱππεὺς μὲν γὰρ ἔην βασιλήϊος ἄλκιμος οὗτος,   5
κύδιμος, ἀρτιεπής, θεοείκελος· ἐν δ' ἄρα μύθοις
Σωκράτεος μίμημα παρ' Αὐσονίοισιν ἐτύχθη·
παισὶ δὲ καλλείψας πατρῷον αἴσιον ὄλβον,
ὠμογέρων τέθνηκε, λιπὼν ἀπερείσιον ἄλγος
εὐγενέεσσι φίλοισι καὶ ἄστεϊ καὶ πολιήταις.   10

364.—ΜΑΡΚΟΥ ΑΡΓΕΝΤΑΡΙΟΥ

Ἀκρίδι καὶ τέττιγι Μυρὼ τόδε θήκατο σῆμα,
λιτὴν ἀμφοτέροις χερσὶ βαλοῦσα κόνιν,
ἵμερα δακρύσασα πυρῆς ἔπι· τὸν γὰρ ἀοιδὸν
Ἅδης, τὴν δ' ἑτέρην ἥρπασε Περσεφόνη.

365.—ΖΩΝΑ ΣΑΡΔΙΑΝΟΥ, τοῦ καὶ ΔΙΟΔΩΡΟΥ

Ἀΐδη ὃς ταύτης καλαμώδεος ὕδατι λίμνης
κωπεύεις νεκύων βᾶριν, †ἐλῶν ὀδύνην,
τῷ Κινύρου τὴν χεῖρα βατηρίδος ἐμβαίνοντι
κλίμακος ἐκτείνας, δέξο, κελαινὲ Χάρον·
πλάζει γὰρ τὸν παῖδα τὰ σάνδαλα· γυμνὰ δὲ θεῖναι   5
ἴχνια δειμαίνει ψάμμον ἔπ' ἠονίην.

Hades went his body, but his soul in Olympus rejoices with Zeus and the other gods . . . . . , but neither eloquence nor God can make man immortal.

363.—ANONYMOUS

THIS tomb of polished metal covers the body of the great hero Zenodotus; but his soul has found in heaven, where Orpheus and Plato are, a holy seat fit to receive a god. He was a valiant knight in the Emperor's service, famous, eloquent, god-like; in his speech he was a Latin copy of Socrates. Bequeathing to his children a handsome fortune, he died while still a vigorous old man, leaving infinite sorrow to his noble friends, city and citizens.

364.—MARCUS ARGENTARIUS

MYRO made this tomb for her grasshopper and cicada, sprinkling a little dust over them both and weeping regretfully over their pyre; for the songster was seized by Hades and the other by Persephone.

365

ZONAS OF SARDIS, ALSO CALLED DIODORUS

DARK Charon, who through the water of this reedy lake rowest the boat of the dead to Hades . . . reach out thy hand from the mounting-ladder to the son of Cinyras as he embarks, and receive him; for the boy cannot walk steadily in his sandals,[1] and he fears to set his bare feet on the sand of the beach.

[1] The meaning is that he died at an age when he had not yet begun to wear sandals, so these were his first pair.

366.—ΑΝΤΙΣΤΙΟΥ

Ἀῴου προχοαὶ σέ, Μενέστρατε, καὶ σέ, Μένανδρε,
λαῖλαψ Καρπαθίη, καὶ σὲ πόρος Σικελὸς
ὤλεσεν ἐν πόντῳ, Διονύσιε· φεῦ πόσον ἄλγος
Ἑλλάδι· τοὺς πάντων κρέσσονας ἀθλοφόρων.

367.—ΑΝΤΙΠΑΤΡΟΥ

Αὔσονος Ἡγερίου με λέγειν νέκυν, ᾧ μετιόντι
νύμφην ὀφθαλμοὺς ἀμβλὺ κατέσχε νέφος,
ὄμμασι δὲ πνοιὴν συναπέσβεσε μοῦνον ἰδόντος
κούρην. φεῦ κείνης, Ἥλιε, θευμορίης·
ἔρροι δὴ κεῖνο φθονερὸν σέλας, εἴθ᾽ Ὑμέναιος   5
ἦψέ μιν οὐκ ἐθέλων, εἴτ᾽ Ἀΐδης ἐθέλων.

368.—ΕΡΥΚΙΟΥ

Ἀτθὶς ἐγώ· κείνη γὰρ ἐμὴ πόλις· ἐκ δέ μ᾽ Ἀθηνῶν
λοιγὸς Ἄρης Ἰταλῶν πρίν ποτ᾽ ἐληΐσατο,
καὶ θέτο Ῥωμαίων πολιήτιδα· νῦν δὲ θανούσης
ὀστέα νησαίη Κύζικος ἠμφίασε.
χαίροις ἡ θρέψασα, καὶ ἡ μετέπειτα λαχοῦσα   5
χθών με, καὶ ἡ κόλποις ὕστατα δεξαμένη.

369.—ΑΝΤΙΠΑΤΡΟΥ

Ἀντιπάτρου ῥητῆρος ἐγὼ τάφος· ἡλίκα δ᾽ ἔπνει
ἔργα, Πανελλήνων πεύθεο μαρτυρίης.
κεῖται δ᾽ ἀμφήριστος, Ἀθηνόθεν, εἴτ᾽ ἀπὸ Νείλου
ἦν γένος· ἠπείρων δ᾽ ἄξιος ἀμφοτέρων.
ἄστεα καὶ δ᾽ ἄλλως ἑνὸς αἵματος, ὡς λόγος, Ἕλλην   5
κλήρῳ δ᾽ ἡ μὲν ἀεὶ Παλλάδος, ἡ δὲ Διός.

196

366.—ANTISTIUS

To thee, Menestratus, the mouth of the Aous was fatal; to thee, Menander, the tempest of the Carpathian Sea; and thou, Dionysius, didst perish at sea in the Sicilian Strait. Alas, what grief to Hellas! the best of all her winners in the games gone.

367.—ANTIPATER OF THESSALONICA

Say that I am the corpse of Italian Egerius whose eyes when he went to meet his bride were veiled by a dim cloud, which extinguished his life together with his eyesight, after he had but seen the girl. Alas, O Sun, that heaven allotted him such a fate! Cursed be that envious wedding torch, whether unwilling Hymen lit or willing Hades.

368.—ERYCIUS

I am a woman of Athens, for that is my birthplace, but the destroying sword of the Italians long ago took me captive at Athens and made me a citizen of Rome, and now that I am dead island Cyzicus covers my bones. Hail ye three lands, thou which didst nourish me, thou to which my lot took me afterwards and thou that didst finally receive me in thy bosom.

369.—ANTIPATER OF THESSALONICA

I am the tomb of the orator Antipater. Ask all Greece to testify to his inspiration. He lies here, and men dispute whether his birth was from Athens or from Egypt; but he was worthy of both continents. For the matter of that, the lands are of one blood, as Greek legend says, but the one is ever allotted to Pallas and the other to Zeus.

370.—ΔΙΟΔΩΡΟΥ

Βάκχῳ καὶ Μούσῃσι μεμηλότα, τὸν Διοπείθους,
  Κεκροπίδην ὑπ᾽ ἐμοί, ξεῖνε, Μένανδρον ἔχω,
ἐν πυρὶ τὴν ὀλίγην ὃς ἔχει κόνιν· εἰ δὲ Μένανδρον
  δίζηαι, δήεις ἐν Διὸς ἢ μακάρων.

371.—ΚΡΙΝΑΓΟΡΟΥ

Γῆ μευ καὶ μήτηρ κικλήσκετο· γῆ με καλύπτει
  καὶ νέκυν. οὐ κείνης ἥδε χερειοτέρη·
ἔσσομαι ἐν ταύτῃ δηρὸν χρόνον· ἐκ δέ με μητρὸς
  ἥρπασεν ἠελίου καῦμα τὸ θερμότατον.
κεῖμαι δ᾽ ἐν ξείνῃ, ὑπὸ χερμάδι, μακρὰ γοηθείς,   5
  Ἴναχος, εὐπειθὴς Κριναγόρου θεράπων.

372.—ΛΟΛΛΙΟΥ ΒΑΣΣΟΥ

Γαῖα Ταραντίνων, ἔχε μείλιχος ἀνέρος ἐσθλοῦ
  τόνδε νέκυν. ψεῦσται δαίμονες ἀμερίων·
ἢ γὰρ ἐὼν Θήβηθεν Ἀτύμνιος οὐκέτι πρόσσω
  ἤνυσεν, ἀλλὰ τεὴν βῶλον ὑπῳκίσατο·
ὀρφανικῷ δ᾽ ἐπὶ παιδὶ λιπὼν βίον, εὖνιν ἔθηκεν   5
  ὀφθαλμῶν. κείνῳ[1] μὴ βαρὺς ἔσσο τάφος.

373.—ΘΑΛΛΟΥ ΜΙΛΗΣΙΟΥ

Δισσὰ φάη, Μίλητε, τεῆς βλαστήματα γαίης,
  Ἰταλὶς ὠκυμόρους ἀμφεκάλυψε κόνις·
πένθεα δὲ στεφάνων ἠλλάξαο· λείψανα δ᾽, αἰαῖ,
  ἔδρακες ἐν βαιῇ κάλπιδι κευθόμενα.
φεῦ, πάτρα τριτάλαινα· πόθεν πάλιν ἢ πότε τοίους   5
  ἀστέρας αὐχήσεις Ἑλλάδι λαμπομένους;

---

[1] Stadtmüller suggests ξείνῳ, and I render so.

370.—DIODORUS

MENANDER of Athens, the son of Diopeithes, the friend of Bacchus and the Muses, rests beneath me, or at least the little dust he shed in the funeral fire. But if thou seekest Menander himself thou shalt find him in the abode of Zeus or in the Islands of the Blest.

371.—CRINAGORAS

EARTH was my mother's name,[1] and earth too covers me now I am dead.   No worse is this earth than the other : in this I shall lie for long, but from my mother the violent heat of the sun snatched me away and in a strange earth I lie under a stone, Inachus, the much bewept and the obedient servant of Crinagoras.

372.—LOLLIUS BASSUS

EARTH of Tarentum, keep gently this body of a good man.   How false are the guardian divinities of mortal men !   Atymnius, coming from Thebes,[2] got no further, but settled under thy soil.   He left an orphan son, whom his death deprived, as it were, of his eyes.   Lie not heavy upon the stranger.

373.—THALLUS OF MILETUS

Two shining lights, Miletus, sprung from thee, doth the Italian earth cover, dead each ere his prime. Thou hast put on mourning instead of garlands, and thou seeest, alas, their remains hidden in a little urn.   Alack, thrice unhappy country !   Whence and when shalt thou have again two such stars to boast of, shedding their light on Greece ?

---

[1] I take this literally.   The name of the slave's mother was Γῆ (Earth).   [2] A place in Italy not far from Tarentum.

374.—ΜΑΡΚΟΥ ΑΡΓΕΝΤΑΡΙΟΥ

Δύσμορος ἐκρύφθην πόντῳ νέκυς, ὃν παρὰ κῦμα
   ἔκλαυσεν μήτηρ μυρία Λυσιδίκη,
ψεύστην αὐγάζουσα κενὸν τάφον· ἀλλά με δαίμων
   ἄπνουν αἰθυίαις θῆκεν ὁμορρόθιον
Πινυταγόρην· ἔσχον δὲ κατ' Αἰγαίην ἅλα πότμον,
   πρυμνούχους στέλλων ἐκ Βορέαο κάλους.
ἀλλ' οὐδ' ὡς ναύτην ἔλιπον δρόμον, ἀλλ' ἀπὸ νηὸς
   ἄλλην πὰρ φθιμένοις εἰσανέβην ἄκατον.

375.—ΑΝΤΙΦΙΛΟΥ ΒΥΖΑΝΤΙΟΥ

Δώματά μοι σεισθέντα κατήριπεν· ἀλλ' ἐμὸς ἀπτὼς
   ἦν θάλαμος, τοίχων ὀρθὰ τιναξαμένων,
οἷς ὑποφωλεύουσαν ὑπήλυθον αἱ κακόμοιροι
   ὠδῖνες· σεισμῷ δ' ἄλλον ἔμιξα φόβον.
μαῖα δέ μοι λοχίων αὐτὴ φύσις· ἀμφότεροι δὲ
   κοινὸν ὑπὲρ γαίης εἴδομεν ἠέλιον.

376.—ΚΡΙΝΑΓΟΡΟΥ

Δείλαιοι, τί κεναῖσιν ἀλώμεθα θαρσήσαντες
   ἐλπίσιν, ἀτηροῦ ληθόμενοι θανάτου;
ἦν ὅδε καὶ μύθοισι καὶ ἤθεσι πάντα Σέλευκος
   ἄρτιος, ἀλλ' ἥβης βαιὸν ἐπαυρόμενος,
ὑστατίοις ἐν Ἴβηρσι, τόσον δίχα τηλόθι Λέσβου,
   κεῖται ἀμετρήτων ξεῖνος ἐπ' αἰγιαλῶν.

377.—ΕΡΥΚΙΟΥ

Εἰ καὶ ὑπο χθονὶ κεῖται, ὅμως ἔτι καὶ κατὰ πίσσαν
   τοῦ μιαρογλώσσου χεύατε Παρθενίου,

374.—MARCUS ARGENTARIUS

My ill-fated body was covered by the sea, and beside the waves my mother, Lysidice, wept for me much, gazing at my false and empty tomb, while my evil genius sent my lifeless corpse to be tossed with the sea-gulls on the deep. My name was Pnytagoras and I met my fate on the Aegean, when taking in the stern cables because of the north-wind. Yet not even so did I end my voyage, but from my ship I embarked on another boat among the dead.[1]

375.—ANTIPHILUS OF BYZANTIUM
(*Not Sepulchral*)

My house collapsed with the earthquake; yet my chamber remained erect, as its walls stood the shock. There while I lay, as if hiding in a cave, the unhappy labour-pains overtook me, and another dread was mingled with that of the earthquake. Nature herself was the midwife, and the child and I both together saw the sun above the earth.

376.—CRINAGORAS

Unhappy men! why do we wander confiding in empty hopes, oblivious of painful death? Here was this Seleucus so perfect in speech and character; but after enjoying his prime but for a season, in Spain, at the end of the world, so far from Lesbos, he lies a stranger on that uncharted coast.

377.—ERYCIUS

Even though he lies under earth, still pour pitch on foul-mouthed Parthenius, because he vomited on the

---

[1] *i.e.* Charon's.

οὕνεκα Πιερίδεσσιν ἐνήμεσε μυρία κεῖνα
φλέγματα καὶ μυσαρῶν ἀπλυσίην ἐλέγων.
ἤλασε καὶ μανίης ἐπὶ δὴ τόσον, ὥστ' ἀγορεῦσαι   5
πηλὸν Ὀδυσσείην καὶ βάτον Ἰλιάδα.
τοιγὰρ ὑπὸ ζοφίαισιν Ἐρινύσιν ἀμμέσον ἧπται
Κωκυτοῦ κλοιῷ λαιμὸν ἀπαγχόμενος.

378.—ΑΠΟΛΛΩΝΙΔΟΥ

Ἔφθανεν Ἡλιόδωρος, ἐφέσπετο δ', οὐδ' ὅσον ὥρῃ
ὕστερον, ἀνδρὶ φίλῳ Διογένεια δάμαρ.
ἄμφω δ', ὡς ἅμ' ἔναιον, ὑπὸ πλακὶ τυμβεύονται,
ξυνὸν ἀγαλλόμενοι καὶ τάφον ὡς θάλαμον.

A. Esdaile, *Lux Juventutis*, p. 81.

379.—ΑΝΤΙΦΙΛΟΥ ΒΥΖΑΝΤΙΟΥ

α. Εἰπέ, Δικαιάρχεια, τί σοι τόσον εἰς ἅλα χῶμα
βέβληται, μέσσου γευόμενον πελάγους;
Κυκλώπων τάδε χεῖρες ἐνιδρύσαντο θαλάσσῃ
τείχεα· μέχρι πόσου, Γαῖα, βιαζόμεθα;
β. Κόσμου νηΐτην δέχομαι στόλον· εἴσιδε Ῥώμην
ἐγγύθεν, εἰ ταύτης μέτρον ἔχω λιμένα.

380.—ΚΡΙΝΑΓΟΡΟΥ

Εἰ καὶ τὸ σῆμα λυγδίνης ἀπὸ πλακὸς
καὶ ξεστὸν ὀρθῇ λαοτέκτονος στάθμῃ,
οὐκ ἀνδρὸς ἐσθλοῦ.   μὴ λίθῳ τεκμαίρεο,

Muses those floods of bile, and the filth of his re-
pulsive elegies. So far gone was he in madness
that he called the Odyssey mud and the Iliad a
bramble. Therefore he is bound by the dark Furies
in the middle of Cocytus, with a dog-collar that
chokes him round his neck.[1]

378.—APOLLONIDES

HELIODORUS went first, and in even less than an
hour his wife, Diogenia, followed her dear husband.
Both, even as they dwelt together, are interred
under one stone, happy to share one tomb, as erst
to share one chamber.

379.—ANTIPHILUS OF BYZANTIUM

(Not Sepulchral)

A. "TELL me, Dicaearchia,[2] why thou hast built
thee so vast a mole in the sea, reaching out to the
middle of the deep? They were Cyclopes' hands
that planted such walls in the sea. How long, O
Land, shalt thou do violence to us?" *B.* "I can
receive the navies of the world. Look at Rome hard
by; is not my harbour as great as she?"

380.—CRINAGORAS

THOUGH the monument be of Parian marble, and
polished by the mason's straight rule, it is not a good
man's. Do not, good sir, estimate the dead by the

---

[1] This Parthenius, who lived in the time of Hadrian, was
known as the "scourge of Homer."
[2] Puteoli. The sea is supposed to be addressing the town.

ὦ λῷστε, τὸν θανόντα.   κωφὸν ἡ λίθος,
τῇ καὶ ζοφώδης ἀμφιέννυται νέκυς.
κεῖται δὲ τῇδε τὠλιγηπελὲς ῥάκος
Εὐνικίδαο, σήπεται δ᾽ ὑπὸ σποδῷ.

381.—ΕΤΡΟΤΣΚΟΤ ΑΠΟ ΜΕΣΣΗΝΗΣ

Ἡ μία καὶ βιότοιο καὶ Ἄϊδος ἤγαγεν εἴσω
    ναῦς Ἱεροκλείδην, κοινὰ λαχοῦσα τέλη.
ἔτρεφεν ἰχθυβολεῦντα, κατέφλεγε τεθνειῶτα,
    σύμπλοος εἰς ἄγρην, σύμπλοος εἰς Ἀΐδην.
ὄλβιος ὁ γριπεὺς ἰδίῃ καὶ πόντον ἐπέπλει
    νηΐ, καὶ ἐξ ἰδίης ἔδραμεν εἰς Ἀΐδην.

382.—ΦΙΛΙΠΠΟΤ ΘΕΣΣΑΛΟΝΙΚΕΩΣ

Ἠπείρῳ μ᾽ ἀποδοῦσα νέκυν, τρηχεῖα θάλασσα,
    σύρεις καὶ τέφρης λοιπὸν ἔτι σκύβαλον.
κἤν Ἀΐδῃ ναυηγὸς ἐγὼ μόνος, οὐδ᾽ ἐπὶ χέρσου
    εἰρήνην ἔξω φρικαλέης σπιλάδος.
ἢ τύμβευε κενοῦσα καθ᾽ ὕδατος, ἢ παραδοῦσα
    γαίῃ, τὸν κείνης μηκέτι κλέπτε νέκυν.

383.—ΤΟΤ ΑΤΤΟΤ

Ἠόνιον τόδε σῶμα βροτοῦ παντλήμονος ἄθρει
    σπαρτόν, ἁλιρραγέων ἐκχύμενον σκοπέλων·
τῇ μὲν ἐρημοκόμης κεῖται καὶ χῆρος ὀδόντων
    κόρσῃ· τῇ δὲ χερῶν πενταφυεῖς ὄνυχες,
πλευρά τε σαρκολιπῆ, ταρσοὶ δ᾽ ἑτέρωθεν ἄμοιροι
    νεύρων, καὶ κώλων ἔκλυτος ἁρμονίη.
οὗτος ὁ πουλυμερὴς εἷς ἦν ποτε.   φεῦ μακαριστοί,
    ὅσσοι ἀπ᾽ ὠδίνων οὐκ ἴδον ἠέλιον.

stone.   The stone is senseless and can cover a foul black corpse as well as any other.   Here lies that weak rag the body of Eunicides and rots under the ashes.

381.—ETRUSCUS OF MESSENE

THE same boat, a double task exacted of it, carried Hieroclides to his living and into Hades.   It fed him by his fishing, and it burnt him dead, travelling with him to the chase and travelling with him to Hades.   Indeed the fisherman was very well off, as he sailed the seas in his own ship and raced to Hades by means of his own ship.

382.—PHILIPPUS OF THESSALONICA

THOU gavest me up dead to the land, cruel sea, and now thou carriest off the little remnant of my ashes. I alone am shipwrecked even in Hades, and not even on land shall I cease to be dashed on the dreadful rocks.   Either bury me, hiding (?) me in thy waters, or if thou givest me up to the land, steal not a corpse that now belongs to the land.

383.—BY THE SAME

LOOK on this corpse of a most unhappy man scattered on the beach shredded by the sea-dashed rocks.   Here lies the hairless and toothless head and here the five fingers of a hand, here the fleshless ribs, the feet without their sinews and the disjointed legs.   This man of many parts once was one.   Blest indeed are those who were never born to see the sun !

384.—ΜΑΡΚΟΥ ΑΡΓΕΝΤΑΡΙΟΥ

Ἡ Βρόμιον στέρξασα πολὺ πλέον ἢ τροφὸς Ἰνώ,
ἡ λάλος ἀμπελίνη γρῆϋς Ἀριστομάχη,
ἡνίκα τὴν ἱερὴν ὑπέδυ χθόνα, πᾶν τ᾽ ἐμαράνθη
πνεῦμα πάρος κυλίκων πλεῖστον ἐπαυρομένη,
εἶπε τάδ᾽· "Ὦ Μινοῖ, πήλαι, φέρε, κάλπιν ἐλαφρήν·   5
οἴσω κυάνεον τοὺξ Ἀχέροντος ὕδωρ·
καὐτὴ παρθένιον γὰρ ἀπώλεσα." τοῦτο δ᾽ ἔλεξε
ψευδές, ἵν᾽ αὐγάζῃ κἢν φθιμένοισι πίθον.

385.—ΦΙΛΙΠΠΟΥ

Ἥρως Πρωτεσίλαε, σὺ γὰρ πρώτην ἐμύησας
Ἴλιον Ἑλλαδικοῦ θυμὸν ἰδεῖν δόρατος,
καὶ περὶ σοῖς τύμβοις ὅσα δένδρεα μακρὰ τέθηλε,
πάντα τὸν εἰς Τροίην ἐγκεκύηκε χόλον·
Ἴλιον ἢν ἐσίδῃ γὰρ ἀπ᾽ ἀκρεμόνων κορυφαίων,   5
καρφοῦται, πετάλων κόσμον ἀναινόμενα.
θυμὸν ἐπὶ Τροίῃ πόσον ἔζεσας, ἡνίκα τὴν σὴν
σώζει καὶ στελέχη μῆνιν ἐπ᾽ ἀντιπάλους.

386.—ΒΑΣΣΟΥ ΛΟΛΛΙΟΥ

Ἥδ᾽ ἐγὼ ἡ τοσάκις Νιόβη λίθος, ὁσσάκι μήτηρ·
δύσμορος ἢ μαστῶν [θερμὸν] ἔπηξα γάλα·
Ἀΐδεω πολὺς ὄλβος ἐμῆς ὠδῖνος ἀριθμός,
ᾧ τέκον. ὢ μεγάλης λείψανα πυρκαϊῆς.

387.—ΒΙΑΝΟΡΟΣ

Θειονόης ἔκλαιον ἐμῆς μόρον, ἀλλ᾽ ἐπὶ παιδὸς
ἐλπίσι κουφοτέρας ἔστενον εἰς ὀδύνας.

---

[1] i.e. condemn me.   cp. Virg. Aen. vi. 492.

384.—MARCUS ARGENTARIUS

OLD Aristomache the talkative friend of the vine, who loved Bacchus much more than did his nurse Ino, when she went under holy earth, and the spirit of her who had enjoyed so many a cup had utterly faded, said "Shake, Minos, the light urn.[1] I will fetch the dark water from Acheron; for I too slew a young husband." [2] This falsehood she told in order that even among the dead she should be able to look at a jar.

385.—PHILIPPUS

HERO Protesilaus, for that thou didst first initiate Ilion into looking on the wrath of Grecian spears, the tall trees also that grow round thy tomb are all big with hatred of Troy. If from their topmost branches they see Ilion, they wither and cast off the beauty of their foliage. How great was thy boiling wrath against Troy, if tree-trunks preserve the spite thou didst bear thy foes.[3]

386.—BASSUS LOLLIUS

HERE am I, Niobe, as many times a stone (*sic*) as I was a mother; so unhappy was I that the milk in my breast grew hard. Great wealth for Hades was the number of my children—to Hades for whom I brought them forth. Oh relics of that great pyre!

387.—BIANOR

I WEPT the death of my Theonoe, but the hopes I had of our child lightened my grief. But now

[2] *i.e.* like the daughters of Danaus, who were compelled to carry water in hell.   [3] *cp.* No. 141.

νῦν δέ με καὶ παιδὸς φθονερή γ' ἀπενόσφισε Μοῖρα·
φεῦ· βρέφος ἐψεύσθην καὶ σὲ τὸ λειπόμενον.
Περσεφόνη, τόδε πατρὸς ἐπὶ θρήνοισιν ἄκουσον·   5
θὲς βρέφος ἐς κόλπους μητρὸς ἀποιχομένης.

388.—ΤΟΥ ΑΥΤΟΥ

Ἰχθύσι καὶ ποταμῷ Κλειτώνυμον ἐχθρὸς ὅμιλος
ὦσεν, ὅτ' εἰς ἄκρην ἦλθε τυραννοφόνος.
ἀλλὰ Δίκα μιν ἔθαψεν· ἀποσπασθεῖσα γὰρ ὄχθα
πᾶν δέμας ἐς κορυφὴν ἐκ ποδὸς ἐκτέρισεν·
κεῖται δ' οὐχ ὑδάτεσσι διάβροχος· αἰδομένα δὲ   5
Γᾶ κεύθει τὸν ἑᾶς ὅρμον ἐλευθερίας.

389.—ΑΠΟΛΛΩΝΙΔΟΥ

Καὶ τίς ὃς οὐκ ἔτλη κακὸν ἔσχατον υἱέα κλαύσας;
ἀλλ' ὁ Ποσειδίππου πάντας ἔθαψε δόμος
τέσσαρας, οὓς Ἀΐδαο συνήριθμον ἥρπασεν ἦμαρ,
τὴν πολλὴν παίδων ἐλπίδα κειραμένου.
πατρὸς δ' ὄμματα λυγρὰ κατομβρηθέντα γόοισιι   5
ὤλετο· κοινή που νὺξ μία πάντας ἔχει.

390.—ΑΝΤΙΠΑΤΡΟΥ

Κυλλήνην ὄρος Ἀρκάδων ἀκούεις·
αὕτη σῆμ' ἐπίκειτ' Ἀπολλοδώρῳ.
Πίσηθέν μιν ἰόντα νυκτὸς ὥρῃ
ἔκτεινεν Διόθεν πεσὼν κεραυνός.
τηλοῦ δ' Αἰανέης τε καὶ Βεροίης   5
νικηθεὶς Διὸς ὁ δρομεὺς καθεύδει.

envious fate has bereft me of the boy too. Alas
my child, all that was left to me, I am cheated of
thee! Persephone, give ear to the prayer of a
mourning father, and lay the child in the bosom of
its dead mother.

388.—By the Same

THE hostile crowd threw Clitonymus to the fish
and the river when he came to the castle to kill the
tyrant. But Justice buried him, for the bank falling
in honoured with funeral his whole body from head
to foot, and he lies unwetted by the water, the earth
in reverence covering him, her haven [1] of freedom.

389.—APOLLONIDES

WHO is there that has not suffered the extremity
of woe, weeping for a son? But the house of Posi-
dippus buried all four, taken from him in four days
by death, that cut short all his hopes of them. The
father's mourning eyes drenched with tears have lost
their sight, and one may say that a common night
now holds them all.

390.—ANTIPATER OF THESSALONICA

YOU have heard of Cyllene the Arcadian mountain.
That is the monument that covers Apollodorus. As
he journeyed from Pisa by night the thunderbolt
from Zeus killed him; and far from Aeanae and
Beroea [2] the racer sleeps, conquered by Zeus.

---

[1] i.e. the protector of her freedom.
[2] Towns in Macedonia.

391.—ΒΑΣΣΟΥ ΛΟΛΛΙΟΥ

Κλειδοῦχοι νεκυων, πάσας Ἀΐδαο κελεύθου\
  φράγνυτε· καὶ στομίοις κλεῖθρα δέχοισθε, πύλαι.\
αὐτὸς ἐγὼν Ἀΐδας ἐνέπω· Γερμανικὸς ἄστρων,\
  οὐκ ἐμός· οὐ χωρεῖ νῆα τόσην Ἀχέρων.

392.—ΗΡΑΚΛΕΙΔΟΥ ΣΙΝΩΠΕΩΣ

Λαῖλαψ καὶ πολὺ κῦμα καὶ ἀντολαὶ Ἀρκτούροιο,\
  καὶ σκότος, Αἰγαίου τ᾽ οἶδμα κακὸν πελάγευς,\
ταῦθ᾽ ἅμα πάνθ᾽ ἐκύκησεν ἐμὴν νέα· τριχθὰ δὲ\
    κλασθεὶς\
ἱστὸς ὁμοῦ φόρτῳ κἀμὲ κάλυψε βυθῷ.\
ναυηγὸν κλαίοιτε παρ᾽ αἰγιαλοῖσι, γονῆες,   5\
  Τλησιμένη, κωφὴν στησάμενοι λίθακα.

393.—ΔΙΟΚΛΕΟΥΣ ΚΑΡΥΣΤΙΟΥ

Μή με κόνι κρύψητε, τί γάρ; πάλι, μηδ᾽ ἔτι ταύτης\
  ἠόνος οὐκ ὀνοτὴν γαῖαν ἐμοὶ τίθετε.\
μαίνεται εἴς με θάλασσα, καὶ ἐν χέρσοιό με δειλὸν\
  εὑρίσκει ῥαχίαις· οἱδέ με κὴν Ἀΐδη.\
χέρσῳ ἐπεκβαίνειν εἰ ἐμεῦ χάριν ὕδατι θυμός,   5\
  †πάρκειμαι σταθερῇ μιμνέμεν ὡς ἄταφος.

394.—ΦΙΛΙΠΠΟΥ ΘΕΣΣΑΛΟΝΙΚΕΩΣ

Μυλεργάτας ἀνήρ με κὴν ζωᾶς χρόνοις\
  βαρυβρομήταν εἶχε δινητὸν πέτρον,

---

[1] By Germanicus we should understand Tiberius' nephew. The connection between the two couplets is not obvious. and something seems to be missing.

391.—BASSUS LOLLIUS

YE janitors of the dead, block all the roads of Hades, and be bolted, ye entrance doors. I myself, Hades, order it. Germanicus belongs to the stars, not to me; Acheron has no room for so great a ship.[1]

392.—HERACLIDES OF SINOPE

THE gale and great waves and the tempestuous rising of Arcturus[2] and the darkness and the evil swell of the Aegean, all these dashed my ship to pieces, and the mast broken in three plunged me in the depths together with my cargo. Weep on the shore, parents, for your shipwrecked Tlesimenes, erecting a cenotaph.

393.—DIOCLES OF CARYSTUS

COVER me not with dust again. What avails it? Nor continue to put on me the guiltless earth of this strand. The sea is furious with me and discovers me, wretched man, even on the surf-beaten land: even in Hades it knows me. If it is the will of the waves to mount on the land for my sake, I prefer[3] to remain on the firm land thus unburied.

394.—PHILIPPUS OF THESSALONICA

THE miller possessed me also during his life, the deep-voiced revolving stone, the wheat-crushing

---

[2] In the middle of September.
[3] Some such sense is required. Jacobs suggested ἀρκοῦμαι, "I am content."

πυρηφάτον Δάματρος εὐκάρπου λάτριν,
καὶ κατθανὼν στάλωσε τῷδ᾽ ἐπ᾽ ἠρίῳ,
σύνθημα τέχνας· ὡς ἔχει μ᾽ ἀεὶ βαρύν,   5
καὶ ζῶν ἐν ἔργοις, καὶ θανὼν ἐπ᾽ ὀστέοις.

395.—ΜΑΡΚΟΥ ΑΡΓΕΝΤΑΡΙΟΥ

Οὗτος ὁ Καλλαίσχρου κενεὸς τάφος, ὃν βαθὺ χεῦμα
ἔσφηλεν Λιβυκῶν ἐνδρομέοντα πόρων,
συρμὸς ὅτ᾽ Ὠρίωνος ἀνεστρώφησε θαλάσσης
βένθος ὑπὸ στυγερῆς οἴδματα πανδυσίης.
καὶ τὸν μὲν δαίσαντο κυκώμενον εἰν ἁλὶ θῆρες,   5
κωφὸν δὲ στήλη γράμμα λέλογχε τόδε.

396.—ΒΙΑΝΟΡΟΣ ΒΙΘΥΝΟΥ

Οἰδίποδος παίδων Θήβη τάφος· ἀλλ᾽ ὁ πανώλης
τύμβος ἔτι ζώντων αἰσθάνεται πολέμων.
κείνους οὔτ᾽ Ἀΐδης ἐδαμάσσατο, κἠν Ἀχέροντι
μάρνανται· κείνων χὠ τάφος ἀντίπαλος,
καὶ πυρὶ πῦρ ἤλεγξαν ἐναντίον. ὦ ἐλεεινοὶ   5
παῖδες, ἀκοιμήτων ἀψάμενοι δοράτων.

397.—ΕΡΥΚΙΟΥ ΘΕΤΤΑΛΟΥ

Οὐχ ὅδε δειλαίου Σατύρου τάφος, οὐδ᾽ ὑπὸ ταύτῃ,
ὡς λόγος, εὔνηται πυρκαϊῇ Σάτυρος·
ἀλλ᾽ εἴ που τινὰ πόντον ἀκούετε, πικρὸν ἐκεῖνον,
τὸν πέλας αἰγονόμου κλυζόμενον Μυκάλας,
κείνῳ δινήεντι καὶ ἀτρυγέτῳ ἔτι κεῖμαι   5
ὕδατι, μαινομένῳ μεμφόμενος Βορέῃ.

---

[1] Literally "at the season of the swelling."

servant of fertile Demeter, and on his death he set
me up on this tomb, an emblem of his calling. So
he finds me ever heavy, in his work while he lived,
and now he is dead, on his bones.

395.—MARCUS ARGENTARIUS

THIS is the cenotaph of Callaeschrus, whom the
deep undid as he was crossing the Libyan main, then
when the force of Orion at the stormy season [1] of his
baneful setting [2] stirred the sea from its depths. The
sea-monsters devoured his wave-tossed corpse, and
the stone bears but this empty inscription.

396.—BIANOR OF BITHYNIA

THEBES is the tomb of the sons of Oedipus, but the
all-destroying tomb feels their still living quarrel.
Not even Hades subdued them, and by Acheron they
still fight; even their tombs are foes and they
dispute still on their funeral pyres.[3] O children
much to be pitied, who grasped spears never to be
laid to rest.

397.—ERYCIUS OF THESSALY

THIS is not the tomb of poor Satyrus; Satyrus
sleeps not, as they tell, under the ashes of this
pyre. But perchance ye have heard of a sea some-
where, the bitter sea that beats on the shore near
Mycale where the wild-goats feed, and in that
eddying and desert water yet I lie, reproaching
furious Boreas.

[2] Early in November.
[3] See No. 399 for the meaning of this.

398.—ΑΝΤΙΠΑΤΡΟΥ

Οὐκ οἶδ᾽ εἰ Διόνυσον ὀνόσσομαι, ἢ Διὸς ὄμβρον
  μέμψομ᾽· ὀλισθηροὶ δ᾽ εἰς πόδας ἀμφότεροι.
ἀγρόθε γὰρ κατιόντα Πολύξενον ἔκ ποτε δαιτὸς
  τύμβος ἔχει γλίσχρων ἐξεριπόντα λόφων·
κεῖται δ᾽ Αἰολίδος Σμύρνης ἑκάς. ἀλλά τις ὄρφνης   5
  δειμαίνοι μεθύων ἀτραπὸν ὑετίην.

399.—ΑΝΤΙΦΙΛΟΥ

Τηλοτάτω χεύασθαι ἔδει τάφον Οἰδιπόδαο
  παισὶν ἀπ᾽ ἀλλήλων, οἷς πέρας οὐδ᾽ Ἀΐδας·
ἀλλὰ καὶ εἰς Ἀχέροντος ἕνα πλόον ἠρνήσαντο,
  χὠ στυγερὸς ζώει κἢν φθιμένοισιν Ἄρης.
ἠνίδε πυρκαϊῆς ἄνισον φλόγα· δαιομένα γὰρ   5
  ἐξ ἑνὸς εἰς δισσὰν δῆριν ἀποστρέφεται.

400.—ΣΕΡΑΠΙΩΝΟΣ ΑΛΕΞΑΝΔΡΕΩΣ

Τοῦτ᾽ ὀστεῦν φωτὸς πολυεργέος. ἦ ῥά τις ἦσθα
  ἔμπορος, ἢ τυφλοῦ κύματος ἰχθυβόλος.
ἄγγειλον θνητοῖσιν ὅτι σπεύδοντες ἐς ἄλλας
  ἐλπίδας εἰς τοίην ἐλπίδα λυόμεθα.

401.—ΚΡΙΝΑΓΟΡΟΥ

Τήνδ᾽ ὑπὸ δύσβωλον θλίβει χθόνα φωτὸς ἀλιτροῦ
  ὀστέα μισητῆς τύμβος ὑπὲρ κεφαλῆς,
στέρνα τ᾽ ἐποκριόεντα, καὶ οὐκ εὔοδμον ὀδόντων
  πρίονα, καὶ κώλων δούλιον οἰοπέδην,

214

398.—ANTIPATER OF THESSALONICA

I know not whether to blame Bacchus or the rain ;
both are treacherous for the feet.   For this tomb
holds Polyxenus who once, returning from the country
after a banquet, fell from the slippery hill-side.   Far
from Aeolian Smyrna he lies.   Let everyone at night
when drunk dread the rain-soaked path.

399.—ANTIPHILUS

Far from each other should the tombs of Oedipus'
sons have been built, for even Hades ends not their
strife.   They refused even to travel in one boat to
the house of Acheron, and hateful Ares lives in
them even now they are dead.   Look at the uneven
flame of their pyre, how it separates from one into
two quarrelling tongues.

400.—SERAPION OF ALEXANDRIA

This bone is that of some man who laboured much.
Either wast thou a merchant or a fisher in the blind,
uncertain sea.   Tell to mortals that eagerly pursuing
other hopes we all rest at the end in the haven of
such a hope.

401.—CRINAGORAS

The tomb above his odious head crushes the bones
of the scoundrel who lies in this unhappy earth ;
it crushes the protruding breast and the unsavoury
sawlike teeth and the servilely fettered legs and

ἄτριχα καὶ κόρσην, Εὐνικίδου ἡμιπύρωτα
λείψαν', ἔτι χλωρῆς ἔμπλεα τηκεδόνος.
χθὼν ὦ δυσνύμφευτε, κακοσκήνευς ἐπὶ τέφρης
ἀνδρὸς μὴ κούφη κέκλισο, μηδ' ὀλίγη.

402.—ΑΝΤΙΠΑΤΡΟΥ

Χειμερίου νιφετοῖο περὶ θριγκοῖσι τακέντος
δῶμα πεσὸν τὴν γραῦν ἔκτανε Λυσιδίκην·
σῆμα δέ οἱ κωμῆται ὁμώλακες οὐκ ἀπ' ὀρυκτῆς
γαίης, ἀλλ' αὐτὸν πύργον ἔθεντο τάφον.

403.—ΜΑΡΚΟΥ ΑΡΓΕΝΤΑΡΙΟΥ

Ψύλλος, ὁ τὰς ποθινὰς ἐπιμισθίδας αἰὲν ἑταίρας
πέμπων ἐς τὰ νέων ἡδέα συμπόσια,
οὗτος ὁ θηρεύων ἀταλόφρονας, ἐνθάδε κεῖται,
αἰσχρὸν ἀπ' ἀνθρώπων μισθὸν ἐνεγκάμενος.
ἀλλὰ λίθους ἐπὶ τύμβον, ὁδοιπόρε, μήτε σὺ βάλλε,
μήτ' ἄλλον πείσῃς· σῆμα λέλογχε νέκυς.
φεῖσαι δ' οὐχ ὅτι κέρδος ἐπῄνεσεν, ἀλλ' ὅτι κοινὰς
θρέψας, μοιχεύειν οὐκ ἐδίδαξε νέους.

404.—ΖΩΝΑ ΣΑΡΔΙΑΝΟΥ

Ψυχράν σευ κεφαλᾶς ἐπαμήσομαι αἰγιαλῖτιν
θῖνα κατὰ κρυεροῦ χευάμενος νέκυος·
οὐ γάρ σευ μήτηρ ἐπιτύμβια κωκύουσα
εἶδεν ἁλίξαντον σὸν μόρον εἰνάλιον·
ἀλλά σ' ἐρημαῖοί τε καὶ ἄξεινοι πλαταμῶνες
δέξαντ' Αἰγαίης γείτονες ἠϊόνος·
ὥστ' ἔχε μὲν ψαμάθου μόριον βραχύ, πουλὺ δὲ δάκρυ
ξεῖν', ἐπεὶ εἰς ὀλοὴν ἔδραμες ἐμπορίην.

hairless head, the half consumed remains of Eunicides still full of green putrescence. O earth, who hast espoused an evil bridegroom, rest not light or thinly-sprinkled on the ashes of the deformed being.[1]

402.—ANTIPATER OF THESSALONICA

On the winter snow melting at the top of her house it fell in and killed old Lysidice. Her neighbours of the village did not make her a tomb of earth dug up for the purpose, but put her house itself over her as a tomb.

403.—MARCUS ARGENTARIUS

Psyllus, who used to take to the pleasant banquets of the young men the venal ladies that they desired, that hunter of weak girls, who earned a disgraceful wage by dealing in human flesh, lies here. But cast not thou stones at his tomb, wayfarer, nor bid another do so. He is dead and buried. Spare him, not because he was content to gain his living so, but because as keeper of common women he dissuaded young men from adultery.

404.—ZONAS OF SARDIS

On thy head I will heap the cold shingle of the beach, shedding it on thy cold corpse. For never did thy mother wail over thy tomb or see the sea-battered body of her shipwrecked son. But the desert and inhospitable strand of the Aegean shore received thee. So take this little portion of sand, stranger, and many a tear; for fated was the journey on which thou didst set out to trade.

[1] cp. No. 380, an imitation of this.

405.—ΦΙΛΙΠΠΟΥ

'Ω ξεῖνε, φεῦγε τὸν χαλαζεπῆ τάφον
τὸν φρικτὸν Ἱππώνακτος, οὗτε χὰ τέφρα
ἰαμβιάζει Βουπάλειον ἐς στύγος,
μή πως ἐγείρῃς σφῆκα τὸν κοιμώμενον,
ὃς οὐδ' ἐν ᾅδῃ νῦν κεκοίμικεν χόλον,
σκάζουσι μέτροις ὀρθὰ τοξεύσας ἔπη.

406.—ΘΕΟΔΩΡΙΔΑ

Εὐφορίων, ὁ περισσὸν ἐπιστάμενός τι ποῆσαι,
    Πειραϊκοῖς κεῖται τοῖσδε παρὰ σκέλεσιν.
ἀλλὰ σὺ τῷ μύστῃ ῥοιὴν ἢ μῆλον ἄπαρξαι,
    ἢ μύρτον· καὶ γὰρ ζωὸς ἐὼν ἐφίλει.

407.—ΔΙΟΣΚΟΡΙΔΟΥ

Ἥδιστον φιλέουσι νέοις προσανάκλιμ' ἐρώτων,
    Σαπφώ, σὺν Μούσαις ἦ ῥά σε Πιερίη
ἢ Ἑλικὼν εὔκισσος, ἴσα πνείουσαν ἐκείναις,
    κοσμεῖ, τὴν Ἐρέσῳ Μοῦσαν ἐν Αἰολίδι,
ἢ καὶ Ὑμὴν Ὑμέναιος ἔχων εὐφεγγέα πεύκην
    σὺν σοὶ νυμφιδίων ἵσταθ' ὑπὲρ θαλάμων·
ἢ Κινύρεω νέον ἔρνος ὀδυρομένῃ Ἀφροδίτῃ
    σύνθρηνος, μακάρων ἱερὸν ἄλσος ὁρῇς·
πάντῃ, πότνια, χαῖρε θεοῖς ἴσα· σὰς γὰρ ἀοιδὰς
    ἀθανάτων ἄγομεν νῦν ἔτι θυγατέρας.

---

[1] He wrote in iambics called "lame" because ending in a
spondee.

405.—PHILIPPUS

Avoid, O stranger, this terrible tomb of Hipponax, which hails forth verses, Hipponax whose very ashes cry in iambics his hatred of Bupalus, lest thou wake the sleeping wasp, who not even in Hades has lulled his spite to rest, but in a halting[1] measure launcheth straight shafts of song.

406.—THEODORIDAS

Euphorion, the exquiste writer of verse, lies by these long walls of the Piraeus.   Offer to the initiated singer a pomegranate or apple, or myrtle-berries,[2] for in his life he loved them.

407.—DIOSCORIDES

Sappho, who dost most sweetly pillow the loves of young men, thee verily Pieria or ivied Helicon honour together with the Muses; for thy breath is like to theirs, thou Muse of Aeolian Eresus.   Either Hymen Hymenaeus bearing his bright torch stands with thee over the bridal couch; or thou lookest on the holy grove of the Blessed, mourning in company with Aphrodite the fair young son of Cinyras.[3]   Wherever thou be, I salute thee, my queen, as divine, for we still deem thy songs to be daughters of the gods.

[2] They were all used in the mysteries.
[3] Adonis.

408.—ΛΕΩΝΙΔΑ

Ἀτρέμα τὸν τύμβον παραμείβετε, μὴ τὸν ἐν ὕπνῳ
πικρὸν ἐγείρητε σφῆκ᾽ ἀναπαυόμενον.
ἄρτι γὰρ Ἱππώνακτος ὁ καὶ τοκέωνε βαΰξας
ἄρτι κεκοίμηται θυμὸς ἐν ἡσυχίῃ.
ἀλλὰ προμηθήσασθε· τὰ γὰρ πεπυρωμένα κείνου   5
ῥήματα πημαίνειν οἶδε καὶ εἰν Ἀΐδῃ.

409.—ΑΝΤΙΠΑΤΡΟΥ [ΘΕΣΣΑΛΟΝΙΚΕΩΣ]

Ὄβριμον ἀκαμάτου στίχον αἴνεσον Ἀντιμάχοιο,
ἄξιον ἀρχαίων ὀφρύος ἡμιθέων,
Πιερίδων χαλκευτὸν ἐπ᾽ ἄκμοσιν, εἰ τορὸν οὖας
ἔλλαχες, εἰ ζαλοῖς τὰν ἀγέλαστον ὄπα,
εἰ τὰν ἄτριπτον καὶ ἀνέμβατον ἀτραπὸν ἄλλοις   5
μαίεαι. εἰ δ᾽ ὕμνων σκᾶπτρον Ὅμηρος ἔχει,
καὶ Ζεύς τοι κρέσσων Ἐνοσίχθονος· ἀλλ᾽ Ἐνοσίχθων
τοῦ μὲν ἔφυ μείων, ἀθανάτων δ᾽ ὕπατος·
καὶ ναετὴρ Κολοφῶνος ὑπέζευκται μὲν Ὁμήρῳ,
ἁγεῖται δ᾽ ἄλλων πλάθεος ὑμνοπόλων.   10

410.—ΔΙΟΣΚΟΡΙΔΟΥ

Θέσπις ὅδε, τραγικὴν ὃς ἀνέπλασε πρῶτος ἀοιδὴν
κωμήταις νεαρὰς καινοτομῶν χαριτας,
Βάκχος ὅτε τριετῇ[1] κατάγοι χορόν, ᾧ τράγος ἄθλων
χὠττικὸς ἦν σύκων ἄρριχος ἆθλον ἔτι.
οἱ δὲ μεταπλάσσουσι νέοι τάδε· μυρίος αἰὼν
πολλὰ προσευρήσει χἄτερα· τἀμὰ δ᾽ ἐμα.

---

[1] Wilamowitz: τριθῦν MS.

408.—LEONIDAS

Go quietly by the tomb, lest ye awake the malignant wasp that lies asleep; for only just has it been laid to rest, the spite of Hipponax that snarled even at his parents.   Have a care then; for his verses, red from the fire, have power to hurt even in Hades.

409.—ANTIPATER OF SIDON

Praise the sturdy verse of tireless Antimachus, worthy of the majesty of the demigods of old, beaten on the anvil of the Muses, if thou art gifted with a keen ear, if thou aspirest to gravity of words, if thou wouldst pursue a path untrodden and unapproached by others.   If Homer holds the sceptre of song, yet, though Zeus is greater than Poseidon, Poseidon his inferior is the chief of the immortals; so the Colophonian bows before Homer, but leads the crowd of other singers.

410.—DIOSCORIDES

I am Thespis, who first modelled tragic song, inventing a new diversion for the villagers, at the season when Bacchus led in the triennial chorus whose prize was still a goat and a basket of Attic figs.   Now my juniors remodel all this; countless ages will beget many new inventions, but my own is mine.

411.—ΤΟΥ ΑΥΤΟΥ

Θέσπιδος εὕρεμα τοῦτο, τά τ᾽ ἀγροιῶτιν ἀν᾽ ὕλαι
παίγνια, καὶ κώμους τούσδε, τελειοτέρους
Αἰσχύλος ἐξύψωσεν, ὁ μὴ σμιλευτὰ χαράξας
γράμματα, χειμάρρῳ δ᾽ οἷα καταρδόμενα,
καὶ τὰ κατὰ σκηνὴν μετεκαίνισεν. ὦ στόμα πάντη   5
δεξιόν, ἀρχαίων ἦσθά τις ἡμιθέων.

412.—ΑΛΚΑΙΟΥ ΜΕΣΣΗΝΙΟΥ

Πᾶσά τοι οἰχομένῳ, Πυλάδη, κωκύεται Ἑλλάς,
ἄπλεκτον χαίταν ἐν χροῒ κειραμένα·
αὐτὸς δ᾽ ἀτμήτοιο κόμας ἀπεθήκατο δάφνας
Φοῖβος, ἑὸν τιμῶν ᾗ θέμις ὑμνοπόλον·
Μοῦσαι δ᾽ ἐκλαύσαντο· ῥόον δ᾽ ἔστησεν ἀκούων   5
Ἀσωπὸς γοερῶν ἦχον ἀπὸ στομάτων·
ἔλληξεν δὲ μέλαθρα Διωνύσοιο χορείης,
εὖτε σιδηρείην οἶμον ἔβης Ἀΐδεω.

413.—ΑΝΤΙΠΑΤΡΟΥ

Οὐχὶ βαθυστόλμων Ἱππαρχία ἔργα γυναικῶν,
τῶν δὲ Κυνῶν ἑλόμαν ῥωμαλέον βίοτον·
οὐδέ μοι ἀμπεχόναι περονήτιδες, οὐ βαθύπελμος
εὐμαρίς, οὐ λιπόων εὔαδε κεκρύφαλος·
οὐλὰς δὲ σκίπωνι συνέμπορος, ἅ τε συνῳδὸς   5
δίπλαξ, καὶ κοίτας βλῆμα χαμαιλεχέος.
ἄμμι δὲ Μαιναλίας κάρρων †ἄμιν[1] Ἀταλάντας
τόσσον, ὅσον σοφία κρέσσον ὀριδρομίας.

[1] Hecker suggests μνᾶμα, and I render so.

411.—By the Same

This invention of Thespis and the greenwood games and revels were raised to greater perfection by Aeschylus who carved letters not neatly chiselled, but as if water-worn by a torrent. In matters of the stage he was also an innovator. O mouth in every respect accomplished, thou wast one of the demigods of old!

412.—ALCAEUS OF MESSENE

Pylades,[1] now thou art gone, all Hellas wails shearing her loosened hair, and Phoebus himself took off the laurels from his flowing locks, honouring his singer as is meet. The Muses wept and Asopus stayed his stream when he heard the voice of mourning. The dance of Dionysus ceased in the halls, when thou didst go down the iron road of Hades.

413.—ANTIPATER OF SIDON

I, Hipparchia,[2] chose not the tasks of amply-robed woman, but the manly life of the Cynics. Nor do tunics fastened with brooches and thick-soled slippers, and the hair-caul wet with ointment please me, but rather the wallet and its fellow-traveller the staff and the course double mantle suited to them, and a bed strewn on the ground. I shall have a greater name than that of Arcadian Atalanta by so much as wisdom is better than racing over the mountains.

---

[1] A celebrated actor.   [2] Wife of the Cynic Crates.

414.—ΝΟΣΣΙΔΟΣ ΤΗΣ ΜΕΛΟΠΟΙΟΥ

Καὶ καπυρὸν γελάσας παραμείβεο, καὶ φίλον εἰπὼν
ῥῆμ' ἐπ' ἐμοί. 'Ρίνθων εἴμ' ὁ Συρακόσιος,
Μουσάων ὀλίγη τις ἀηδονίς· ἀλλὰ φλυάκων
ἐκ τραγικῶν ἴδιον κισσὸν ἐδρεψάμεθα.

415.—ΚΑΛΛΙΜΑΧΟΥ

Βαττιάδεω παρὰ σῆμα φέρεις πόδας, εὖ μὲν ἀοιδὴν
εἰδότος, εὖ δ' οἴνῳ καίρια συγγελάσαι.

416.—ΑΛΛΟ

Εὐκράτεω Μελέαγρον ἔχω, ξένε, τὸν σὺν Ἔρωτι
καὶ Μούσαις κεράσανθ' ἡδυλόγους Χάριτας.

417.—ΜΕΛΕΑΓΡΟΥ

Νᾶσος ἐμὰ θρέπτειρα Τύρος· πάτρα δέ με τεκνοῖ
Ἀτθὶς ἐν Ἀσσυρίοις ναιομένα, Γάδαρα·
Εὐκράτεω δ' ἔβλαστον ὁ σὺν Μούσαις Μελέαγρος
πρῶτα Μενιππείοις συντροχάσας Χάρισιν.
εἰ δὲ Σύρος, τί τὸ θαῦμα; μίαν, ξένε, πατρίδα κόσμον
ναίομεν· ἐν θνατοὺς πάντας ἔτικτε Χάος.
πουλυετὴς δ' ἐχάραξα τάδ' ἐν δέλτοισι πρὸ τύμβου·
γήρως γὰρ γείτων ἐγγύθεν Ἀΐδεω.
ἀλλά με τὸν λαλιὸν καὶ πρεσβύτην προτιειπὼν
χαίρειν, εἰς γῆρας καὐτὸς ἵκοιο λάλον.

414.—NOSSIS

LAUGH frankly as thou passest by and speak a kind word over me. I am the Syracusan Rhintho, one of the lesser nightingales of the Muses; but from my tragic burlesques I plucked for myself a special wreath of ivy.

415.—CALLIMACHUS

THIS is the tomb of Callimachus that thou art passing. He could sing well, and laugh well at the right time over the wine.

416.—ANONYMOUS

I HOLD, stranger, Meleager, son of Eucrates, who mixed the sweet-spoken Graces with Love and the Muses.

417.—MELEAGER

ISLAND Tyre was my nurse, and Gadara, which is Attic,[1] but lies in Syria, gave birth to me. From Eucrates I sprung, Meleager, who first by the help of the Muses ran abreast of the Graces of Menippus.[2] If I am a Syrian, what wonder? Stranger, we dwell in one country, the world; one Chaos gave birth to all mortals. In my old age I wrote these lines in my tablets before my burial; for eld and death are near neighbours. Speak a word to wish me, the loquacious old man, well, and mayst thou reach a loquacious old age thyself.

[1] As regards culture.
[2] He wrote besides his epigrams satires in which he imitated Menippus.

418.—ΤΟΥ ΑΥΤΟΥ

Πρῶτά μοι Γαδάρων κλεινὰ πόλις ἔπλετο πάτρα,
ἤνδρωσεν δ᾽ ἱερὰ δεξαμένα με Τύρος·
εἰς γῆρας δ᾽ ὅτ᾽ ἔβην, ἁ καὶ Δία θρεψαμένα Κῶς
κἀμὲ θετὸν Μερόπων ἀστὸν ἐγηροτρόφει.
Μοῦσαι δ᾽ εἰν ὀλίγοις με, τὸν Εὐκράτεω Μελέαγρον   5
παῖδα, Μενιππείοις ἠγλάϊσαν Χάρισιν.

419.—ΤΟΥ ΑΥΤΟΥ

Ἀτρέμας, ὦ ξένε, βαῖνε· παρ᾽ εὐσεβέσιν γὰρ ὁ
    πρέσβυς
εὕδει, κοιμηθεὶς ὕπνον ὀφειλόμενον,
Εὐκράτεω Μελέαγρος, ὁ τὸν γλυκύδακρυν Ἔρωτα
καὶ Μούσας ἱλαραῖς συστολίσας Χάρισιν·
ὃν θεόπαις ἤνδρωσε Τύρος Γαδάρων θ᾽ ἱερὰ χθών·   5
Κῶς δ᾽ ἐρατὴ Μερόπων πρέσβυν ἐγηροτρόφει.
ἀλλ᾽ εἰ μὲν Σύρος ἐσσί, Σάλαμ· εἰ δ᾽ οὖν σύ γε Φοῖνιξ,
Ναίδιος· εἰ δ᾽ Ἕλλην, Χαῖρε· τὸ δ᾽ αὐτὸ φράσον.

420.—ΔΙΟΤΙΜΟΥ ΑΘΗΝΑΙΟΥ

Ἐλπίδες ἀνθρώπων, ἐλαφραὶ θεαί—οὐ γὰρ ἂν ὧδε
Λέσβον· ὁ λυσιμελὴς ἀμφεκάλυψ᾽ Ἀΐδης,
ὅς ποτε καὶ βασιλῆϊ συνέδραμε,—ναὶ μετ᾽ Ἐρώτων
χαίρετε κουφόταται δαίμονες ἀθανάτων.
αὐλοὶ δ᾽ ἄφθεγκτοι καὶ ἀπευθέες, οἷς ἐνέπνευσε,   5
κεῖσθ᾽, ἐπεὶ οὐ θιάσους . . . οἶδ᾽ Ἀχέρων.

---

[1] Ptolemy Philadelphus, who was brought up in Cos ; cf.
Theocr. 17. 58.

418.—By the Same

My first country was famous Gadara; then Tyre received me and brought me up to manhood. When I reached old age, Cos, which nurtured Zeus,[1] made me one of her Meropian [2] citizens and cared for my declining years. But the Muses adorned me, Meleager, son of Eucrates, more than most men with the Graces of Menippus.

419.—By the Same

Go noiselessly by, stranger; the old man sleeps among the pious dead, wrapped in the slumber that is the lot of all. This is Meleager, the son of Eucrates, who linked sweet tearful Love and the Muses with the merry Graces. Heavenborn Tyre and Gadara's holy soil reared him to manhood, and beloved Cos of the Meropes tended his old age. If you are a Syrian, Salam! if you are a Phoenician, Naidius [3]! if you are a Greek, Chaire! (Hail) and say the same yourself.

420.—DIOTIMUS OF ATHENS

Ye Hopes of men, light goddesses—for never, were ye not so, had Hades, who bringeth our strength to naught, covered Lesbon, once as blest as the Great King—yea, ye Hopes and ye Loves too, lightest of all deities, farewell! And ye, the flutes he once breathed in, must lie dumb and unheard; for Acheron knoweth no troops of musicians.

[2] The city of Cos, to distinguish it from an earlier capital of the island, was known as Cos Meropis.

[3] This Phoenician word for "Hail" is uncertain. Plautus gives it as "haudoni."

GREEK ANTHOLOGY

421.—ΜΕΛΕΑΓΡΟΤ

Αἰνιγματῶδες

Πτανέ, τί σοὶ σιβύνης, τί δὲ καὶ συὸς εὔαδε δέρμα;
   καὶ τίς ἐὼν στάλας σύμβολον ἐσσὶ τίνος;
οὐ γὰρ Ἔρωτ᾽ ἐνέπω σε—τί γάρ; νεκύεσσι πάροικος
   ἵμερος; αἰάζειν ὁ θρασὺς οὐκ ἔμαθεν—
οὐδὲ μὲν οὐδ᾽ αὐτὸν ταχύπουν Κρόνον· ἔμπαλι
     γὰρ δὴ
   κεῖνος μὲν τριγέρων, σοὶ δὲ τέθηλε μέλη.
ἀλλ᾽ ἄρα, ναὶ δοκέω γάρ, ὁ γᾶς ὑπένερθε σοφιστὰς
   ἐστί· σὺ δ᾽ ὁ πτερόεις, τοὔνομα τοῦδε, λόγος.
Λατῴας δ᾽ ἀμφῆκες ἔχεις γέρας, ἔς τε γέλωτα
   καὶ σπουδάν, καί που μέτρον ἐρωτογράφον.
ναὶ μὲν δὴ Μελέαγρον ὁμώνυμον Οἰνέος υἱῷ
   σύμβολα σημαίνει ταῦτα συοκτασίης.
χαῖρε καὶ ἐν φθιμένοισιν, ἐπεὶ καὶ Μοῦσαν Ἔρωτι
   καὶ Χάριτας σοφίαν εἰς μίαν ἡρμόσαο.

422.—ΛΕΩΝΙΔΑ ΤΑΡΑΝΤΙΝΟΤ

Τί στοχασώμεθά σου, Πεισίστρατε, χῖον ὁρῶντες
   γλυπτὸν ὑπὲρ τύμβου κείμενον ἀστράγαλον;
ἦ ῥά γε μὴ ὅτι Χῖος; ἔοικε γάρ· ἤ ῥ᾽ ὅτι παίκτας
   ἦσθά τις, οὐ λίην δ᾽, ὦ ᾽γαθέ, πλειστοβόλος;
ἦ τὰ μὲν οὐδὲ σύνεγγυς, ἐν ἀκρήτῳ δὲ κατέσβης
   Χίῳ; ναὶ δοκέω, τῷδε προσηγγίσαμεν.

423.—ΑΝΤΙΠΑΤΡΟΤ ΣΙΔΩΝΙΟΤ

Τὰν μὲν ἀεὶ πολύμυθον, ἀεὶ λάλον, ὦ ξένε, κίσσα
   φάσει, τὰν δὲ μέθας σύντροφον ἅδε κύλιξ,

421.—MELEAGER

An enigmatic epitaph on himself

Thou with the wings, what pleasure hast thou in the hunting spear and boar-skin? Who art thou, and the emblem of whose tomb? For Love I cannot call thee. What! doth Desire dwell next the dead? No! the bold boy never learnt to wail. Not yet art thou swift-footed Cronos; on the contrary, he is as old as old can be, and thy limbs are in the bloom of youth. Then—yes, I think I am right—he beneath the earth was a sophist, and thou art the winged word for which he was famed. The double-edged attribute of Artemis[1] thou bearest in allusion to his laughter mixed with gravity and perhaps to the metre of his love verses. Yea, in truth, these symbols of boar-slaying point to his name-sake, Meleager, son of Oeneus. Hail, even among the dead, thou who didst fit together into one work of wisdom, Love, the Muses and the Graces.

422.—LEONIDAS OF TARENTUM

What shall we conjecture about you, Pisistratus, when we see a Chian die carved on your tomb?[2] Shall we not say that you were a Chian? That seems probable. Or shall we say that you were a gamester and not a particularly lucky one, my friend? Or are we still far from the truth, and was your life's light put out by Chian wine? Yes, I think now we are near it.

423.—ANTIPATER OF SIDON

The jay, stranger, will tell you I was ever a woman of many words, ever talkative, and the cup

[1] The hunting spear.
[2] The worst cast of the dice was called Chian.

229

τὰν Κρῆσσαν δὲ τὰ τόξα, τὰ δ᾽ εἴρια τὰν φιλοεργόν,
 ἄνδεμα δ᾽ αὖ μίτρας τὰν πολιοκρόταφον·
τοιάνδε σταλοῦχος ὅδ᾽ ἔκρυφε Βιττίδα τύμβος   5
 †τιμελάχραντον νυμφιδίαν ἄλοχον.
ἀλλ᾽, ὦνερ, καὶ χαῖρε, καὶ οἰχομένοισιν ἐς ἅδαν
 τὰν αὐτὰν μύθων αὖθις ὄπαζε χάριν.

424.—ΤΟΥ ΑΥΤΟΥ

ἁ. Μαστεύω τί σευ Ἆγις ἐπὶ σταλίτιδι πέτρᾳ,
 Λυσιδίκα, γλυπτὸν τόνδ᾽ ἐχάραξε νόον·
ἀνία γὰρ καὶ κημός, ὅ τ᾽ εὐόρνιθι Τανάγρᾳ
 οἰωνὸς βλαστῶν, θοῦρος ἐγερσιμάχας,
οὐχ ἅδεν οὐδ᾽ ἐπέοικεν ὑπωροφίαισι γυναιξίν,   5
 ἀλλὰ τὰ τ᾽ ἠλακάτας ἔργα τά θ᾽ ἱστοπόδων.
β. Τὰν μὲν ἀνεγρομέναν με ποτ᾽ εἴρια νύκτερος ὄρνις,
 ἀνία δ᾽ αὐδάσει δώματος ἀνίοχον·
ἱππαστὴρ δ᾽ ὅδε κημὸς ἀείσεται οὐ πολύμυθον,
 οὐ λάλον, ἀλλὰ καλᾶς ἔμπλεον ἀσυχίας.   10

425.—ΤΟΥ ΑΥΤΟΥ

Μὴ θάμβει, μάστιγα Μυροῦς ἐπὶ σάματι λεύσσων,
 γλαῦκα, βιόν, χαροπὰν χᾶνα, θοὰν σκύλακα.
τόξα μὲν αὐδάσει με πανεύτονον ἀγέτιν οἴκου,
 ἁ δὲ κύων τέκνων γνήσια καδομέναν·
μάστιξ δ᾽ οὐκ ὀλοάν, ξένε, δεσπότιν, οὐδ᾽ ἀγέρωχον   5
 δμωσί, κολάστειραν δ᾽ ἔνδικον ἀμπλακίας·
χὰν δὲ δόμων φυλακᾶς μελεδήμονα· τὰν δ᾽ ἄ<ρ᾽
 ἄγρυπνον>
γλαῦξ ἅδε γλαυκᾶς Παλλάδος ἀμφίπολον.
τοιοῖσδ᾽ ἀμφ᾽ ἔργοισιν ἐγάθεον· ἔνθεν ὅμευνος
 τοιάδ᾽ ἐμᾷ στάλᾳ σύμβολα τεῦξε Βίτων.   10

that I was of a convivial habit. The bow proclaims
me Cretan, the wool a good workwoman, and the
snood that tied up my hair shows that I was grey-
headed. Such was the Bittis that this tomb with
its stele covers, the wedded wife of . . . . But, hail,
good sir, and do us who are gone to Hades the
favour to bid us hail likewise in return.

424.—By the Same

A. "I seek to discover what the meaning of these
carvings is that Agis made upon your stele, Lysidice.
For the reins and muzzle and the bird who comes
from Tanagra celebrated for its fowls, the bold
awaker of battles, such are not things that please
or become sedentary women, but rather the works
of the spindle and the loom." B. "The bird of the
night proclaims me one who rises in the night to
work, the reins tell that I directed my house, and
this horse's muzzle that I was not fond of many
words and talkative, but full of admirable silence."

425.—By the Same

Do not wonder at seeing on Myro's tomb a whip,
an owl, a bow, a grey goose and a swift bitch. The
bow proclaims that I was the strict well-strung
directress of my house, the bitch that I took true
care of my children, the whip that I was no cruel
or overbearing mistress, but a just chastiser of faults,
the goose that I was a careful guardian of the house,
and this owl that I was a faithful servant of owl-eyed
Pallas. Such were the things in which I took delight,
wherefore my husband Biton carved these emblems
on my grave-stone.

426.—ΤΟΥ ΑΥΤΟΥ

α. Εἰπέ, λέων, φθιμένοιο τίνος τάφον ἀμφιβέβηκας,
  βουφάγε; τίς τᾶς σᾶς ἄξιος ἦν ἀρετᾶς;
β. Υἱὸς Θευδώροιο Τελευτίας, ὃς μέγα πάντων
  φέρτερος ἦν, θηρῶν ὅσσον ἐγὼ κέκριμαι.
 οὐχὶ μάταν ἔστακα, φέρω δέ τι σύμβολον ἀλκᾶς
  ἀνέρος· ἦν γὰρ δὴ δυσμενέεσσι λέων.

427.—ΤΟΥ ΑΥΤΟΥ

Ἀ στάλα, φέρ' ἴδω, τίν' ἔχει νέκυν. ἀλλὰ δέδορκα
  γράμμα μὲν οὐδέν πω τμαθὲν ὕπερθε λίθου,
ἐννέα δ' ἀστραγάλους πεπτηότας· ὧν πίσυρες μὲν
  πρᾶτοι Ἀλεξάνδρου μαρτυρέουσι βόλον,
οἱ δὲ τὸ τᾶς νεότατος ἐφήλικος ἄνθος, Ἔφηβον,
  εἰς δ' ὅ γε μανύει Χῖον ἀφαυρότερον.
ἦ ῥα τόδ' ἀγγέλλοντι, καὶ ὁ σκάπτροισι μεγαυχὴς
  χὠ θάλλων ἥβᾳ τέρμα τὸ μηδὲν ἔχει;
ἢ τὸ μὲν οὔ· δοκέω δὲ ποτὶ σκοπὸν ἰθὺν ἐλάσσειν
  ἰόν, Κρηταιεὺς ὥς τις ὀϊστοβόλος.
ἧς ὁ θανὼν Χῖος μέν, Ἀλεξάνδρου δὲ λελογχὼς
  οὔνομ', ἐφηβαίῃ δ' ὤλετ' ἐν ἁλικίᾳ.
ὣς εὖ τὸν φθίμενον νέον ἄκριτα καὶ τὸ κυβευθὲν
  πνεῦμα δι' ἀφθέγκτων εἶπέ τις ἀστραγάλων.

428.—ΜΕΛΕΑΓΡΟΥ

Εἰς Ἀντίπατρον τὸν Σιδώνιον

Ἀ στάλα, σύνθημα τί σοι γοργωπὸς ἀλέκτωρ
  ἔστα, καλλαΐνᾳ σκαπτοφόρος πτέρυγι,
ποσσὶν ὑφαρπάζων Νίκας κλάδον; ἄκρα δ' ἐπ' αὐτᾶς
  βαθμίδος προπεσὼν κέκλιται ἀστράγαλος.

426.—By the Same

A. "Tell, lion, thou slayer of kine, on whose tomb thou standest there and who was worthy of thy valour." *B.* "Teleutias, the son of Theodorus, who was far the most valiant of men, as I am judged to be of beasts. Not in vain stand I here, but I emblem the prowess of the man, for he was indeed a lion to his enemies."

427.—By the Same

Come let us see who lies under this stone. But I see no inscription cut on it, only nine cast dice, of which the first four represent the throw called Alexander, the next four that called Ephebus—the bloom of youthful maturity—and the one the more unlucky throw called Chian. Is their message this, that both the proud sceptred potentate and the young man in his flower end in nothing, or is that not so?—I think now like a Cretan archer I shall shoot straight at the mark. The dead man was a Chian, his name was Alexander and he died in youth. How well one told through dumb dice of the young man dead by ill-chance and the life staked and lost!

428.—MELEAGER

On Antipater of Sidon

Tell me, thou stone, why does this bright-eyed cock stand on thee as an emblem, bearing a sceptre in his lustred wing and seizing in his claws the branch of victory, while cast at the very edge of the

ἢ ῥά γε νικάεντα μάχᾳ σκαπτοῦχον ἄνακτα   5
   κρύπτεις; ἀλλὰ τί σοι παίγνιον ἀστράγαλος;
πρὸς δέ, τί λιτὸς ὁ τύμβος; ἐπιπρέπει ἀνδρὶ πενι-
   χρῷ,
   ὄρνιθος κλαγγαῖς νυκτὸς ἀνεγρομένῳ.
οὐ δοκέω· σκᾶπτρον γὰρ ἀναίνεται. ἀλλὰ σὺ κεύθεις
   ἀθλοφόρον, νίκαν ποσσὶν ἀειράμενον.   10
οὐ ψαύω καὶ τῇδε· τί γὰρ ταχὺς εἴκελος ἀνὴρ
   ἀστραγάλῳ; νῦν δὴ τὠτρεκὲς ἐφρασάμαν·
φοῖνιξ οὐ νίκαν ἐνέπει, πάτραν δὲ μεγαυχῆ
   ματέρα Φοινίκων, τὰν πολύπαιδα Τύρον·
ὄρνις δ᾿, ὅττι γεγωνὸς ἀνήρ, καί που περὶ Κύπριν   15
   πρᾶτος κὴν Μούσαις ποικίλος ὑμνοθέτας.
σκᾶπτρα δ᾿ ἔχει σύνθημα λόγου· θνάσκειν δὲ
   πεσόντα
   οἰνοβρεχῆ, προπετὴς ἐννέπει ἀστράγαλος.
καὶ δὴ σύμβολα ταῦτα· τὸ δ᾿ οὔνομα πέτρος ἀείδει,
   Ἀντίπατρον, προγόνων φύντ᾿ ἀπ᾿ ἐρισθενέων.   20

429.—ΑΛΚΑΙΟΥ ΜΙΤΤΛΗΝΑΙΟΥ

Δίζημαι κατὰ θυμὸν ὅτου χάριν ἁ παροδῖτις
   δισσάκι φῖ μοῦνον γράμμα λέλογχε πέτρος,
λαοτύποις σμίλαις κεκολαμμένον. ἆρα γυναικὶ
   τᾷ χθονὶ κευθομένᾳ Χιλιὰς ἦν ὄνομα;
τοῦτο γὰρ ἀγγέλλει κορυφούμενος εἰς ἓν ἀριθμός.   5
   ἢ τὸ μὲν εἰς ὀρθὰν ἀτραπὸν οὐκ ἔμολεν,
ἁ δ᾿ οἰκτρὸν ναίουσα τόδ᾿ ἠρίον ἔπλετο Φιδίς;
   νῦν σφιγγὸς γρίφους Οἰδίπος ἐφρασάμην.
αἰνετὸς οὐκ δισσοῖο καμὼν αἴνιγμα τύποιο,
   φέγγος μὲν ξυνετοῖς, ἀξυνέτοις δ᾿ ἔρεβος   10

base lies a die? Dost thou cover some sceptred king victorious in battle? But why the die thy plaything? And besides, why is the tomb so simple? It would suit a poor man woke up o'nights by the crowing of the cock. But I don't think that is right, for the sceptre tells against it. Then you cover an athlete, a winner in the foot-race? No, I don't hit it off so either, for what resemblance does a swift-footed man bear to a die? Now I have it: the palm does not mean victory, but prolific Tyre, the proud mother of palms, was the dead man's birthplace; the cock signifies that he was a man who made himself heard, a champion too I suppose in love matters and a versatile songster. The sceptre he holds is emblematic of his speech and the die cast wide means that in his cups he fell and died. Well, these are symbols, but the stone tells us his name, Antipater, descended from most puissant ancestors.

429.—ALCAEUS OF MITYLENE

I ASK myself why this road-side stone has only two phis chiselled on it. Was the name of the woman who is buried here Chilias?[1] The number which is the sum of the two letters points to this. Or am I astray in this guess and was the name of her who dwells in this mournful tomb Phidis?[2] Now am I the Oedipus who has solved the sphinx's riddle. He deserves praise, the man who made this puzzle out of two letters, a light to the intelligent and darkness to the unintelligent.

---

[1] φ stands for 500.   [2] *i.e.* φ δίς, twice φ.

430.—ΔΙΟΣΚΟΡΙΔΟΤ

Τίς τὰ νεοσκύλευτα ποτὶ δρυὶ τᾷδε καθᾶψεν
   ἔντεα; τῷ πέλτα Δωρὶς ἀναγράφεται;
πλάθει γὰρ Θυρεᾶτις ὑφ' αἵματος ἅδε λοχιτᾶν,
   χάμες ἀπ' Ἀργείων τοὶ δύο λειπόμεθα.
πάντα νέκυν μάστευε δεδουπότα, μή τις, ἔτ' ἔμπνους
   λειπόμενος, Σπάρτᾳ κῦδος ἔλαμψε νόθον.
ἴσχε βάσιν. νίκα γὰρ ἐπ' ἀσπίδος ὧδε Λακώνων
   φωνεῖται θρόμβοις αἵματος Ὀθρυάδα,
χὠ τόδε μοχθήσας σπαίρει πέλας. ἆ πρόπατορ Ζεῦ,
   στύξον ἀνικάτω σύμβολα φυλόπιδος.   1

431.—ΑΔΗΛΟΝ, οἱ δὲ ΣΙΜΩΝΙΔΟΤ

Οἵδε τριηκόσιοι, Σπάρτα πατρί, τοῖς συναρίθμοις
   Ἰναχίδαις Θυρεᾶν ἀμφὶ μαχεσσάμενοι,
αὐχένας οὐ στρέψαντες, ὅπᾳ ποδὸς ἴχνια πρᾶτον
   ἁρμόσαμεν, ταύτᾳ καὶ λίπομεν βιοτάν.
ἄρσενι δ' Ὀθρυάδαο φόνῳ κεκαλυμμένον ὅπλον
   καρύσσει· "Θυρέα, Ζεῦ, Λακεδαιμονίων."
αἰ δέ τις Ἀργείων ἔφυγεν μόρον, ἦς ἀπ' Ἀδράστου·
   Σπάρτᾳ δ' οὐ τὸ θανεῖν, ἀλλὰ φυγεῖν θάνατος.

432.—ΔΑΜΑΓΗΤΟΤ

Ὦ Λακεδαιμόνιοι, τὸν ἀρήϊον ὔμμιν ὁ τύμβος
   Γύλλιν ὑπὲρ Θυρέας οὗτος ἔχει φθίμενον,
ἄνδρας ὃς Ἀργείων τρεῖς ἔκτανε, καὶ τόδ' ἔειπεν·
   "Τεθναίην Σπάρτας ἄξια μησάμενος."

---

[1] This refers to the celebrated fight at Thyreae between
three hundred Argives and as many Spartans. Two Argives
survived at the end, who, thinking all the Spartans dead,
went off to announce the victory; but the Spartan Othryadas

130.—DIOSCORIDES

Who hung the newly-stripped arms on this oak? By whom is the Dorian shield inscribed? For this land of Thyrea is soaked with the blood of champions and we are the only two left of the Argives. Seek out every fallen corpse, lest any left alive illuminate Sparta in spurious glory. Nay! stay thy steps, for here on the shield the victory of the Spartans is announced by the clots of Othryadas' blood, and he who wrought this still gasps hard by. O Zeus our ancestor, look with loathing on those tokens of a victory that was not won.[1]

431.—Anonymous, some say by SIMONIDES

We the three hundred, O Spartan fatherland, fighting for Thyrea with as many Argives, never turning our necks, died there where we first planted our feet. The shield, covered with the brave blood of Othryadas proclaims "Thyrea, O Zeus, is the Lacedemonians'." But if any Argive escaped death he was of the race of Adrastus.[2] For a Spartan to fly, not to die, is death.

432.—DAMAGETUS

O Spartans, the tomb holds your martial Gyllis who fell for Thyrea. He killed three Argives, and exclaimed, "Let me die having wrought a deed worthy of Sparta."

remained on the field and, according at least to this epigram, the next, and No. 526, erected a trophy and inscribed it with his blood.

[2] The only one of the seven Argive leaders who returned from Thebes.

433.—ΤΥΜΝΕΩ

Τὸν παραβάντα νόμους Δαμάτριον ἔκτανε μάτηρ
  ἁ Λακεδαιμονία τὸν Λακεδαιμόνιον.
θηκτὸν δ᾽ ἐν προβολᾷ θεμένα ξίφος, εἶπεν, ὀδόντα
  ὀξὺν ἐπιβρύκουσ᾽, οἷα Λάκαινα γυνά·
"Ἔρρε κακὸν σκυλάκευμα, κακὰ μερίς, ἔρρε ποθ᾽
  ἅδαν,
ἔρρε· τὸν οὐ Σπάρτας ἄξιον οὐδ᾽ ἔτεκον."

434.—ΔΙΟΣΚΟΡΙΔΟΥ

Εἰς δηΐων πέμψασα λόχους Δημαινέτη ὀκτὼ
  παῖδας, ὑπὸ στήλῃ πάντας ἔθαπτε μιᾷ.
δάκρυα δ᾽ οὐκ ἔρρηξ᾽ ἐπὶ πένθεσιν· ἀλλὰ τόδ᾽ εἶπεν
  μοῦνον· "Ἰώ, Σπάρτα, σοὶ τέκνα ταῦτ᾽ ἔτεκον."

435.—ΝΙΚΑΝΔΡΟΥ

Εὐπυλίδας, Ἐράτων, Χαῖρις, Λύκος, Ἆγις, Ἀλέξων,
  ἐξ Ἰφικρατίδα παῖδες, ἀπωλόμεθα
Μεσσάνας ὑπὸ τεῖχος· ὁ δ᾽ ἕβδομος ἄμμε Γύλιππος
  ἐν πυρὶ θεὶς μεγάλαν ἦλθε φέρων σποδιάν,
Σπάρτᾳ μὲν μέγα κῦδος, Ἀλεξίππᾳ δὲ μέγ᾽ ἄχθος
  ματρί· τὸ δ᾽ ἐν πάντων καὶ καλὸν ἐντάφιον.

436.—ΗΓΕΜΟΝΟΣ

Εἴποι τις παρὰ τύμβον ἰὼν ἀγέλαστος ὁδίτας
  τοῦτ᾽ ἔπος· "Ὀγδώκοντ᾽ ἐνθάδε μυριάδας
Σπάρτας χίλιοι ἄνδρες ἐπέσχον λήματι Περσῶν,
  καὶ θάνον ἀστρεπτεί· Δώριος ἁ μελέτα."

433.—TYMNES

His Spartan mother slew the Spartan Demetrius for transgressing the law. Bringing her sharp sword to the guard, she said, gnashing her teeth, like a Laconian woman as she was: "Perish, craven whelp, evil piece, to Hell with thee! He who is not worthy of Sparta is not my son."

434.—DIOSCORIDES

Demaeneta sent eight sons to encounter the phalanx of the foes, and she buried them all beneath one stone. No tear did she shed in her mourning, but said this only: "Ho! Sparta, I bore these children for thee."

435.—NICANDER

We the six sons of Iphicratides, Eupylidas, Eraton, Chaeris, Lycus, Agis, and Alexon fell before the wall of Messene, and our seventh brother Gylippus having burnt our bodies came home with a heavy load of ashes, a great glory to Sparta, but a great grief to Alexippa our mother. One glorious shroud wrapped us all.

436.—HEGEMON

Some stranger passing gravely by the tomb might say, "Here a thousand Spartans arrested by their valour the advance of eighty myriads of Persians, and died without turning their backs. That is Dorian discipline."

437.—ΦΑΕΝΝΟΥ

Οὐκ ἔτλας, ὥριστε Λεωνίδα, αὖτις ἱκέσθαι
   Εὐρώταν, χαλεπῷ σπερχόμενος πολέμῳ·
ἀλλ' ἐπὶ Θερμοπύλαισι τὸ Περσικὸν ἔθνος ἀμύνων
   ἐδμάθης, πατέρων ἀζόμενος νόμιμα.

438.—ΔΑΜΑΓΗΤΟΥ

Ὤλεο δὴ πατέρων περὶ ληΐδα καὶ σύ, Μαχάτα,
   δριμὺν ἐπ' Αἰτωλοῖς ἀντιφέρων πόλεμον,
πρωθήβας· χαλεπὸν γὰρ Ἀχαιϊκὸν ἄνδρα νοῆσαι
   ἄλκιμον, εἰς πολιὰν ὅστις ἔμεινε τρίχα.

439.—ΘΕΟΔΩΡΙΔΑ

Οὕτω δὴ Πύλιον τὸν Ἀγήνορος, ἄκριτε Μοῖρα,
   πρώϊον ἐξ ἥβας ἔθρισας Αἰολέων,
Κῆρας ἐπισσεύσασα βίου κύνας. ὦ πόποι, ἀνὴρ
   οἷος ἀμειδήτῳ κεῖται ἕλωρ Ἀΐδῃ.

440.—ΛΕΩΝΙΔΑ ΤΑΡΑΝΤΙΝΟΥ

Ἠρίον, οἷον νυκτὶ καταφθιμένοιο καλύπτεις
   ὀστέον, οἵην, γαῖ', ἀμφέχανες κεφαλήν,
πολλὸν μὲν ξανθαῖσιν ἀρεσκομένου Χαρίτεσσι,
   πολλοῦ δ' ἐν μνήμῃ πᾶσιν Ἀριστοκράτευς.
ᾔδει Ἀριστοκράτης καὶ μείλιχα δημολογῆσαι,
   [στρεβλὴν οὐκ ὀφρὺν ἐσθλὸς ἐφελκόμενος·
ᾔδει καὶ Βάκχοιο παρὰ κρητῆρος ἄδηριν]
   ἰθῦναι κείνην εὐκύλικα λαλιήν·
ᾔδει καὶ ξείνοισι καὶ ἐνδήμοισι προσηνέα
   ἔρδειν. γαῖ' ἐρατή, τοῖον ἔχεις φθίμενον.

437.—PHAENNUS

Leonidas, bravest of men, thou couldst not endure to return to the Eurotas when sore pressed by the war, but in Thermopylae resisting the Persians thou didst fall reverencing the usage of thy fathers.

438.—DAMAGETUS

In thy first youth thou didst perish too, Machatas, grimly facing the Aetolians in the portion of thy fathers. It is hard to find a brave Achaean who hath survived till his hairs are grey.

439.—THEODORIDAS

Undiscerning Fate, hounding on thy pack of demons that hunt life, thus thou hast cut off from the Aeolian youth before his time Pylius the son of Agenor. Ye gods, what a man lies low, the spoil of sombre Hades!

440.—LEONIDAS OF TARENTUM

O tomb, what a man was he, the dead whose bones thou dost hide in the night: O earth, what a head thou hast engulphed! Very pleasing was Aristocrates to the flaxen-haired Graces; much is his memory treasured by all. Aristocrates could converse sweetly, without a frown, and over the wine [1] he could guide well the convivial flow of talk; and well he knew how to confer kindness on compatriots and strangers. Such, beloved earth, is the dead who is thine.

[1] The bracketed verses which I render only summarily are supplied by Planudes and probably not genuine.

441.—ΑΡΧΙΛΟΧΟΥ

Ὑψηλοὺς Μεγάτιμον Ἀριστοφόωντά τε Νάξου
κίονας, ὦ μεγάλη γαῖ᾽, ὑπένερθεν ἔχεις.

442.—ΣΙΜΩΝΙΔΟΥ

Εὐθυμάχων ἀνδρῶν μνησώμεθα, τῶν ὅδε τύμβος,
οἳ θάνον εὔμηλον ῥυόμενοι Τεγέαν,
αἰχμηταὶ πρὸ πόληος, ἵνα σφίσι μὴ καθέληται
Ἑλλὰς ἀποφθιμένου κρατὸς ἐλευθερίαν.

443.—ΤΟΥ ΑΥΤΟΥ

Τῶνδε ποτὲ στέρνοισι τανυγλώχινας ὀϊστοὺς
λοῦσεν φοινίσσᾳ θοῦρος Ἄρης ψακάδι.
ἀντὶ δ᾽ ἀκοντοδόκων ἀνδρῶν μνημεῖα θανόντων.
ἄψυχ᾽ ἐμψύχων, ἅδε κέκευθε κόνις.

444.—ΘΕΑΙΤΗΤΟΥ

Χείματος οἰνωθέντα τὸν Ἀνταγόρεω μέγαν οἶκον
ἐκ νυκτῶν ἔλαθεν πῦρ ὑπονειμάμενον·
ὀγδώκοντα δ᾽ ἀριθμὸν ἐλεύθεροι ἄμμιγα δούλοις
τῆς ἐχθρῆς ταύτης πυρκαϊῆς ἔτυχον.
οὐκ εἶχον διελεῖν προσκηδέες ὀστέα χωρίς·   5
ξυνὴ δ᾽ ἦν κάλπις, ξυνὰ δὲ τὰ κτέρεα·
εἷς καὶ τύμβος ἀνέστη· ἀτὰρ τὸν ἕκαστον ἐκείνων
οἶδε καὶ ἐν τέφρῃ ῥηϊδίως Ἀΐδης.

445.—ΠΕΡΣΟΥ ΘΗΒΑΙΟΥ

Μαντιάδας, ὦ ξεῖνε, καὶ Εὔστρατος, υἷες Ἐχέλλου,
Δυμαῖοι, κραναῇ κείμεθ᾽ ἐνὶ ξυλόχῳ,
ἄγραυλοι γενεῆθεν ὀροιτύποι. οἱ δ᾽ ἐπὶ τύμβῳ,
μανυταὶ τέχνας, δουροτόμοι πελέκεις.

441.—ARCHILOCHUS

GREAT earth, thou hast beneath thee the tall pillars of Naxos, Megatimus and Aristophon.

442.—SIMONIDES

LET us ever remember the men whose tomb this is, who turned not from the battle but fell in arms before their city, defending Tegea rich in flocks, that Greece should never strip from their dead heads the crown of freedom.

443.—By THE SAME

ONCE in the breasts of these men did Ares wash with red rain his long-barbed arrows. Instead of men who stood and faced the shafts this earth covers memorials of the dead, lifeless memorials of their living selves.

444.—THEAETETUS

THE secretly creeping flames, on a winter night, when all were heavy with wine, consumed the great house of Antagoras. Free men and slaves together, eighty in all, perished on this fatal pyre. Their kinsmen could not separate their bones, but one common urn, one common funeral was theirs, and one tomb was erected over them. Yet readily can Hades distinguish each of them in the ashes.

445.—PERSES OF THEBES

WE lie, stranger, in the rough woodland, Mantiades and Eustratus of Dyme, the sons of Echellus, rustic wood-cutters as our fathers were ; and to shew our calling the woodman's axes stand on our tomb.

243

446.—ΗΓΗΣΙΠΠΟΥ

Ἑρμιονεὺς ὁ ξεῖνος, ἐν ἀλλοδαπῶν δὲ τέθαπται,
Ζωΐλος, Ἀργείαν γαῖαν ἐφεσσάμενος,
ἂν ἐπί οἱ βαθύκολπος ἀμάσατο δάκρυσι νύμφα
λειβομένα, παῖδές τ᾽ εἰς χρόα κειράμενοι.

447.—ΚΑΛΛΙΜΑΧΟΥ

Σύντομος ἦν ὁ ξεῖνος· ὃ καὶ στίχος· οὐ μακρὰ λέξω·
"Θῆρις Ἀρισταίου, Κρὴς" ἐπ᾽ ἐμοὶ δόλιχος.

448.—ΛΕΩΝΙΔΑ ΤΑΡΑΝΤΙΝΟΥ

Πραταλίδα τὸ μνᾶμα Λυκαστίω, ἄκρον ἐρώτων
εἰδότος, ἄκρα μάχας, ἄκρα λινοστασίας,
ἄκρα χοροιτυπίας. χθόνιοι, <Μίνωϊ τὸν ἄνδρα>
τοῦτον, Κρηταιεῖς Κρῆτα, παρῳκίσατε.

449.—ΑΛΛΟ

Πραταλίδα παιδεῖον Ἔρως πόθον, Ἄρτεμις ἄγραν,
Μοῦσα χορούς, Ἄρης ἐγγυάλιξε μάχαν.
πῶς οὐκ εὐαίων ὁ Λυκάστιος, ὃς καὶ ἔρωτι
ἆρχε καὶ ἐν μολπᾷ, καὶ δορὶ καὶ στάλικι;

450.—ΔΙΟΣΚΟΡΙΔΟΥ

Τῆς Σαμίης τὸ μνῆμα Φιλαινίδος· ἀλλὰ προσειπεῖν
τλῆθί με, καὶ στήλης πλησίον, ὦνερ, ἴθι.
οὐκ εἴμ᾽ ἢ τὰ γυναιξὶν ἀναγράψασα προσάντη
ἔργα, καὶ Αἰσχύνην οὐ νομίσασα θεόν·

446.—HEGESIPPUS

THE stranger is Zoilus of Hermione, but he lies buried in a foreign land, clothed in this Argive earth, which his deep-bosomed wife, her cheeks bedewed with tears, and his children, their hair close cut, heaped on him.

447.—CALLIMACHUS

THE stranger was brief; so shall the verse be. I will not tell a long story "Theris Aristaeus' son, a Cretan."—For me it is too long.

448.—LEONIDAS OF TARENTUM

THE tomb is that of Protalidas of Lycastus who was supreme in love, war, the chase and the dance. Ye judges of the under-world, yourselves Cretans, ye have taken the Cretan to your company.

449.—ANONYMOUS

LOVE gave to Protalidas success in the pursuit of his boy loves, Artemis in the chase, the Muse in the dance and Ares in war. Must we not call him blest, the Lycastian supreme in love and song, with the spear and the hunting-net !

450.—DIOSCORIDES

THE tomb is that of Samian Philaenis; but be not ashamed, Sir, to speak to me and to approach the stone. I am not she who wrote those works offensive to ladies, and who did not acknowledge Modesty to

245

ἀλλὰ φιλαιδήμων, ναὶ ἐμὸν τάφον· εἰ δέ τις ἡμέας
αἰσχύνων λαμυρὴν ἔπλασεν ἱστορίην,
τοῦ μὲν ἀναπτύξαι χρόνος οὔνομα· τἀμὰ δὲ λυγρὴν
ὀστέα τερφθείη κληδόν᾽ ἀπωσαμένης.

451.—ΚΑΛΛΙΜΑΧΟΥ

Τᾷδε Σάων ὁ Δίκωνος Ἀκάνθιος ἱερὸν ὕπνον
κοιμᾶται. θνάσκειν μὴ λέγε τοὺς ἀγαθούς.

J. A. Pott, *Greek Love Songs and Epigrams*, i. p. 36.

452.—ΛΕΩΝΙΔΑ

Μέμνησθ᾽ Εὐβούλοιο σαόφρονος, ὦ παριόντες.
πίνωμεν· κοινὸς πᾶσι λιμὴν Ἀΐδης.

453.—ΚΑΛΛΙΜΑΧΟΥ

Δωδεκέτη τὸν παῖδα πατὴρ ἀπέθηκε Φίλιππος
ἐνθάδε, τὴν πολλὴν ἐλπίδα, Νικοτέλην.

454.—ΤΟΥ ΑΥΤΟΥ

Τὸν βαθὺν οἰνοπότην Ἐρασίξενον ἡ δὶς ἐφεξῆς
ἀκρήτου προποθεῖσ᾽ ᾤχετ᾽ ἔχουσα κύλιξ.

455.—ΛΕΩΝΙΔΑ

Μαρωνὶς ἡ φίλοινος, ἡ πίθων σποδός,
ἐνταῦθα κεῖται γρῆῢς, ἧς ὑπὲρ τάφου
γνωστὸν πρόκειται πᾶσιν Ἀττικὴ κύλιξ.
στένει δὲ καὶ γᾶς νέρθεν, οὐχ ὑπὲρ τέκνων,
οὐδ᾽ ἀνδρός, οὓς λέλοιπεν ἐνδεεῖς βίου·
ἓν δ᾽ ἀντὶ πάντων, οὕνεχ᾽ ἡ κύλιξ κενή.

be a goddess. But I was of a chaste disposition, I swear it by my tomb, and if anyone, to shame me, composed a wanton treatise, may Time reveal his name and may my bones rejoice that I am rid of the abominable report.[1]

451.—CALLIMACHUS

HERE Saon, son of Dicon of Acanthus, sleeps the holy sleep. Say not that the good are dead.

452.—LEONIDAS OF TARENTUM

REMEMBER temperate Eubulus, ye passers-by. Let us drink, we all end in the haven of Hades.

453.—CALLIMACHUS

HERE Philippus laid his twelve-year-old son, Nicoteles, his great hope.

454.—BY THE SAME

THE cup of unmixed wine drained twice straight off has run away with Erasixenus the deep drinker.

455.—LEONIDAS OF TARENTUM

WINE-BIBBING old Maronis, the jar-drier, lies here, and on her tomb, significant to all, stands an Attic cup. She laments beneath the earth not for her husband and children whom she left in indigence, but solely because the cup is empty.

[1] cp. No. 345.

456.—ΔΙΟΣΚΟΡΙΔΟΥ

Τὴν τιτθὴν Ἱέρων Σειληνίδα, τήν, ὅτε πίνοι
ζωρόν, ὑπ' οὐδεμιῆς θλιβομένην κύλικος,
ἀγρῶν ἐντὸς ἔθηκεν, ἵν' ἡ φιλάκρητος ἐκείνη
καὶ φθιμένη ληνῶν γείτονα τύμβον ἔχοι.

457.—ΑΡΙΣΤΩΝΟΣ

Ἀμπελὶς ἡ φιλάκρητος ἐπὶ σκήπωνος ὁδηγοῦ
ἤδη τὸ σφαλερὸν γῆρας ἐρειδομένη,
λαθριδίη Βάκχοιο νεοθλιβὲς ἦρ' ἀπὸ ληνοῦ
πῶμα Κυκλωπείην πλησομένη κύλικα·
πρὶν δ' ἀρύσαι μογερὰν ἔκαμεν χέρα· γραῦς δὲ
  παλαιή,
ναῦς ἅθ' ὑποβρύχιος ζωρὸν ἔδυ πέλαγος.
Εὐτέρπη δ' ἐπὶ τύμβῳ ἀποφθιμένης θέτο σῆμα
λάϊνον, οἰνηρῶν γείτονα θειλοπέδων.

458.—ΚΑΛΛΙΜΑΧΟΥ

Τὴν Φρυγίην Αἴσχρην, ἀγαθὸν γάλα, πᾶσιν ἐν ἐσθλῷ
  Μίκκος καὶ ζωὴν οὖσαν ἐγηροκόμει,
καὶ φθιμένην ἀνέθηκεν, ἐπεσσομένοισιν ὁρᾶσθαι
  ἡ γρῆϋς μαστῶν ὡς ἀπέχει χάριτας.

459.—ΤΟΥ ΑΥΤΟΥ

Κρηθίδα τὴν πολύμυθον, ἐπισταμένην καλὰ παίζειν
  δίζηνται Σαμίων πολλάκι θυγατέρες,
ἡδίστην συνέριθον, ἀείλαλον· ἡ δ' ἀποβρίζει
  ἐνθάδε τὸν πάσαις ὕπνον ὀφειλόμενον.

R. Garnett, *A Chaplet from the Greek Anthology*, cv.

456.—DIOSCORIDES

HERE lies Hiero's nurse Silenis, who when she began to drink untempered wine never made a grievance of being offered one cup more. He laid her to rest in his fields, that she who was so fond of wine should even dead and buried be near to vats.

457.—ARISTO

THE tippler Ampelis, already supporting her tottering old age on a guiding staff, was covertly abstracting from the vat the newly pressed juice of Bacchus, and about to fill a cup of Cyclopean size, but before she could draw it out her feeble hand failed her and the old woman, like a ship submerged by the waves, disappeared in the sea of wine. Euterpe erected this stone monument on her tomb near the pressing-floor of the vineyard.

458.—CALLIMACHUS

ON Phrygian Aeschra, his good nurse, did Miccus while she lived bestow every comfort that soothes old age, and when she died he erected her statue, that future generations may see how he rewarded the old woman for her milk.

459.—By THE SAME

OFTEN do the daughters of Samos miss prattling Crethis who could sport so well, their sweetest work-mate, never silent; but she sleeps here the sleep that is the portion of all

460.—ΤΟΥ ΑΥΤΟΥ

Εἶχον ἀπὸ σμικρῶν ὀλίγον βίον, οὔτε τι δεινὸν
ῥέζων, οὔτ᾽ ἀδικῶν οὐδένα. γαῖα φίλη,
Μικύλος εἴ τι πονηρὸν ἐπήνεσα, μήτε συ κούφη
γίνεο, μήτ᾽ ἄλλοι δαίμονες, οἵ μ᾽ ἔχετε.

461.—ΜΕΛΕΑΓΡΟΥ

Παμμῆτορ γῆ, χαῖρε· σὺ τὸν πάρος οὐ βαρὺν εἰς σὲ
Αἰσιγένην καὐτὴ νῦν ἐπέχοις ἀβαρής.

462.—ΔΙΟΝΥΣΙΟΥ

Ἀγχιτόκον Σατύραν Ἀΐδας λάχε, Σιδονία δὲ
κρύψε κόνις, πάτρα δ᾽ ἐστονάχησε Τύρος.

463.—ΛΕΩΝΙΔΑ

Αὗτα Τιμόκλει᾽, αὗτα Φιλώ, αὗτα Ἀριστώ,
αὗτα Τιμαιθώ, παῖδες Ἀριστοδίκου,
πᾶσαι ὑπ᾽ ὠδῖνος πεφονευμέναι· αἷς ἔπι τοῦτο
σᾶμα πατὴρ στάσας κάτθαν᾽ Ἀριστόδικος.

464.—ΑΝΤΙΠΑΤΡΟΥ

Ἦπου σὲ χθονίας, Ἀρετημιάς, ἐξ ἀκάτοιο
Κωκυτοῦ θεμέναν ἴχνος ἐπ᾽ ἀϊόνι,
οἰχόμενον βρέφος ἄρτι νέῳ φορέουσαν ἀγοστῷ
ᾤκτειραν θαλεραὶ Δωρίδες εἰν ἀΐδα,
πευθόμεναι τέο κῆρα· σὺ δὲ ῥαίνουσα παρειὰς
δάκρυσιν, ἄγγειλας κεῖν᾽ ἀνιαρὸν ἔπος·
"Διπλόον ὠδίνασα, φίλαι, τέκος, ἄλλο μὲν ἀνδρὶ
Εὔφρονι καλλιπόμαν, ἄλλο δ᾽ ἄγω φθιμένοις."

460.—By the Same

I got a little living from my possessions, never doing any wickedness or injuring any one. Dear earth, if Micylus ever consented to any evil may neither thou be light to me nor the other powers who hold me.

461.—MELEAGER

Hail earth, Mother of all! Aesigenes was never a burden to thee, and do thou too hold him without weighing heavy on him.

462.—DIONYSIUS

Satyra with child and near her time has been taken by Hades. The earth of Sidon covers her, and Tyre her country bewails her.

463.—LEONIDAS OF TARENTUM

This is Timoclea, this is Philo, this is Aristo, this is Timaetho, the daughters of Aristodicus, all dead in childbirth. Their father Aristodicus died after erecting this monument to them.

464.—ANTIPATER OF SIDON

Of a surety, Aretemias, when descending from the boat, thou didst set thy foot on the beach of Cocytus, carrying in thy young arms thy babe newly dead, the fair daughters of the Dorian land pitied thee in Hades and questioned thee concerning thy death; and thou, thy cheeks bedewed with tears, didst give them these mournful tidings "My dears, I brought forth twin children; one I left with Euphron my husband, and the other I bring to the dead."

465.—ΗΡΑΚΛΕΙΤΟΥ

Ἁ κόνις ἀρτίσκαπτος, ἐπὶ στάλας δὲ μετώπων
    σείονται φύλλων ἡμιθαλεῖς στέφανοι·
γράμμα διακρίναντες, ὁδοιπόρε, πέτρον ἴδωμεν,
    λευρὰ περιστέλλειν ὀστέα φατὶ τίνος.—
" Ξεῖν᾿, Ἀρετημιάς εἰμι· πάτρα Κνίδος· Εὔφρονος
        ἦλθον
    εἰς λέχος· ὠδίνων οὐκ ἄμορος γενόμαν·
δισσὰ δ᾿ ὁμοῦ τίκτουσα, τὸ μὲν λίπον ἀνδρὶ ποδηγὸν
    γήρως· ὃν δ᾿ ἀπάγω μναμόσυνον πόσιος."

466.—ΛΕΩΝΙΔΑ

Ἁ δείλ᾿ Ἀντίκλεις, δειλὴ δ᾿ ἐγὼ ἡ τὸν ἐν ἥβης
    ἀκμῇ καὶ μοῦνον παῖδα πυρωσαμένη,
ὀκτωκαιδεκέτης ὃς ἀπώλεο, τέκνον· ἐγὼ δὲ
    ὀρφάνιον κλαίω γῆρας ὀδυρομένη.
βαίην εἰς Ἄιδος σκιερὸν δόμον· οὔτε μοι ἠὼς
    ἡδεῖ᾿ οὔτ᾿ ἀκτὶς ὠκέος ἠελίου.
ἆ δείλ᾿ Ἀντίκλεις, μεμορημένε, πένθεος εἴης
    ἰητήρ, ζωῆς ἔκ με κομισσάμενος.

467.—ΑΝΤΙΠΑΤΡΟΥ

Τοῦτό τοι, Ἀρτεμίδωρε, τεῷ ἐπὶ σάματι μάτηρ
    ἴαχε, δωδεκέτη σὸν γοόωσα μόρον·
" Ὤλετ᾿ ἐμᾶς ὠδῖνος ὁ πᾶς πόνος εἰς σποδὸν εἰς πῦρ,
    ὤλεθ᾿ ὁ παμμέλεος γεινομένου κάματος·
ὤλετο χἀ ποθινὰ τέρψις σέθεν· ἐς γὰρ ἄκαμπτον,
    ἐς τὸν ἀνόστητον χῶρον ἔβης ἐνέρων·
οὐδ᾿ ἐς ἐφηβείαν ἦλθες, τέκος· ἀντὶ δὲ σεῖο
    στάλα καὶ κωφὰ λείπεται ἄμμι κόνις."

465.—HERACLITUS

THE earth is newly dug and on the faces of the tomb-stone wave the half-withered garlands of leaves. Let us decipher the letters, wayfarer, and learn whose smooth bones the stone says it covers. " Stranger, I am Aretemias, my country Cnidus. I was the wife of Euphro and I did not escape travail, but bringing forth twins, I left one child to guide my husband's steps in his old age, and I took the other with me to remind me of him."

466.—LEONIDAS OF TARENTUM

O UNHAPPY Anticles, and I most unhappy who have laid on the pyre my only son in the bloom of his youth ! At eighteen didst thou perish, my child, and I weep and bewail my old age bereft of thee. Would I could go to the shadowy house of Hades ! Nor dawn nor the rays of the swift sun are sweet to me. Unhappy Anticles, gone to thy doom, be thou healer of my mourning by taking me away from life to thee.

467.—ANTIPATER OF SIDON

THIS is the lament thy mother, Artemidorus, uttered over thy tomb, bewailing thy death at twelve years of age. " All the fruit of my travail hath perished in fire and ashes, it hath perished all thy miserable father's toil for thee, and it hath perished all the winsome delight of thee ; for thou art gone to the land of the departed, from which there is no turning back or home-coming. Nor didst thou reach thy prime, my child, and in thy stead naught is left us but thy grave-stone and dumb dust."

468.—ΜΕΛΕΑΓΡΟΥ

Οἰκτρότατον μάτηρ σε, Χαρίξενε, δῶρον ἐς ἅδαν,
  ὀκτωκαιδεκέταν ἐστόλισεν χλαμύδι.
ἦ γὰρ δὴ καὶ πέτρος ἀνέστενεν, ἁνίκ᾽ ἀπ᾽ οἴκων
  ἅλικες οἰμωγᾷ σὸν νέκυν ἠχθοφόρευν.
πένθος δ᾽, οὐχ ὑμέναιον ἀνωρύοντο γονῆες·   5
  αἰαῖ, τὰς μαστῶν ψευδομένας χάριτας,
καὶ κενεὰς ὠδῖνας· ἰὼ κακοπάρθενε Μοῖρα,
  στεῖρα γονὰς στοργὰν ἔπτυσας εἰς ἀνέμους.
τοῖς μὲν ὁμιλήσασι ποθεῖν πάρα, τοῖς δὲ τοκεῦσι
  πενθεῖν, οἷς δ᾽ ἀγνώς, πευθομένοις ἐλεεῖν.   1

W. G. Headlam, *Fifty Poems of Meleager*, xxxiv.

469.—ΧΑΙΡΗΜΟΝΟΣ

Εὔβουλον τέκνωσεν Ἀθηναγόρης περὶ πάντων
  ἥσσονα μὲν μοίρᾳ, κρέσσονα δ᾽ εὐλογίᾳ.

470.—ΜΕΛΕΑΓΡΟΥ

α. Εἶπον ἀνειρομένῳ τίς καὶ τίνος ἐσσί. β. Φίλαυλος
  Εὐκρατίδεω. α. Ποδαπὸς δ᾽ εὔχεαι . . .
α. Ἔζησας δὲ τίνα στέργων βίον; β. Οὐ τὸν ἀρότρου
  οὐδὲ τὸν ἐκ νηῶν, τὸν δὲ σοφοῖς ἕταρον.
α. Γήραϊ δ᾽ ἢ νούσῳ βίον ἔλλιπες; β. Ἤλυθον
    Ἅδαν
  αὐτοθελεί, Κείων γευσάμενος κυλίκων.

---

¹ The short cloak worn by ephebi.

468.—MELEAGER

AT eighteen, Charixenus, did thy mother dress thee in thy chlamys [1] to offer thee, a woeful gift, to Hades. Even the very stones groaned aloud, when the young men thy mates bore thy corpse with wailing from the house. No wedding hymn, but a song of mourning did thy parents chant. Alack for the breasts that suckled thee cheated of their guerdon, alack for the travail endured in vain! O Fate, thou evil maiden, barren thou art and hast spat to the winds a mother's love for her child. What remains but for thy companions to regret thee, for thy parents to mourn thee, and for those to whom thou wast unknown to pity when they are told of thee.

469.—CHAEREMON

ATHENAGORES begot Eubulus, excelled by all in fate, excelling all in good report.

470.—MELEAGER

A. "TELL him who enquires, who and whose son thou art." *B.* "Philaulus son of Eucratides." *A.* " And from whence dost thou say?" *B.* ". . ." *A.* "What livelihood didst thou choose when alive?" *B.* "Not that from the plough nor that from ships, but that which is gained in the society of sages." *A.* "Didst thou depart this life from old age or from sickness?" *B.* "Of my own will I came to Hades, having drunk of the Cean cup." [2] *A.* "Wast thou

---

[2] In Ceos old men, when incapable of work, are said to have been compelled to drink poison.

α. Ἡ πρέσβυς; β. Καὶ κάρτα.   α. Λάχοι νύ σε
  βῶλος ἐλαφρὴ
σύμφωνον πινυτῷ σχόντα λόγῳ βίοτον.

471.—ΚΑΛΛΙΜΑΧΟΥ

Εἴπας "ἥλιε, χαῖρε" Κλεόμβροτος ὠμβρακιώτης
  ἥλατ' ἀφ' ὑψηλοῦ τείχεος εἰς ἀΐδαν,
ἄξιον οὐδὲν ἰδὼν θανάτου κακόν, ἀλλὰ Πλάτωνος
  ἓν τὸ περὶ ψυχῆς γράμμ' ἀναλεξάμενος.

472.—ΛΕΩΝΙΔΑ

Μυρίος ἦν, ἄνθρωπε, χρόνος προτοῦ, ἄχρι πρὸς ἠῶ
  ἦλθες, χὠ λοιπὸς μυρίος εἰς ἀΐδην.
τίς μοῖρα ζωῆς ὑπολείπεται, ἢ ὅσον ὅσσον
  στιγμὴ καὶ στιγμῆς εἴ τι χαμηλότερον;
μικρή σευ ζωὴ τεθλιμμένη· οὐδὲ γὰρ αὐτὴ
  ἡδεῖ', ἀλλ' ἐχθροῦ στυγνοτέρη θανάτου.
ἐκ τοίης ὤνθρωποι ἀπηκριβωμένοι ὀστῶν
  ἁρμονίης, †ὕψιστ' ἠέρα καὶ νεφέλας·
ὦνερ, ἴδ' ὡς ἀχρεῖον, ἐπεὶ περὶ νήματος ἄκρον
  εὐλὴ ἀκέρκιστον λῶπος ἐφεζομένη·
οἷον τὸ †ψαλα, θρῖον ἀπεψιλωμένον οἷον,
  πόλλον ἀραχναίου στυγνότερον σκελέτου.
ἠοῦν ἐξ ἠοῦς ὅσσον σθένος, ὦνερ, ἐρευνῶν
  εἴης ἐν λιτῇ κεκλιμένος βιοτῇ·
αἰὲν τοῦτο νόῳ μεμνημένος ἄχρις ὁμιλῇς
  ζωοῖς, ἐξ οἵης ἡρμόνισαι καλάμης.

J. A. Pott, *Greek Love Songs and Epigrams*, i. p. 30 (part only).

old?" *B.* "Yea, very old." *A.* "May the earth that rests on thee be light, for the life thou didst lead was in accordance with wisdom and reason."

471.—CALLIMACHUS

CLEOMBROTUS the Ambracian saying, "Farewell, O Sun," leapt from a high wall to Hades, not that he saw any evil worthy of death, but that he had read one treatise of Plato, that on the soul.

472.—LEONIDAS OF TARENTUM

O MAN, infinite was the time ere thou camest to the light, and infinite will be the time to come in Hades. What is the portion of life that remains to thee, but a pin-prick, or if there be aught tinier than a pin-prick? A little life and a sorrowful is thine; for even that little is not sweet, but more odious than death the enemy. Men built as ye are, of such a frame of bones, do ye lift yourselves up to the air and the clouds? See, man, how little use it is; for at the end of the thread[1] a worm seated on the loosely woven vesture[2] reduces it to a thing like a skeleton leaf, a thing more loathly than a cobweb. Enquire of thyself at the dawn of every day, O man, what thy strength is and learn to lie low, content with a simple life; ever remembering in thy heart, as long as thou dwellest among the living, from what stalks of straw thou art pieced together.[3]

[1] *i.e.* of life.   [2] The flesh.
[3] The epigram was doubtless written under a figure of a skeleton. Lines 11, 12 are corrupt and the sense uncertain.

472b.—ΤΟΥ ΑΥΤΟΥ

Χειμέριον ζωὴν ὑπαλεύεο, νεῖο δ' ἐς ὅρμον,
  ὡς κἠγὼ Φείδων ὁ Κρίτου εἰς ἀΐδην.

473.—ΑΡΙΣΤΟΔΙΚΟΥ

Δαμὼ καὶ Μάθυμνα τὸν ἐν τριετηρίσιν Ἥρας
  Εὔφρονα λυσσατὰν ὡς ἐπύθοντο νέκυν,
ζωὰν ἀρνήσαντο, τανυπλέκτων δ' ἀπὸ μιτρᾶν
  χερσὶ δεραιούχους ἐκρεμάσαντο βρόχους.

474.—ΑΔΗΛΟΝ

Εἷς ὅδε Νικάνδρου τέκνων τάφος· ἓν φάος ἀς ὗς
  ἄνυσε τὰν ἱερὰν Λυσιδίκας γενεάν.

475.—ΔΙΟΤΙΜΟΥ

Νυμφίον Εὐαγόρην ποτὶ πενθερὸν ἡ Πολυαίνου
  Σκυλλὶς ἀν' εὐρείας ἦλθε βοῶσα πύλας,
παῖδα τὸν Ἡγεμάχειον ἐφέστιον· οὐδ' ἄρ' ἐκείνη
  χήρη πατρῴους αὖθις ἐσῆλθε δόμους,
δαιμονίη· τριτάτῳ δὲ κατέφθιτο μηνὶ δυσαίων   5
  οὐλομένη ψυχῆς δύσφρονι τηκεδόνι.
τοῦτο δ' ἐπ' ἀμφοτέροισι πολύκλαυτον φιλότητος
  ἕστηκεν λείῃ μνῆμα παρὰ τριόδῳ.

476.—ΜΕΛΕΑΓΡΟΥ

Δάκρυά σοι καὶ νέρθε διὰ χθονός, Ἡλιοδώρα,
  δωροῦμαι, στοργᾶς λείψανον, εἰς ἀΐδαν,
δάκρυα δυσδάκρυτα· πολυκλαύτῳ δ' ἐπὶ τύμβῳ
  σπένδω μνᾶμα πόθων, μνᾶμα φιλοφροσύνας.

258

472B.—BY THE SAME

AVOID the storms of life and hie ye to the haven,
to Hades, as I, Pheidon the son of Critas, did.

473.—ARISTODICUS

DEMO and Methymna when they heard that
Euphron, the frenzied devotee at the triennial
festivals of Hera, was dead, refused to live longer,
and made of their long knitted girdles nooses for
their necks to hang themselves.

474.—ANONYMOUS

THIS single tomb holds all Nicander's children ;
the dawn of one day made an end of the holy
offspring of Lysidice.

475.—DIOTIMUS

SCYLLIS the daughter of Polyaenus went to her
father-in-law's, lamenting, as she entered the wide
gates, the death of her bridegroom, Evagoras the
son of Hegemachus, who dwelt there. She came
not back, poor widowed girl, to her father's house,
but within three months she perished, her spirit
wasted by deadly melancholy. This tearful memorial
of their love stands on the tomb of both beside the
smooth high-way.

476.—MELEAGER

TEARS, the last gift of my love, even down through
the earth I send to thee in Hades, Heliodora—tears
ill to shed, and on thy much-wept tomb I pour them
in memory of longing, in memory of affection.

οἰκτρὰ γὰρ οἰκτρὰ φίλαν σε καὶ ἐν φθιμένοις
  Μελέαγρος   5
αἰάζω, κενεὰν εἰς Ἀχέροντα χάριν.
αἰαῖ, ποῦ τὸ ποθεινὸν ἐμοὶ θάλος; ἅρπασεν Ἅδας,
  ἅρπασεν· ἀκμαῖον δ᾽ ἄνθος ἔφυρε κόνις.
ἀλλά σε γουνοῦμαι, Γᾶ παντρόφε, τὰν πανόδυρτον
  ἠρέμα σοῖς κόλποις, μᾶτερ, ἐναγκάλισαι.   10

H. C. Beeching, *In a Garden*, p. 99 ; A. Lang, *Grass of
Parnassus*, ed. 2, p. 189 ; J. A. Pott, *Greek Love Songs and
Epigrams*, i. p. 76.

477.—ΤΥΜΝΕΩ

Μή σοι τοῦτο, Φιλαινί, λίην ἐπικάρδιον ἔστω,
  εἰ μὴ πρὸς Νείλῳ γῆς μορίης ἔτυχες,
ἀλλά σ᾽ Ἐλευθέρνης ὅδ᾽ ἔχει τάφος· ἔστι γὰρ ἴση
  πάντοθεν εἰς ἁίδην ἐρχομένοισιν ὁδός.

478.—ΛΕΩΝΙΔΟΥ

Τίς ποτ᾽ ἄρ᾽ εἶ; τίνος ἆρα παρὰ τρίβον ὀστέα ταῦτα
  τλῆμον᾽ ἐν ἡμιφαεῖ λάρνακι γυμνὰ μένει;
μνῆμα δὲ καὶ τάφος αἰὲν ἁμαξεύοντος ὁδίτεω
  ἄξονι καὶ τροχιῇ λιτὰ παραξέεται·
ἤδη σου καὶ πλευρὰ παρατρίψουσιν ἅμαξαι,   5
  σχέτλιε, σοὶ δ᾽ οὐδεὶς οὐδ᾽ ἐπὶ δάκρυ βαλεῖ.

479.—ΘΕΟΔΩΡΙΔΑ

Πέτρος ἐγὼ τὸ πάλαι γυρὴ καὶ ἄτριπτος ἐπιβλὴς
  τὴν Ἡρακλείτου ἔνδον ἔχω κεφαλήν·
αἰών μ᾽ ἔτριψεν κροκάλαις ἴσον· ἐν γὰρ ἁμάξῃ
  παμφόρῳ αἰζηῶν εἰνοδίη τέταμαι.
ἀγγέλλω δὲ βροτοῖσι, καὶ ἄστηλός περ ἐοῦσα,   5
  θεῖον ὑλακτητὴν δήμου ἔχουσα κύνα.

Piteously, piteously doth Meleager lament for thee
who art still dear to him in death, paying a vain
tribute to Acheron.   Alas! Alas! Where is my
beautiful one, my heart's desire?   Death has taken
her, has taken her, and the flower in full bloom is
defiled by the dust.   But Earth my mother, nurturer
of all, I beseech thee, clasp her gently to thy bosom,
her whom all bewail.

477.—TYMNES

Let not this, Philaenis, weigh on thy heart, that
the earth in which it was thy fate to lie is not
beside the Nile, but that thou art laid in this tomb
at Eleutherna.   From no matter where the road is
the same to Hades.

478.—LEONIDAS OF TARENTUM

Who ever canst thou be?   Whose poor bones are
these that remain exposed beside the road in a
coffin half open to the light, the mean tomb and
monument ever scraped by the axle and wheel of
the traveller's coach?   Soon the carriages will crush
thy ribs, poor wretch, and none to shed a tear for
thee.

479.—THEODORIDES

I, the stone coffin that contain the head of Hera-
clitus, was once a rounded and unworn cylinder, but
Time has worn me like the shingle, for I lie in the
road, the highway for all sorts and conditions of men.
I announce to mortals, although I have no stele,
that I hold the divine dog who used to bark at the
commons.

480.—ΛΕΩΝΙΔΑ

Ἤδη μευ τέτριπται ὑπεκκεκαλυμμένον ὀστεῦν
  ἁρμονίη τ', ὦνερ, πλὰξ ἐπικεκλιμένη·
ἤδη καὶ σκώληκες ὑπὲκ σοροῦ αὐγάζονται
  ἡμετέρης· τί πλέον γῆν ἐπιεννύμεθα;
ἢ γὰρ τὴν οὔπω πρὶν ἰτὴν ὁδὸν ἐτμήξαντο   5
  ἄνθρωποι, κατ' ἐμῆς νισσόμενοι κεφαλῆς.
ἀλλὰ πρὸς ἐγγαίων, Ἀϊδωνέος Ἑρμεία τε
  καὶ Νυκτός, ταύτης ἐκτὸς ἴτ' ἀτραπιτοῦ.

481.—ΦΙΛΗΤΑ ΣΑΜΙΟΥ

Ἁ στάλα βαρύθουσα λέγει τάδε· "Τὰν μινύωρον,
  τὰν μικκὰν Ἀΐδας ἅρπασε Θειοδόταν."
χἀ μικκὰ τάδε πατρὶ λέγει πάλιν· "Ἴσχεο λύπας,
  Θειόδοτε· θνατοὶ πολλάκι δυστυχέες."

482.—ΑΔΗΛΟΝ

Οὔπω τοι πλόκαμοι τετμημένοι, οὐδὲ σελάνας
  τοὶ τριετεῖς μηνῶν ἀνιοχεῦντο δρόμοι,
Κλεύδικε, Νικασὶς ὅτε σὰν περὶ λάρνακα μάτηρ,
  τλῆμον, ἐπ' αἰακτᾷ πόλλ' ἐβόα στεφάνα,
καὶ γενέτας Περίκλειτος· ἐπ' ἀγνώτῳ δ' Ἀχέροντι   5
  ἡβάσεις ἥβαν, Κλεύδικ', ἀνοστοτάταν.

483.—ΑΔΗΛΟΝ

Ἀΐδη ἀλλιτάνευτε καὶ ἄτροπε, τίπτε τοι οὕτω
  Κάλλαισχρον ζωᾶς νήπιον ὠρφάνισας;
ἔσται μὰν ὅ γε παῖς ἐν δώμασι Φερσεφονείοις
  παίγνιον· ἀλλ' οἴκοι λυγρὰ λέλοιπε πάθη.

ﾠ

BOOK VII. EPIGRAMS 480–483

480.—LEONIDAS OF TARENTUM

ALREADY, Sirrah, my bones and the slab that lies on my skeleton are exposed and crushed, already the worms are visible, looking out of my coffin. What avails it to clothe ourselves with earth; for men travelling over my head have opened here a road untrodden before. But I conjure you by the infernal powers, Pluto, Hermes and Night, keep clear of this path.

481.—PHILETAS OF SAMOS

THE grave-stone heavy with grief says "Death has carried away short-lived little Theodota," and the little one says again to her father, "Theodotus, cease to grieve; mortals are often unfortunate."

482.—ANONYMOUS

NOT yet had thy hair been cut, Cleodicus, nor had the moon yet driven her chariot for thrice twelve periods across the heaven, when Nicasis thy mother and thy father Periclitus, on the brink of thy lamented tomb, poor child, wailed much over thy coffin. In unknown Acheron, Cleodicus, shalt thou bloom in a youth that never, never may return here.

483.—ANONYMOUS

HADES, inexorable and unbending, why hast thou robbed baby Callaeschron of life? In the house of Persephone the boy shall be her plaything, but at home he leaves bitter suffering.

GREEK ANTHOLOGY

484.—ΔΙΟΣΚΟΡΙΔΟΥ

Πέντε κόρας καὶ πέντε Βιὼ Διδύμωνι τεκοῦσα
ἄρσενας, οὐδὲ μιᾶς οὐδ᾽ ἑνὸς ὠνάσατο·
ἢ μέγ᾽ ἀρίστη ἐοῦσα καὶ εὔτεκνος οὐχ ὑπὸ παίδων,
ὀθνείαις δ᾽ ἐτάφη χερσὶ θανοῦσα Βιώ.

485.—ΤΟΥ ΑΥΤΟΥ

Βάλλεθ᾽ ὑπὲρ τύμβου πολιὰ κρίνα, καὶ τὰ συνήθη
τύμπαν᾽ ἐπὶ στήλῃ ῥήσσετ᾽ Ἀλεξιμένους,
καὶ περιδινήσασθε μακρῆς ἀνελίγματα χαίτης
Στρυμονίην ἄφετοι Θυιάδες ἀμφὶ πόλιν,
ἢ γλυκερὰ πνεύσαντος ἐφ᾽ ὑμετέροισιν †ἀδάπταις
πολλάκι πρὸς μαλακοὺς τοῦδ᾽ ἐχόρευε νόμους.

486.—ΑΝΥΤΗΣ ΜΕΛΟΠΟΙΟΥ

Πολλάκι τῷδ᾽ ὀλοφυδνὰ κόρας ἐπὶ σάματι Κλείνα
μάτηρ ὠκύμορον παῖδ᾽ ἐβόασε φίλαν,
ψυχὰν ἀγκαλέουσα Φιλαινίδος, ἃ πρὸ γάμοιο
χλωρὸν ὑπὲρ ποταμοῦ χεῦμ᾽ Ἀχέροντος ἔβα.

487.—ΠΕΡΣΟΥ ΜΑΚΕΔΟΝΟΣ

Ὤλεο δὴ πρὸ γάμοιο, Φιλαίνιον, οὐδέ σε μάτηρ
Πυθιὰς ὡραίους ἤγαγεν εἰς θαλάμους
νυμφίου· ἀλλ᾽ ἐλεεινὰ καταδρύψασα παρειὰς
τεσσαρακαιδεκέτιν τῷδ᾽ ἐκάλυψε τάφῳ.

488.—ΜΝΑΣΑΛΚΟΥ

Αἰαῖ Ἀριστοκράτεια, σὺ μὲν βαθὺν εἰς Ἀχέροντα
οἴχεαι ὡραίου κεκλιμένα πρὸ γάμου·
ματρὶ δὲ δάκρυα σᾷ καταλείπεται, ἅ σ᾽ ἐπὶ τύμβῳ
πολλάκι κεκλιμένα κωκύει ἐκ †κεφαλᾶς.

264

484.—DIOSCORIDES

Five daughters and five sons did Bio bear to Didymon, but she got no joy from one of either. Bio herself so excellent and a mother of such fine babes, was not buried by her children, but by strange hands.

485.—By the Same

Cast white lilies on the tomb and beat by the stele of Aleximenes the drums he used to love; whirl your long flowing locks, ye Thyiades, in freedom by the city on the Strymon, whose people often danced to the tender strains of his flute that breathed sweetly on your ———.

486.—ANYTE

Often on this her daughter's tomb did Cleina call on her dear short-lived child in wailing tones, summoning back the soul of Philaenis, who ere her wedding passed across the pale stream of Acheron.

487.—PERSES OF MACEDONIA

Thou didst die before thy marriage, Philaenion, nor did thy mother Pythias conduct thee to the chamber of the bridegroom who awaited thy prime: but wretchedly tearing her cheeks, she laid thee in this tomb at the age of fourteen.

488.—MNASALCAS

Alas! Aristocrateia, thou art gone to deep Acheron, gone to rest before thy prime, before thy marriage; and naught but tears is left for thy mother, who reclining on thy tomb often bewails thee.

489.—ΣΑΠΦΟΥΣ

Τιμάδος ἅδε κόνις, τὰν δὴ πρὸ γάμοιο θανοῦσαν
δέξατο Φερσεφόνας κυάνεος θάλαμος,
ἇς καὶ ἀποφθιμένας πᾶσαι νεοθᾶγι σιδάρῳ
ἅλικες ἱμερτὰν κρατὸς ἔθεντο κόμαν.

490.—ΑΝΥΤΗΣ

Παρθένον Ἀντιβίαν κατοδύρομαι, ἇς ἐπὶ πολλοὶ
νυμφίοι ἱέμενοι πατρὸς ἵκοντο δόμον,
κάλλευς καὶ πινυτᾶτος ἀνὰ κλέος· ἀλλ' ἐπὶ πάντων
ἐλπίδας οὐλομένα Μοῖρ' ἐκύλισε πρόσω.

491.—ΜΝΑΣΑΛΚΟΥ

Αἰαῖ παρθενίας ὀλοόφρονος, ἇς ἄπο φαιδρὰν
ἔκλασας ἁλικίαν, ἱμερόεσσα Κλεοῖ·
καδδέ σ' ἀμυξάμεναι περιδάκρυες αἵδ' ἐπὶ τύμβῳ
λᾶες Σειρήνων ἔσταμες εἰδάλιμοι.

492.—ΑΝΥΤΗΣ ΜΙΤΥΛΗΝΑΙΑΣ

Ὠιχόμεθ', ὦ Μίλητε, φίλη πατρί, τῶν ἀθεμίστων
τὰν ἄνομον Γαλατᾶν κύπριν ἀναινόμεναι,
παρθενικαὶ τρισσαὶ πολιήτιδες, ἇς ὁ βιατὰς
Κελτῶν εἰς ταύτην μοῖραν ἔτρεψεν Ἄρης.
οὐ γὰρ ἐμείναμεν ἅμμα τὸ δυσσεβὲς οὐδ' Ὑμέναιον
νυμφίον, ἀλλ' Ἀΐδην κηδεμόν' εὑρόμεθα.

---

[1] This seems to be on a girl who killed herself to preserve her virginity.

489.—SAPPHO

THIS is the dust of Timas, whom, dead before her marriage, the dark chamber of Persephone received. When she died, all her girl companions with newly sharpened steel shore their lovely locks.

490.—ANYTE

I BEWAIL virgin Antibia, eager to wed whom came many suitors to her father's house, led by the report of her beauty and discretion ; but destroying Fate, in the case of all, sent their hopes rolling far away.

491.—MNASALCAS

WOE worth baleful virginity, for which, delightful Cleo, thou didst cut short thy bright youth ! We stones in the semblance of Sirens stand on thy tomb tearing our cheeks for thee and weeping.[1]

492.—ANYTE OF MITYLENE (?)

WE leave thee, Miletus, dear fatherland, refusing the lawless love of the impious Gauls, three maidens, thy citizens, whom the sword of the Celts forced to this fate. We brooked not the unholy union nor such a wedding, but we put ourselves in the wardship of Hades.[2]

[2] This tale seems to be derived from some romance. According to Jerome (*Adv. Jovianum*, Lib. I., p. 186) the maidens were seven in number.

493.—ΑΝΤΙΠΑΤΡΟΥ ΘΕΣΣΑΛΟΝΙΚΕΩΣ

Οὐ νούσῳ ῾Ροδόπα τε καὶ ἁ γενέτειρα Βοΐσκα
οὐδ᾽ ὑπὸ δυσμενέων δούρατι κεκλίμεθα·
ἀλλ᾽ αὐταί, πάτρας ὁπότ᾽ ἔφλεγεν ἄστυ Κορίνθου
γοργὸς ῎Αρης, ἀΐδαν ἄλκιμον εἱλόμεθα.
ἔκτανε γὰρ μάτηρ με διασφακτῆρι σιδάρῳ,   5
οὐδ᾽ ἰδίου φειδὼ δύσμορος ἔσχε βίου,
ἇψε δ᾽ ἐναυχενίῳ δειρὰν βρόχῳ· ἦς γὰρ ἀμείνων
δουλοσύνας ἀμῖν πότμος ἐλευθέριος.

494.—ΑΔΕΣΠΟΤΟΝ

᾽Εν πόντῳ Σώδαμος ὁ Κρὴς θάνεν, ᾧ φίλα, Νηρεῦ,
δίκτυα καὶ τὸ σὸν ἦν κεῖνο σύνηθες ὕδωρ,
ἰχθυβολεὺς ὁ περισσὸς ἐν ἀνδράσιν. ἀλλὰ θάλασσα
οὔ τι διακρίνει χείματος οὐδ᾽ ἁλιεῖς.

495.—ΑΛΚΑΙΟΥ ΜΕΣΣΗΝΙΟΥ

Στυγνὸς ἐπ᾽ ᾽Αρκτούρῳ ναύταις πλόος· ἐκ δὲ βορείης
λαίλαπος ᾽Ασπάσιος πικρὸν ἔτευξα μόρον,
οὔ στείχεις παρὰ τύμβον, ὁδοιπόρε· σῶμα δὲ πόντος
ἔκρυψ᾽ Αἰγαίῳ ῥαινόμενον πελάγει.
ἠϊθέων δακρυτὸς ἅπας μόρος· ἐν δὲ θαλάσσῃ   5
πλεῖστα πολυκλαύτου κήδεα ναυτιλίης.

496.—ΣΙΜΩΝΙΔΟΥ

᾽Ηερίη Γεράνεια, κακὸν λέπας, ὤφελεν ῎Ιστρον
τῆλε καὶ ἐκ Σκυθέων μακρὸν ὁρᾶν Τάναϊν,

268

493.—ANTIPATER OF THESSALONICA

I, RHODOPE, and my mother Boisca neither died of sickness, nor fell by the sword of the foes, but ourselves, when dreadful Ares burnt the city of Corinth our country, chose a brave death. My mother slew me with the slaughtering knife, nor did she, unhappy woman, spare her own life, but tied the noose round her neck ; for it was better than slavery to die in freedom.

494.—ANONYMOUS

IN the sea, Nereus, died Sodamus the Cretan who loved thy nets and was at home on these thy waters. He excelled all men in his skill as a fisher, but the sea in a storm makes no distinction between fishermen and others.

495.—ALCAEUS OF MESSENE

ARCTURUS' rising [1] is an ill season for sailors to sail at, and I, Aspasius, whose tomb thou passest, traveller, met my bitter fate by the blast of Boreas. My body, washed by the waters of the Aegaean main, is lost at sea. Lamentable ever is the death of young men, but most mournful of all is the fate of travellers who perish in the sea.

496.—SIMONIDES

LOFTY Gerania,[2] evil cliff, would that from the far Scythian land thou didst look down on the Danube and the long course of the Tanais, and didst not

---

[1] Middle of September.   [2] North of the Isthmus of Corinth.

μηδὲ πέλας ναίειν Σκειρωνικὸν οἶδμα θαλάσσης,
  ἄγκεα νιφομένης ἀμφὶ Μεθουριάδος.
νῦν δ' ὁ μὲν ἐν πόντῳ κρυερὸς νέκυς· οἱ δὲ βαρεῖαν   5
  ναυτιλίην κενεοὶ τῇδε βοῶσι τάφοι.

497.—ΔΑΜΑΓΗΤΟΥ

Καί ποτε Θυμώδης, τὰ παρ' ἐλπίδα κήδεα κλαίων,
  παιδὶ Λύκῳ κενεὸν τοῦτον ἔχευε τάφον·
οὐδὲ γὰρ ὀθνείην ἔλαχεν κόνιν, ἀλλά τις ἀκτὴ
  Θυνιὰς ἢ νήσων Ποντιάδων τις ἔχει·
ἔνθ' ὅγε που πάντων κτερέων ἄτερ ὀστέα φαίνει   5
  γυμνὸς ἐπ' ἀξείνου κείμενος αἰγιαλοῦ.

498.—ΑΝΤΙΠΑΤΡΟΥ

Δᾶμις ὁ Νυσαιεὺς ἐλαχὺ σκάφος ἔκ ποτε πόντου
  Ἰονίου ποτὶ γᾶν ναυστολέων Πέλοπος,
φορτίδα μὲν καὶ πάντα νεὼς ἐπιβήτορα λαόν,
  κύματι καὶ συρμῷ πλαζομένους ἀνέμων,
ἀσκηθεῖς ἐσάωσε· καθιεμένης δ' ἐπὶ πέτραις   5
  ἀγκύρης, ψυχρῶν κάτθανεν ἐκ νιφάδων
ἡμύσας ὁ πρέσβυς. ἴδ' ὡς λιμένα γλυκὺν ἄλλοις
  δούς, ξένε, τὸν Λήθης αὐτὸς ἔδυ λιμένα.

499.—ΘΕΑΙΤΗΤΟΥ

Ναυτίλοι ὦ πλώοντες, ὁ Κυρηναῖος Ἀρίστων
  πάντας ὑπὲρ Ξενίου λίσσεται ὔμμε Διός,
εἰπεῖν πατρὶ Μένωνι, παρ' Ἰκαρίαις ὅτι πέτραις
  κεῖται, ἐν Αἰγαίῳ θυμὸν ἀφεὶς πελάγει.

dwell near the waves of the Scironian sea and by the ravines of snowy Methurias.[1]   Now he is in the sea, a cold corpse, and the empty tomb here laments his unhappy voyage.

497.—DAMAGETUS

THYMODES too,[2] on a time, weeping for his un-expected sorrow built this empty tomb for his son Lycus; for not even does he lie under foreign earth, but some Bithynian strand, some island of the Black Sea holds him.   There he lies, without funeral, showing his bare bones on the inhospitable shore.

498.—ANTIPATER OF SIDON

DAMIS of Nysa once navigating a small vessel from the Ionian Sea to the Peloponnesus, brought safe and sound to land the ship with all on board, which the waves and winds had swept out of its course; but just as they were casting anchor on the rocks the old man died from the chilling snow-storm, having fallen asleep.   Mark, stranger, how having found a sweet haven for others, he himself entered the haven of Lethe.

499.—THEAETETUS

YE sailors on the sea, Aristo of Cyrene prays you all by Zeus the Protector of strangers to tell his father Meno that he lost his life in the Aegaean main, and lies by the rocks of Icaria.

[1] The only Methuriades known are small islands near Troezen.

[2] Because there were other similar tombs close by.

500.—ΑΣΚΛΗΠΙΑΔΟΥ

'Ω παρ' ἐμὸν στείχων κενὸν ἠρίον, εἶπον, ὁδῖτα,
εἰς Χίον εὖτ' ἂν ἵκῃ, πατρὶ Μελησαγόρῃ,
ὡς ἐμὲ μὲν καὶ νῆα καὶ ἐμπορίην κακὸς Εὖρος
ὤλεσεν, Εὐίππου δ' αὐτὸ λέλειπτ' ὄνομα.

501.—ΠΕΡΣΟΥ

Εὔρου χειμέριαί σε καταιγίδες ἐξεκύλισαν,
Φίλλι, πολυκλύστῳ γυμνὸν ἐπ' ἠϊόνι,
οἰνηρῆς Λέσβοιο παρὰ σφυρόν· αἰγίλιπος δὲ
πέτρου ἁλιβρέκτῳ κεῖσαι ὑπὸ πρόποδι.

502.—ΝΙΚΑΙΝΕΤΟΥ

'Ηρίον εἰμὶ Βίτωνος, ὁδοιπόρε· εἰ δὲ Τορώνην
λείπων εἰς †αὐτὴν ἔρχεαι 'Αμφίπολιν,
εἰπεῖν Νικαγόρᾳ, παίδων ὅτι τὸν μόνον αὐτῷ
Στρυμονίης ἐρίφων ὤλεσε πανδυσίῃ.

503.—ΛΕΩΝΙΔΑ

α. 'Αρχαίης ὦ θινὸς ἐπεστηλωμένον ἄχθος,
εἴποις ὅντιν' ἔχεις, ἢ τίνος, ἢ ποδαπόν.
β. Φίντων' Ἑρμιονῆα Βαθυκλέος, ὃν πολὺ κῦμα
ὤλεσεν, 'Αρκτούρου λαίλαπι χρησάμενον.

504.—ΤΟΥ ΑΥΤΟΥ

Πάρμις ὁ Καλλιγνώτου ἐπακταῖος καλαμευτής,
ἄκρος καὶ κίχλης καὶ σκάρου ἰχθυβολεύς,

500.—ASCLEPIADES

WAYFARER who passest by my empty tomb, when thou comest to Chios tell my father Melesagoras that the evil south-easter destroyed me, my ship, and my merchandise, and naught but the name of Euippus is left.

501.—PERSES

THE wintry blasts of the east wind cast thee out naked, Phillis, on the surf-beaten shore beside a spur of Lesbos rich in wine, and thou liest on the sea-bathed foot of the lofty cliff.

502.—NICAENETUS

I AM the tomb, traveller, of Bito, and if leaving Torone thou comest to Amphipolis, tell Nicagoras that the Strymonian wind at the setting of the Kids was the death of his only son.

503.—LEONIDAS OF TARENTUM

A. "O stone standing a burden on the ancient beach, tell me whom thou holdest, whose son and whence." *B.* "Phinto the son of Bathycles of Hermione, who perished in the heavy sea, encountering the blast of Arcturus."[1]

504.—BY THE SAME

PARMIS, Callignotus' son, the shore-fisher, a first class hand at catching wrasse and scaros and the

---

[1] *i.e.* a September gale.

GREEK ANTHOLOGY

καὶ λάβρου πέρκης δελεάρπαγος, ὅσσα τε κοίλας
  σήραγγας πέτρας τ' ἐμβυθίους νέμεται,
ἄγρης ἐκ πρώτης ποτ' ἰουλίδα πετρήεσσαν   5
  δακνάζων, ὀλοὴν ἐξ ἁλὸς ἀράμενος,
ἔφθιτ'· ὀλισθηρὴ γὰρ ὑπ' ἐκ χερὸς ἀΐξασα
  ᾤχετ' ἐπὶ στεινὸν παλλομένη φάρυγα.
χὠ μὲν μηρίνθων καὶ δούνακος ἀγκίστρων τε
  ἐγγὺς ἀπὸ πνοιὴν ἧκε κυλινδόμενος,   10
νήματ' ἀναπλήσας ἐπιμοίρια· τοῦ δὲ θανόντος
  Γρίπων ὁ γριπεὺς τοῦτον ἔχωσε τάφον.

505.—ΣΑΠΦΟΥΣ

Τῷ γριπεῖ Πελάγωνι πατὴρ ἐπέθηκε Μενίσκος
  κύρτον καὶ κώπαν, μνᾶμα κακοζοΐας.

Sir C. A. Elton, *Specimens of the Classic Poets*, i. p. 108.

506.—ΛΕΩΝΙΔΑ

Κἠν γῇ καὶ πόντῳ κεκρύμμεθα· τοῦτο περισσὸν
  ἐκ Μοιρέων Θάρσυς Χαρμίδου ἤνυσατο.
ἦ γὰρ ἐπ' ἀγκύρης ἔνοχον βάρος εἰς ἅλα δύνων,
  Ἰόνιόν θ' ὑγρὸν κῦμα κατερχόμενος,
τὴν μὲν ἔσωσ', αὐτὸς δὲ μετάτροπος ἐκ βυθοῦ ἔρρων   5
  ἤδη καὶ ναύταις χεῖρας ὀρεγνύμενος,
ἐβρώθην· τοῖόν μοι ἐπ' ἄγριον εὖ μέγα κῆτος
  ἦλθεν, ἀπέβροξεν δ' ἄχρις ἐπ' ὀμφαλίου.
χἤμισυ μὲν ναῦται, ψυχρὸν βάρος, ἐξ ἁλὸς ἡμῶν
  ἤρανθ', ἥμισυ δὲ πρίστις ἀπεκλάσατο·   10
ἠόνι δ' ἐν ταύτῃ κακὰ λείψανα Θάρσυος, ὦνερ,
  ἔκρυψαν· πάτρην δ' οὐ πάλιν ἱκόμεθα.

274

perch, greedy seizer of the bait, and all fish that live in crevices and on rocky bottoms, met his death by biting[1] a rock-dwelling iulis[2] from his first catch of the day, a fish he lifted from the sea for his destruction; for slipping from his fingers, it went wriggling down his narrow gullet. So breathed he his last, rolling over in agony, near his lines, rod, and hooks, fulfilling the doom the destinies spun for him, and Gripo the fisherman built him this tomb.

505.—SAPPHO

His father, Meniscus, placed on Pelagon's tomb a weel and oar, a memorial of the indigent life he led.

506.—LEONIDAS OF TARENTUM

I AM buried both on land and in the sea; this is the exceptional fate of Tharsys, son of Charmides. For diving to loosen the anchor, which had become fixed, I descended into the Ionian sea; the anchor I saved, but as I was returning from the depths and already reaching out my hands to the sailors, I was eaten; so terrible and great a monster of the deep came and gulped me down as far as the navel. The half of me, a cold burden, the sailors drew from the sea, but the shark bit off the other half. On this beach, good Sir, they buried the vile remains of Tharsys, and I never came home to my country.

[1] To kill it.
[2] Now called "yilos," not a wrasse (as L. and S.), but a small, rather prickly rock-fish.

507ᴀ.—ΣΙΜΩΝΙΔΟΥ

Ἄνθρωπ', οὐ Κροίσου λεύσσεις τάφον, ἀλλὰ γὰρ ἀνδρὸς
χερνήτεω μικρὸς τύμβος, ἐμοὶ δ' ἱκανός.

507ʙ.—ΤΟΥ ΑΥΤΟΥ

Οὐκ ἐπιδὼν νύμφεια λέχη κατέβην τὸν ἄφυκτον
Γόργιππος ξανθῆς Φερσεφόνης θάλαμον.

508.—ΤΟΥ ΑΥΤΟΥ

Παυσανίην ἰητρὸν ἐπώνυμον, Ἀγχίτεω υἱόν,
τόνδ', Ἀσκληπιάδην, πατρὶς ἔθαψε Γέλα,
ὃς πλείστους κρυεραῖσι μαραινομένους ὑπὸ νούσοις
φῶτας ἀπέστρεψεν Φερσεφόνης θαλάμων.

509.—ΤΟΥ ΑΥΤΟΥ

Σῆμα Θεόγνιδος εἰμὶ Σινωπέος, ᾧ μ' ἐπέθηκεν
Γλαῦκος ἑταιρείης ἀντὶ πολυχρονίου.

510.—ΤΟΥ ΑΥΤΟΥ

Σῶμα μὲν ἀλλοδαπὴ κεύθει κόνις· ἐν δέ σε πόντῳ,
Κλείσθενες, Εὐξείνῳ μοῖρ' ἔκιχεν θανάτου
πλαζόμενον· γλυκεροῦ δὲ μελίφρονος οἴκαδε νόστου
ἤμπλακες, οὐδ' ἵκευ Χίον ἐπ' ἀμφιρύτην.

A. Esdaile, *The Poetry Review*, Sept. 1913.

511.—ΤΟΥ ΑΥΤΟΥ

Σῆμα καταφθιμένοιο Μεγακλέος εὖτ' ἂν ἴδωμαι,
οἰκτείρω σε, τάλαν Καλλία, οἷ' ἔπαθες.

507A.—SIMONIDES

Thou seest not the grave of Croesus, but a poor labourer's tomb is this, yet sufficient for me.

507B.—By the Same

I, Gorgippus, without having looked on the bridal bed, descended to the chamber that none may escape of fair-haired Persephone.

508.—By the Same

His city Gela buried here Pausanias, son of Anchites, a physician of the race of Asclepius, bearing a name [1] expressive of his calling, who turned aside from the chambers of Persephone many men wasted by chilling disease.

509.—By the Same

I am the monument of Theognis of Sinope, erected over him by Glaucus for the sake of their long companionship.

510.—By the Same

The earth of a strange land lies on thy body, Cleisthenes, but the doom of death overtook thee wandering on the Euxine sea. Thou wast cheated of sweet, honied home-coming, nor ever didst thou return to sea-girt Chios.

511.—By the Same

When I look on the tomb of Megacles dead, I pity thee, poor Callias, for what thou hast suffered.

[1] Stiller of pain.

512.—ΤΟΥ ΑΥΤΟΥ

Τῶνδε δι᾽ ἀνθρώπων ἀρετὰν οὐχ ἵκετο καπνὸς
    αἰθέρα δαιομένης εὐρυχόρου Τεγέας,
οἳ βούλοντο πόλιν μὲν ἐλευθερίᾳ τεθαλυῖαν
    παισὶ λιπεῖν, αὐτοὶ δ᾽ ἐν προμάχοισι θανεῖν.

513.—ΤΟΥ ΑΥΤΟΥ

Φῆ ποτε Πρωτόμαχος, πατρὸς περὶ χεῖρας ἔχοντος
    ἡνίκ᾽ ἀφ᾽ ἱμερτὴν ἔπνεεν ἡλικίην·
"Ὦ Τιμηνορίδη, παιδὸς φίλου οὔ ποτε λήξεις
    οὔτ᾽ ἀρετὴν ποθέων οὔτε σαοφροσύνην."

514.—ΤΟΥ ΑΥΤΟΥ

Αἰδὼς καὶ Κλεόδημον ἐπὶ προχοῇσι Θεαίρου
    ἀενάου στονόεντ᾽ ἤγαγεν εἰς θάνατον,
Θρηϊκίῳ κύρσαντα λόχῳ· πατρὸς δὲ κλεεννὸν
    Διφίλου αἰχμητὴς υἱὸς ἔθηκ᾽ ὄνομα.

515.—ΤΟΥ ΑΥΤΟΥ

Αἰαῖ, νοῦσε βαρεῖα· τί δὴ ψυχαῖσι μεγαίρεις
    ἀνθρώπων ἐρατῇ πὰρ νεότητι μένειν ;
ἦ καὶ Τίμαρχον γλυκερῆς αἰῶνος ἄμερσας
    ἤϊθεον, πρὶν ἰδεῖν κουριδίην ἄλοχον.

516.—ΤΟΥ ΑΥΤΟΥ

Οἳ μὲν ἐμὲ κτείναντες ὁμοίων ἀντιτύχοιεν,
    Ζεῦ Ξένι᾽· οἳ δ᾽ ὑπὸ γᾶν θέντες ὄναιντο βίου.

512.—By the Same

Through the valour of these men the smoke of spacious Tegea in flames never went up to heaven. They resolved to leave to their children their city prospering in freedom and to die themselves in the forefront of the fight.

513.—By the Same

Protomachus said, when his father was holding him in his arms as he breathed forth his lovely youth, "Timenorides, never shalt thou cease to regret thy dear son's valour and virtue."

514.—By the Same

Shame of retreat led Cleodemus, too, to mournful death when on the banks of ever-flowing Theaerus he engaged the Thracian troop, and his warrior son made the name of his father, Diphilus, famous.

515.—By the Same

Alas, cruel sickness, why dost thou grudge the souls of men their sojourn with lovely youth? Timarchus, too, in his youth thou hast robbed of his sweet life ere he looked on a wedded wife.

516.—By the Same

Zeus, Protector of strangers, let them who slew me meet with the same fate, but may they who laid me in earth live and prosper.[1]

---

[1] On the grave of one slain by robbers. *cp.* Nos. 310, 581.

517.—ΚΑΛΛΙΜΑΧΟΥ

Ἠῶοι Μελάνιππον ἐθάπτομεν, ἠελίου δὲ
δυομένου Βασιλὼ κάτθανε παρθενικὴ
αὐτοχερί· ζώειν γάρ, ἀδελφεὸν ἐν πυρὶ θεῖσα,
οὐκ ἔτλη. δίδυμον δ' οἶκος ἐσεῖδε κακὸν
πατρὸς Ἀριστίπποιο· κατήφησεν δὲ Κυρήνη
πᾶσα, τὸν εὔτεκνον χῆρον ἰδοῦσα δόμον.

518.—ΤΟΥ ΑΥΤΟΥ

Ἀστακίδην τὸν Κρῆτα, τὸν αἰπόλον, ἥρπασε Νύμφη
ἐξ ὄρεος· καὶ νῦν ἱερὸς Ἀστακίδης.
οὐκέτι Δικταίῃσιν ὑπὸ δρυσίν, οὐκέτι Δάφνιν
ποιμένες, Ἀστακίδην δ' αἰὲν ἀεισόμεθα.

519.—ΤΟΥ ΑΥΤΟΥ

Δαίμονα τίς δ' εὖ οἶδε τὸν αὔριον, ἀνίκα καὶ σέ,
Χάρμι, τὸν ὀφθαλμοῖς χθιζὸν ἐν ἀμετέροις,
τᾷ ἑτέρᾳ κλαύσαντες ἐθάπτομεν; οὐδὲν ἐκείνου
εἶδε πατὴρ Διοφῶν χρῆμ' ἀνιαρότερον.

520.—ΤΟΥ ΑΥΤΟΥ

Ἢν δίζῃ Τίμαρχον ἐν Ἄϊδος, ὄφρα πύθηαι
ἤ τι περὶ ψυχῆς, ἢ πάλι πῶς ἔσεαι,
δίζεσθαι φυλῆς Πτολεμαΐδος, υἱέα πατρὸς
Παυσανίου· δήεις δ' αὐτὸν ἐν εὐσεβέων.

521.—ΤΟΥ ΑΥΤΟΥ

Κύζικον ἢν ἔλθῃς, ὀλίγος πόνος Ἱππακὸν εὑρεῖν
καὶ Διδύμην· ἀφανὴς οὔτι γὰρ ἡ γενεή·
καί σφιν ἀνιηρὸν μὲν ἐρεῖς ἔπος, ἔμπα δὲ λέξαι
τοῦθ', ὅτι τὸν κείνων ὧδ' ἐπέχω Κριτίην.

517.—CALLIMACHUS

It was morning when we buried Melanippus, and at sunset the maiden Basilo died by her own hand; for after laying her brother on the pyre she could not abide to live. The house of their father Aristippus witnessed a double woe, and all Cyrene stood with downcast eyes, seeing the home bereft of its lovely children.

518.—By the Same

A nymph from the mountains carried off Astacides the Cretan goat-herd, and now Astacides is holy. No more, ye shepherds, beneath the oaks of Dicte shall we sing of Daphnis, but ever of Astacides.

519.—By the Same

Who knows well to-morrow's fate, when thee, Charmis, who wast yesterday in our eyes, we bewailed and buried next day. Thy father Diophon never looked upon any more grievous thing.

520.—By the Same

If thou wouldst seek Timarchus in Hades to enquire anything about the soul, or about how it shall be with thee hereafter, ask for Pausanias' son of the tribe Ptolemais, and it is in the abode of the pious that thou shalt find him.

521.—By the Same

If thou comest to Cyzicus, it will be little trouble to find Hippacus and Didyme; for the family is by no means obscure. Then give them this message, grievous indeed, but fail not to give it, that I hold their Critias.

281

522.—ΤΟΥ ΑΥΤΟΥ

Τιμονόη, τίς δ' ἐσσί; μὰ δαίμονας, οὔ σ' ἂν ἐπέγνων,
εἰ μὴ Τιμοθέου πατρὸς ἐπῆν ὄνομα
στήλῃ, καὶ Μήθυμνα τεῇ πόλις. ἦ μέγα φημὶ
χῆρον ἀνιᾶσθαι σὸν πόσιν Εὐθυμένη.

523.—ΤΟΥ ΑΥΤΟΥ

Οἵτινες Ἀλείοιο παρέρπετε σᾶμα Κίμωνος
ἴστε τὸν Ἱππαίου παῖδα παρερχόμενοι.

524.—ΤΟΥ ΑΥΤΟΥ

α. Ἦ ῥ' ὑπὸ σοὶ Χαρίδας ἀναπαύεται; β. Εἰ τὸν
   Ἀρίμμα
   τοῦ Κυρηναίου παῖδα λέγεις, ὑπ' ἐμοί.
α. Ὦ Χαρίδα, τί τὰ νέρθε; γ. Πολὺς σκότος.
   α. Αἱ δ' ἄνοδοι τί:
γ. Ψεῦδος. α. Ὁ δὲ Πλούτων; γ. Μῦθος.
   α. Ἀπωλόμεθα.
γ. Οὗτος ἐμὸς λόγος ὔμμιν ἀληθινός· εἰ δὲ τὸν ἡδὺν
   βούλει, πελλαίου βοῦς μέγας εἰν ἀΐδῃ.

525.—ΤΟΥ ΑΥΤΟΥ

Ὅστις ἐμὸν παρὰ σῆμα φέρεις πόδα, Καλλιμάχου με
   ἴσθι Κυρηναίου παῖδά τε καὶ γενέτην.
εἰδείης δ' ἄμφω κεν· ὁ μέν κοτε πατρίδος ὅπλων
   ἦρξεν· ὁ δ' ἤεισεν κρέσσονα βασκανίης.
οὐ νέμεσις· Μοῦσαι γὰρ ὅσους ἴδον ὄμματι παῖδας
   μὴ λοξῷ πολιοὺς οὐκ ἀπέθεντο φίλους.

522.—By the Same

Timonoe! But who art thou? By heaven I would not have recognised thee, had not thy father's name Timotheus and thy city's Methymna stood on the grave-stone. I know of a truth that thy widowed husband Euthymenes is in sore distress.

523.—By the Same

Ye who pass by the monument of Cimon of Elis, know that it is Hippaeus' son whom ye pass by.

524.—By the Same

A. "Doth Charidas rest beneath thee?" *B.* "If it is the son of Arimmas of Cyrene that you mean, he does." *A.* "What is it like below, Charidas?" *C.* "Very dark." *A.* "And what about return?" *C.* "All lies." *A.* "And Pluto?" *C.* "A myth." *A.* "I am done for." [1] *C.* "This is the truth that I tell you, but if you want to hear something agreeable, a large ox in Hades costs a shilling." (?)

525.—By the Same

Know thou who passest my monument that I am the son and father of Callimachus of Cyrene. Thou wilt have heard of both; the one once held the office of general in his city and the other sang songs which overcame envy. No marvel, for those on whom the Muses did not look askance in boyhood they do not cast off when they are grey.

---

[1] *i.e.* all my hopes are gone.

526.—ΝΙΚΑΝΔΡΟΥ ΚΟΛΟΦΩΝΙΟΥ

Ζεῦ πάτερ, Ὀθρυάδα τίνα φέρτερον ἔδρακες ἄλλον,
ὃς μόνος ἐκ Θυρέας οὐκ ἐθέλησε μολεῖν
πατρίδ᾽ ἐπὶ Σπάρταν, διὰ δὲ ξίφος ἤλασε πλευρᾶν,
δοῦλα καταγράψας σκῦλα κατ᾽ Ἰναχιδᾶν;

527.—ΘΕΟΔΩΡΙΔΑ

Θεύδοτε, κηδεμόνων μέγα δάκρυον, οἵ σε θανόντα
κώκυσαν, μέλεον πυρσὸν ἀναψάμενοι,
αἰνόλινε, τρισάωρε· σὺ δ᾽ ἀντὶ γάμου τε καὶ ἥβης
κάλλιπες ἡδίστῃ ματρὶ γόους καὶ ἄχη.

528.—ΤΟΥ ΑΥΤΟΥ

Εὐρύσορον περὶ σῆμα τὸ Φαιναρέτης ποτὲ κοῦραι
κέρσαντο ξανθοὺς Θεσσαλίδες πλοκάμους,
πρωτοτόκον καὶ ἄποτμον ἀτυζόμεναι περὶ νύμφην·
Λάρισσαν δὲ φίλην ἤκαχε καὶ τοκέας.

529.—ΤΟΥ ΑΥΤΟΥ

Τόλμα καὶ εἰς ἀΐδαν καὶ ἐς οὐρανὸν ἄνδρα κομίζει,
ἃ καὶ Σωσάνδρου παῖδ᾽ ἐπέβασε πυρᾶς,
Δωρόθεον· Φθίᾳ γὰρ ἐλεύθερον ἦμαρ ἰάλλων
ἐρραίσθη Σηκῶν μεσσόθι καὶ Χιμέρας.

530.—ΑΝΤΙΠΑΤΡΟΥ ΘΕΣΣΑΛΟΝΙΚΕΩΣ

Μούναν σὺν τέκνοις νεκυοστόλε δέξο με πορθμεῦ
τὰν λάλον· ἀρκεῖ σοι φόρτος ὁ Τανταλίδης·
πληρώσει γαστὴρ μία σὸν σκάφος· εἴσιδε κούρους
καὶ κούρας, Φοίβου σκῦλα καὶ Ἀρτέμιδος.

526.—NICANDER OF COLOPHON

O FATHER Zeus, didst thou ever see a braver than Othryadas, who would not return alone from Thyrea to Sparta his country, but transfixed himself with his sword after having inscribed the trophy signifying the subjection of the Argives.[1]

527.—THEODORIDAS

THEODOTUS, cause of many tears to thy kinsmen, who lamented thee dead, lighting the mournful pyre, ill-fated, dead all too early, instead of joy in thy marriage and thy youth, to thy sweet mother is left but groaning and grief.

528.—BY THE SAME

THE daughters of Thessaly sheared their yellow locks at the spacious tomb of Phaenarete, distraught with grief for the luckless bride dead in her first childbed, and her dear Larissa and her parents were stricken with sorrow.

529.—BY THE SAME

DARING leads a man to Hades and to heaven; daring laid Dorotheus, Sosander's son, on the pyre; for winning freedom for Phthia he was smitten midway between Sekoi and Chimera.

530.—ANTIPATER OF THESSALONICA
On Niobe and her children

THOU ferry-man of the dead, receive me, who could not hold my tongue, alone with my children; a boat-load from the house of Tantalus is sufficient for thee. One womb shall fill thy boat; look on my boys and girls, the spoils of Phoebus and Artemis.

[1] *cp.* Nos. 430, 431.

531.—ΤΟΥ ΑΥΤΟΥ

Αὐτά τοι, τρέσσαντι παρὰ χρέος, ὤπασεν ἅδαν,
  βαψαμένα κοίλων ἐντὸς ἄρη λαγόνων,
μάτηρ ἅ σ' ἔτεκεν, Δαμάτριε· φᾶ δὲ σίδαρον
  παιδὸς ἑοῦ φύρδαν μεστὸν ἔχουσα φόνου,
ἀφριόεν κοναβηδὸν ἐπιπρίουσα γένειον,
  δερκομένα λοξαῖς, οἷα Λάκαινα, κόραις·
" Λεῖπε τὸν Εὐρώταν, ἴθι Τάρταρον· ἁνίκα δειλὰν
  οἶσθα φυγάν, τελέθεις οὔτ' ἐμὸς οὔτε Λάκων."

532.—ΙΣΙΔΩΡΟΥ ΑΙΓΕΑΤΟΥ

Ἔκ με γεωμορίης Ἐτεοκλέα πόντιος ἐλπὶς
  εἵλκυσεν, ὀθνείης ἔμπορον ἐργασίης·
νῶτα δὲ Τυρσηνῆς ἐπάτευν ἁλός· ἀλλ' ἅμα νηὶ
  πρηνιχθεὶς κείνης ὕδασιν ἐγκατέδυν,
ἀθρόον ἐμβρίσαντος ἀήματος. οὐκ ἄρ' ἁλωὰς
  αὐτὸς ἐπιπνείει κεἰς ὀθόνας ἄνεμος.

533.—ΔΙΟΝΥΣΙΟΥ ΑΝΔΡΙΟΥ

Καὶ Διὶ καὶ Βρομίῳ με διάβροχον οὐ μέγ' ὀλισθεῖν,
  καὶ μόνον ἐκ δοιῶν, καὶ βροτὸν ἐκ μακάρων.

534.—ΑΥΤΟΜΕΔΟΝΤΟΣ ΑΙΤΩΛΟΥ

Ἄνθρωπε, ζωῆς περιφείδεο, μηδὲ παρ' ὥρην
  ναυτίλος ἴσθι· καὶ ὡς οὐ πολὺς ἀνδρὶ βίος.
δείλαιε Κλεόνικε, σὺ δ' εἰς λιπαρὴν Θάσον ἐλθεῖν
  ἠπείγευ, Κοίλης ἔμπορος ἐκ Συρίης,
ἔμπορος, ὦ Κλεόνικε· δύσιν δ' ὑπὸ Πλειάδος αὐτὴν
  ποντοπορῶν, αὐτῇ Πλειάδι συγκατέδυς.

H. C. Beeching, *In a Garden*, p. 97.

531.—BY THE SAME

THE very mother who bore thee, Demetrius, gave thee death when forgetful of thy duty thou didst fly, driving the sword into thy flanks. Holding the steel that reeked with her son's blood, gnashing her teeth, foaming at the mouth, and looking askance like a Spartan woman as she was, she exclaimed " Leave the Eurotas ; go to Tartarus.   Since thou couldst fly like a coward, thou art neither mine nor Sparta's."

532.—ISIDORUS OF AEGAE

I AM Eteocles whom the hopes of the sea drew from husbandry and made a merchant in place of what I was by nature.   I was travelling on the surface of the Tyrrhenian Sea, but with my ship I sunk head-long into its depths in a sudden fierce squall.   It is not then the same wind that blows on the threshing-floor and fills the sails.

533.—DIONYSIUS OF ANDROS

IT is no great marvel that I slipped when soaked by Zeus[1] and Bacchus.   It was two to one, and gods against a mortal.

534.—AUTOMEDON OF AETOLIA

MAN, spare thy life, and go not to sea in ill season. Even as it is, man's life is not long.   Unhappy Cleonicus, thou wast hastening to reach bright Thasos, trading from Coelesyria—trading, O Cleonicus ; but on thy voyage at the very setting of the Pleiads,[2] with the Pleiads thou didst set.

[1] *i.e.* rain.   [2] Beginning of November.

GREEK ANTHOLOGY

535.—ΜΕΛΕΑΓΡΟΥ

Οὐκέθ' ὁμοῦ χιμάροισιν ἔχειν βίον, οὐκέτι ναίειν
  ὁ τραγόπους ὀρέων Πὰν ἐθέλω κορυφάς.
τί γλυκύ μοι, τί ποθεινὸν ἐν οὔρεσιν; ὤλετο Δάφνις,
  Δάφνις ὃς ἡμετέρῃ πῦρ ἔτεκε κραδίῃ.
ἄστυ τόδ' οἰκήσω· θηρῶν δέ τις ἄλλος ἐπ' ἄγρην
  στελλέσθω. τὰ πάροιθ' οὐκέτι Πανὶ φίλα.

536.—ΑΛΚΑΙΟΥ [ΜΙΤΥΛΗΝΑΙΟΥ]

Οὐδὲ θανὼν ὁ πρέσβυς ἑῷ ἐπιτέτροφε τύμβῳ
  βότρυν ἀπ' οἰνάνθης ἥμερον, ἀλλὰ βάτον,
καὶ πνιγόεσσαν ἄχερδον, ἀποστύφουσαν ὁδιτῶν
  χείλεα καὶ δίψει καρφαλέον φάρυγα.
ἀλλά τις Ἱππώνακτος ἐπὴν παρὰ σῆμα νέηται,
  εὐχέσθω κνώσσειν εὐμενέοντα νέκυν.

537.—ΦΑΝΙΟΥ [ΓΡΑΜΜΑΤΙΚΟΥ]

Ἠρίον οὐκ ἐπὶ πατρί, πολυκλαύτου δ' ἐπὶ παιδὸς
  Λῦσις ἄχει κενεὴν τήνδ' ἀνέχωσε κόνιν,
οὔνομα ταρχύσας, ἐπεὶ οὐχ ὑπὸ χεῖρα τοκήων
  ἤλυθε δυστήνου λείψανα Μαντιθέου.

538.—ΑΝΥΤΗΣ

Μάνης οὗτος ἀνὴρ ἦν ζῶν ποτέ· νῦν δὲ τεθνηκὼς
  ἴσον Δαρείῳ τῷ μεγάλῳ δύναται.

J. A. Pott, *Greek Love Songs and Epigrams*, i. p. 24.

535.—MELEAGER

No longer do I, goat-footed Pan, desire to dwell among the goats or on the hill-tops. What pleasure, what delight have I in mountains? Daphnis is dead, Daphnis who begot a fire in my heart. Here in the city will I dwell; let some one else set forth to hunt the wild beasts; Pan no longer loves his old life.

536.—ALCAEUS[1]

Not even now the old man is dead, do clusters of the cultivated vine grow on his tomb, but brambles and the astringent wild pear that contracts the traveller's lips and his throat parched with thirst. But he who passes by the tomb of Hipponax should pray his corpse to rest in sleep.

537.—PHANIAS

No monument for his father, but in mournful memory of his lamented son did Lysis build this empty mound of earth, burying but his name, since the remains of unhappy Mantitheus never came into his parents' hands.

538.—ANYTE

This man when alive was Manes,[2] but now he is dead he is as great as great Darius.

---

[1] Probably the Messenian.   [2] A slave's name.

539.—ΠΕΡΣΟΥ ΠΟΙΗΤΟΥ

Οὐ προϊδών, Θεότιμε, κακὴν δύσιν ὑετίοιο
    Ἀρκτούρου, κρυερῆς ἥψαο ναυτιλίης,
ἤ σε, δι' Αἰγαίοιο πολυκλήϊδι θέοντα
    νηΐ, σὺν οἷς ἑτάροις ἤγαγεν εἰς ἀΐδην.
αἰαῖ, Ἀριστοδίκη δὲ καὶ Εὔπολις, οἵ σ' ἐτέκοντο,
    μύρονται, κενεὸν σῆμα περισχόμενοι.

540.—ΔΑΜΑΓΗΤΟΥ

Πρὸς σὲ Διὸς Ξενίου γουνούμεθα, πατρὶ Χαρίνῳ
    ἄγγειλον Θήβην, ὦνερ, ἐπ' Αἰολίδα
Μῆνιν καὶ Πολύνικον ὀλωλότε, καὶ τόδε φαίης,
    ὡς οὐ τὸν δόλιον κλαίομεν ἄμμι μόρον,
καίπερ ὑπὸ Θρῃκῶν φθίμενοι χερός, ἀλλὰ τὸ κείνου
    γῆρας ἐν ἀργαλέῃ κείμενον ὀρφανίῃ.

541.—ΤΟΥ ΑΥΤΟΥ

Ἔστης ἐν προμάχοις, Χαιρωνίδη, ὧδ' ἀγορεύσας,
    "'Ἢ μόρον, ἢ νίκαν, Ζεῦ, πολέμοιο δίδου,"
ἡνίκα τοι περὶ Τάφρον Ἀχαιΐδα τῇ τότε νυκτὶ
    δυσμενέες θρασέος δῆριν ἔθεντο πόνου.
ναὶ μὴν ἀντ' ἀρετῆς σε διακριδὸν Ἅλις ἀείδει,
    θερμὸν ἀνὰ ξείνην αἷμα χέαντα κόνιν.

542.—ΦΛΑΚΚΟΥ

Ἕβρου χειμερίοις ἀταλὸς κρυμοῖσι δεθέντος
    κοῦρος ὀλισθηροῖς ποσσὶν ἔθραυσε πάγον,

---

[1] In November.
[2] The scene of a battle in which the Spartans defeated the

539.—PERSES

HEEDLESS, Theotimus, of the coming evil setting of rainy Arcturus[1] didst thou set out on thy perilous voyage, which carried thee and thy companions, racing over the Aegaean in the many-oared galley, to Hades. Alas for Aristodice and Eupolis, thy parents, who mourn thee, embracing thy empty tomb.

540.—DAMAGETES

BY Zeus, the Protector of strangers, we adjure thee, Sir, tell our father Charinus, in Aeolian Thebes, that Menis and Polynicus are no more ; and say this, that though we perished at the hands of the Thracians, we do not lament our treacherous murder, but his old age left in bereavement ill to bear.

541.—BY THE SAME

STANDING in the forefront of the battle, Chaeronidas, so spokest thou, "Zeus, grant me death or victory," on that night when by Achaean Taphros,[2] the foe made thee meet him in stubborn battle strife : verily doth Elis sing of thee above all men for thy valour, who didst then shed thy warm blood on the foreign earth.

542.—FLACCUS

THE tender boy, slipping, broke the ice of the Hebrus frozen by the winter cold, and as he was

Messenians, but this epigram must refer to some later combat on the same spot.

τοῦ παρασυρομένοιο περιρραγὲς αὐχέν' ἔκοψεν
θηγαλέον ποταμοῦ Βιστονίοιο τρύφος.
καὶ τὸ μὲν ἡρπάσθη δίναις μέρος· ἡ δὲ τεκοῦσα
λειφθὲν ὕπερθε τάφῳ μοῦνον ἔθηκε κάρα.
μυρομένη δὲ τάλαινα, "Τέκος, τέκος," εἶπε, "τὸ
            μέν σου
πυρκαϊή, τὸ δέ σου πικρὸν ἔθαψεν ὕδωρ."

543.—ΑΔΕΣΠΟΤΟΝ

Πάντα τις ἀρήσαιτο φυγεῖν πλόον, ὁπότε καὶ σύ,
Θεύγενες, ἐν Λιβυκῷ τύμβον ἔθευ πελάγει,
ἡνίκα σοι κεκμηὸς ἐπέπτατο φορτίδι νηὶ
οὖλον ἀνηρίθμων κεῖνο νέφος γεράνων.

544.—ΑΔΕΣΠΟΤΟΝ

Εἰπέ, ποτὶ Φθίαν εὐάμπελον ἤν ποθ' ἵκηαι
καὶ πόλιν ἀρχαίαν, ὦ ξένε, Θαυμακίαν.
ὡς δρυμὸν Μαλεαῖον ἀναστείβων ποτ' ἔρημον
εἶδες Λάμπωνος τόνδ' ἐπὶ παιδὶ τάφον
Δερξία, ὅν ποτε μοῦνον ἕλον δόλῳ, οὐδ' ἀναφανδόν,
κλῶπες ἐπὶ Σπάρταν δῖαν ἐπειγόμενον.

545.—ΗΓΗΣΙΠΠΟΥ

Τὴν ἀπὸ πυρκαϊῆς ἐνδέξια φασὶ κέλευθον
Ἑρμῆν τοὺς ἀγαθοὺς εἰς Ῥαδάμανθυν ἄγειν,
ᾗ καὶ Ἀριστόνοος, Χαιρεστράτου οὐκ ἀδάκρυτος
παῖς, ἡγησίλεω δῶμ' Ἄιδος κατέβη.

---

[1] cp. Bk. IX. No. 56.

carried away by the current, a sharp fragment of the
Bistonian river breaking away cut through his neck.
Part of him was carried away by the flood, but his
mother laid in the tomb all that was left to her
above the ice, his head alone. And, wailing, she
cried, " My child, my child, part of thee hath the
pyre buried and part the cruel water." [1]

543.—ANONYMOUS

ONE should pray to be spared sea-voyages alto-
gether, Theogenes, since thou, too, didst make thy
grave in the Libyan Sea, when that tired close-
packed flock of countless cranes descended like a
cloud on thy loaded ship. [2]

544.—ANONYMOUS

TELL, stranger, if ever thou dost come to Phthia,
the land of vines, and to the ancient city of Thaumacia
that, mounting once through the lonely woodland of
Malea, thou didst see this tomb of Derxias the son
of Lampo, whom once, as he hastened on his way to
glorious Sparta, the bandits slew by treachery and
not in open fight.

545.—HEGESIPPUS

THEY say that Hermes leads the just from the
pyre to Rhadamanthus by the right-hand path, the
path by which Aristonous, the not unwept son of
Chaerestratus, descended to the house of Hades, the
gatherer of peoples.

[1] Pliny (*N.H.* x. 13) tells of ships being similarly sunk
by flocks of quails alighting on them at night.

546.—ΑΔΕΣΠΟΤΟΝ

Εἶχε κορωνοβόλον πενίης λιμηρὸν Ἀρίστων
ὄργανον, ᾧ πτηνὰς ἠκροβόλιζε χένας,
ἦκα παραστείχων δολίην ὁδόν, οἷος ἐκείνας
ψεύσασθαι λοξοῖς ὄμμασι φερβομένας.
νῦν δ᾽ ὁ μὲν εἰν ἀΐδῃ· τὸ δέ οἱ βέλος ὀρφανὸν ἤχου
καὶ χερός· ἡ δ᾽ ἄγρη τύμβον ὑπερπέταται.

547.—ΛΕΩΝΙΔΟΥ ΑΛΕΞΑΝΔΡΕΩΣ

Τὰν στάλαν ἐχάραξε Βίανωρ οὐκ ἐπὶ ματρί,
οὐδ᾽ ἐπὶ τῷ γενέτᾳ, πότμον ὀφειλόμενον,
παρθενικᾷ δ᾽ ἐπὶ παιδί· κατέστενε δ᾽, οὐχ Ὑμεναίῳ
ἀλλ᾽ Ἀΐδᾳ νύμφαν δωδεκέτιν κατάγων.

548.—ΤΟΥ ΑΥΤΟΥ

α. Τίς Δαίμων Ἀργεῖος ἐπ᾽ ἠρίῳ; ἆρα σύναιμος
ἐστὶ Δικαιοτέλους; β. Ἐστὶ Δικαιοτέλους.
α. Ἠχὼ τοῦτ᾽ ἐλάλησε πανύστατον, ἢ τόδ᾽ ἀληθές,
κεῖνος ὅδ᾽ ἐστὶν ἀνήρ; β. Κεῖνος ὅδ᾽ ἐστὶν ἀνήρ

549.—ΤΟΥ ΑΥΤΟΥ

Πέτρος ἔτ᾽ ἐν Σιπύλῳ Νιόβη θρήνοις ἀναλύζει
ἑπτὰ δὶς ὠδίνων δυρομένη θάνατον·
λήξει δ᾽ οὐδ᾽ αἰῶνι γόου. τί δ᾽ ἀλαζόνα μῦθον
φθέγξατο, τὸν ζωῆς ἄρπαγα καὶ τεκέων;

546.—ANONYMOUS

ARISTO had his sling, a weapon procuring him a
scanty living, with which he was wont to shoot the
winged geese, stealing softly upon them so as to
elude them as they fed with sidelong-glancing eyes.
Now he is in Hades and the sling noiseless and idle
with no hand to whirl it, and the game fly over his
tomb.

547–550 ARE BY LEONIDAS OF ALEXANDRIA
AND ARE ISOPSEPHA, LIKE BOOK VI. Nos. 321–329.

547

BIANOR engraved the stone, not for his mother or
father, as had been their meet fate, but for his un-
married daughter, and he groaned as he led the
bride of twelve years not to Hymenaeus but to
Hades.

548

"WHO is the Argive Daemon on the tomb? Is he
a brother of Dicaeoteles?" (*Echo*) "A brother of
Dicaeoteles." "Did Echo speak the last words, or
is it true that this is the man?" (*Echo*) "This is
the man."

549

NIOBE, a rock in Sipylus, still sobs and wails,
mourning for the death of twice seven children, and
never during the ages shall she cease from her plaint.
Why did she speak the boastful words that robbed
her of her life and her children?

550.—ΤΟΥ ΑΥΤΟΥ

Ναυηγὸς γλαυκοῖο φυγὼν Τρίτωνος ἀπειλὰς
  Ἀνθεὺς Φθιώτην οὐ φύγεν αἰνόλυκον·
Πηνειοῦ παρὰ χῦμα γὰρ ὤλετο. φεῦ τάλαν ὅστις
  Νηρείδων Νύμφας ἔσχεν ἀπιστοτέρας.

551.—ΑΓΑΘΙΟΥ ΣΧΟΛΑΣΤΙΚΟΥ

Λητόϊος καὶ Παῦλος ἀδελφεὼ ἄμφω ἐόντε
  ξυνὴν μὲν βιότου συζυγίην ἐχέτην,
ξυνὰ δὲ καὶ Μοίρης λαχέτην λίνα, καὶ παρὰ θῖνα
  Βοσπορίην ξυνὴν ἀμφεβάλοντο κόνιν.
οὐδὲ γὰρ ἀλλήλοιν ζώειν ἀπάνευθε δυνάσθην,   5
  ἀλλὰ συνετρεχέτην καὶ παρὰ Φερσεφόνην.
χαίρετον ὦ γλυκερὼ καὶ ὁμόφρονε· σήματι δ᾽ ὑμέων
  ὤφελεν ἱδρῦσθαι βωμὸς Ὁμοφροσύνης.

552.—ΤΟΥ ΑΥΤΟΥ

α. Ὦ ξένε, τί κλαίεις; β. Διὰ σὸν μόρον. α. Οἶσθα
    τίς εἰμι;
  β. Οὐ μὰ τόν· ἀλλ᾽ ἔμπης οἰκτρὸν ὁρῶ τὸ τέλος.
  ἐσσὶ δὲ τίς; α. Περίκλεια. β. Γυνὴ τίνος; α. Ἀν-
    δρὸς ἀρίστου,
  ῥήτορος, ἐξ Ἀσίης, οὔνομα Μεμνονίου.
β. Πῶς δέ σε Βοσπορίη κατέχει κόνις; α. Εἴρεο
    Μοῖραν,   5
  ἥ μοι τῆλε πάτρης ξεῖνον ἔδωκε τάφον.
β. Παῖδα λίπες; α. Τριέτηρον, ὃς ἐν μεγάροισιν
    ἀλύων
  ἐκδέχεται μαζῶν ἡμετέρων σταγόνα.
β. Αἴθε καλῶς ζώοι. α. Ναί, ναί, φίλος, εὔχεο κείνῳ,
  ὄφρα μοι ἡβήσας δάκρυ φίλον σταλάοι.   10

550

ANTHEUS, who escaped the threats of sea-green Trito, escaped not the terrible Phthian wolf. For by the stream of Peneus he perished. Unfortunate! to whom the Nymphs were more treacherous than the Nereids.[1]

551.—AGATHIAS SCHOLASTICUS

LETOEUS and Paulus, being two brothers, were united in life, and united in the predestined hour of their death, they lie by the Bosporus clothed in one shroud of dust. For they could not live apart from each other, but ran together to Persephone. Hail, sweet pair, ever of one mind; on your tomb should stand an altar of Concord.

552.—BY THE SAME

A. "STRANGER, why mournest thou?" B. "For thy fate." A. "Dost know who I am?" B. "No, by ——! but still I see thy end was wretched, and who art thou?" A. "Periclea." B. "Whose wife?" A. "The wife of a noble man, an orator from Asia, by name Memnonius." B. "And how is it that thou liest by the Bosporus?" A. "Ask Fate who gave me a tomb in a strange land far from my own country." B. "Didst thou leave a son?" A. "One of three years old, who wanders up and down the house seeking the milk of my breasts." B. "May he live and prosper." A. "Yea, yea, my friend, pray for him, that he may grow up and shed sweet tears for me."

[1] cp. No. 289.

553.—ΔΑΜΑΣΚΙΟΥ ΦΙΛΟΣΟΦΟΥ

Ζωσίμη, ἡ πρὶν ἐοῦσα μόνῳ τῷ σώματι δούλη,
καὶ τῷ σώματι νῦν εὗρεν ἐλευθερίην.

554.—ΦΙΛΙΠΠΟΥ ΘΕΣΣΑΛΟΝΙΚΕΩΣ

Λατύπος Ἀρχιτέλης Ἀγαθάνορι παιδὶ θανόντι
χερσὶν ὀϊζυραῖς ἡρμολόγησε τάφον,
αἰαῖ, πέτρον ἐκεῖνον, ὃν οὐκ ἐκόλαψε σίδηρος,
ἀλλ᾽ ἐτάκη πυκινοῖς δάκρυσι τεγγόμενος.
φεῦ, στήλη φθιμένῳ κούφη μένε, κεῖνος ἵν᾽ εἴπῃ·   5
"Ὄντως πατρῴη χεὶρ ἐπέθηκε λίθον."

555.—ΙΩΑΝΝΟΥ ΠΟΙΗΤΟΥ

Ἐς πόσιν ἀθρήσασα παρ᾽ ἐσχατίης λίνα μοίρης
ᾔνεσα καὶ χθονίους, ᾔνεσα καὶ ζυγίους·
τοὺς μέν, ὅτι ζώων λίπον ἀνέρα· τοὺς δ᾽, ὅτι τοῖον.
ἀλλὰ πατὴρ μίμνοι παισὶν ἐφ᾽ ἡμετέροις.

555в.—ΤΟΥ ΑΥΤΟΥ

Τοῦτο σαοφροσύνας ἀντάξιον εὕρεο, Νοστώ·
δάκρυά σοι γαμέτας σπεῖσε καταφθιμένᾳ.

556.—ΘΕΟΔΩΡΟΥ ΤΟΥ ΑΝΘΥΠΑΤΟΥ

Νηλειὴς Ἀΐδης· ἐπὶ σοὶ δ᾽ ἐγέλασσε θανόντι,
Τίτυρε, καὶ νεκύων θῆκέ σε μιμολόγον.

557.—ΚΥΡΟΥ ΠΟΙΗΤΟΥ

Τρεῖς ἐτέων δεκάδες, Μαίης χρόνος· ἐς τρία δ᾽ ἄλλα
ἔτρεχεν, ἀλλ᾽ Ἀΐδης πικρὸν ἔπεμψε βέλος·
θηλυτέρην δ᾽ ἥρπαξε ῥόδων καλύκεσσιν ὁμοίην,
πάντ᾽ ἀπομαξαμένην ἔργα τὰ Πηνελόπης.

553.—DAMASCIUS THE PHILOSOPHER

Zosime who was never a slave but in body, has now gained freedom for her body too.

554.—PHILIPPUS OF THESSALONICA

The mason Architeles with mourning hands constructed a tomb for Agathanor his son. Alas! alas! this stone no chisel cut, but drenched by many tears it crumbled. Thou, tablet, rest lightly on the dead, that he may say " Of a truth it was my father's hand which placed this stone on me."

555.—JOANNES THE POET

Looking at my husband, as my life was ebbing away, I praised the infernal gods, and those of wedlock, the former because I left my husband alive, the latter that he was so good a husband. But may their father live to bring up our children.

555b.—By the Same

This, Nosto, was the reward thy virtue gained, that thy husband shed tears for thee at thy death.

556.—THEODORUS PROCONSUL
On a mime

Hades is grim, but he laughed at thy death, Tityrus, and made thee the mime of the dead.

557.—CYRUS THE POET

Maia had passed her thirtieth year and was approaching her thirty-third, when Hades cast at her his cruel dart and carried off the woman who was like a rosebud, a very counterpart of Penelope in her work.

558.—ΑΔΕΣΠΟΤΟΝ

Ἅδης μὲν σύλησεν ἐμῆς νεότητος ὀπώρην,
   κρύψε δὲ παππῴῳ μνήματι τῷδε λίθος.
οὔνομα Ῥουφῖνος γενόμην, πάϊς Αἰθερίοιο,
   μητρὸς δ᾽ ἐξ ἀγαθῆς· ἀλλὰ μάτην γενόμην.
ἐς γὰρ ἄκρον μούσης τε καὶ ἥβης ἦκον ἐλάσσας,   5
   φεῦ, σοφὸς εἰς ἀΐδην, καὶ νέος εἰς ἔρεβος.
κώκυε καὶ σὺ βλέπων τάδε γράμματα μακρόν, ὁδῖτα·
   δὴ γὰρ ἔφυς ζωῶν ἢ πάϊς ἠὲ πατήρ.

559.—ΘΕΟΣΕΒΕΙΑΣ

Εἶδεν Ἀκεστορίη τρία πένθεα· κείρατο χαίτην
   πρῶτον ἐφ᾽ Ἱπποκράτει, καὶ δεύτερον ἀμφὶ Γαληνῷ·
καὶ νῦν Ἀβλαβίου γοερῷ περὶ σήματι κεῖται,
   αἰδομένη μετὰ κεῖνον ἐν ἀνθρώποισι φανῆναι.

560.—ΠΑΥΛΟΥ ΣΙΛΕΝΤΙΑΡΙΟΥ

Εἰ καὶ ἐπὶ ξείνης σε, Λεόντιε, γαῖα καλύπτει,
   εἰ καὶ ἐρικλαύτων τῆλ᾽ ἔθανες γονέων,
πολλά σοι ἐκ βλεφάρων ἐχύθη περιτύμβια φωτῶν
   δάκρυα, δυστλήτῳ πένθεϊ δαπτομένων.
πᾶσι γὰρ ἦσθα λίην πεφιλημένος, οἷά τε πάντων   5
   ξυνὸς ἐὼν κοῦρος, ξυνὸς ἐὼν ἕταρος.
αἰαῖ, λευγαλέη καὶ ἀμείλιχος ἔπλετο Μοῖρα,
   μηδὲ τεῆς ἥβης, δύσμορε, φεισαμένη.

561.—ΙΟΥΛΙΑΝΟΥ ΑΠΟ ΥΠΑΡΧΩΝ ΑΙΓΥΠΤΙΟΥ

Ἡ Φύσις ὠδίνασα πολὺν χρόνον ἀνέρ᾽ ἔτικτεν
   ἄξιον εἰς ἀρετὴν τῶν προτέρων ἐτέων,

558.—Anonymous

Hades spoiled the ripe fruit of my youth and the stone hid me in this ancestral tomb. My name was Rufinus, the son of Aetherius and I was born of a noble mother, but in vain was I born; for after reaching the perfection of education and youth, I carried, alas! my learning to Hades and my youth to Erebus. Lament long, O traveller, when thou readest these lines, for without doubt thou art either the father or the son of living men.

559.—THEOSEBEIA

Three sorrows Medicine[1] met with. First she shore her hair for Hippocrates, and next for Galen, and now she lies on the tearful tomb of Ablabius, ashamed, now he is gone, to shew herself among men.

560.—PAULUS SILENTIARIUS

Though the earth cover thee in a strange land, Leontius, though thou didst die far from thy afflicted parents, yet many funeral tears were shed for thee by mortals consumed by insufferable sorrow. For thou wert greatly beloved by all and it was just as if thou wert the common child, the common companion of every one. Ah! direful and merciless was Fate that spared not even thy youth.

561.—JULIANUS, PREFECT OF EGYPT

Nature after long labour gave birth to a man whose virtue was worthy of former years, Craterus

---

[1] 'Ακεστορία is the same as 'Ακέσω daughter of Aesculapius.

τὸν Κρατερὸν σοφίην τε καὶ οὔνομα, τὸν καὶ ἀνιγροῖς
κινήσαντα γόῳ δάκρυον ἀντιπάλοις.
εἰ δὲ νέος τέθνηκεν, ὑπέρτερα νήματα Μοίρης   5
μέμφεο, βουλομένης κόσμον ἄκοσμον ἔχειν.

562.—ΤΟΥ ΑΥΤΟΥ

Ὦ φθέγμα Κρατεροῖο, τί σοι πλέον εἴ γε καὶ αὐδῆς
ἔπλεο καὶ σιγῆς αἴτιον ἀντιπάλοις;
ζῶντος μὲν γὰρ ἅπαντες ἐφώνεον· ἐκ δὲ τελευτῆς
ὑμετέρης ἰδίην αὖθις ἔδησαν ὄπα.
οὔτις γὰρ μετὰ σεῖο μόρον τέτληκε τανύσσαι   5
ὦτα λόγοις· Κρατερῷ δ᾽ ἓν τέλος ἠδὲ λόγοις.

563.—ΠΑΥΛΟΥ ΣΙΛΕΝΤΙΑΡΙΟΥ

Σιγᾷς Χρυσεόμαλλε τὸ χάλκεον, οὐκέτι δ᾽ ἡμῖν
εἰκόνας ἀρχεγόνων ἐκτελέεις μερόπων
νεύμασιν ἀφθόγγοισι· τεὴ δ᾽, ὄλβιστε, σιωπὴ
νῦν στυγερὴ τελέθει, τῇ πρὶν ἐθελγόμεθα.

564.—ΑΔΕΣΠΟΤΟΝ

Τῇδέ ποτ᾽ ἀκτερέϊστον ἐδέξατο γαῖα χανοῦσα
Λαοδίκην, δηίων ὕβριν ἀλευομένην.
σῆμα δ᾽ ἀμαλδύναντος ἀνωίστοιο χρόνοιο,
Μάξιμος ἔκδηλον θῆκ᾽ Ἀσίης ὕπατος,
καὶ κούρης χάλκειον ἐπεὶ τύπον ἐφράσατ᾽ ἄλλῃ   5
κείμενον ἀκλειῶς, τῷδ᾽ ἐπέθηκε κύκλῳ.

(strong) in name and in wisdom, whose death moved to tears even his grievous opponents. If he died young, blame the supreme decree of Fate who willed that the world should be despoiled of its ornament.[1]

562.—By the Same

O eloquence of Craterus, what profits it thee if thou wast a cause of speech or of silence to thy adversaries? When thou didst live, all cried out in applause; but after thy death the mouths of all are sealed; for none any more would lend an ear to speeches. The art of speaking perished with Craterus.

563.—PAULUS SILENTIARIUS

Thou art bound in brazen silence, Chryseomallus, and no longer dost thou figure to us the men of old time in dumb show.[2] Now, most gifted man, is thy silence, in which we once took delight, grievous to us.

564.—Anonymous

Here on a time the earth opened to receive Laodice,[3] not duly laid to rest, but flying from the violence of the enemy. Unreckonable Time having effaced the monument, Maximus the Proconsul of Asia brought it again to light, and having noticed the girl's bronze statue lying elsewhere unhonoured, he set it up on this circular barrow.

---

[1] The play on the two senses of "cosmos" cannot be reproduced.
[2] He was a mime.   [3] The daughter of Priam.

565.—ΙΟΥΛΙΑΝΟΥ ΑΠΟ ΥΠΑΡΧΩΝ ΑΙΓΥΠΤΙΟΥ

Αὐτὴν Θειοδότην ὁ ζωγράφος. αἴθε δὲ τέχνης
ἤμβροτε, καὶ λήθην δῶκεν ὀδυρομένοις.

566.—ΜΑΚΗΔΟΝΙΟΥ ΥΠΑΤΟΥ

Γαῖα, καὶ Εἰλείθυια, σὺ μὲν τέκες, ἡ δὲ καλύπτεις·
χαίρετον· ἀμφοτέρας ἤνυσα τὸ στάδιον.
εἶμι δέ, μὴ νοέων πόθι νίσομαι· οὐδὲ γὰρ ὑμέας
ἢ τίνος ἢ τίς ἐὼν οἶδα πόθεν μετέβην.

567.—ΑΓΑΘΙΟΥ ΣΧΟΛΑΣΤΙΚΟΥ

Κανδαύλου τόδε σῆμα· δίκη δ᾽ ἐμὸν οἶτον ἰδοῦσα
οὐδὲν ἀλιτραίνειν τὴν παράκοιτιν ἔφη.
ἤθελε γὰρ δισσοῖσιν ὑπ᾽ ἀνδράσι μηδὲ φανῆναι,
ἀλλ᾽ ἢ τὸν πρὶν ἔχειν, ἢ τὸν ἐπιστάμενον.
χρῆν ἄρα Κανδαύλην παθέειν κακόν· οὐ γὰρ ἂν ἔτλη 5
δεῖξαι τὴν ἰδίην ὄμμασιν ἀλλοτρίοις.

568.—ΤΟΥ ΑΥΤΟΥ

Ἑπτά με δὶς λυκάβαντας ἔχουσαν ἀφήρπασε δαίμων,
ἣν μούνην Διδύμῳ πατρὶ Θάλεια τέκεν.
ἆ Μοῖραι, τί τοσοῦτον ἀπηνέες, οὐδ᾽ ἐπὶ παστοὺς
ἠγάγετ᾽ οὐδ᾽ ἐρατῆς ἔργα τεκνοσπορίης;
οἱ μὲν γὰρ γονέες με γαμήλιον εἰς Ὑμέναιον 5
μέλλον ἄγειν· στυγεροῦ δ᾽ εἰς Ἀχέροντος ἔβην.
ἀλλὰ θεοί, λίτομαι, μητρός γε γόους πατέρος τε
παύσατε, τηκομένων εἵνεκ᾽ ἐμεῦ φθιμένης.

565.—JULIANUS, PREFECT OF EGYPT

THE painter limned Theodote just as she was. Would his art had failed him and he had given forgetfulness to us who mourn her.

566.—MACEDONIUS CONSUL

EARTH and Ilithyia, one of you brought me to birth, the other covers me.   Farewell! I have run the race of each.[1]   I depart, not knowing whither I go, for neither do I know who I was or whose or from whence when I came to you.

567.—AGATHIAS SCHOLASTICUS

THIS is the monument of Candaules,[2] and Justice seeing my fate said that my wife committed no crime; for she wished not to be seen by two men, but wished either her first husband or him who knew her charms to possess her.   It was fated for Candaules to come to an evil end; otherwise he would never have ventured to show his own wife to strange eyes.

568.—BY THE SAME

FATE carried me off but fourteen years old, the only child that Thalia bore to Didymus.   Ah, ye Destinies, why were ye so hard-hearted, never bringing me to the bridal chamber or the sweet task of conceiving children?   My parents were on the point of leading me to Hymen, but I went to loathed Acheron.   But, ye gods, still, I pray, the plaints of my father and mother who wither away because of my death.

[1] What he means is "the race of life and death."
[2] See Herod. i. 11.

569.—ΤΟΥ ΑΥΤΟΥ

Ναὶ λίτομαι, παροδῖτα, φίλῳ κατάλεξον ἀκοίτῃ,
  εὖτ' ἂν ἐμὴν λεύσσῃς πατρίδα Θεσσαλίην·
" Κάτθανε σὴ παράκοιτις, ἔχει δέ μιν ἐν χθονὶ τύμβος,
  αἰαῖ, Βοσπορίης ἐγγύθεν ἠιόνος·
ἀλλά μοι αὐτόθι τεῦχε κενήριον ἐγγύθι σεῖο,
  ὄφρ' ἀναμιμνήσκῃ τῆς ποτὲ κουριδίης."

570.—ΑΔΕΣΠΟΤΟΝ

Δουλκίτιον μὲν ἄνακτες ἄκρον βιότοιο πρὸς ὄλβον
  ἤγαγον ἐξ ἀρετῆς καὶ κλέος ἀνθυπάτων·
ὡς δὲ φύσις μιν ἔλυσεν ἀπὸ χθονός, ἀθάνατοι μὲν
  αὐτὸν ἔχουσι θεοί, σῶμα δὲ σηκὸς ὅδε.

571.—ΛΕΟΝΤΙΟΥ ΣΧΟΛΑΣΤΙΚΟΥ

Ὀρφέος οἰχομένου, τάχα τις τότε λείπετο Μοῦσα·
  σεῦ δέ, Πλάτων, φθιμένου, παύσατο καὶ κιθάρη·
ἦν γὰρ ἔτι προτέρων μελέων ὀλίγη τις ἀπορρὼξ
  ἐν σαῖς σωζομένη καὶ φρεσὶ καὶ παλάμαις.

572.—ΑΓΑΘΙΟΥ ΣΧΟΛΑΣΤΙΚΟΥ

Οὐχ ὁσίοις λεχέεσσιν ἐτέρπετο λάθριος ἀνήρ,
  λέκτρον ὑποκλέπτων ἀλλοτρίης ἀλόχου·
ἐξαπίνης δὲ δόμων ὀροφὴ πέσε, τοὺς δὲ κακούργους
  ἔσκεπεν, ἀλλήλοις εἰσέτι μισγομένους.
ξυνὴ δ' ἀμφοτέρους κατέχει παγίς· εἰν ἑνὶ δ' ἄμφω
  κεῖνται, συζυγίης οὐκέτι παυόμενοι.

569.—By the Same

Yea, I pray thee, traveller, tell my dear husband, when thou seest my country Thessaly, "Thy wife is dead and rests in her tomb, alas, near the shore of the Bosporus. But build me at home a cenotaph near thee, so that thou mayest be reminded of her who was once thy spouse."

570.—Anonymous

Our princes, owing to his virtues, promoted Dulcitius to great wealth and proconsular rank; and now that Nature has released him from earth, the immortal gods possess himself, but this enclosure his body.

571.—LEONTIUS SCHOLASTICUS

When Orpheus departed, perchance some Muse survived, but at thy death, Plato,[1] the lyre ceased to sound. For in thy mind and in thy fingers there yet survived some little fragment at least of ancient music.

572.—AGATHIAS SCHOLASTICUS

A certain man secretly took his pleasure in unholy intercourse, stealing the embraces of another man's wife; but of a sudden the roof fell in and buried the sinners still coupled. One trap holds both, and together they lie in an embrace that never ceases.

---

[1] A contemporary musician.

573.—ΛΕΟΝΤΙΟΥ ΣΧΟΛΑΣΤΙΚΟΥ

Χειρεδίου τόδε σῆμα, τὸν ἔτρεφεν Ἀτθὶς ἄρουρα
εἰκόνα ῥητήρων τῆς προτέρης δεκάδος,
ῥηϊδίως πείθοντα δικασπόλον· ἀλλὰ δικάζων
οὔποτε τῆς ὀρθῆς οὐδ᾽ ὅσον ἐτράπετο.

574.—ΑΓΑΘΙΟΥ ΣΧΟΛΑΣΤΙΚΟΥ

Θεσμοὶ μὲν μεμέληντο συνήθεες Ἀγαθονίκῳ·
Μοῖρα δὲ δειμαίνειν οὐ δεδάηκε νόμους·
ἀλλά μιν ἁρπάξασα σοφῶν ἤμερσε θεμίστων,
οὔπω τῆς νομίμης ἔμπλεον ἡλικίης.
οἰκτρὰ δ᾽ ὑπὲρ τύμβοιο κατεστονάχησαν ἑταῖροι
κείμενον, οὐ θιάσου κόσμον ὀδυρόμενοι·
ἡ δὲ κόμην τίλλουσα γόῳ πληκτίζετο μήτηρ,
αἰαῖ, τὸν λαγόνων μόχθον ἐπισταμένη.
ἔμπης ὄλβιος οὗτος, ὃς ἐν νεότητι μαρανθεὶς
ἔκφυγε τὴν βιότου θᾶσσον ἀλιτροσύνην.

575.—ΛΕΟΝΤΙΟΥ ΣΧΟΛΑΣΤΙΚΟΥ

Σῆμα Ῥόδης· Τυρίη δὲ γυνὴ πέλεν· ἀντὶ δὲ πάτρης
ἵκετο τήνδε πόλιν, κηδομένη τεκέων.
αὐτὴ ἀειμνήστοιο λέχος κόσμησε Γεμέλλου,
ὃς πάρος εὐνομίης ἴδμονα θῆκε πόλιν.
γρηῦς μὲν μόρον εὗρεν, ὄφελλε δὲ μυρία κύκλα
ζώειν· τῶν ἀγαθῶν οὐ δεχόμεσθα κόρον.

576.—ΙΟΥΛΙΑΝΟΥ ΑΠΟ ΥΠΑΡΧΩΝ ΑΙΓΥΠΤΙΟΥ

α. Κάτθανες, ὦ Πύρρων; β. Ἐπέχω. α. Πυμάτην
    μετὰ μοῖραν
φῂς ἐπέχειν; β. Ἐπέχω. α. Σκέψιν ἔπαυσε
    τάφος.

BOOK VII. EPIGRAMS 573-576

573.—LEONTIUS SCHOLASTICUS

THIS is the tomb of Cheiredius whom the Attic land
nourished, an orator the image of the ancient ten,[1]
ever easily convincing the judge, but when himself
a judge never swerving a hair's breadth from the
straight path.

574.—AGATHIAS SCHOLASTICUS

AGATHONICUS had diligently studied jurisprudence,
but Fate has not learnt to fear the laws, and laying
hands on him tore him from his learning in it, before
he was of lawful age to practise. His fellow-students
bitterly lamented over his tomb, mourning for the
ornament of their company, and his mother tearing
her hair in her mourning beat herself, remembering,
alas, the labour of her womb. Yet blest was he
in fading young and escaping early the iniquity of
life.

575.—LEONTIUS SCHOLASTICUS

THE tomb is Rhode's. She was a Tyrian woman,
and quitting her country came to this city for the
sake of her children. She adorned the bed of
Gemellus of eternal memory, who formerly was a
professor of law in this city. She died in old age,
but should have lived for thousands of years: we
never feel we have enough of the good.

576.—JULIANUS, PREFECT OF EGYPT

A. " ARE you dead, Pyrrho?"[2] *B.* "I doubt it."
A. "Even after your final dissolution, do you say you
doubt?" *B.* "I doubt." *A.* "The tomb has put an
end to doubt."

[1] The celebrated ten Attic orators.
[2] The Sceptic philosopher.

GREEK ANTHOLOGY

577.—ΤΟΥ ΑΥΤΟΥ

Ὅστις με τριόδοισι μέσαις τάρχυσε θανόντα,
λυγρὰ παθὼν τύμβου μηδ᾽ ὀλίγοιο τύχοι,
πάντες ἐπεὶ Τίμωνα νέκυν πατέουσιν ὁδῖται,
καὶ μόρος ἄμμι μόνοις ἄμμορος ἡσυχίης.

578.—ΑΓΑΘΙΟΥ ΣΧΟΛΑΣΤΙΚΟΥ

Τὸν κρατερὸν Πανόπηα, τὸν ἀγρευτῆρα λεόντων,
τὸν λασιοστέρνων κέντορα παρδαλίων,
τύμβος ἔχει· γλαφυρῆς γὰρ ἀπὸ χθονὸς ἔκτανε δεινὸς
σκορπίος, οὐτήσας ταρσὸν ὀρεσσιβάτην.
αἰγανέη δὲ τάλαινα σίγυνά τε πὰρ χθονὶ κεῖται,
αἰαῖ, θαρσαλέων παίγνια δορκαλίδων.

579.—ΛΕΟΝΤΙΟΥ ΣΧΟΛΑΣΤΙΚΟΥ

Πέτρου ὁρᾷς ῥητῆρος ἀεὶ γελόωσαν ὀπωπήν,
ἐξόχου εἰν ἀγοραῖς, ἐξόχου ἐν φιλίῃ.
ἐν δὲ Διωνύσου θηεύμενος ὤλετο μοῦνος,
ὑψόθεν ἐκ τέγεος σὺν πλεόνεσσι πεσών,
βαιὸν ἐπιζήσας, ὅσον ἤρκεσε. τοῦτον ἔγωγε
ἄγριον οὐ καλέω, τὸν δὲ φύσει θάνατον.

580.—ΙΟΥΛΙΑΝΟΥ ΑΙΓΥΠΤΙΟΥ

Οὔποτέ με κρύψεις ὑπὸ πυθμένα νείατον αἴης
τόσσον, ὅσον κρύψαι πάνσκοπον ὄμμα Δίκης.

581.—ΤΟΥ ΑΥΤΟΥ

Ἀντὶ φόνου τάφον ἄμμι χαρίζεαι, ἀλλὰ καὶ αὐτὸς
ἴσων ἀντιτύχοις οὐρανόθεν χαρίτων.

---

[1] i.e. long enough to set his affairs in order.

577.—By the Same

May he who buried me at the cross-roads come to
an ill end and get no burial at all; since all the
travellers tread on Timon and in death, the portion
of all, I alone have no portion of repose.

578.—AGATHIAS SCHOLASTICUS

In this tomb rests strong Panopeus the lion-hunter,
the piercer of shaggy-breasted panthers; for a terrible
scorpion issuing from a hole in the earth smote his
heel as he walked on the hills and slew him.
On the ground, alas, lie his poor javelin and spear,
to be the playthings of impudent deer.

579.—LEONTIAS SCHOLASTICUS

Thou seest the ever-smiling face of Peter the
orator, excellent in debate, excellent in friendship.
In the theatre whilst looking at the performance he
fell from the roof with others and was the only one
who died, after surviving a short time, sufficient for
his needs.[1] I call this no violent death, but a natural
one.

580.—JULIANUS, PREFECT OF EGYPT

Never shalt thou hide me even in the very bottom
of the earth in a manner that shall hide the all-
seeing eye of Justice.[2]

581.—By the Same

Thou givest me a tomb in return for murdering me,
but may heaven grant thee in return the same kind-
ness.

[2] This and the following are supposed to be addressed to
his murderers by a man killed by robbers. *cp.* No. 310.

582.—ΤΟΥ ΑΥΤΟΥ

Χαῖρέ μοι, ὦ ναυηγέ, καὶ εἰς Ἀίδαο περήσας
μέμφεο μὴ πόντου κύμασιν, ἀλλ᾿ ἀνέμοις.
κεῖνοι μέν σ᾿ ἐδάμασσαν· ἁλὸς δέ σε μείλιχον ὕδωρ
ἐς χθόνα καὶ πατέρων ἐξεκύλισε τάφους.

583.—ΑΓΑΘΙΟΥ ΣΧΟΛΑΣΤΙΚΟΥ

Ἀβάλε μηδ᾿ ἐγένοντο γάμοι, μὴ νύμφια λέκτρα·
οὐ γὰρ ἂν ὠδίνων ἐξεφάνη πρόφασις.
νῦν δ᾿ ἡ μὲν τριτάλαινα γυνὴ τίκτουσα κάθηται,
γαστρὶ δὲ δυσκόλπῳ νεκρὸν ἔνεστι τέκος·
τρισσὴ δ᾿ ἀμφιλύκη δρόμον ἤνυσεν, ἐξότε μίμνει   5
τὸ βρέφος ἀπρήκτοις ἐλπίσι τικτόμενον.
κούφη σοὶ τελέθει γαστήρ, τέκος, ἀντὶ κονίης·
αὕτη γάρ σε φέρει, καὶ χθονὸς οὐ χατέεις.

584.—ΙΟΥΛΙΑΝΟΥ ΑΙΓΥΠΤΙΟΥ

Πλώεις ναυηγόν με λαβὼν καὶ σήματι χώσας ;
πλῶε, Μαλειάων ἄκρα φυλασσόμενος·
αἰεὶ δ᾿ εὐπλοΐην μεθέποις φίλος· ἢν δέ τι ῥέξῃ
ἄλλο Τύχη, τούτων ἀντιάσαις χαρίτων.

585.—ΤΟΥ ΑΥΤΟΥ

Μύγδων τέρμα βίοιο λαχών, αὐτόστολος ἦλθεν
εἰς ἀίδην, νεκύων πορθμίδος οὐ χατέων.
ἣν γὰρ ἔχε ζώων βιοδώτορα, μάρτυρα μόχθων,
ἄγραις εἰναλίαις πολλάκι βριθομένην,

582.—By THE SAME

HAIL! thou ship-wrecked man, and when thou landest in Hades, blame not the waves of the sea, but the winds. It was they who overcame thee, but the kindly water of the sea cast thee out on the land by the tombs of thy fathers.

583.—AGATHIAS SCHOLASTICUS

O WOULD that marriage and bridal beds had never been, for then there would have been no occasion for child-bed. But now the poor woman sat in labour and in the unhappy recess of her womb lay the dead child. Three days passed and ever the babe remained with unfulfilled hope of its being born. The womb, O babe, instead of the dust rests lightly on thee, for it enwraps thee and thou hast no need of earth.

584.—JULIANUS, PREFECT OF EGYPT

DOST thou travel on the sea, thou who didst take up my ship-wrecked body and bury it in a tomb? Travel, but avoid Cape Malea, and mayst thou ever, my friend, find fair weather. But if Fortune be adverse, mayst thou meet with the same kindness.

585.—By THE SAME

MYGDON, the span of his life finished, went to Hades in his own boat, not requiring the ferry-boat of the dead. For she who was in life his support and the witness of his toil, often loaded with his

τήνδε καὶ ἐν θανάτῳ λάχε σύνδρομον, εὖτε τελευτὴν
εὕρετο συλλήξας ὁλκάδι καιομένη.
οὕτω πιστὸν ἄνακτι πέλεν σκάφος, οἶκον ἀέξον
Μύγδονι, καὶ σύμπλουν ἐς βίον, ἐς θάνατον.

586.—ΤΟΥ ΑΥΤΟΥ

Οὔτι σε πόντος ὄλεσσε καὶ οὐ πνείοντες ἀῆται,
ἀλλ᾽ ἀκόρητος ἔρως φοιτάδος ἐμπορίης.
εἴη μοι γαίης ὀλίγος βίος· ἐκ δὲ θαλάσσης
ἄλλοισιν μελέτω κέρδος ἀελλομάχον.

587.—ΤΟΥ ΑΥΤΟΥ

Εἰς Πάμφιλον φιλόσοφον

Χθών σε τέκεν, πόντος δὲ διώλεσε, δέκτο δὲ θῶκος
Πλουτῆος· κεῖθεν δ᾽ οὐρανὸν εἰσανέβης.
οὐχ ὡς ναυηγὸς δὲ βυθῷ θάνες, ἀλλ᾽ ἵνα πάντων
κλήροις ἀθανάτων, Πάμφιλε, κόσμον ἄγῃς.

588.—ΠΑΥΛΟΥ ΣΙΛΕΝΤΙΑΡΙΟΥ

Δαμόχαρις Μοίρης πυμάτην ὑπεδύσατο σιγήν.
φεῦ· τὸ καλὸν Μούσης βάρβιτον ἠρεμέει·
ὤλετο Γραμματικῆς ἱερὴ βάσις. ἀμφιρύτη Κῶς,
καὶ πάλι πένθος ἔχεις οἶον ἐφ᾽ Ἱπποκράτει.

589.—ΑΓΑΘΙΟΥ ΣΧΟΛΑΣΤΙΚΟΥ

Μηδὲν ἀπαγγείλειας ἐς Ἀντιόχειαν, ὁδῖτα,
μὴ πάλιν οἰμώξῃ χεύματα Κασταλίης,

prey from the sea, was his fellow-traveller in death too, when he came to his end in company with the burning boat; so faithful to her master was she, increasing his substance and travelling with him to life[1] and to death.

586.—By the Same

It was not the sea which was thy end, and the gales, but insatiable love of that commerce which turned thee mad. Give me a little living from the land; let others pursue profit from the sea gained by fighting the storms.

587.—By the Same

On Pamphilus the Philosopher

The earth bore thee, the sea destroyed thee, and Pluto's seat received thee, and thence thou didst ascend to heaven. Thou didst not perish in the deep, Pamphilus, as one shipwrecked, but in order to add an ornament to the domains of all the immortals.

588.—PAULUS SILENTIARIUS

Damocharis passed into the final silence of Fate; alas! the Muses' lovely lyre is silent; the holy foundation of Grammar has perished. Sea-girt Cos, thou art again in mourning as for Hippocrates.

589.—AGATHIAS SCHOLASTICUS

Bear not the message, traveller, to Antioch, lest again the streamlets of Castalia lament, because of a

[1] *i.e.* to get his living. See No. 381 of which this is an imitation.

οὕνεκεν ἐξαπίνης Εὐστόργιος ἔλλιπε μοῦσαν,
  θεσμῶν τ' Αὐσονίων ἐλπίδα μαψιδέην,
ἑβδόματον δέκατόν τε λαχὼν ἔτος· ἐς δὲ κονίην
  ἠμείφθη κενεὴν εὔσταχυς ἡλικίη.
καὶ τὸν μὲν κατέχει χθόνιος τάφος· ἀντὶ δ' ἐκείνου
  οὔνομα καὶ γραφίδων χρώματα δερκόμεθα.

590.—ΙΟΥΛΙΑΝΟΥ ΑΙΓΥΠΤΙΟΥ

α. Κλεινὸς Ἰωάννης. β. Θνητός, λέγε. α. Γαμ-
  βρὸς ἀνάσσης.
β. Θνητὸς ὅμως. α. Γενεῆς ἄνθος Ἀναστασίου.
β. Θνητοῦ κἀκείνου. α. Βίον ἔνδικος. β. Οὐκέτι
  τοῦτο
    θνητὸν ἔφης· ἀρεταὶ κρείσσονές εἰσι μόρου.

591.—ΤΟΥ ΑΥΤΟΥ

Ὑπατίου τάφος εἰμί· νέκυν δ' οὔ φημι καλύπτειν
  τόσσου τόσσος ἐὼν Αὐσονίων προμάχου·
γαῖα γὰρ αἰδομένη λιτῷ μέγαν ἀνέρα χῶσαι
  σήματι, τῷ πόντῳ μᾶλλον ἔδωκεν ἔχειν.

592.—ΤΟΥ ΑΥΤΟΥ

Αὐτὸς ἄναξ νεμέσησε πολυφλοίσβοισι θαλάσσης
  κύμασιν, Ὑπατίου σῶμα καλυψαμένοις·
ἤθελε γάρ μιν ἔχειν γέρας ὕστατον, οἷα θανόντα,
  καὶ μεγαλοφροσύνης κρύψε θάλασσα χάριν.
ἔνθεν, πρηϋνόου κραδίης μέγα δεῖγμα, φαεινὸν
  τίμησεν κενεῷ σήματι τῷδε νέκυν.

---

[1] One of Justinian's generals.
[2] The poet in these epigrams does not mention that Jus-

sudden at the age of seventeen Eustorgius left
the Muse and his unfulfilled hope of learning in
Roman Law, and to empty dust was changed the
bloom of his youth. He lies in the tomb and
instead of him we see his name and the colours of
the brush.

590.—JULIANUS, PREFECT OF EGYPT

A. " FAMOUS was Ioannes." *B.* " Mortal, say."
A. " The son-in-law of an empress." *B.* " Yes, but
mortal." *A.* " The flower of the family of Anas-
tasius." *B.* " And mortal too was he." *A.* " Right-
eous in his life." *B.* " That is no longer mortal.
Virtue is stronger than death."

591.—BY THE SAME

I AM the tomb of Hypatius [1] and I do not say that
I contain in this little space the remains of the great
Roman general. For the earth, ashamed of burying
so great a man in so small a tomb, preferred to give
him to the sea to keep.

592.—BY THE SAME

THE emperor himself was wrath with the roaring
sea for covering the body of Hypatius; for now he
was dead he wished the last honours to be paid to
him, and the sea hid him from the favour of his
magnanimity. Hence, a great proof of the mildness
of his heart, he honoured the distinguished dead
with this cenotaph. [2]

tinian had Hypatius strangled and thrown into the sea as
an indignity ; but perhaps the poems are sarcastic rather
than courtly.

593.—ΑΓΑΘΙΟΥ ΣΧΟΛΑΣΤΙΚΟΥ

Τὰν πάρος ἀνθήσασαν ἐν ἀγλαΐᾳ καὶ ἀοιδᾷ,
τὰν πολυκυδίστου μνάμονα θεσμοσύνας,
Εὐγενίαν κρύπτει χθονία κόνις· αἱ δ' ἐπὶ τύμβῳ
κείραντο πλοκάμους Μοῦσα, Θέμις, Παφίη.

594.—ΙΟΥΛΙΑΝΟΥ ΑΙΓΥΠΤΙΟΥ

Μνῆμα σόν, ὦ Θεόδωρε, πανατρεκές, οὐκ ἐπὶ τύμβῳ,
ἀλλ' ἐνὶ βιβλιακῶν μυριάσιν σελίδων,
αἷσιν ἀνεζώγρησας ἀπολλυμένων, ἀπὸ λήθης
ἁρπάξας, νοερῶν μόχθον ἀοιδοπόλων.

595.—ΤΟΥ ΑΥΤΟΥ

Κάτθανε μὲν Θεόδωρος· ἀοιδοπόλων δὲ παλαιῶν
πληθὺς οἰχομένη νῦν θάνεν ἀτρεκέως.
πᾶσα γὰρ ἐμπνείοντι συνέπνεε, πᾶσα δ' ἀπέσβη
σβεννυμένου· κρύφθη δ' εἰν ἑνὶ πάντα τάφῳ.

596.—ΑΓΑΘΙΟΥ ΣΧΟΛΑΣΤΙΚΟΥ

Ναὶ μὰ τὸν ἐν γαίῃ πύματον δρόμον, οὔτε μ' ἄκοιτις
ἔστυγεν, οὔτ' αὐτὸς Θεύδοτος Εὐγενίης
ἐχθρὸς ἑκὼν γενόμην· ἀλλὰ φθόνος ἠέ τις ἄτη
ἡμέας ἐς τόσσην ἤγαγεν ἀμπλακίην.
νῦν δ' ἐπὶ Μινώην καθαρὴν κρηπῖδα μολόντες
ἀμφότεροι λευκὴν ψῆφον ἐδεξάμεθα.

593.—AGATHIAS SCHOLASTICUS

On Eugenia his Sister

THE earth covers Eugenia who once bloomed in beauty and poesy, who was learned in the revered science of the law. On her tomb the Muse, Themis, and Aphrodite all shore their hair.

594.—JULIANUS, PREFECT OF EGYPT

THY truest monument, Theodorus,[1] is not on thy tomb, but in the many thousand pages of thy books, in which, snatching them from oblivion, thou didst recall to life the labours of thoughtful poets.

595.—BY THE SAME

THEODORUS died, and now the crowd of ancient poets is really dead and gone; for all breathed as long as he breathed, and the light of all is quenched with his; all are hidden in one tomb.

596.—AGATHIAS SCHOLASTICUS

On Theodotus his brother-in-law

NAY! by this our last journey in the earth, neither did my wife hate me nor did I, Theodotus, willingly become Eugenia's enemy; but some envy or fatality led us into that great error. Now, having come to the pure bench of Minos, we were both pronounced not guilty.

---

[1] Seemingly a grammarian.

597.—ΙΟΤΛΙΑΝΟΤ ΑΙΓΤΠΤΙΟΤ

Ἡ γλυκερὸν μέλψασα καὶ ἄλκιμον, ἡ θρόον αὐδῆς
μούνη θηλυτέρης στήθεσι ῥηξαμένη,
κεῖται σιγαλέη· τόσον ἔσθενε νήματα Μοίρης,
ὡς λιγυρὰ κλεῖσαι χείλεα Καλλιόπης.

598.—ΤΟΥ ΑΥΤΟΥ

Οὔτε φύσις θήλεια, καὶ οὐ πολιοῖο καρήνου
ἀδρανίη φωνῆς σῆς κατέλυσε βίην·
ἀλλὰ μόλις ξυνοῖσι νόμοις εἴξασα τελευτῆς,
φεῦ, φεῦ, Καλλιόπη, σὴν κατέλυσας ὄπα.

599.—ΤΟΥ ΑΥΤΟΥ

Οὔνομα μὲν ΚΑΛΗ, φρεσὶ δὲ πλέον ἠὲ προσώπῳ,
κάτθανε· φεῦ, Χαρίτων ἐξαπόλωλεν ἔαρ.
καὶ γὰρ ἔην Παφίη πανομοίιος, ἀλλὰ συνεύνῳ
μούνῳ· τοῖς δ' ἑτέροις Παλλὰς ἐρυμνοτάτη.
τίς λίθος οὐκ ἐγόησεν, ὅτ' ἐξήρπαξεν ἐκείνην   5
εὐρυβίης Ἀίδης ἀνδρὸς ἀπ' ἀγκαλίδων ;

600.—ΤΟΥ ΑΥΤΟΥ

Ὤριος εἶχέ σε παστάς, ἀώριος εἶλέ σε τύμβος,
εὐθαλέων Χαρίτων ἄνθος, Ἀναστασίη.
σοὶ γενέτης, σοὶ πικρὰ πόσις κατὰ δάκρυα λείβει,
σοὶ τάχα καὶ πορθμεὺς δακρυχέει νεκύων·
οὐ γὰρ ὅλον λυκάβαντα διήνυσας ἄγχι συνεύνου,   5
ἀλλ' ἐκκαιδεκέτιν, φεῦ, κατέχει σε τάφος.

320

BOOK VII. EPIGRAMS 597-600

597.—JULIANUS, PREFECT OF EGYPT

Silent she lies, whose voice was sweet and brave, from whose bosom alone of women burst the fulness of song; so strong were the threads of Fate that they closed the tuneful lips of Calliope.

598.—By the Same

Neither the weakness of thy sex, Calliope, nor that of old age, relaxed the strength of thy voice, but yielding with a hard struggle to the common law of death thou didst relax it, alas, alas!

599.—By the Same

She is dead, Kale (Beautiful) by name and more so in mind than in face. Alas! the spring of the Graces has perished utterly. For very like was she to Aphrodite, but only for her lord; for others she was an unassailable Pallas. What stone did not mourn when the strong hand of Hades tore her from her husband's arms.

600.—By the Same

Anastasia, flower of the blooming Graces, the marriage bed received thee in due season and the tomb before thy season. Both thy father and husband shed bitter tears for thee, and perchance even the ferry-man of the dead weeps for thee. For not even a whole year didst thou pass with thy husband, but the tomb holds thee aged alas! but sixteen.

321

GREEK ANTHOLOGY

601.—ΤΟΥ ΑΥΤΟΥ

Φεῦ, φεῦ, ἀμετρήτων χαρίτων ἔαρ ἡδὺ μαραίνει
ἀμφὶ σοὶ ὠμοφάγων χεῖμα τὸ νερτερίων.
καὶ σὲ μὲν ἥρπασε τύμβος ἀπ' ἠελιώτιδος αἴγλης,
πέμπτον ἐφ' ἑνδεκάτῳ πικρὸν ἄγουσαν ἔτος,
σὸν δὲ πόσιν γενέτην τε κακαῖς ἀλάωσεν ἀνίαις,   5
οἷς πλέον ἠελίου λάμπες, Ἀναστασίη.

602.—ΑΓΑΘΙΟΥ ΣΧΟΛΑΣΤΙΚΟΥ

Εὐστάθιε, γλυκερὸν μὲν ἔχεις τύπον· ἀλλά σε κηρὸν
δέρκομαι, οὐδ' ἔτι σοι κεῖνο τὸ λαρὸν ἔπος
ἕζεται ἐν στομάτεσσι· τεῇ δ' εὐάνθεμος ἥβη,
αἰαῖ, μαψιδίη νῦν χθονός ἐστι κόνις.
πέμπτου καὶ δεκάτου γὰρ ἐπιψαύσας ἐνιαυτοῦ   5
τετράκις ἐξ μούνους ἔδρακες ἠελίους·
οὐδὲ τεοῦ πάππου θρόνος ἤρκεσεν, οὐ γενετῆρος
ὄλβος.   πᾶς δὲ τεὴν εἰκόνα δερκόμενος
τὴν ἄδικον Μοῖραν καταμέμφεται, οὕνεκα τοίην,
ἃ μέγα νηλειής, ἔσβεσεν ἀγλαΐην.   10

603.—ΙΟΥΛΙΑΝΟΥ ΑΠΟ ΥΠΑΡΧΩΝ ΑΙΓΥΠΤΙΟΥ

α. Ἄγριός ἐστι Χάρων. β. Πλέον ἤπιος. α. Ἥρ-
πασεν ἤδη
τὸν νέον. β. Ἀλλὰ νόῳ τοῖς πολιοῖσιν ἴσον.
α. Τερπωλῆς δ' ἀπέπαυσεν. β. Ἀπεστυφέλιξε δὲ
μόχθων.
α. Οὐκ ἐνόησε γάμους. β. Οὐδὲ γάμων ὀδύνας.

601.—By the Same

Alas! Alas! the winter of savage Hell nips the spring of thy countless charms; the tomb has torn thee from the light of the sun at the sad age of sixteen years, and has blinded with evil grief thy husband and thy father, for whom, Anastasia, thou didst shine brighter than the sun.

602.—AGATHIAS SCHOLASTICUS

Eustathius, sweet is thy image, but I see thee in wax, and no longer doth that pleasant speech dwell in thy mouth. Alas, thy blooming youth is now futile dust of earth. For after reaching thy fifteenth year thou didst look only on twenty-four suns. Neither thy grandfather's high office helped thee, nor the riches of thy father. All who look on thy image blame unjust Fate, ah! so merciless, for quenching the light of such beauty.

603.—JULIANUS, PREFECT OF EGYPT

A. "Charon is savage." *B.* "Kind rather." *A.* "He carried off the young man so soon." *B.* "But in mind he was the equal of greybeards." *A.* "He cut him off from pleasure." *B.* "But he thrust him out of the way of trouble." *A.* "He knew not wedlock." *B.* "Nor the pains of wedlock."

604.—ΠΑΥΛΟΥ ΣΙΛΕΝΤΙΑΡΙΟΥ

Λέκτρα σοι ἀντὶ γάμων ἐπιτύμβια, παρθένε κούρη,
ἐστόρεσαν παλάμαις πενθαλέαις γενέται.
καὶ σὺ μὲν ἀμπλακίας βιότου καὶ μόχθον Ἐλευθοῦς
ἔκφυγες· οἱ δὲ γόων πικρὸν ἔχουσι νέφος.
δωδεκέτιν γὰρ μοῖρα, Μακηδονίη, σε καλύπτει,   5
κάλλεσιν ὁπλοτέρην, ἤθεσι γηραλέην.

605.—ΙΟΥΛΙΑΝΟΥ ΑΠΟ ΥΠΑΡΧΩΝ
ΑΙΓΥΠΤΙΟΥ

Σοὶ σορὸν εὐλάϊγγα, Ῥοδοῖ, καὶ τύμβον ἐγείρει,
ῥύσιά τε ψυχῆς δῶρα πένησι νέμει,
ἀντ᾽ εὐεργεσίης γλυκερὸς πόσις· ὅττι θανοῦσα
ὠκύμορος κείνῳ δῶκας ἐλευθερίην.

606.—ΠΑΥΛΟΥ ΣΙΛΕΝΤΙΑΡΙΟΥ

Πρηΰς, ἐλευθερίην ἐπιειμένος, ἡδὺς ἰδέσθαι,
ἐν βιότῳ προλιπὼν υἱέα γηροκόμον,
τύμβον ἔχει Θεόδωρος ἐπ᾽ ἐλπίδι κρέσσονι μοίρης,
ὄλβιος ἐν καμάτοις, ὄλβιος ἐν θανάτῳ.

607.—ΠΑΛΛΑΔΑ ΑΛΕΞΑΝΔΡΕΩΣ

Ψυλλὼ πρεσβυγενὴς τοῖς κληρονόμοις φθονέσασα,
αὐτὴ κληρονόμος τῶν ἰδίων γέγονεν·
ἁλλομένη δὲ τάχος κατέβη δόμον εἰς Ἀΐδαο,
ταῖς δαπάναις τὸ ζῆν σύμμετρον εὑρομένη.
πάντα φαγοῦσα βίον συναπώλετο ταῖς δαπάναισιν·
ἥλατο δ᾽ εἰς ἀΐδην, ὡς ἀπεκερμάτισεν.

604.—PAULUS SILENTIARIUS

MAIDEN, thy parents with sorrowing hands made thy funeral, not thy wedding bed. The errors of life and the labour of childbed thou hast escaped, but a bitter cloud of mourning sits on them. For Fate hath hidden thee, Macedonia, aged but twelve, young in beauty, old in behaviour.

605.—JULIANUS, PREFECT OF EGYPT

YOUR sweet husband, Rhodo, builds a sarcophagus of fine marble and a tomb for you and gives alms to the poor to redeem your soul, in return for your kindness in dying early and giving him freedom.

606.—PAULUS SILENTIARIUS

GENTLE, clothed in freedom, sweet of aspect, leaving alive a son who tended his old age, Theodorus rests here in hope of better things than death, happy in his labour and happy in his death.

607.—PALLADAS OF ALEXANDRIA

OLD Psyllo, grudging her heirs, made herself her own heir and with a quick leap went down to the house of Hades, contriving to end her life and her outlay at the same time. Having eaten up all her fortune, she perished together with her spending power, and jumped to Hades when her last penny was gone.

608.—ΕΥΤΟΛΜΙΟΥ ΣΧΟΛΑΣΤΙΚΟΥ
ΙΛΛΟΥΣΤΡΙΟΥ

Υίέος ὠκυμόρου θάνατον πενθοῦσα Μενίππη
κωκυτῷ μεγάλῳ πνεῦμα συνεξέχεεν,
οὐδ᾽ ἔσχεν παλίνορσον ἀναπνεύσασα γοῆσαι·
ἀλλ᾽ ἅμα καὶ θρήνου παύσατο καὶ βιότου.

609.—ΠΑΥΛΟΥ ΣΙΛΕΝΤΙΑΡΙΟΥ

Ἀττικὸς ἐς ξυνήν με παναγρέος ἐλπίδα μοίρης
θυμῷ θαρσαλέῳ ζῶν ἐλάχηνε τάφον,
παίζων ἐξ ἀρετῆς θανάτου φόβον. ἀλλ᾽ ἐπὶ δηρὸν
ἠέλιος σοφίης μιμνέτω ἠελίῳ.

610.—ΠΑΛΛΑΔΑ ΑΛΕΞΑΝΔΡΙΟΥ

Ἥρπασέ τις νύμφην, καὶ τὸν γάμον ἥρπασε δαίμων,
ψυχῶν συλήσας τερπομένην ἀγέλην.
εἰς γάμος εἰκοσιπέντε τάφους ἔπλησε θανόντων.
πάνδημος δὲ νεκρῶν εἷς γέγονεν θάλαμος.
νύμφη Πενθεσίλεια πολύστονε, νυμφίε Πενθεῦ,
ἀμφοτέρων ὁ γάμος πλούσιος ἐν θανάτοις.

611.—ΕΥΤΟΛΜΙΟΥ ΣΧΟΛΑΣΤΙΚΟΥ
ΙΛΛΟΥΣΤΡΙΟΥ

Παρθενικὴν Ἑλένην μετ᾽ ἀδελφεὸν ἄρτι θανόντα
δειλαίη μήτηρ κόψατο διπλασίως.
μνηστῆρες δ᾽ ἐγόησαν ἴσον γόον· ἦν γὰρ ἑκάστῳ
θρηνεῖν τὴν μήπω μηδενὸς ὡς ἰδίην.

326

608.—EUTOLMIUS SCHOLASTICUS, ILLUSTRIS

MENIPPE, mourning the early death of her son, sent forth her spirit together with her loud dirge, nor could she recover it to utter another wail, but at the same moment ceased from lament and from life.

609.—PAULUS SILENTIARIUS

ATTICUS with a bold heart dug me this tomb in his life-time, in anticipation of the common fate that overtakes all men, mocking the fear of death owing to his virtue. But long may the sun of wisdom remain beneath the sun.

610.—PALLADAS OF ALEXANDRIA

ONE carried off a bride and Fate carried off the wedding party, despoiling of life the merry company. One wedding sent four and twenty corpses to their graves, and one chamber became their common mortuary. Penthesilea,[1] unhappy bride, Pentheus[1] bridegroom of sorrow, rich in deaths was your marriage!

611.—EUTOLMIUS SCHOLASTICUS, ILLUSTRIS

IN double grief her wretched mother bewailed maiden Helen dead just after her brother. Her suitors too lamented her equally, for each could mourn for her as his own who was yet no one's.

[1] Both names derived from *penthos*, "mourning," and of course fictitious.

612.—ΑΓΑΘΙΟΥ ΣΧΟΛΑΣΤΙΚΟΥ

Φεῦ, φεῦ, τὴν δεκάτην Ἑλικωνίδα, τὴν λυραοιδὸν
  Ῥώμης καὶ Φαρίης, ἥδε κέκευθε κόνις.
ὤλετο φορμίγγων τερετίσματα, λῆξαν ἀοιδαί,
  ὥσπερ Ἰωάννῃ πάντα συνολλύμενα.
καὶ τάχα θεσμὸν ἔθηκαν ἐπάξιον ἐννέα Μοῦσαι,   5
  τύμβον Ἰωάννης ἀνθ᾽ Ἑλικῶνος ἔχειν.

613.—ΔΙΟΓΕΝΟΥΣ ΕΠΙΣΚΟΠΟΥ ΑΜΙΣΟΥ

Ἐπὶ Διογένει ἀδελφόπαιδι

Σοὶ τόδε, Διόγενες, θαλερῆς μνημήιον ἥβης
  Πόντῳ ἐν Εὐξείνῳ θήκατο Φρὺξ γενέτης,
φεῦ, πάτρης ἑκὰς ὅσσον. ἄγεν δέ σε νεῦμα θεοῖο,
  πατρὸς ἀδελφειῷ πένθος ὀφειλόμενον,
ὅς σε περιστείλας ἱερῇ παλάμῃ τε καὶ εὐχῇ   5
  γείτονα τῆς μακάρων θῆκε χοροστασίης.

614.—ΑΓΑΘΙΟΥ ΣΧΟΛΑΣΤΙΚΟΥ

Ἑλλανὶς τριμάκαιρα καὶ ἁ χαρίεσσα Λάμαξις
  ἤστην μὲν πάτρας φέγγεα Λεσβιάδος·
ὅκκα δ᾽ Ἀθηναίῃσι σὺν ὁλκάσιν ἐνθάδε κέλσας
  τὰν Μυτιληναίων γᾶν ἀλάπαξε Πάχης,
τὰν κουρᾶν ἀδίκως ἠράσσατο, τὼς δὲ συνεύνως   5
  ἔκτανεν, <ὡς> τήνας τῇδε βιησόμενος.
ταὶ δὲ κατ᾽ Αἰγαίοιο ῥόου πλατὺ λαῖτμα φερέσθην,
  καὶ ποτὶ τὰν κραναὰν Μοψοπίαν δραμέτην·
δάμῳ δ᾽ ἀγγελέτην ἀλιτήμονος ἔργα Πάχητος,
  μέσφα μιν εἰς ὀλοὴν κῆρα συνηλασάτην.   10

328

612.—AGATHIAS SCHOLASTICUS

ALAS! alas! this earth covers the tenth Muse, the lyric chanter of Rome and Alexandria. They have perished, the notes of the lyre; song hath perished as if dying together with Joanna. Perchance the nine Muses have imposed on themselves a law worthy of them—to dwell in Joanna's tomb instead of on Helicon.

613.—DIOGENES, BISHOP OF AMISUS

On his nephew Diogenes

THIS monument of thy radiant youth, Diogenes, did thy Phrygian father erect to thee on the Euxine Sea—alas! how far from thy home. The decree of God brought thee here to die, a sorrow fore-doomed for me, thy father's brother, who having laid thee out with my consecrated hand and with prayer, put thee to rest here beside the dancing-place of the blest.[1]

614.—AGATHIAS SCHOLASTICUS

THRICE blessed Hellanis and lovely Lamaxis were the stars of their Lesbian home; and when Paches, sailing here with the Athenian ships, ravaged the territory of Mytilene, he conceived a guilty passion for the young matrons and killed their husbands, thinking thus to force them. They, taking ship across the wide Aegean main, hurried to steep Mopsopia[2] and complained to the people of the actions of wicked Paches, until they drove him to an evil

[1] *i.e.* the church.   [2] Athens.

τοῖα μέν, ὦ κούρα, πεπονήκατον· ἂψ δ' ἐπὶ πάτραν
ἤκετον, ἐν δ' αὐτᾷ κεῖσθον ἀποφθιμένα·
εὖ δὲ πόνων ἀπόνασθον, ἐπεὶ ποτὶ σᾶμα συνεύνων
εὕδετον, ἐς κλεινᾶς μνᾶμα σαοφροσύνας·
ὑμνεῦσιν δ' ἔτι πάντες ὁμόφρονας ἡρωΐνας,   15
πάτρας καὶ ποσίων πήματα τισαμένας.

615.—ΑΔΕΣΠΟΤΟΝ

Εὐμόλπου φίλον υἱὸν ἔχει τὸ Φαληρικὸν οὖδας
Μουσαῖον, φθίμενον σῶμ' ὑπὸ τῷδε τάφῳ.

616.—ΑΛΛΟ

Ὧδε Λίνον Θηβαῖον ἐδέξατο γαῖα θανόντα,
Μούσης Οὐρανίης υἱὸν ἐϋστεφάνου.

617.—ΑΛΛΟ

Θρήϊκα χρυσολύρην τῇδ' Ὀρφέα Μοῦσαι ἔθαψαν,
ὃν κτάνεν ὑψιμέδων Ζεὺς ψολόεντι βέλει.

618.—ΑΛΛΟ

Ἄνδρα σοφὸν Κλεόβουλον ἀποφθίμενον καταπενθεῖ
ἥδε πάτρα Λίνδος πόντῳ ἀγαλλομένη.

619.—ΑΛΛΟ

Πλούτου καὶ σοφίης πρύτανιν πατρὶς ἥδε Κόρινθος
κόλποις ἀγχίαλος γῆ Περίανδρον ἔχει.

doom. This, ladies, ye accomplished, and returning to your country lie in it dead. And a good guerdon ye have for your pains, since ye sleep hard by your husbands, a monument of glorious virtue, and all still sing the praises of the heroines, one in heart, who avenged the sufferings of their country and of their lords.[1]

615.—Anonymous

THE earth of Phaleron holds Musaeus, Eumolpus' dear son, dead under this tomb

616.—Anonymous

HERE the earth received at his death Linus of Thebes, son of the fair-wreathed Muse Urania.

617.—Anonymous

HERE the Muses buried Thracian Orpheus of the golden lyre, whom Zeus, who reigneth on high, slew with his smoking bolt.

618.—Anonymous

THIS, his country Lindos, that glories in the sea, mourns wise Cleobulus dead.

619.—Anonymous

THIS, his country Corinth, that lies near the sea, holds in her bosom Periander, supreme in wealth and wisdom.

[1] This incident, like that in No. 492, is probably derived from a romance.

620.—ΔΙΟΓΕΝΟΤΣ ΛΑΕΡΤΙΟΤ

Μήποτε λυπήσῃ σε τὸ μή σε τυχεῖν τινος, ἀλλὰ
  τέρπεο πᾶσιν ὁμῶς οἷσι δίδωσι θεύς·
καὶ γὰρ ἀθυμήσας ὁ σοφὸς Περίανδρος ἀπέσβη,
  οὕνεκεν οὐκ ἔτυχεν πρήξιος ἧς ἔθελεν.

621.—ΑΔΕΣΠΟΤΟΝ

Ἐνθάδ' ἐγὼ Σοφοκλῆς στυγερὸν δόμον Ἄιδος ἔσβην
  κάμμορος, εἴδατι Σαρδῴῳ σελίνοιο γελάσκων.
ὣς μὲν ἐγών, ἕτεροι δ' ἄλλως· πάντες δέ τε πάντως.

622.—ΑΝΤΙΦΙΛΟΤ ΒΤΖΑΝΤΙΟΤ

Βόρχος ὁ βουποίμην ὅτ' ἐπὶ γλυκὺ κηρίον εἷρπεν,
  αἰγίλιπα σχοίνῳ πέτρον ἐπερχόμενος,
εἵπετό οἱ σκυλάκων τις ὁ καὶ βοσίν, ὃς φάγε λεπτὴν
  σχοῖνον ἀνελκομένῳ χραινομένην μέλιτι·
κάππεσε δ' εἰς Ἀίδαο· τὸ δ' ἀτρυγὲς ἀνδράσιν ἄλλοις
  κεῖνο μέλι ψυχῆς ὤνιον εἰρύσατο.

623.—ΑΙΜΙΛΙΑΝΟΤ

Ἕλκε, τάλαν, παρὰ μητρὸς ὃν οὐκέτι μαστὸν ἀμέλξεις,
  ἕλκυσον ὑστάτιον νᾶμα καταφθιμένης·
ἤδη γὰρ ξιφέεσσι λιπόπνοος· ἀλλὰ τὰ μητρὸς
  φίλτρα καὶ εἰν ἀίδῃ παιδοκομεῖν ἔμαθεν.

---

[1] This poisonous herb contracted the muscles, so as to give
the appearance of grinning. We do not know who this
Sophocles was.

620.—DIOGENES LAERTIUS

NEVER be vexed at not getting anything, but rejoice in all the gifts of God. For wise Periander died of disappointment at not attaining the thing he wished.

621.—ANONYMOUS

HERE I, unhappy Sophocles, entered the house of Hades, laughing, because I ate Sardinian celery.[1] So perished I, and others otherwise, but all in some way or other.

622.—ANTIPHILUS OF BYZANTIUM

WHEN Borchus the neat-herd went to get the sweet honey-comb, climbing the steep rock by a rope, one of his dogs who used to follow the herd followed him, and, as he was pulling himself up, bit through the thin rope which was trickling with honey. He fell into Hades, grasping, at the cost of his life, that honey which no other man could harvest.

623.—AEMILIANUS

SUCK, poor child, at the breast whereat thy mother will never more suckle thee; drain the last drops from the dead. She hath already rendered up her spirit, pierced by the sword, but a mother's love can cherish her child even in death.[2]

---

[1] This probably refers to a picture by Aristides of Thebes.

624.—ΔΙΟΔΩΡΟΥ

Ἔρροις, Ἰονίοιο πολυπτοίητε θάλασσα,
νηλής, Ἀΐδεω πορθμὲ κελαινοτάτου,
ἢ τόσσους κατέδεξο. τίς ἂν τεά, κάμμορε, λέξαι
αἴσυλα, δυστήνων αἶσαν ὀπιζόμενος;
Αἰγέα καὶ Λαβέωνα σὺν ὠκυμόροισιν ἑταίροις
νηΐ τε σὺν πάσῃ βρύξας ἁλιρροθίῃ.

625.—ΑΝΤΙΠΑΤΡΟΥ ΣΙΔΩΝΙΟΥ

Εἰδότα κἠπ' Ἄτλαντα τεμεῖν πόρον, εἰδότα Κρήτης
κύματα καὶ πόντου ναυτιλίην μέλανος,
Καλλιγένευς Διόδωρον Ὀλύνθιον ἴσθι θανόντα
ἐν λιμένι, πρῴρης νύκτερον ἐκχύμενον,
δαιτὸς ἐκεῖ τὸ περισσὸν ὅτ' ἤμεεν. ἆ πόσον ὕδωρ
ὤλεσε τὸν τόσσῳ κεκριμένον πελάγει.

626.—ΑΔΕΣΠΟΤΟΝ

Ἐσχατιαὶ Λιβύων Νασαμωνίδες, οὐκέτι θηρῶν
ἔθνεσιν ἠπείρου νῶτα βαρυνόμεναι,
ἠχοῖ ἐρημαίαισιν ἐπηπύσεσθε λεόντων
ὠρυγαῖς ψαμάθους ἄχρις ὑπὲρ Νομάδων,
φῦλον ἐπεὶ νήριθμον ἐν ἰχνοπέδαισιν ἀγρευθὲν
ἐς μίαν αἰχμηταῖς Καῖσαρ ἔθηκεν ὁ παῖς·
αἱ δὲ πρὶν ἀγραύλων ἐγκοιτάδες ἀκρώρειαι
θηρῶν, νῦν ἀνδρῶν εἰσὶ βοηλασίαι.

Not the Euxine, but a part of the Thracian Sea.

624.—DIODORUS

Out on thee, dreaded Ionian Sea, pitiless water, ferrier of men to blackest Hades, thou who hast engulfed so many. Who, with the fate of the unfortunates before his eyes, shall tell all thy crimes, ill-starred sea ? Thou hast swallowed in thy surges Aegeus and Labeo, with their short-lived companions and their whole ship.

625.—ANTIPATER OF SIDON

Know that Diodorus, the son of Calligenes of Olynthus, who could make his way even as far as Atlas, and knew the Cretan waters and the navigation of the Black Sea,[1] died in port, falling off the prow at night, while he was spewing out the excess of the feast. Ah, how small a bit of water was fatal to him who had been proved in so vast an expanse of ocean !

626.—Anonymous

(*Not Sepulchral*)

Ye furthest Nasamonian wilds of Libya, no longer, your expanse vexed by the hordes of wild beasts of the continent, shall ye ring in echo, even beyond the sands of the Nomads, to the voice of lions roaring in the desert, since Caesar the son has trapped the countless tribe and brought it face to face with his fighters.[2] Now the heights once full of the lairs of prowling beasts are pasturage for the cattle of men.

[1] *i.e.* the *bestiarii* in the circus.

627.—ΔΙΟΔΩΡΟΥ

Ἡμιτελῆ θάλαμόν τε καὶ ἐγγύθι νυμφικὰ λέκτρα,
  κοῦρε, λιπὼν ὁλοὴν οἶμον ἔβης Ἀΐδου·
Θύνιον Ἀστακίην δὲ μάλ' ἤκαχες, ἤ σε μάλιστα
  οἰκτρὰ τὸν ἡβητὴν κώκυεν ἤθεον,
Ἱππάρχου κλαίουσα κακὸν μόρον, εἴκοσι ποίας   5
  μοῦνον ἐπεὶ βιότου πλήσαο καὶ πίσυρας.

628.—ΚΡΙΝΑΓΟΡΟΥ

Ἠρνήσαντο καὶ ἄλλαι ἐὸν πάρος οὔνομα νῆσοι
  ἀκλεές, ἐς δ' ἀνδρῶν ἦλθον ὁμωνυμίην·
κληθείητε καὶ ὕμμες Ἐρωτίδες· οὐ νέμεσίς τοι,
  Ὀξεῖαι, ταύτην κλῆσιν ἀμειψαμέναις.
παιδὶ γάρ, ὃν τύμβῳ Δίης ὑπεθήκατο βώλου,   5
  οὔνομα καὶ μορφὴν αὐτὸς ἔδωκεν Ἔρως.
ὦ χθὼν σηματόεσσα, καὶ ἡ παρὰ θινὶ θάλασσα,
  παιδὶ σὺ μὲν κούφη κεῖσο, σὺ δ' ἡσυχίη.

629.—ΑΝΤΙΠΑΤΡΟΥ

Ἡ χθαμαλὴν ὑπέδυς ὁ τόσος κόνιν; εἰς σέ τις ἀθρῶν,
  Σώκρατες, Ἑλλήνων μέμψεται ἀκρισίην·
νηλέες, οἳ τὸν ἄριστον ἀπώλεσαν, οὐδὲ ἐν αἰδοῖ
  δόντες. τοιοῦτοι πολλάκι Κεκροπίδαι.

630.—ΑΝΤΙΦΙΛΟΥ ΒΥΖΑΝΤΙΟΥ

Ἤδη που πάτρης πελάσας σχεδόν, " Αὔριον," εἶπον,
  " ἡ μακρὴ κατ' ἐμοῦ δυσπλοΐη κοπάσει."
οὔπω χεῖλος ἔμυσε, καὶ ἦν ἴσος Ἅιδι πόντος,
  καί με κατέτρυχεν κεῖνο τὸ κοῦφον ἔπος.
πάντα λόγον πεφύλαξο τὸν αὔριον· οὐδὲ τὰ μικρὰ   5
  λήθει τὴν γλώσσης ἀντίπαλον Νέμεσιν.

336

BOOK VII. EPIGRAMS 627–630

627.—DIODORUS

LEAVING thy bridal-chamber half prepared, thy wedding close at hand, thou hast gone, young man, down the baneful road of Hades; and sorely hast thou afflicted Thynion of Astacus, who most piteously of all lamented for thee, dead in thy prime, weeping for the evil fate of her Hipparchus, seeing thou didst complete but twenty-four years.

628.—CRINAGORAS

OTHER islands ere this have rejected their inglorious names and named themselves after men. Be called Erotides (Love islands), ye Oxeiai (Sharp islands); it is no shame for you to change; for Eros himself gave both his name and his beauty to the boy whom Dies laid here beneath a heap of clods. O earth, crowded with tombs, and sea that washest on the shore, do thou lie light on the boy, and thou lie hushed for his sake.

629.—ANTIPATER OF THESSALONICA

DOST thou who art so great rest in so shallow a soil? He who looks at thee, Socrates, must blame the unwisdom of the Greeks. Merciless judges! who slew the best of men, nor shamed them one jot. Such often are the Athenians.

630.—ANTIPHILUS OF BYZANTIUM

Now nearing my country I said, "To-morrow shall this wind that blew so long against me abate." Scarce had I closed my lips when the sea became like hell, and that light word I spoke was my destruction. Beware ever of that word "to-morrow"; not even little things are unnoticed by the Nemesis that is the foe of our tongues.

631.—ΑΠΟΛΛΩΝΙΔΟΥ

Ἦν ἄρα Μιλήτου Φοιβήϊον <ὅρμον> ἵκησθε,
  λέξατε Διογένει πένθιμον ἀγγελίην,
παῖς ὅτι οἱ ναυηγὸς ὑπὸ χθονὶ κεύθεται Ἄνδρου
  Δίφιλος, Αἰγαίου κῦμα πιὼν πελάγευς.

632.—ΔΙΟΔΩΡΟΥ

Κλίμακος ἐξ ὀλίγης ὀλίγον βρέφος ἐν Διοδώρου
  κάππεσεν, ἐκ δ᾽ ἐάγη καίριον ἀστράγαλον,
δινηθεὶς προκάρηνος. ἐπεὶ δ᾽ ἴδε θεῖον ἄνακτα
  ἀντόμενον, παιδνὰς αὐτίκ᾽ ἔτεινε χέρας.
ἀλλὰ σὺ νηπιάχου δμωός, κόνι, μήποτε βρίθειν   5
  ὀστέα, τοῦ διετοῦς φειδομένη Κόρακος.

633.—ΚΡΙΝΑΓΟΡΟΥ

Καὶ αὐτὴ ἤχλυσεν ἀκρέσπερος ἀντέλλουσα
  μήνη, πένθος ἑὸν νυκτὶ καλυψαμένη,
οὕνεκα τὴν χαρίεσσαν ὁμώνυμον εἶδε Σελήνην
  ἄπνουν εἰς ζοφερὸν δυομένην ἀΐδην.
κείνη γὰρ καὶ κάλλος ἑοῦ κοινώσατο φωτός,   5
  καὶ θάνατον κείνης μίξεν ἑῷ κνέφεϊ.

634.—ΑΝΤΙΦΙΛΟΥ ΒΥΖΑΝΤΙΟΥ

Νεκροδόκον κλιντῆρα Φίλων ὁ πρέσβυς ἀείρων
  ἐγκλιδόν, ὄφρα λάβοι μισθὸν ἐφημέριον,
σφάλματος ἐξ ὀλίγοιο πεσὼν θάνεν· ἦν γὰρ ἕτοιμος
  εἰς ἀΐδην, ἐκάλει δ᾽ ἡ πολιὴ πρόφασιν·
ὃν δ᾽ ἄλλοις ἐφόρει νεκυοστόλον, αὐτὸς ἐφ᾽ αὑτῷ   5
  ἀσκάντην ὁ γέρων ἀχθοφορῶν ἔλαθεν.

338

631.—APOLLONIDES

IF thou comest to Apollo's harbour at Miletus, give to Diogenes the mournful message that his shipwrecked son Diphilus lies in Andrian earth, having drunk the water of the Aegean Sea.

632.—DIODORUS

A LITTLE child in Diodorus' house fell from a little ladder, but falling head first broke the vertebra of its neck, to break which is fatal. But when it saw its revered master running up, it at once stretched out its baby arms to him. Earth, never lie heavy on the bones of the little slave child, but be kind to two-year-old Corax.

633.—CRINAGORAS

THE moon herself, rising at early eve, dimmed her light, veiling her mourning in night, because she saw her namesake, pretty Selene, going down dead to murky Hades. On her she had bestowed the beauty of her light, and with her death she mingled her own darkness.

634.—ANTIPHILUS

OLD Philo, stooping to lift the bier to gain his daily wage, stumbled slightly, but fell and was killed; for he was ripe for Hades, and old age was on the look out for an opportunity; and so all unawares he lifted for himself that bier on which he used to carry the corpses of others.

635.—ΤΟΥ ΑΥΤΟΥ

Ναῦν Ἱεροκλείδης ἔσχεν σύγγηρον, ὁμόπλουν,
    τὴν αὐτὴν ζωῆς καὶ θανάτου σύνοδον,
πιστὴν ἰχθυβολεῦντι συνέμπορον· οὔτις ἐκείνης
    πώποτ᾽ ἐπέπλωσεν κῦμα δικαιοτέρη·
γήραος ἄχρις ἔβοσκε πονευμένη· εἶτα θανόντα   5
    ἐκτέρισεν· συνέπλω δ᾽ ἄχρι καὶ Ἀΐδεω.

636.—ΚΡΙΝΑΓΟΡΟΥ

Ποιμὴν ὦ μάκαρ, εἴθε κατ᾽ οὔρεος ἐπροβάτευον
    κἠγώ, ποιηρὸν τοῦτ᾽ ἀνὰ λευκόλοφον,
κριοῖς ἀγητῆρσι ποτ᾽ ἐβληχημένα βάζων,
    ἢ πικρῇ βάψαι νήοχα πηδάλια
ἅλμῃ. τοιγὰρ ἔδυν ὑποβένθιος· ἀμφὶ δὲ ταύτην   5
    θῖνά με ῥοιβδήσας Εὖρος ἐφωρμίσατο.

637.—ΑΝΤΙΠΑΤΡΟΥ

Πύρρος ὁ μουνερέτης ὀλίγῃ νηῒ λεπτὰ ματεύων
    φυκία καὶ τριχίνης μαινίδας ἐκ καθέτης,
ἠιόνων ἀποτῆλε τυπεὶς κατέδουπε κεραυνῷ·
    νηῦς δὲ πρὸς αἰγιαλοὺς ἔδραμεν αὐτομάτη
ἀγγελίην θείῳ καὶ λιγνύϊ μηνύουσα,
    καὶ φράσαι Ἀργῴην οὐκ ἐπόθησε τρόπιν.

638.—ΚΡΙΝΑΓΟΡΟΥ

Παίδων ἀλλαχθέντι μόρῳ ἔπι τοῦτ᾽ ἐλεεινὴ
    μήτηρ ἀμφοτέρους εἶπε περισχομένη·
" Καὶ νέκυν οὐ σέο, τέκνον, ἐπ᾽ ἤματι τῷδε γοήσειν
    ἤλπισα, καὶ ζωοῖς οὐ σὲ μετεσσόμενον
ὄψεσθαι· νῦν δ᾽ οἱ μὲν ἐς ὑμέας ἠμείφθησαν
    δαίμονες, ἄψευστον δ᾽ ἵκετο πένθος ἐμοί."

635.—By the Same

HIEROCLES' boat grew old with him, always travelled with him, and accompanied him in life and in death. It was his faithful fishing partner, and no juster boat ever sailed the waves. It laboured to keep him until his old age, and then it buried him when he was dead, and travelled with him to Hades.[1]

636.—CRINAGORAS

O HAPPY shepherd, would that I, too, had led my sheep down this grassy white knoll, answering the bleatings of the rams that lead the flock, rather than dipped in the bitter brine the rudder to guide my ship. Therefore I sunk to the depths, and the whistling east wind brought me to rest on this beach.

637.—ANTIPATER OF THESSALONICA

PYRRHUS the solitary oarsman, fishing with his hair-line for small hakes and sprats from his little boat, fell, struck by a thunderbolt, far away from the shore. The boat came ashore of itself, bearing the message by sulphur and smoke, and had no need of a speaking keel like that of Argo.

638.—CRINAGORAS

THE poor mother, when the expected fate of her two sons was reversed, spoke thus, clasping both of them : "Neither did I hope, my child, to weep for thee to-day, nor, my child, to see thee yet among the living. Now your fates have been interchanged, but sorrow undeniable has come to me."

[1] *cp.* Nos. 305, 381, 585, above.

639.—ΑΝΤΙΠΑΤΡΟΥ

Πᾶσα θάλασσα θάλασσα· τί Κυκλάδας ἢ στενὸν
  Ἕλλης
  κῦμα καὶ Ὀξείας ἠλεὰ μεμφόμεθα;
ἄλλως τοὔνομ᾽ ἔχουσιν· ἐπεὶ τί με, τὸν προφυγόντα
  κεῖνα, Σκαρφαιεὺς ἀμφεκάλυψε λιμήν;
νόστιμον εὐπλοΐην ἀρῷτό τις· ὡς τά γε πόντου   5
  πόντος, ὁ τυμβευθεὶς οἶδεν Ἀρισταγόρης.

640.—ΤΟΥ ΑΥΤΟΥ

Ῥιγηλὴ ναύταις ἐρίφων δύσις, ἀλλὰ Πύρωνι
  πουλὺ γαληναίη χείματος ἐχθροτέρη·
νῆα γὰρ ἀπνοΐῃ πεπεδημένου ἔφθασε ναύταις
  ληϊστέων ταχινὴ δίκροτος ἐσσυμένη·
χεῖμα δέ μιν προφυγόντα γαληναίῳ ἐπ᾽ ὀλέθρῳ   5
  ἔκτανον· ἃ λυγρῆς δειλὲ καχορμισίης.

641.—ΑΝΤΙΦΙΛΟΥ

Σῆμα δυωδεκάμοιρον ἀφεγγέος ἠελίοιο,
  τοσσάκις ἀγλώσσῳ φθεγγόμενον στόματι,
εὖτ᾽ ἂν θλιβομένοιο ποτὶ στενὸν ὕδατος ἀὴρ
  αὐλὸν ἀποστείλῃ πνεῦμα διωλύγιον,
θῆκεν Ἀθήναιος δήμῳ χάριν, ὡς ἂν ἐναργὴς   5
  εἴη κἢν φθονεραῖς ἠέλιος νεφέλαις.

642.—ΑΠΟΛΛΩΝΙΔΟΥ

Σύρου καὶ Δήλοιο κλύδων μέσος υἷα Μενοίτην
  σὺν φόρτῳ Σαμίου κρύψε Διαφανέος,
εἰς ὅσιον σπεύδοντα πλόου τάχος· ἀλλὰ θάλασσα
  ἐχθρὴ καὶ νούσῳ πατρὸς ἐπειγομένοις.

342

639.—ANTIPATER OF THESSALONICA

Every sea is sea. Why do we foolishly blame the Cyclades, or the Hellespont, and the Sharp Isles?[1] They merit not their evil fame; for why, when I had escaped them, did the harbour of Scarphaea[2] drown me? Let who will pray for fair weather to bring him home; Aristagoras, who is buried here, knows that the sea is the sea.

640.—By the Same

Fearsome for sailors is the setting of the Kids, but for Pyro calm was far more adverse than storm. For his ship, stayed by calm, was overtaken by a swift double-oared pirate galley. He was slain by them, having escaped the storm but to perish in the calm. Alas, in what an evil harbour ended his voyage!

641.—ANTIPHILUS

(Not Sepulchral, but on a Water-clock)

This recorder of the invisible sun, divided into twelve parts, and as often speaking with tongueless mouth, each time that, the water being compressed in the narrow pipe, the air sends forth a sonorous blast, was erected by Athenaeus for the public, so that the sun might be visible even when covered by envious clouds.

642.—APOLLONIDES

Between Syrus and Delos the waves engulfed Menoetes of Samos, son of Diaphanes, together with his cargo. For a pious purpose was he hurrying home, but the sea is the enemy even of those who are hastening to be with their fathers in sickness.

[1] See No. 628.   [2] A harbour of Locris.   343

643.—ΚΡΙΝΑΓΟΡΟΥ

Ὑμνίδα τὴν Εὐάνδρου, ἐράσμιον αἰὲν ἄθυρμα
  οἰκογενές, κούρην αἱμύλον εἰναέτιν,
ἥρπασας, ὦ ἄλλιστ' Ἀΐδη, τί πρόωρον ἐφίεις
  μοῖραν τῇ πάντως σεῖό ποτ' ἐσσομένῃ;

644.—ΒΙΑΝΟΡΟΣ ΓΡΑΜΜΑΤΙΚΟΥ

Ὕστατον ἐθρήνησε τὸν ὠκύμορον Κλεαρίστη
  παῖδα, καὶ ἀμφὶ τάφῳ πικρὸν ἔπαυσε βίον·
κωκύσασα γὰρ ὅσσον ἐχάνδανε μητρὸς ἀνίη,
  οὐκέτ' ἐπιστρέψαι πνεύματος ἔσχε τόνους.
θηλύτεραι, τί τοσοῦτον ἐμετρήσασθε τάλαιναι
  θρῆνον, ἵνα κλαύσητ' ἄχρι καὶ Ἀΐδεω;

645.—ΚΡΙΝΑΓΟΡΟΥ

Ὦ δύστην' ὄλβοιο Φιλόστρατε, ποῦ σοι ἐκεῖνα
  σκῆπτρα καὶ αἱ βασιλέων ἄφθονοι ἐντυχίαι,[1]
αἷσιν ἐπηώρησας ἀεὶ βίον; ἦ ἐπὶ Νείλῳ
  . . . . δαίοις ὢν περίοπτος ὅροις;
ὀθνεῖοι καμάτους τοὺς σοὺς διεμοιρήσαντο,
  σὸς δὲ νέκυς ψαφαρῇ κεῖσετ' ἐν Ὀστρακίνῃ.

646.—ΑΝΥΤΗΣ ΜΕΛΟΠΟΙΟΥ

Λοίσθια δὴ τάδε πατρὶ φίλῳ περὶ χεῖρε βαλοῦσα
  εἶπ' Ἐρατώ, χλωροῖς δάκρυσι λειβομένα·
"Ὦ πάτερ, οὔ τοι ἔτ' εἰμί, μέλας δ' ἐμὸν ὄμμα
    καλύπτει
  ἤδη ἀποφθιμένης κυάνεος θάνατος."

---

[1] εὐτυχίαι MS. : I correct.

BOOK VII. EPIGRAMS 643–646

643.—CRINAGORAS

O HADES the inexorable, thou hast carried off
Hymnis, Evander's daughter, ever the loveable pet
of his house, the coaxing nine-year-old girl. Why
didst thou send such early death to her who must
one day in any case be thine?

644.—BIANOR THE GRAMMARIAN

CLEARISTE mourned her last for the early death of
her son, and on the tomb ended her embittered life.
For, wailing with all the force a mother's sorrow
could give her, she could not recover force to draw
her breath. Women, why give ye such ample
measure to your grief as to wail even till it brings
you to Hades?

645.—CRINAGORAS

O PHILOSTRATUS,[1] unhappy for all thy wealth, where
are those sceptres and constant intercourse with
princes on which thy fortune ever depended? Shall
thy tomb be (?) by the Nile conspicuous in the region
of . . . .? Foreigners have shared among them the
fruit of thy toil, and thy corpse shall lie in sandy
Ostracine.[2]

646.—ANYTE

THESE were the last words that Erato spoke,
throwing her arms round her dear father's neck, her
cheeks wet with fresh tears: "Father, I am thine no
longer; I am gone, and sombre death casts already
his black veil over my eyes."

[1] An Academic philosopher, a favourite of Anthony and
Cleopatra. [2] Between Egypt and Palestine. By
"foreigners" he means probably Roman soldiers.

647.—ΣΙΜΩΝΙΔΟΥ, οἱ δὲ ΣΙΜΙΟΥ

Ὕστατα δὴ τάδ' ἔειπε φίλην ποτὶ μητέρα Γοργὼ
    δακρυόεσσα, δέρης χερσὶν ἐφαπτομένη·
" Αὖθι μένοις παρὰ πατρί, τέκοις δ' ἐπὶ λῴονι μοίρᾳ
    ἄλλαν, σῷ πολιῷ γήραϊ καδεμόνα."

648.—ΛΕΩΝΙΔΑ ΤΑΡΑΝΤΙΝΟΥ

Ἐσθλὸς Ἀριστοκράτης ὅτ' ἀπέπλεεν εἰς Ἀχέροντα,
    εἶπ' ὀλιγοχρονίης ἁψάμενος κεφαλῆς·
" Παίδων τις μνήσαιτο, καὶ ἑδνώσαιτο γυναῖκα,
    εἰ καί μιν δάκνοι δυσβίοτος πενίη·
ζωὴν στυλώσαιτο· κακὸς δ' ἄστυλος ἰδέσθαι
    οἶκος· ὁ δ' αὖ λῶστον,[1] τἀνέρος ἐσχαρεῶν
εὐκίων φαίνοιτο, καὶ ἐν πολυκαέϊ ὄγκῳ
    ἐμπρέποι,[2] αὐγάζων δαλὸν ἐπεσχάριον."
ᾔδει Ἀριστοκράτης τὸ κρήγυον· ἀλλὰ γυναικῶν,
    ὤνθρωπ', ἤχθαιρεν τὴν ἀλιτοφροσύνην.

649.—ΑΝΥΤΗΣ ΜΕΛΟΠΟΙΟΥ

Ἀντί τοι εὐλεχέος θαλάμου σεμνῶν θ' ὑμεναίων
    μάτηρ στῆσε τάφῳ τῷδ' ἐπὶ μαρμαρίνῳ
παρθενικάν, μέτρον τε τεὸν καὶ κάλλος ἔχοισαν,
    Θερσί· ποτιφθεγκτὰ δ' ἔπλεο καὶ φθιμένα.

650.—[ΦΛΑΚΚΟΥ ἢ] ΦΑΛΑΙΚΟΥ

Φεῦγε θαλάσσια ἔργα, βοῶν δ' ἐπιβάλλευ ἐχέτλῃ,
    εἴ τί τοι ἡδὺ μακρῆς πείρατ' ἰδεῖν βιοτῆς·
ἠπείρῳ γὰρ ἔνεστι μακρὸς βίος· εἰν ἁλὶ δ' οὔ πως
    εὐμαρὲς εἰς πολιὴν ἀνδρὸς ἰδεῖν κεφαλήν.

[1] λῷστος MS. : I correct.
[2] I write so : ἔνστη MS.

346

647.—SIMONIDES or SIMIAS

THESE were the very last words that Gorgo spoke to her dear mother, in tears throwing her hands round her neck : " Stay here with father and mayest thou bear another daughter, more fortunate than I was, to tend thy grey old age."

648.—LEONIDAS OF TARENTUM

GOOD Aristocrates, as he was taking ship for Acheron, resting his doomed head on his hand, said : " Let every man seek to have children and get him a wife, even if miserable poverty pinch him. Let him support his life with pillars ; a house without pillars is ill to look on. Nay ! what is best, may the room where his hearth is have many fair columns, and shining with the luxury of many lights, illumine the log that burns on the hearth." [1] Aristocrates knew what was best, but, O man, he hated the evil-mindedness of women.

649.—ANYTE

THY mother, Thersis, instead of a bridal chamber and solemn wedding rites, gave thee to stand on this thy marble tomb a maiden like to thee in stature and beauty, and even now thou art dead we may speak to thee.

650.—PHALAECUS

AVOID busying thee with the sea, and put thy mind to the plough that the oxen draw, if it is any joy for thee to see the end of a long life.   For on land there is length of days, but on the sea it is not easy to find a man with grey hair.

---

[1] Lines 6-8 are somewhat obscure.   Children seem to be meant by the lights as well as by the pillars or columns.

651.—ΕΥΦΟΡΙΩΝΟΣ

Οὐχ ὁ τρηχὺς Ἐλαιὸς ἐπ᾿ ὀστέα κεῖνα καλύπτει,
οὐδ᾿ ἡ κυάνεον γράμμα λαλοῦσα πέτρη·
ἀλλὰ τὰ μὲν Δολίχης τε καὶ αἰπεινῆς Δρακάνοιο
Ἰκάριον ῥήσσει κῦμα περὶ κροκάλαις·
ἀντὶ δ᾿ ἐγὼ ξείνης Πολυμήδεος ἡ κενεὴ χθὼν   5
ὠγκώθην Δρυόπων διψάσιν ἐν βοτάναις.

652.—ΛΕΩΝΙΔΑ ΤΑΡΑΝΤΙΝΟΥ

Ἠχήεσσα θάλασσα, τί τὸν Τιμάρεος οὕτως
πλώοντ᾿ οὐ πολλῇ νηὶ Τελευταγόρην,
ἄγρια χειμήνασα, κατεπρηνώσαο πόντῳ
σὺν φόρτῳ, λάβρον κῦμ᾿ ἐπιχευαμένη;
χὠ μέν που καὶ ἦξιν ἢ ἰχθυβόροις λαρίδεσσιν   5
τεθρήνητ᾿ ἄπνους εὐρεῖ ἐπ᾿ αἰγιαλῷ·
Τιμάρης δὲ κενὸν τέκνου κεκλαυμένον ἀθρῶν
τύμβον, δακρύει παῖδα Τελευταγόρην.

653.—ΠΑΓΚΡΑΤΟΥΣ

Ὤλεσεν Αἰγαίου διὰ κύματος ἄγριος ἀρθεὶς
Λὶψ Ἐπιηρείδην Ὑάσι δυομέναις,
αὐτὸν ἑῇ σὺν νηὶ καὶ ἀνδράσιν· ᾧ τόδε σῆμα
δακρύσας κενεὸν παιδὶ πατὴρ ἔκαμεν.

654.—ΛΕΩΝΙΔΑ ΤΑΡΑΝΤΙΝΟΥ

Αἰεὶ λῃσταὶ καὶ ἀλιφθόροι, οὐδὲ δίκαιοι
Κρῆτες· τίς Κρητῶν οἶδε δικαιοσύνην;
ὡς καὶ ἐμὲ πλώοντα σὺν οὐκ εὐπίονι φόρτῳ
Κρηταιεῖς ὦσαν Τιμόλυτον καθ᾿ ἁλός,
δείλαιον. κἠγὼ μὲν ἁλιζώοις λαρίδεσσι   5
κέκλαυμαι, τύμβῳ δ᾿ οὐχ ὕπο Τιμόλυτος.

BOOK VII. EPIGRAMS 651–654

651.—EUPHORION

CRAGGY Elaeus doth not cover those thy bones, nor this stone that speaks in blue letters. They are broken by the Icarian sea on the shingly beach of Doliche[1] and lofty Dracanon,[2] and I, this empty mound of earth, am heaped up here in the thirsty herbage of the Dryopes[3] for the sake of old friendship with Polymedes.

652.—LEONIDAS OF TARENTUM

THOU booming sea, why didst thou rise in angry storm, and striking with a huge wave send headlong to the deep, cargo and all, Teleutagoras, son of Timares, as he sailed in his little ship? He, lying somewhere dead on the broad beach, is bewailed over by terns and fish-eating gulls, and Timares, looking on his son's empty tear-bedewed tomb, weeps for his child Teleutagoras.

653.—PANCRATES

AT the setting of the Hyades the fierce Sirocco rose and destroyed Epierides in the Aegean Sea, himself, his ship and crew; and for him his father in tears made this empty tomb.

654.—LEONIDAS OF TARENTUM

THE Cretans are ever brigands and pirates, and never just; who ever heard of the justice of a Cretan? So they were Cretans who threw me unhappy Timolytus into the sea, when I was travelling with no very rich cargo. I am bewailed by the sea-gulls, and there is no Timolytus in this tomb.

[1] Another name of the island Icaria.
[2] A cape on this island.   [3] The inhabitants of Doris.

655.—ΤΟΥ ΑΥΤΟΥ

Ἀρκεῖ μοι γαίης μικρὴ κόνις· ἡ δὲ περισσὴ
ἄλλον ἐπιθλίβοι πλούσια κεκλιμένον
στήλη, τὸ σκληρὸν νεκρῶν βάρος· εἴ με θανόντα
γνώσοντ᾽, Ἀλκάνδρῳ τοῦτο τί Καλλιτέλευς;

656.—ΤΟΥ ΑΥΤΟΥ

Τὴν ὀλίγην βῶλον καὶ τοῦτ᾽ ὀλιγήριον, ὦνερ,
σῆμα ποτίφθεγξαι τλάμονος Ἀλκιμένευς,
εἰ καὶ πᾶν κέκρυπται ὑπ᾽ ὀξείης παλιούρου
καὶ βάτου, ἥν ποτ᾽ ἐγὼ δήϊον Ἀλκιμένης.

657.—ΤΟΥ ΑΥΤΟΥ

Ποιμένες οἳ ταύτην ὄρεος ράχιν οἰοπολεῖτε
αἶγας κευθείρους ἐμβοτέοντες ὄϊς,
Κλειταγόρῃ, πρὸς Γῆς, ὀλίγην χάριν, ἀλλὰ προσηνῆ
τίνοιτε, χθονίης εἵνεκα Φερσεφόνης.
βληχήσαιντ᾽ ὄϊές μοι, ἐπ᾽ ἀξέστοιο δὲ ποιμὴν
πέτρης συρίζοι πρηέα βοσκομέναις·
εἴαρι δὲ πρώτῳ λειμώνιον ἄνθος ἀμέρσας
χωρίτης στεφέτω τύμβον ἐμὸν στεφάνῳ,
καί τις ἀπ᾽ εὐάρνοιο καταχραίνοιτο γάλακτι
οἰός, ἀμολγαῖον μαστὸν ἀνασχόμενος,
κρηπῖδ᾽ ὑγραίνων ἐπιτύμβιον· εἰσὶ θανόντων
εἰσὶν ἀμοιβαῖαι κἀν φθιμένοις χάριτες.

658.—ΘΕΟΚΡΙΤΟΥ, οἱ δὲ ΛΕΩΝΙΔΟΥ ΤΑΡΑΝΤΙΝΟΥ

Γνώσομαι εἴ τι νέμεις ἀγαθοῖς πλέον, ἢ καὶ ὁ δειλὸς
ἐκ σέθεν ὡσαύτως ἶσον, ὁδοιπόρ᾽, ἔχει.
"Χαιρέτω οὗτος ὁ τύμβος," ἐρεῖς, "ἐπεὶ Εὐρυμέδοντος
κεῖται τῆς ἱερῆς κοῦφος ὑπὲρ κεφαλῆς."

350

655.—By the Same

A LITTLE dust of the earth is enough for me, and may a rich and useless monument, a weight ill for the dead to bear, crush some other man in his rest. What is that to Alexander, son of Calliteles, if they know who I am or not, now that I am dead?

656.—By the Same

SALUTE, Sir, this little mound and modest monument of hapless Alcimenes, though it be all overgrown by the sharp buckthorn and brambles on which I, Alcimenes, once waged war.

657.—By the Same

YE shepherds who roam over this mountain ridge feeding your goats and fleecy sheep, do, in the name of Earth, a little kindness, but a pleasant one, to Cleitagoras, for the sake of Persephone underground. May the sheep bleat to me, and the shepherd seated on the unhewn rock pipe soft notes to them as they feed, and may the villager in early spring gather meadow flowers and lay a garland on my grave. May one of you bedew it with the milk of a ewe, mother of pretty lambs, holding her udder up and wetting the edge of the tomb. There are ways, I assure you, even among the dead of returning a favour done to the departed.

658.—THEOCRITUS or LEONIDAS OF TARENTUM

I SHALL discover, wayfarer, if thou honourest more the good, or if a worthless man hath as much of thy esteem. In the first case thou wilt say, "All hail to this tomb because it lies light on the holy head of Eurymedon."

659. <ΘΕΟΚΡΙΤΟΥ>

Νήπιον υἱὸν ἔλειπες· ἐν ἡλικίῃ δὲ καὶ αὐτός,
  Εὐρύμεδον, τύμβου τοῦδε θανὼν ἔτυχες.
σοὶ μὲν ἕδρη θείοισι παρ' ἀνδράσι· τὸν δὲ πολῖται
  τιμησεῦντι, πατρὸς μνώμενοι ὡς ἀγαθοῦ.

660.—ΛΕΩΝΙΔΑ ΤΑΡΑΝΤΙΝΟΥ

Ξεῖνε, Συρακόσιός τοι ἀνὴρ τόδ' ἐφίεται Ὄρθων,
  " Χειμερίας μεθύων μηδαμὰ νυκτὸς ἴῃς· "
καὶ γὰρ ἐγὼ τοιοῦτον ἔχω μόρον, ἀντὶ δὲ †πολλῆς
  πατρίδος ὀθνείαν κεῖμαι ἐφεσσάμενος.

661.—ΤΟΥ ΑΥΤΟΥ

Εὐσθένεος τὸ μνῆμα· φυσιγνώμων ὁ σοφιστής,
  δεινὸς ἀπ' ὀφθαλμοῦ καὶ τὸ νόημα μαθεῖν.
εὖ μιν ἔθαψαν ἑταῖροι ἐπὶ ξείνης ξένον ὄντα,
  χὐμνοθέτης ἐν τοῖς δαιμονίως φίλος ὤν.
πάντων ὧν ἐπέοικεν ἔχειν τεθνεῶθ' ὁ σοφιστής,   5
  καίπερ ἄκικυς ἐών, εἶχ' ἄρα κηδεμόνας.

662.—ΛΕΩΝΙΔΟΥ

Ἡ παῖς ᾤχετ' ἄωρος ἐν ἑβδόμῳ ἥδ' ἐνιαυτῷ
  εἰς ἀΐδην, πολλῆς ἡλικίης προτέρη,
δειλαίη, ποθέουσα τὸν εἰκοσάμηνον ἀδελφόν,
  νήπιον ἀστόργου γευσάμενον θανάτου.
αἰαῖ, λυγρὰ παθοῦσα Περιστέρη, ὡς ἐν ἑτοίμῳ   5
  ἀνθρώποις δαίμων θῆκε τὰ δεινότατα.

659.—THEOCRITUS

(On the same Tomb)

Thou hast left an infant son, but thyself, Eurymedon, didst die in thy prime and liest in this tomb. Thy abode is with the divine among men, but him the citizens will honour, mindful of his father's goodness.

660.—LEONIDAS OF TARENTUM

Stranger, a Syracusan named Orthon enjoins this upon thee: "Never go out drunk on a winter night." For that was what caused my death, and instead of resting in my ample country I lie clothed in foreign soil.

661.—By the Same

The tomb is that of Eusthenes the sophist, who was a reader of character, skilled in discovering our thought from our eyes. Well did his companions bury him, a stranger in a strange land, and among them was a poet marvellously dear to him. So the sophist, although he was feeble, had those who took care that he should have on his death all proper honour.

662.—By the Same

The girl is gone to Hades before her time in her seventh year, before all her many playmates, hapless child, longing for her little brother, who twenty months old tasted of loveless death. Alas Peristera[1] for thy sad fate! How hath Heaven decreed that the very path of men should be sown with calamities!

[1] Little dove.

663.—ΤΟΥ ΑΥΤΟΥ

Ὁ μικκὸς τοδ' ἔτευξε τᾷ Θραΐσσᾳ
Μήδειος τὸ μνᾶμ' ἐπὶ τᾷ ὁδῷ, κἠπέγραψε Κλείτας.
ἑξεῖ τὰν χάριν ἁ γυνὰ ἀντ' ἐκείνων
ὧν τὸν κῶρον ἔθρεψε. τί μάν; ἔτι χρησίμα καλεῖται.

664.—ΑΛΛΟ

Ἀρχίλοχον καὶ στᾶθι καὶ εἴσιδε τὸν πάλαι ποιητάν,
τὸν τῶν ἰάμβων, οὗ τὸ μυρίον κλέος
διῆλθε κἠπὶ νύκτα καὶ ποτ' ἀῶ.
ἦ ῥά νιν αἱ Μοῦσαι καὶ ὁ Δάλιος ἠγάπευν Ἀπόλλων,
ὡς ἐμμελής τ' ἔγεντο κἠπιδέξιος
ἔπεά τε ποιεῖν, πρὸς λύραν τ' ἀείδειν.

665.—ΤΟΥ ΑΥΤΟΥ ΛΕΩΝΙΔΟΥ

Μήτε μακρῇ θαρσέων ναυτίλλεο μήτε βαθείῃ
νηΐ· κρατεῖ παντὸς δούρατος εἷς ἄνεμος.
ὤλεσε καὶ Πρόμαχον πνοιὴ μία, κῦμα δ' ἐν αὔτως
ἀθρόον ἐς κοίλην ἐστυφέλιξεν ἅλα.
οὐ μήν οἱ δαίμων πάντῃ κακός· ἀλλ' ἐνὶ γαίῃ
πατρίδι καὶ τύμβου καὶ κτερέων ἔλαχεν
κηδεμόνων ἐν χερσίν, ἐπεὶ τρηχεῖα θάλασσα
νεκρὸν πεπταμένους θῆκεν ἐπ' αἰγιαλούς.

666.—ΑΝΤΙΠΑΤΡΟΥ ΘΕΣΣΑΛΟΝΙΚΕΩΣ

Οὗτος ὁ Λειάνδροιο διάπλοος, οὗτος ὁ πόντου
πορθμός, ὁ μὴ μούνῳ τῷ φιλέοντι βαρύς·
ταῦθ' Ἡροῦς τὰ πάροιθεν ἐπαύλια, τοῦτο τὸ πύργου
λείψανον, ὁ προδότης ὧδ' ἐπέκειτο λύχνος.
κοινὸς δ' ἀμφοτέρους ὅδ' ἔχει τάφος, εἰσέτι καὶ νῦν
κείνῳ τῷ φθονερῷ μεμφομένους ἀνέμῳ.

663.—By the Same

LITTLE Medeus made this tomb by the wayside for his Thracian nurse, and inscribed it with the name of Clita. She will have her reward for nursing the boy. Why? She is still called "useful"![1]

664.—ANONYMOUS

STAND and look on Archilochus, the iambic poet of old times, whose vast renown reached to the night and to the dawn. Verily did the Muses and Delian Apollo love him; so full of melody was he, so skilled to write verse and to sing it to the lyre.

665.—LEONIDAS OF TARENTUM

TRUST not in the length or depth of the ship thou voyagest in; one wind lords it over every keel. One blast destroyed Promachus, and one huge wave dashed him into the trough of the sea. Yet Heaven was not entirely unkind to him, but he got funeral and a tomb in his own country by the hands of his own people, since the rude sea cast out his body on the expanse of the beach.

666.—ANTIPATER OF THESSALONICA

THIS is the place where Leander crossed, these are the straits, unkind not only to one lover. This is where Hero once dwelt, here are the ruins of the tower, the treacherous lamp rested here. In this tomb they both repose, still reproaching that envious wind.

[1] This epithet is occasionally found on the tombs of slaves.

667.—ΑΔΕΣΠΟΤΟΝ

Ἐν τῷ ναῷ τῆς ἁγίας Ἀναστασίας ἐν Θεσσαλόνικῃ

Τίπτε μάτην γοόωντες ἐμῷ παραμίμνετε τύμβῳ;
  οὐδὲν ἔχω θρήνων ἄξιον ἐν φθιμένοις.
λῆγε γόων καὶ παῦε, πόσις, καὶ παῖδες ἐμεῖο
  χαίρετε, καὶ μνήμην σώζετ᾽ Ἀμαζονίης.

668.—ΛΕΩΝΙΔΟΥ

Οὐδ᾽ εἴ μοι γελόωσα καταστορέσειε Γαλήνη
  κύματα, καὶ μαλακὴν φρῖκα φέροι Ζέφυρος,
νηοβάτην ὄψεσθε· δέδοικα γὰρ οὓς πάρος ἔτλην
  κινδύνους ἀνέμοις ἀντικορυσσόμενος.

669.—ΠΛΑΤΩΝΟΣ ΤΟΥ ΦΙΛΟΣΟΦΟΥ

Ἀστέρας εἰσαθρεῖς ἀστὴρ ἐμός.   εἴθε γενοίμην
  Οὐρανός, ὡς πολλοῖς ὄμμασιν εἰς σὲ βλέπω.

A. J. Butler, *Amaranth and Asphodel*, p. 14 ; A. Esdaile,
Poems and Translations, p. 48.

670.—ΤΟΥ ΑΥΤΟΥ

Ἀστὴρ πρὶν μὲν ἔλαμπες ἐνὶ ζωοῖσιν Ἑῷος·
  νῦν δὲ θανὼν λάμπεις Ἕσπερος ἐν φθιμένοις.

P. B. Shelley, "Thou wert the morning-star . . .," *Works*
(Oxford ed.), p. 712.

671.—ΑΔΗΛΟΝ, οἱ δὲ ΒΙΑΝΟΡΟΣ

Πάντα Χάρων ἄπληστε, τί τὸν νέον ἥρπασας αὔτως
  Ἄτταλον; οὐ σὸς ἔην, κἂν θάνε γηραλέος;

667.—Anonymous

In the Church of St. Anastasia in Thessalonica

Why, lamenting in vain, do you stay beside my tomb? I, among the dead, suffer naught worthy of tears. Cease from lament, my husband, and ye, my children, rejoice and preserve the memory of Amazonia.

668.—LEONIDAS OF ALEXANDRIA

Not even if smiling calm were to smooth the waves for me, and gently rippling Zephyr were to blow, shall ye see me take ship; for I dread the perils I encountered formerly battling with the winds.

669.—PLATO

Thou lookest on the stars, my Star.[1] Would I were heaven, to look on thee with many eyes.

670.—By the Same

Of old among the living thou didst shine the Star of morn; now shinest thou in death the Star of eve.

671.—By Some Attributed to BIANOR

Ever insatiable Charon, why didst thou wantonly take young Attalus? Was he not thine even had he died old?

[1] Aster (Star) is said to have been the name of a youth whom Plato admired.

357

672.—ΑΔΕΣΠΟΤΟΝ

᾿Εν Κορίνθῳ γέγραπται

Χθὼν μὲν ἔχει δέμας ἐσθλόν, ἔχει κλυτὸν οὐρανὸς
    ἦτορ
᾿Ανδρέω, ὃς Δαναοῖσι καὶ ᾿Ιλλυριοῖσι δικάσσας,
οὐχ ὁσίων κτεάνων καθαρὰς ἐφυλάξατο χεῖρας.

673.—ΑΔΗΛΟΝ

Εἰ γένος εὐσεβέων ζώει μετὰ τέρμα βίοιο,
ναιετάον κατὰ θεσμὸν ἀνὰ στόμα φωτὸς ἑκάστου,
᾿Ανδρέα, σὺ ζώεις, οὐ κάτθανες· ἀλλά σε χῶρος
ἄμβροτος ἀθανάτων ἁγίων ὑπέδεκτο καμόντα.

674.—ΑΔΡΙΑΝΟΥ

᾿Αρχιλόχου τόδε σῆμα, τὸν ἐς λυσσῶντας ἰάμβους
ἤγαγε Μαιονίδῃ Μοῦσα χαριζομένη.

675.—ΛΕΩΝΙΔΟΥ

῎Ατρομος ἐκ τύμβου λύε πείσματα ναυηγοῖο·
χἠμῶν ὀλλυμένων ἄλλος ἐνηοπόρει.

676.—ΑΔΗΛΟΝ

Δοῦλος ᾿Επίκτητος γενόμην, καὶ σῶμ᾿ ἀνάπηρος,
καὶ πενίην ῎Ιρος, καὶ φίλος ἀθανάτοις.

---

[1] i.e. otherwise he would have excelled Homer in epic
verse.

672.—ANONYMOUS

Inscribed at Corinth

THE earth holds the comely body, heaven the glorious spirit of Andreas, who, administering justice in Greece and Illyria, kept his hands clean of ill-gotten gain.

673.—ANONYMOUS

IF pious folk live after the end of this life, dwelling, as is fit, in the mouths of all men, thou, Andreas, livest and art not dead, but the divine place of the immortal holy ones has received thee after life's labour.

674.—ADRIANUS

THIS is the tomb of Archilochus, whom the Muse, out of kindness to Homer,[1] guided to furious iambics.

675.—LEONIDAS OF ALEXANDRIA

Isopsephon

TREMBLE not in loosing thy cable from the tomb of the shipwrecked man. While I was perishing another was travelling unhurt.[2]

676.—ANONYMOUS

I, EPICTETUS,[3] was a slave, and not sound in all my limbs, and poor as Irus,[4] and beloved by the gods.

[2] Imitated from No. 282. [3] The celebrated philosopher.
[4] The beggar in the *Odyssey*.

359

GREEK ANTHOLOGY

677.—ΣΙΜΩΝΙΔΟΥ

Μνῆμα τόδε κλεινοῖο Μεγιστίου, ὅν ποτε Μῆδοι
Σπερχειὸν ποταμὸν κτεῖναν ἀμειψάμενοι,
μάντιος, ὃς τότε κῆρας ἐπερχομένας σάφα εἰδὼς
οὐκ ἔτλη Σπάρτης ἡγεμόνας προλιπεῖν.

678.—ΑΔΕΣΠΟΤΟΝ

Πληρώσας στρατιὴν Σωτήριχος ἐνθάδε κεῖμαι,
ὄλβον ἐμῶν καμάτων γλυκεροῖς τεκέεσσιν ἐάσας.
ἦρξα δ' ἐν ἱππήεσσι, Γερήνιος οἷά τε Νέστωρ·
ἐξ ἀδίκων τε πόνων κειμήλιον οὐδὲν ἔτευξα.
τοὔνεκα καὶ μετὰ πότμον ὁρῶ φάος Οὐλύμποιο.

679.—ΤΟΥ ΑΓΙΟΥ ΣΩΦΡΟΝΙΟΥ ΠΑΤΡΙ- ΑΡΧΟΥ

a. Τύμβε, τίς ἢ πόθεν, ἦν δ' ἔτι παῖς τίνος, ἔργα
καὶ ὄλβον,
νεκρός, ὃν ἔνδον ἔχεις, ἔννεπε, κευθόμενον.
β. Οὗτος Ἰωάννης, Κύπριος γένος, υἱὸς ἐτύχθη
εὐγενέος Στεφάνου· ἦν δὲ νομεὺς Φαρίης.
κτήμασι μὲν πολύολβος ὅλων πλέον ὢν τρέφε
Κύπρος,
ἐκ πατέρος πατέρων, ἐξ ὁσίων τε πόνων·
ἔργα δὲ θέσκελα πάντα λέγειν, ἅπερ ἐν χθονὶ τεῦξει
οὐδ' ἐμοῦ ἐστι νόου, οὐδ' ἑτέρων στομάτων·
πάντα γὰρ ἄνδρα παρῆλθε φαεινοτάταις ἀρετῆσι
δόξαντα κρατέειν ταῖς ἀρεταῖς ἑτέρων.
τοῦ καὶ κάλλεα πάντα, τάπερ πτόλις ἔλλαχεν αὗτη,
εἰσὶ φιλοφροσύνης κόσμος ἀρειοτάτης.

360

677.—SIMONIDES

THIS is the tomb of famous Megistias[1] the prophet, whom the Persians slew after crossing the Spercheius. Though he well knew then the impending fate, he disdained to desert the Spartan leaders.

678.—ANONYMOUS

HAVING accomplished my military service, I, Soterichus, lie here, leaving to my sweet children the wealth I gained by my labours. I commanded in the cavalry, like Gerenian Nestor, and I never amassed any treasure from unjust actions. Therefore after death too I see the light of Olympus.

679.—SAINT SOPHRONIUS THE PATRIARCH

A. "TELL me, tomb, of him whom thou hast hidden within thee, who and whence he was, whose son, his profession, and substance." *B.* "This man was Joannes of Cyprus, the son of noble Stephanus, and he was the pastor of Alexandria. He was wealthiest of all the Cyprians by inheritance and by his holy labours; and to tell all the divine deeds he did on earth is beyond my understanding or the tongue of others; for he surpassed in most brilliant virtues even men who seemed to surpass others. All the beautiful public works which this city possesses are ornaments due to his most praiseworthy munificence."

[1] The prophet who was with the Spartans at Thermopylae. Leonidas wished to send him home, but he refused to go.

361

680.—ΤΟΥ ΑΥΤΟΥ

Ἀρχὸς Ἰωάννης Φαρίης ἀρετῶν ἱερήων
ἐνθάδε νῦν μετὰ τέρμα φίλῃ παρὰ πατρίδι κεῖται·
θνητὸν γὰρ λάχε σῶμα, καὶ εἰ βίον ἄφθιτον ἕξει,
ἀθανάτους πρήξεις τε κατὰ χθόνα ῥέξεν ἀπείρους.

681.—ΠΑΛΛΑΔΑ ΑΛΕΞΑΝΔΡΕΩΣ

Οὐκ ἀπεδήμησας τιμῆς χάριν, ἀλλὰ τελευτῆς·
  καὶ χωλός περ ἐὼν ἔδραμες εἰς ἀίδην,
Γέσσιε Μοιράων τροχαλώτερε· ἐκ προκοπῆς γὰρ
  ἧς εἶχες κατὰ νοῦν, ἐξεκόπης βιότου.

682.—ΤΟΥ ΑΥΤΟΥ

Γέσσιος οὐ τέθνηκεν ἐπειγόμενος παρὰ Μοίρης·
  αὐτὸς τὴν Μοῖραν προὔλαβεν εἰς ἀίδην.

683.—ΤΟΥ ΑΥΤΟΥ

" Μηδὲν ἄγαν " τῶν ἑπτὰ σοφῶν ὁ σοφώτατος εἶπεν·
  ἀλλὰ σὺ μὴ πεισθείς, Γέσσιε, ταῦτ' ἔπαθες·
καὶ λόγιός περ ἐὼν ἀλογώτατον ἔσχες ὄνειδος,
  ὡς ἐπιθυμήσας οὐρανίης ἀνόδου.
οὕτω Πήγασος ἵππος ἀπώλεσε Βελλεροφόντην,
  βουληθέντα μαθεῖν ἀστροθέτους κανόνας·
ἀλλ' ὁ μὲν ἵππον ἔχων καὶ θαρσαλέον σθένος ἥβης,
  Γέσσιος οὐδὲ χέσειν εὔτονον ἦτορ ἔχων.

680.—By the Same

Joannes, both chief in virtue and chief priest of Alexandria, lies here after his death in his dear country. For his body was mortal, although he shall have immortal life and did countless immortal works on earth.

681–688 are by PALLADAS OF ALEXANDRIA,
AND ALL ON THE SAME SUBJECT [1]

681

You did not go abroad for the sake of honour, but of death, and although lame you ran to Hades, Gessius, swifter than the Fates. For you retreated from life owing to the advancement of which you were dreaming.

682

Gessius did not die hurried by Fate, but arrived in Hades before Fate.

683

The wisest of the Seven Sages said "Naught in excess," but you, Gessius, were not convinced of it, and came to this end. Though erudite, you incurred the reproach of the greatest lack of reason in desiring to ascend to heaven. Thus it was that Pegasus was fatal to Bellerophon, because he wished to learn the rules of motion of the stars. But he had a horse and the confident strength of youth, whereas Gessius could not screw his courage up enough even to ease himself.

[1] They are all of course facetious. It is insinuated that Gessius' disappointment at not getting the consulate promised him by astrologers hastened his end.

684.—ΤΟΥ ΑΥΤΟΥ

Μηδεὶς ζητήσῃ μερόπων ποτὲ καὶ θεὸς εἶναι,
μηδ' ἀρχὴν μεγάλην, κόμπον ὑπερφίαλον.
Γέσσιος αὐτὸς ἔδειξε· κατηνέχθη γὰρ ἐπαρθείς,
θνητῆς εὐτυχίης μηκέτ' ἀνασχόμενος.

685.—ΤΟΥ ΑΥΤΟΥ

Ζητῶν ἐξεῦρες βιοτου τέλος εὐτυχίης τε,
ἀρχὴν ζητήσας πρὸς τέλος ἐρχομένην.
ἀλλ' ἔτυχες τιμῆς, ὦ Γέσσιε, καὶ μετὰ μοῖραν
σύμβολα τῆς ἀρχῆς ὕστατα δεξάμενος.

686.—ΤΟΥ ΑΥΤΟΥ

Γέσσιον ὡς ἐνόησεν ὁ Βαύκαλος ἄρτι θανόντα
χωλεύοντα πλέον, τοῖον ἔλεξεν ἔπος·
" Γέσσιε, πῶς, τί παθὼν κατέβης δόμον Ἄϊδος εἴσω
γυμνός, ἀκήδεστος, σχήματι καινοτάφῳ ; "
τὸν δὲ μέγ' ὀχθήσας προσέφη καὶ Γέσσιος εὐθύς·
" Βαύκαλε, τὸ στρῆνος καὶ θάνατον παρέχει."

687.—ΤΟΥ ΑΥΤΟΥ

Τὴν Ἀμμωνιακὴν ἀπάτην ὅτε Γέσσιος ἔγνω
τοῦ ξενικοῦ θανάτου ἐγγύθεν ἐρχόμενος,
τὴν ἰδίαν γνώμην κατεμέμψατο, καὶ τὸ μάθημα,
καὶ τοὺς πειθομένους ἀστρολόγοις ἀλόγοις.

688.—ΤΟΥ ΑΥΤΟΥ

Οἱ δύο Κάλχαντες τὸν Γέσσιον ὤλεσαν ὅρκοις,
τῶν μεγάλων ὑπάτων θῶκον ὑποσχόμενοι.
ὦ γένος ἀνθρώπων ἀνεμώλιον, αὐτοχόλωτον,
ἄχρι τέλους βιότου μηδὲν ἐπιστάμενον.

684

LET no mortal even seek to be a god also, nor pursue the pride of high office. Gessius is the proof of it, for he was first of all puffed up and then collapsed, not content with mortal felicity.

685

You sought and found the end of life and happiness, seeking an office[1] tending to the highest end But you obtained the honour, Gessius, receiving after your death the insignia of office.

686

WHEN Baucalus saw Gessius just after his death. and lamer than ever, he spoke thus : " Gessius, what made thee descend into Hell, naked, without funeral, in new burial guise ? " And to him in great wrath Gessius at once replied : " Baucalus, the pride of wealth may cause death."

687

WHEN Gessius discovered the fraud of the oracle of Ammon not long before his death in a strange land, he blamed his own belief and that science, and those who trust in silly astrologers.

688

THE two soothsayers brought death on Gessius by their oaths, promising him the consular chair. O race of men vain minded, angry with themselves, knowing nothing even until the end of life.

[1] The word also means " beginning."

689.—ΑΔΗΛΟΝ

Ἐνθάδε σῶμα λέλοιπεν Ἀπελλιανὸς μέγ' ἄριστος·
ψυχὴν δ' ἐν χείρεσσιν ἐὴν παρακάτθετο Χριστῷ.

690.—ΑΔΗΛΟΝ

Οὐδὲ θανὼν κλέος ἐσθλὸν ἀπώλεσας ἐς χθόνα πᾶσαν,
ἀλλ' ἔτι σῆς ψυχῆς ἀγλαὰ πάντα μένει,
ὅσσ' ἔλαχές τ' ἔμαθές τε, φύσει μῆτιν πανάριστε·
τῷ ῥα καὶ ἐς μακάρων νῆσον ἔβης, Πυθέα.

691.—ΑΔΕΣΠΟΤΟΝ

Ἄλκηστις νέη εἰμί· θάνον δ' ὑπὲρ ἀνέρος ἐσθλοῦ,
Ζήνωνος, τὸν μοῦνον ἐνὶ στέρνοισιν ἐδέγμην,
ὃν φωτὸς γλυκερῶν τε τέκνων προὔκριν' ἐμὸν ἦτορ,
οὔνομα Καλλικράτεια, βροτοῖς πάντεσσιν ἀγαστή.

692.—ΑΝΤΙΠΑΤΡΟΥ, οἱ δὲ ΦΙΛΙΠΠΟΥ ΘΕΣΣΑΛΟΝΙΚΕΩΣ

Γλύκων, τὸ Περγαμηνὸν Ἀσίδι κλέος,
ὁ παμμάχων κεραυνός, ὁ πλατὺς πόδας,
ὁ καινὸς Ἄτλας, αἵ τ' ἀνίκατοι χέρες
ἔρροντι· τὸν δὲ πρόσθεν οὔτ' ἐν Ἰταλοῖς,
οὔθ' Ἑλλάδι προωστόν, οὔτ' ἐν Ἀσίδι,
ὁ πάντα νικῶν Ἀΐδης ἀνέτραπεν.

693.—ΑΠΟΛΛΩΝΙΔΟΥ

Γλῆνιν παρηονῖτις ἀμφέχω χερμάς,
πικρῇ κατασπασθέντα κύματος δίνῃ,
ὅτ' ἰχθυάζετ' ἐξ ἄκρης ἀπορρῶγος·
χῶσαν δέ μ' ὅσσος λαὸς ἦν συνεργήτης,
Πόσειδον, οὓς σὺ σῷζε, καὶ γαληναίην
αἰὲν διδοίης ὁρμιηβόλοις θῖνα.

689.—ANONYMOUS

HERE Apellianus, most excellent of men, left his body, depositing his soul in the hands of Christ.

690.—ANONYMOUS

NOT even in death hast thou lost on the earth all thy good fame, but the splendid gifts of thy mind all survive, all thy talent and learning, Pytheas, most highly endowed by nature. Therefore art thou gone to the islands of the blest.

691.—ANONYMOUS

I AM a new Alcestis, and died for my good husband Zeno, whom alone I had taken to my bosom. My heart preferred him to the light of day and my sweet children. My name was Callicratia, and all men reverenced me.

692.—ANTIPATER OR PHILIP OF THESSALONICA

GLYCO of Pergamus, the glory of Asia, the thunder-bolt of the pancration,[1] the broad-footed, the new Atlas, has perished; they have perished, those un-vanquished hands, and Hades, who conquers all, has thrown him who never before met with a fall in Italy, Greece, or Asia.

693.—APOLLONIDES

I, THE heap of stones by the shore, cover Glenis, who was swept away by the cruel swirl of a wave as he was angling from a steep projecting rock. All his fellow fishermen raised me. Save them, Poseidon, and grant ever to all casters of the line a calm shore.

[1] A combination of wrestling and boxing.

694.—ΑΔΑΙΟΤ

Ἢν παρίῃς ἥρωα, Φιλοπρήγμων δὲ καλεῖται,
πρόσθε Ποτιδαίης κείμενον ἐν τριόδῳ,
εἰπεῖν οἷον ἐπ᾽ ἔργον ἄγεις πόδας· εὐθὺς ἐκεῖνος
εὑρήσει σὺν σοὶ πρήξιος εὐκολίην.

695.—ΑΔΕΣΠΟΤΟΝ

Ὁρᾷς πρόσωπον Κασσίας τῆς σώφρονος.
εἰ καὶ τέθνηκε, ταῖς ἀρεταῖς γνωρίζεται
ψυχῆς τὸ κάλλος μᾶλλον ἢ τοῦ σώματος.

696.—ΑΡΧΙΟΤ ΜΙΤΤΛΗΝΑΙΟΤ

Αἰωρῇ θήρειον ἱμασσόμενος δέμας αὔραις
    τλᾶμον, ἀορτηθεὶς ἐκ λασίας πίτυος,
αἰωρῇ· Φοίβῳ γὰρ ἀνάρσιον εἰς ἔριν ἔστης,
    πρῶνα Κελαινίτην ναιετάων, Σάτυρε.
σεῦ δὲ βοὰν αὐλοῖο μελίβρομον οὐκέτι Νύμφαι,   5
    ὡς πάρος, ἐν Φρυγίοις οὔρεσι πευσόμεθα.

697.—ΧΡΙΣΤΟΔΩΡΟΤ

Οὗτος Ἰωάννην κρύπτει τάφος, ὅς ῥ᾽ Ἐπιδάμνου
    ἄστρον ἔην, ἣν πρὶν παῖδες ἀριπρεπέες
ἔκτισαν Ἡρακλῆος· ὅθεν καὶ μέρμερος ἥρως
    αἰεὶ τῶν ἀδίκων σκληρὸν ἔκοπτε μένος.
εἶχε δ᾽ ἀπ᾽ εὐσεβέων προγόνων ἐρικυδέα πάτρην   5
    Λυχνιδόν, ἣν Φοῖνιξ Κάδμος ἔδειμε πόλιν.

---

[1] The name means "busybody."   [2] Marsyas.

694.—ADAEUS

(*Not Sepulchral*)

IF thou passest by the shrine of the hero (his name is Philopragmon)[1] that is at the cross-roads outside Potidaea, tell him on what task thou journeyest, and he at once will help thee to find a means of accomplishing it.

695.—ANONYMOUS

THOU seest the face of virtuous Cassia. Though she be dead, the beauty of her soul rather than of her visage is made manifest by her virtues.

696.—ARCHIAS OF MITYLENE

POOR Satyr[2] who didst dwell on the hills of Celaenae, thou hangest from a leafy pine, thy beast-like body flogged by the winds, because thou didst enter on fatal strife with Phoebus; and no longer, as of old, shall we Nymphs hear on the Phrygian hills the honeyed notes of thy flute.

697.—CHRISTODORUS

THIS tomb covers Joannes, who was the star of Epidamnus, the city founded by the famous sons of Heracles,[3] whence it was brought about that this active hero ever reduced the stubborn strength of the unrighteous. The renowned fatherland of his pious parents and himself was Lychnidus, a city built by Phoenician Cadmus. Thence sprung this Heli-

---

[3] It was founded by a certain Phalius who claimed descent from the Heraclidae.

ἔνθεν λύχνος ἔην Ἑλικώνιος, οὕνεκα Κάδμος
στοιχείων Δαναοῖς πρῶτος ἔδειξε τύπον.
εἰς ὑπάτους δ᾽ ἀνέλαμψε, καὶ Ἰλλυριοῖσι δικάζων,
Μούσας καὶ καθαρὴν ἐστεφάνωσε Δίκην.   10

698.—ΤΟΥ ΑΥΤΟΥ

Αὐτὸς Ἰωάννης Ἐπιδάμνιος ἐνθάδε κεῖται,
τηλεφανὴς ὑπάτων κόσμος ἀειφανέων·
ὁ γλυκύ μοι Μουσέων πετάσας φάος, ὁ πλέον ἄλλων
εὐρύνας ξενίου δαίμονος ἐργασίην,
παμφόρβην παλάμην κεκτημένος, ἥντινα μούνην   5
οὐκ ἴδε δωτίνης μέτρον ὁριζόμενον.
αἰπυτάτην δ᾽ ηὔξησε [νόμοις πα]τρίοισιν ἀπήνην,
φαιδρύνας καθαρῆς ἔργα δικαιοσύνης.
ὦ πόποι, οὐκ ἔζησε πολὺν χρόνον, ἀλλ᾽ ἐνιαυτοὺς
μοῦνον ἀναπλήσας τεσσαράκοντα δύο,   10
ᾤχετο μουσοπόλοισι ποθὴν πάντεσσιν ἐάσας,
οὓς ἐπόθει πατέρων φέρτερα γειναμένων.

699.—ΑΔΕΣΠΟΤΟΝ

Ἰκάρου ὦ νεόφοιτον ἐς ἠέρα πωτηθέντος
Ἰκαρίη πικρῆς τύμβε κακοδρομίης,
ἀβάλε μήτε σε κεῖνος ἰδεῖν, μήτ᾽ αὐτὸς ἀνεῖναι
Τρίτων Αἰγαίου νῶτον ὑπὲρ πελάγευς.
οὐ γάρ σοι σκεπανή τις ὑφόρμισις, οὔτε βόρειον   5
ἐς κλίτος, οὔτ᾽ ἀγὴν κύματος ἐς νοτίην.
ἔρροις, ὦ δύσπλωτε, κακόξενε· σεῖο δὲ τηλοῦ
πλώοιμι, στυγεροῦ ὅσσον ἀπ᾽ Ἀΐδεω.

700.—ΔΙΟΔΩΡΟΥ ΓΡΑΜΜΑΤΙΚΟΥ

Ἴστω νυκτὸς ἐμῆς, ἥ μ᾽ ἔκρυφεν, οἰκία ταῦτα
λάϊνα, Κωκυτοῦ τ᾽ ἀμφιγόητον ὕδωρ,

conian lamp,[1] because Cadmus first taught the Greeks letters. He attained the consulate, and administering justice in Illyria, crowned the Muses and pure Justice.

698.—By the Same

Here lies Joannes of Epidamnus, the far-shining ornament of ever brilliant consuls, who spread abroad the sweet light of the Muses, and more than others amplified the work of hospitality, having a hand that fed all, and alone among men knew not any measure to limit its gifts. He ornamented his lofty consular car with the laws of his country, making bright the works of pure justice. Ye gods! he did not live long, but at the age of only forty-two departed this life, regretted by all poets, whom he loved more than his own parents.

699.—Anonymous

Icaria, memorial of the disastrous journey of Icarus flying through the newly-trodden air, would he too had never seen thee, would that Triton had never sent thee up above the expanse of the Aegean Sea. For thou hast no sheltered anchorage, either on the northern side nor where the sea breaks on thee from the south. A curse on thee, inhospitable foe of mariners! May I voyage as far from thee as from loathly Hell.

700.—DIODORUS GRAMMATICUS

Know, thou stone palace of the Night that hides me, and thou, flood of Cocytus, where wailing is loud, it

[1] "Lychnus." There is a poor pun on Lychnidus.

οὔτι μ' ἀνήρ, ὃ λέγουσι, κατέκτανεν ἐς γάμον ἄλλης
  παπταίνων· τί μάτην οὔνομα Ῥουφιανός;
ἀλλά με Κῆρες ἄγουσι μεμορμέναι. οὐ μία δήπου   5
  Παῦλα Ταραντίνη κάτθανεν ὠκύμορος.

701.—ΤΟΥ ΑΥΤΟΥ

Ἰφθίμῳ τόδ' ἐπ' ἀνδρὶ φίλη πόλις ἤνυσ' Ἀχαιῷ
  γράμμα παρ' εὐΰδρου νάμασιν Ἀσκανίης.
κλαῦσε δέ μιν Νίκαια· πατὴρ δ' ἐπί οἱ Διομήδης
  λάϊνον ὑψιφαῆ τόνδ' ἀνέτεινε τάφον,
δύσμορος, αἰάζων ὀλοὸν κακόν. ἦ γὰρ ἐῴκει   5
  υἱέα οἱ τίνειν ταῦτα κατοιχομένῳ.

702.—ΑΠΟΛΛΩΝΙΔΟΥ

Ἰχθυοθηρητῆρα Μενέστρατον ὤλεσεν ἄγρη
  δούνακος, ἐξαμίτης ἐκ τριχὸς ἑλκομένη,
εἶδαρ ὅτ' ἀγκίστρου φονίου πλάνον ἀμφιχανοῦσα
  ὀξείην ἐρυθρὴ φυκὶς ἔβρυξε πάγην·
ἀγνυμένη δ' ὑπ' ὀδόντι κατέκτανεν, ἅλματι λάβρῳ   5
  ἐντὸς ὀλισθηρῶν δυσαμένη φαρύγων.

703.—ΜΥΡΙΝΟΥ

Θύρσις ὁ κωμήτης, ὁ τὰ νυμφικὰ μῆλα νομεύων,
  Θύρσις ὁ συρίζων Πανὸς ἴσον δόνακι,
ἔνδιος οἰνοπότης σκιερὰν ὑπὸ τὰν πίτυν εὕδει·
  φρουρεῖ δ' αὐτὸς ἑλὼν ποίμνια βάκτρον Ἔρως.
ἀ Νύμφαι, Νύμφαι, διεγείρατε τὸν λυκοθαρσῆ   5
  βοσκόν, μὴ θηρῶν κύρμα γένηται Ἔρως.

was not my husband, as they say, who, contemplating another marriage, slew me. Why should Rufinus have that evil name for naught? But the fatal Destinies brought me here. Paula of Tarentum is not the only woman who has died before her time.

701.—By the Same

His dear city set up this inscription by the beautiful waters of Ascania[1] to the strong man Achaeus. Nicaea wept for him, and his father Diomedes erected to him this tall and glittering stone monument, lamenting; for it had been meeter for his son to pay him these honours when he died himself.

702.—APOLLONIDES

The capture of his rod, pulled out of the sea by the six-stranded hair line, was fatal to the fisherman Menestratus; then, when the red phycis, gaping at the errant bait of the murderous hook, swallowed greedily the sharp fraud, as he was cracking its skull with its teeth, it slew him, taking a violent leap and slipping down his throat.[2]

703.—MYRINUS

(*Not Sepulchral*)

Thyrsis the villager who feeds the Nymphs' flocks, Thyrsis whose piping is equal to Pan's, sleeps under the shady pine tree having drunk wine at midday, and Love takes his crook and keeps the flock himself. Ye Nymphs! ye Nymphs! awake the shepherd who fears no wolf, lest Love become the prey of wild beasts.

[1] A lake near Nicaea.   [2] *cp.* No. 504.

704.—ΑΔΗΛΟΝ

Ἐμοῦ θανόντος γαῖα μιχθήτω πυρί·
οὐδὲν μέλει μοι· τἀμὰ γὰρ καλῶς ἔχει.

705.—ΑΝΤΙΠΑΤΡΟΥ

Στρυμόνι καὶ μεγάλῳ πεποτισμένον Ἑλλησπόντῳ
   ἠρίον Ἠδωνῆς Φυλλίδος, Ἀμφίπολι,
λοιπά τοι Αἰθοπίης Βραυρωνίδος ἴχνια νηοῦ
   μίμνει, καὶ ποταμοῦ τἀμφιμάχητον ὕδωρ,
τὴν δέ ποτ᾽ Αἰγείδαις μεγάλην ἔριν ὡς ἁλιανθὲς
   τρῦχος ἐπ᾽ ἀμφοτέραις δερκόμεθ᾽ ἠϊόσιν.

706.—ΔΙΟΓΕΝΟΥΣ

Ἰλιγγίασε Βάκχον ἐκπιὼν χανδὸν
   Χρύσιππος, οὐδ᾽ ἐφείσατο
οὐ τῆς στοᾶς, οὐχ ἧς πάτρας, οὐ τῆς ψυχῆς,
   ἀλλ᾽ ἦλθε δῶμ᾽ ἐς Ἀΐδεω.

707.—ΔΙΟΣΚΟΡΙΔΟΥ

Κἠγὼ Σωσιθέου κομέω νέκυν, ὅσσον ἐν ἄστει
   ἄλλος ἀπ᾽ αὐθαίμων ἡμετέρων Σοφοκλῆν,
Σκίρτος ὁ πυρρογένειος. ἐκισσοφόρησε γὰρ ὡνὴρ
   ἄξια Φλιασίων, ναὶ μὰ χορούς, Σατύρων·
κἠμὲ τὸν ἐν καινοῖς τεθραμμένον ἤθεσιν ἤδη
   ἤγαγεν εἰς μνήμην πατρίδ᾽ ἀναρχαΐσας·

---

[1] Said to have been a favourite quotation of both Tiberius and Nero.

374

704.—Anonymous

WHEN I am dead may earth be mingled with fire. It matters not to me, for with me all is well.[1]

705.—ANTIPATER OF THESSALONICA
(*Not Sepulchral*)

AMPHIPOLIS, tomb of Edonian Phyllis, washed by the Strymon and great Hellespont, all that is left of thee is the ruin of the temple of Brauronian Artemis and the disputed[2] water of thy river. We see her for whom the Athenians strove so long now lying like a torn rag of precious purple on either bank.

706.—DIOGENES LAERTIUS

CHRYSIPPUS became dizzy when he had drunk up the wine at a gulp, and sparing neither the Stoa, nor his country, nor his life, went to the house of Hades.[3]

707.—DIOSCORIDES

I, TOO, red-bearded Scirtus the Satyr, guard the body of Sositheus as one of my brothers guards Sophocles on the Acropolis. For he wielded the ivy-bough, yea by the dance I swear it, in a manner worthy of the Satyrs of Phlius, and restoring ancient usage, led me, who had been reared in new-fangled fashions, back to the tradition of our fathers. Once

---

[2] The Athenian possession of Amphipolis was disputed by the Spartans and later by the Macedonians.

[3] Chrysippus was said to have died in consequence of drinking too much at a banquet given him by his disciples.

καὶ πάλιν εἰσώρμησα τὸν ἄρσενα Δωρίδι Μούσῃ
ῥυθμόν, πρός τ᾽ αὐδὴν ἑλκόμενος μεγάλην
†ἑπτὰ δέ μοι ἐρσων τύπος οὐ χερὶ καινοτομηθεὶς
τῇ φιλοκινδύνῳ φροντίδι Σωσιθέου.

708.—ΤΟΥ ΑΥΤΟΥ

Τῷ κωμῳδογράφῳ, κούφη κόνι, τὸν φιλάγωνα
κισσὸν ὑπὲρ τύμβου ζῶντα Μάχωνι φέροις·
οὐ γὰρ ἔχεις κηφῆνα παλίμπλυτον, ἀλλά τι τέχνης
ἄξιον ἀρχαίης λείψανον ἠμφίεσας.
τοῦτο δ᾽ ὁ πρέσβυς ἐρεῖ· "Κέκροπος πόλι, καὶ
    παρὰ Νείλῳ
ἔστιν ὅτ᾽ ἐν Μούσαις δριμὺ πέφυκε θύμον."

709.—ΑΛΕΞΑΝΔΡΟΥ

Σάρδιες ἀρχαῖαι, πατέρων νομός, εἰ μὲν ἐν ὑμῖν
ἐτρεφόμαν, κερνᾶς ἦν τις ἂν ἢ βακέλας
χρυσοφόρος, ῥήσσων καλὰ τύμπανα· νῦν δέ μοι
    Ἀλκμὰν
οὔνομα, καὶ Σπάρτας εἰμὶ πολυτρίποδος,
καὶ Μούσας ἐδάην Ἑλικωνίδας, αἵ με τυράννων
θῆκαν Δασκύλεω μείζονα καὶ Γύγεω.

710.—ΗΡΙΝΝΗΣ [ΜΙΤΤΛΗΝΑΙΗΣ]

Στᾶλαι, καὶ Σειρῆνες ἐμαί, καὶ πένθιμε κρωσσέ,
ὅστις ἔχεις Ἀΐδα τὰν ὀλίγαν σποδιάν,
τοῖς ἐμὸν ἐρχομένοισι παρ᾽ ἠρίον εἴπατε χαίρειν,
αἴτ᾽ ἀστοὶ τελέθωντ᾽, αἴθ᾽ ἑτέρας πόλιος·

---

[1] Sositheus was a tragic poet of the 4th century. His
Satyric dramas, of which we have some fragments, were
especially celebrated. The Satyric drama is said to have
originated at Phlius.

[2] Macho is known to us chiefly as the author of scandalous

more I forced the virile rhythm on the Doric Muse, and drawn to magniloquence . . . a daring innovation introduced by Sositheus.[1]

708.—By the Same

Light earth, give birth to ivy that loves the stage to flourish on the tomb of Macho[2] the writer of comedies. For thou holdest no re-dyed drone, but he whom thou clothest is a worthy remnant of ancient art. This shall the old man say : " O city of Cecrops, sometimes on the banks of the Nile, too, the strong-scented thyme of poesy grows."

709.—ALEXANDER

Ancient Sardis, home of my fathers, had I been reared in thee I would have been a cernus-bearer[3] or eunuch, wearing ornaments of gold and beating pretty tambourines; but now my name is Alcman, and I am a citizen of Sparta of the many tripods, and have learnt to know the Heliconian Muses who made me greater than the tyrants Dascyles and Gyges.[4]

710.—ERINNA

Ye columns and my Sirens,[5] and thou, mournful pitcher that holdest the little ash of death, bid them who pass by my tomb hail, be they citizens or from another town ; and tell this, too, that I was

anecdotes in verse, many of which are quoted by Athenaeus. This epigram was actually engraved on his tomb at Alexandria where he spent most of his life.

[3] The cernus was a vessel used in the rites of Cybele.

[4] Kings of Lydia.

[5] Figures of Sirens that stood on the tomb.

χὥτι με *νύμφαν εὖσαν* ἔχει τάφος, εἴπατε καὶ τό·
χὥτι πατήρ μ᾽ ἐκάλει Βαυκίδα, χὥτι γένος
Τηνία, ὡς εἰδῶντι· καὶ ὅττι μοι ἁ συνεταιρὶς
Ἤρινν᾽ ἐν τύμβῳ γράμμ᾽ ἐχάραξε τόδε.

711.—ΑΝΤΙΠΑΤΡΟΥ

Ἤδη μὲν κροκόεις Πιτανάτιδι πίτνατο νύμφᾳ
  Κλειναρέτᾳ χρυσέων παστὸς ἔσω θαλάμων,
καδεμόνες δ᾽ ἤλποντο διωλένιον φλόγα πεύκας
  ἄψειν ἀμφοτέραις ἀνσχόμενοι παλάμαις,
Δημὼ καὶ Νίκιππος· ἀφαρπάξασα δὲ νοῦσος
  παρθενικὰν Λάθας ἄγαγεν ἐς πέλαγος·
ἀλγειναὶ δ᾽ ἐκάμοντο συνάλικες, οὐχὶ θυρέτρων,
  ἀλλὰ τὸν Ἀΐδεω στερνοτυπῆ πάταγον.

712.—ΗΡΙΝΝΗΣ

Νύμφας Βαυκίδος ἐμμί· πολυκλαύταν δὲ παρέρπων
  στάλαν τῷ κατὰ γᾶς τοῦτο λέγοις Ἀΐδα·
"Βάσκανος ἔσσ᾽, Ἀΐδα." τὰ δέ τοι καλὰ σάμαθ᾽
  ὁρῶντι
ὠμοτάταν Βαυκοῦς ἀγγελέοντι τύχαν,
ὡς τὰν παῖδ᾽, Ὑμέναιος ἐφ᾽ αἷς ἀείδετο πεύκαις,
  ταῖσδ᾽ ἐπὶ καδεστὰς ἔφλεγε πυρκαϊᾷ·
καὶ σὺ μέν, ὦ Ὑμέναιε, γάμων μολπαῖον ἀοιδὰν
  ἐς θρήνων γοερὸν φθέγμα μεθηρμόσαο.

713.—ΑΝΤΙΠΑΤΡΟΥ

Παυροεπὴς Ἤριννα, καὶ οὐ πολύμυθος ἀοιδαῖς·
  ἀλλ᾽ ἔλαχεν Μούσας τοῦτο τὸ βαιὸν ἔπος.

buried here a bride, and that my father called me Baucis, and that my country was Tenos, that they may know. Say, likewise, that my friend and companion Erinna engraved these lines on my tomb.

711.—ANTIPATER OF SIDON

ALREADY her saffron couch inside the golden wedding-chamber had been laid for Clinareta the bride of Pitana. Already her parents Demo and Nicippus were looking forward to raising on high in both hands the blazing pine-torch, when sickness carried the girl away and took her to the sea of Lethe. All sadly her girl companions instead of beating at her door beat their breasts, as is the rite of death.

712.—ERINNA

I AM the tomb of Baucis the bride, and as thou passest the much bewept pillar, say to Hades who dwells below "Hades, thou art envious." To thee the fair letters thou seest on the stone will tell the most cruel fate of Bauco, how her bridegroom's father lighted her pyre with those very torches that had burnt while they sang the marriage hymn. And thou, Hymenaeus, didst change the tuneful song of wedding to the dismal voice of lamentation.

713.—ANTIPATER OF SIDON

(*Not Sepulchral*)

FEW are Erinna's verses nor is she wordy in her songs, but this her little work is inspired. Therefore

379

τοιγάρτοι μνήμης οὐκ ἤμβροτεν, οὐδὲ μελαίνης
   νυκτὸς ὑπὸ σκιερῇ κωλύεται πτέρυγι·
αἱ δ' ἀναρίθμητοι νεαρῶν σωρηδὸν ἀοιδῶν
   μυριάδες λήθῃ, ξεῖνε, μαραινόμεθα.
λωΐτερος κύκνου μικρὸς θρόος ἠὲ κολοιῶν
   κρωγμὸς ἐν εἰαριναῖς κιδνάμενος νεφέλαις.

714.—ΑΔΕΣΠΟΤΟΝ

Ῥήγιον Ἰταλίης τεναγώδεος ἄκρον ἀείδω,
   αἰεὶ Θρινακίου γευομένη ὕδατος,
οὕνεκα τὸν φιλέοντα λύρην φιλέοντά τε παῖδας
   Ἴβυκον εὐφύλλῳ θῆκεν ὑπὸ πτελέῃ,
ἡδέα πολλὰ παθόντα· πολὺν δ' ἐπὶ σήματι κισσὸν
   χεύατο καὶ λευκοῦ φυταλιὴν καλάμου.

715.—ΛΕΩΝΙΔΟΥ

Πολλὸν ἀπ' Ἰταλίης κεῖμαι χθονός, ἔκ τε Τάραντος
   πάτρης· τοῦτο δέ μοι πικρότερον θανάτου.
τοιοῦτος πλανίων ἄβιος βίος· ἀλλά με Μοῦσαι
   ἔστερξαν, λυγρῶν δ' ἀντὶ μελιχρὸν ἔχω.
οὔνομα δ' οὐκ ἤμυσε Λεωνίδου· αὐτά με δῶρα
   κηρύσσει Μουσέων πάντας ἐπ' ἠελίους.

716.—ΔΙΟΝΥΣΙΟΥ ΡΟΔΙΟΥ

Πρώϊος, ἀλλὰ ποθεινὸς ὅσοι πόλιν Ἰαλύσοιο
   ναίομεν, εἰς λήθης πικρὸν ἔδυς πέλαγος,
δρεψάμενος σοφίην ὀλίγον χρόνον· ἀμφὶ δὲ τύμβῳ
   σεῖο καὶ ἄκλαυτοι γλαῦκες ἔθεντο γόον,
Φαινόκριτ'· οὐδὲν ὅμοιον ἐπεσσομένοισιν ἀοιδὸς
   φθέγξεται, ἀνθρώπους ἄχρι φέρωσι πόδες.

fails she not to be remembered, and is not held hidden under the shadowy wing of black night. But we, stranger, the countless myriads of later singers, lie in heaps withering from oblivion. The low song of the swan is better than the cawing of jackdaws echoing far and wide through the clouds of spring.

714.—ANONYMOUS

I SING of Rhegium, that at the point of the shoaly coast of Italy tastes ever of the Sicilian sea, because under the leafy poplar she laid Ibycus the lover of the lyre, the lover of boys, who had tasted many pleasures ; and over his tomb she shed in abundance ivy and white reeds.

715.—LEONIDAS OF TARENTUM

FAR from the Italian land I lie, far from my country Tarentum, and this is bitterer to me than death. Such is the life of wanderers, ill to live ; but the Muses loved me and instead of sourness sweets are mine. The name of Leonidas hath not sunk into oblivion, but the gifts of the Muses proclaim it to the end of days.

716.—DIONYSIUS OF RHODES

Too early and missed by all us who dwell in the city of Ialysus, hast thou sunk, Phaenocritus, into the sea of oblivion, after plucking for a brief time the flowers of wisdom ; and round thy tomb the very owls that never shed tears lamented. No singer shall ever sing as thou didst to future generations as long as men walk upon their feet.

717.—ΑΔΕΣΠΟΤΟΝ

Νηιάδες καὶ ψυχρὰ βοαύλια ταῦτα μελίσσαις
  οἶμον ἐπ᾽ εἰαρινὴν λέξατε νισσομέναις,
ὡς ὁ γέρων Λεύκιππος ἐπ᾽ ἀρσιπόδεσσι λαγωοῖς
  ἔφθιτο χειμερίη νυκτὶ λοχησάμενος.
σμήνεα δ᾽ οὐκέτι οἱ κομέειν φίλον· αἱ δὲ τὸν ἄκρης ⁵
  γείτονα ποιμένιαι πολλὰ ποθοῦσι νάπαι.

A. Lang, *Grass of Parnassus*, ed. 2, p. 185.

718.—ΝΟΣΣΙΔΟΣ

Ὦ ξεῖν᾽, εἰ τύ γε πλεῖς ποτὶ καλλίχορον Μυτιλάναν,
  τὰν Σαπφὼ χαρίτων ἄνθος ἐναυσαμέναν,
εἰπεῖν, ὡς Μούσαισι φίλαν τήνᾳ τε Λοκρὶς γᾶ
  τίκτεν ἴσαν ὅτι θ᾽ οἱ τοὔνομα Νοσσίς· ἴθι.

719.—ΛΕΩΝΙΔΑ ΤΑΡΑΝΤΙΝΟΥ

Τέλληνος ὅδε τύμβος· ἔχω δ᾽ ὑποβωλέα πρέσβυν
  τῆνον τὸν πρᾶτον γνόντα γελοιομελεῖν.

720.—ΧΑΙΡΗΜΟΝΟΣ

Κλεύας οὑτυμοκλεῖος, ὑπὲρ Θυρεᾶν δόρυ τείνας,
  κάτθανες ἀμφίλογον γᾶν ἀποτεμνόμενος.

721.—ΤΟΥ ΑΥΤΟΥ

Τοῖς Ἄργει Σπάρτηθεν ἴσαι χέρες, ἴσα δὲ τεύχη
  συμβάλομεν· Θυρέαι δ᾽ ἦσαν ἄεθλα δορός.
ἄμφω δ᾽ ἀπροφάσιστα τὸν οἴκαδε νόστον ἀφέντες
  οἰωνοῖς θανάτου λείπομεν ἀγγελίαν.

---

¹ Unfortunately this version of the epigram is quite un-
certain, as it involves considerable departures from the MS.
text, itself unintelligible.

717.—Anonymous

Ye Naiads, and ye cool pastures, tell the bees that start for their spring journeys that old Lysippus perished lying in ambush for the fleet-footed hares on a winter night. No longer does he take joy in tending the swarms, and the dells where feed the flocks miss much their neighbour of the hill.(?)

718.—NOSSIS

Stranger, if thou sailest to Mitylene, the city of lovely dances which kindled (?) Sappho, the flower of the Graces, say that the Locrian land bore one dear to the Muses and equal to her and that her name was Nossis. Go![1]

719.—LEONIDAS

I am the tomb of Tellen,[2] and under ground I hold the old man, who was the first to learn how to compose comic songs.

720.—CHAEREMON

Cleuas, the son of Etymocles, who didst wield the spear for Thyreae, thou didst die allotting to thyself the disputed land.

721.—By the Same

We from Sparta engaged the Argives equal in number and in arms, Thyreae being the prize of the spear, and both abandoning without seeking for pretexts our hope of return home, we leave the birds to tell of our death.

[2] Tellen (4th century B.C.) was by profession a flute-player. Of his comic productions we know nothing.

722.—ΘΕΟΔΩΡΙΔΑ

Δηρίφατον κλαίω Τιμοσθένη, υἷα Μολόσσου,
ξεῖνον ἐπὶ ξείνῃ Κεκροπίᾳ φθίμενον.

723.—ΑΔΕΣΠΟΤΟΝ

Ἁ πάρος ἄδμητος καὶ ἀνέμβατος, ὦ Λακεδαῖμον,
καπνὸν ἐπ' Εὐρώτᾳ δέρκεαι Ὠλένιον,
ἄσκιος· οἰωνοὶ δὲ κατὰ χθονὸς οἰκία θέντες
μύρονται· μήλων δ' οὐκ ἀΐουσι λύκοι.

724.—ΑΝΥΤΗΣ ΜΕΛΟΠΟΙΟΥ

Ἦ ῥα μένος σε, Πρόαρχ', ὄλεσ' ἐν δαΐ, δῶμά τε
πατρὸς
Φειδία ἐν δνοφερῷ πένθει ἔθου φθίμενος·
ἀλλὰ καλόν τοι ὕπερθεν ἔπος τόδε πέτρος ἀείδει,
ὡς ἔθανες πρὸ φίλας μαρνάμενος πατρίδος.

725.—ΚΑΛΛΙΜΑΧΟΥ

α. Αἴνιε, καὶ σὺ γὰρ ὧδε, Μενέκρατες, οὐκ ἐπὶ πουλὺ
ἦσθα· τί σε, ξείνων λῷστε, κατειργάσατο;
ἦ ῥα τὸ καὶ Κένταυρον; β. Ὃ μοι πεπρωμένος
ὕπνος
ἦλθεν, ὁ δὲ τλήμων οἶνος ἔχει πρόφασιν.

726.—ΛΕΩΝΙΔΑ

Ἑσπέριον κήῳον ἀπώσατο πολλάκις ὕπνον
ἡ γρῆϋς πενίην Πλαθὶς ἀμυνομένη·

722.—THEODORIDAS

I weep for Timosthenes, the son of Molossus, slain in battle, dying a stranger on the strange Attic soil.

723.—Anonymous

(*Not Sepulchral*)

Lacedaemon, formerly unconquered and uninvaded, thou seest the Olenian[1] smoke on the banks of Eurotas. No shade of trees hast thou left; the birds nest on the ground and the wolves hear not the bleating of sheep.

724.—ANYTE

Thy valour, Proarchus, slew thee in the fight, and thou hast put in black mourning by thy death the house of thy father Phidias. But the stone above thee sings this good message, that thou didst fall fighting for thy dear fatherland.

725.—CALLIMACHUS

A. "Menecrates of Aenus, you too were not long on earth. Tell me, best of friends, what caused your death? Was it that which caused the Centaur's?"[2] *B.* "The fore-ordained sleep came to me, and the unhappy wine is blamed."

726.—LEONIDAS OF TARENTUM

Old Platthis often repelled from her her evening and morning sleep, keeping poverty away, and near

[1] Achaean. This refers to the invasion of Lacedaemonia by the Achaeans in B.C. 189. [2] *i.e.* wine.

καί τι πρὸς ἠλακάτην καὶ τὸν συνέριθον ἄτρακτον
ἤεισεν, πολιοῦ γήραος ἀγχίθυρος,
κἄτι παριστίδιος δινευμένη ἄχρις ἐπ' ἠοῦς 5
κεῖνον Ἀθηναίης σὺν Χάρισιν δόλιχον,
ἢ ῥικνῇ ῥικνοῦ περὶ γούνατος ἄρκιον ἱστῷ
χειρὶ στρογγύλλουσ' ἱμερόεσσα κρόκην.
ὀγδωκονταέτις δ' Ἀχερούσιον ηὔγασεν ὕδωρ
ἡ καλὴ καλῶς Πλατθὶς ὑφηναμένη. 10

727.—ΘΕΑΙΤΗΤΟΥ

Τὰν γνώμαν ἐδόκει Φιλέας οὐ δεύτερος ἄλλου
εἶμεν· ὁ δὲ φθονερὸς κλαιέτω ἔσκε θάνῃ.
ἀλλ' ἔμπας δόξας κενεὰ χάρις· εἰν ἀίδᾳ γὰρ
Μίνω Θερσίτας οὐδὲν ἀτιμότερος.

728.—ΚΑΛΛΙΜΑΧΟΥ

Ἱερέη Δήμητρος ἐγώ ποτε, καὶ πάλιν Καβείρων,
ὦνερ, καὶ μετέπειτα Δινδυμήνης,
ἡ γρηῢς γενόμην, ἡ νῦν κόνις, ἡνο. . .
πολλῶν προστασίη νέων γυναικῶν.
καί μοι τέκν' ἐγένοντο δύ' ἄρσενα, κἠπέμυσ' ἐκείνων 5
εὐγήρως ἐνὶ χερσίν. ἕρπε χαίρων.

729.—ΤΥΜΝΕΩ

Εὐειδὴς Τριτωνὶς ἐπ' οὐκ ἀγαθαῖς ἐλοχεύθη
κληδόσιν· οὐ γὰρ ἂν ὧδ' ὤλετο δαιμονίη
ἀρτιτόκος· τὰ δὲ πολλὰ κατήγαγεν ἓν βρέφος ᾅδην
σὺν κείνῃ· δεκάτην δ' οὐχ ὑπερῆρεν ἕω.

the door of gray old age used to sing a tune to her spindle and familiar distaff. Still by the loom until the dawn she revolved in company with the Graces that long task of Pallas, or, a loveable figure, smoothed with her wrinkled hand on her wrinkled knee the thread sufficient for the loom. Aged eighty years comely Platthis who wove so well set eyes on the lake of Acheron.

727.—THEAETETUS

Phileas seemed inferior to none in the gifts of his mind ; let him who envies him go and cry himself to death.[1] Yet but empty pleasure hath a man in fame, for in Hades Thersites is as highly honoured as Minos.

728.—CALLIMACHUS

I, the old woman who am now dust was once the priestess of Demeter and again of the Cabiri and afterwards of Cybele. I was the patroness of many young women. I had two male children and closed my eyes at a goodly old age in their arms. Go in peace.

729.—TYMNES

The omens were evil when fair Tritonis was brought to bed, for otherwise she would not have perished, unhappy girl, just after the child was born. With her this one babe brought down to Hades so much happiness, and it did not even live beyond the tenth dawn.

---

[1] A form of imprecation.

730.—ΠΕΡΣΟΥ

Δειλαία Μνάσυλλα, τί τοι καὶ ἐπ' ἠρίῳ οὗτος
  μυρομένᾳ κούραν γραπτὸς ἔπεστι τύπος
Νευτίμας; ἇς δή ποκ' ἄπο ψυχὰν ἐρύσαντο
  ὠδῖνες, κεῖται δ' οἷα κατὰ βλεφάρων
ἀχλύϊ πλημμύρουσα φίλας ὑπὸ ματρὸς ἀγοστῷ   5
  αἰαῖ 'Αριστοτέλης δ' οὐκ ἀπάνευθε πατὴρ
δεξιτερᾷ κεφαλὰν ἐπεμάσσετο. ὢ μέγα δειλοί,
  οὐδὲ θανόντες ἑῶν ἐξελάθεσθ' ἀχέων.

731.—ΛΕΩΝΙΔΑ

"'Άμπελος ὡς ἤδη κάμακι στηρίζομαι αὐτῷ
  σκηπανίῳ· καλέει μ' εἰς ἀΐδην θάνατος.
δυσκώφει μὴ Γόργε· τί τοι χαριέστερον, ἢ τρεῖς
  ἢ πίσυρας ποίας θάλψαι ὑπ' ἠελίῳ;"
ὧδ' εἴπας οὐ κόμπῳ, ἀπὸ ζωὴν ὁ παλαιὸς   5
  ὤσατο, κής πλεόνων ἦλθε μετοικεσίην.

732.—ΘΕΟΔΩΡΙΔΑ

Ὤχευ ἔτ' ἀσκίπων Κινησία, Ἑρμόλα υἱὲ
  ἐκτίσων 'Αΐδῃ χρεῖος ὀφειλόμενον,
γήρᾳ ἔτ' ἄρτια πάντα φέρων· χρήστην δὲ δίκαιον
  εὑρών σε στέρξει παντοβίης 'Αχέρων.

733.—ΔΙΟΤΙΜΟΥ

†Αἰνόμενοι δύο γρῆες ὁμήλικες ἦμεν, 'Αναξὼ
  καὶ Κληνώ, δίδυμοι παῖδες 'Επικράτεος·
Κληνὼ μὲν Χαρίτων ἱερή, Δήμητρι δ' 'Αναξὼ
  ἐν ζωῇ προπολεῦσ'· ἐννέα δ' ἠελίων

730.—PERSES

UNHAPPY Mnasylla, why does it stand on thy tomb, this picture of thy daughter Neotima whom thou lamentest, her whose life was taken from her by the pangs of labour?   She lies in her dear mother's arms, as if a heavy cloud had gathered on her eyelids and, alas, not far away her father Aristoteles rests his head on his right hand.[1]   O most miserable pair, not even in death have ye forgotten your grief.

731.—LEONIDAS OF TARENTUM

"I AM already supported only on a stick, like a vine on a stake; Death calls me to Hades.   Stop not thy ears, Gorgus.   What further pleasure hast thou in basking in the sun yet for three or four summers?" So speaking in no braggart strain the old man cast away his life and settled in the abode of the greater number.

732.—THEODORIDAS

THOU art gone, still without a staff, Cinesias, son of Hermolas, to pay the debt thou owest to Hades, in thy old age but bringing him thyself still complete.   So all-subduing Acheron finding thee a just debtor shall love thee.

733.—DIOTIMUS

WE two old women Anaxo and Cleno the twin daughters of Epicrates were ever together; Cleno was in life the priestess of the Graces and Anaxo served Demeter.   We wanted nine days to complete

---

[1] An attitude of mourning.

ὀγδωκονταέτεις ἔτι λειπόμεθ' ἐς τόδ' ἱκέσθαι   5
    τῆς μοίρης· ἐτέων δ' οὐ φθόνος †ἰσοσίη.
καὶ πόσιας καὶ τέκνα φιλήσαμεν· αἱ δὲ παλαιαὶ
    πρῶθ' ἡμεῖς Ἀΐδην πρῆϋν ἀνυσσάμεθα.

734.—ΑΔΗΛΟΝ

†Ἦξεν ὅλατιτυτειδεστι. τί γάρ; νέκυς ω ποτι παίδων
    τῶν ἀγαθῶν ἠδ' ἦν ἀρχιγέρων ὁ γέρων,
ἀλλὰ φίλος γ' ὦ πρέσβυ, γένοιτο τευ ὄλβια τέκνα
    ἐλθεῖν καὶ λευκῆς ἐς δρόμον ἡλικίης.

735.—ΔΑΜΑΓΗΤΟΥ

Ὑστάτιον, Φώκαια, κλυτὴ πόλι, τοῦτο Θεανὼ
    εἶπεν ἐς ἀτρύγετον νύκτα κατερχομένη·
" Οἴμοι ἐγὼ δύστηνος· Ἀπέλλιχε, ποῖον, ὄμευνε,
    ποῖον ἐπ' ὠκείῃ νηΐ περᾷς πέλαγος;
αὐτὰρ ἐμεῦ σχεδόθεν μόρος ἵσταται. ὡς ὄφελόν γε   5
    χειρὶ φίλην τὴν σὴν χεῖρα λαβοῦσα θανεῖν."

736.—ΛΕΩΝΙΔΑ ΤΑΡΑΝΤΙΝΟΥ

Μὴ φθείρευ, ὤνθρωπε, περιπλάνιον βίον ἕλκων,
    ἄλλην ἐξ ἄλλης εἰς χθόν' ἀλινδόμενος,
μὴ φθείρευ, κἂν εἴ σε περιστέψαιτο καλιὴ
    ἣν θάλποι μικκὸν πῦρ ἀνακαιόμενον,
εἰ καί σοι λιτή τε καὶ οὐκ εὐάλφιτος εἴη   5
    φύστη ἐνὶ γρώνῃ μασσομένη παλάμαις,
ἢ καί σοι γλήχων, ἢ καὶ θύμον, ἢ καὶ ὁ πικρὸς
    ἁδυμιγὴς εἴη χόνδρος ἐποψίδιος.

737.—ΑΔΕΣΠΟΤΟΝ

Ἐνθάδ' ἐγὼ ληστῆρος ὁ τρισδείλαιος ἄρηι
    ἐδμήθην· κεῖμαι δ' οὐδενὶ κλαιόμενος.

our eightieth year. . . . . . We loved our husbands
and children, and we, the old women, won gentle death
before them.

734.—Anonymous

This corrupt epigram seems to be partly in Doric and is
evidently a dialogue.   Lines 1 and 2 are quite unintelligible.
It ends thus :—

O old man, may thy blessed children too reach
the road of gray age.

735.—DAMAGETUS

Phocaea, glorious city, these were the last words
Theano spoke as she descended into the vast night :
" Alas unhappy that I am, Apellichus ! What sea, my
husband, art thou crossing in thy swift ship ?   But by
me death stands close, and would I could die holding
thy dear hand in mine."

736.—LEONIDAS OF TARENTUM

Vex not thyself, O man, leading a vagrant life,
rolled from one land to another.   Vex not thyself
if thou hast a little hut to cover thee, warmed by a
little fire, if thou hast a poor cake of no fine
meal kneaded by thy hands in a stone trough, if thou
hast mint or thyme for a relish or even coarse salt
not unsweetened.

737.—Anonymous

Here I thrice unfortunate was slain by an armed
robber, and here I lie bewept by none.

738.—ΘΕΟΔΩΡΙΔΑ

Κληῖδες Κύπρου σε καὶ ἐσχατιαὶ Σαλαμῖνος,
Τίμαρχ᾽, ὑβριστής τ᾽ ὤλεσε Λὶψ ἄνεμος,
νηΐ τε σὺν φόρτῳ τε· κόνιν δέ σου ἀμφιμέλαιναν
δέξαντ᾽ οἰζυροί, σχέτλιε, κηδεμόνες.

739.—ΦΑΙΔΙΜΟΥ

Αἰάζω Πολύανθον, ὃν εὐνέτις, ὦ παραμείβων,
νυμφίον ἐν τύμβῳ θῆκεν Ἀρισταγόρη,
δεξαμένη σποδιήν τε καὶ ὀστέα (τὸν δὲ δυσαὲς
ὤλεσεν Αἰγαίου κῦμα περὶ Σκίαθον),
δύσμορον ὀρθρινοί μιν ἐπεὶ νέκυν ἰχθυβολῆες,
ξεῖνε, Τορωναίων εἵλκυσαν ἐς λιμένα.

740.—ΛΕΩΝΙΔΑ

Αὕτα ἐπὶ Κρήθωνος ἐγὼ λίθος, οὔνομα κείνου
δηλοῦσα· Κρήθων δ᾽ ἐν χθονίοις σποδιά.
ὁ πρὶν καὶ Γύγῃ παρισεύμενος ὄλβον, ὁ τὸ πρὶν
βουπάμων, ὁ πρὶν πλούσιος αἰπολίοις,
ὁ πρίν—τί πλείω μυθεῦμαι; ὁ πᾶσι μακαρτός,
φεῦ, γαίης ὅσσης ὅσσον ἔχει μόριον.

741.—ΚΡΙΝΑΓΟΡΟΥ

Ὀθρυάδην, Σπάρτης τὸ μέγα κλέος, ἢ Κυνέγειρον
ναύμαχον, ἢ πάντων ἔργα κάλει πολέμων·
Ἄρεος αἰχμητὴς Ἰταλὸς παρὰ χεύμασι Ῥήνου
κλινθείς, ἐκ πολλῶν ἡμιθανὴς βελέων,
αἰετὸν ἁρπασθέντα φίλου στρατοῦ ὡς ἴδ᾽ ὑπ᾽
ἐχθροῖς,
αὖτις ἀρηιφάτων ἄνθορεν ἐκ νεκύων·
κτείνας δ᾽ ὅς σφ᾽ ἐκόμιζεν, ἑοῖς ἀνεσώσατο ταγοῖς,
μοῦνος ἀήττητον δεξάμενος θάνατον.

738.—THEODORIDAS

THE Keys of Cyprus[1] and the promontory of Salamis and the rude south wind destroyed thee, Timarchus, with thy ship and cargo, and thy mourning kinsmen received but the black ashes of thee, ill-fated man.

739.—PHAEDIMUS

I MOURN for Polyanthus, O passer by, whom his wife Aristagora laid in the tomb, her newly wedded lord, receiving his ashes and dust (in the stormy Aegean near Sciathus he had perished) after the fishermen in the early morn had towed his corpse into the harbour of Torone.

740.—LEONIDAS OF TARENTUM

I AM the stone that rests on Cretho and makes known his name, but Cretho is ashes underground, he who once vied with Gyges in wealth, who was lord of many herds and flocks, who was—why need I say more? he who was blessed by all. Alas, what a little share of his vast lands is his!

741.—CRINAGORAS

CITE Othryadas,[2] the great glory of Sparta, or Cynegeirus,[3] the sea-fighter, or all great deeds of arms. The Italian warrior who lay by the streams of the Rhine, half dead from many wounds, when he saw the eagle of his dear legion seized by the enemy, again arose from amid the corpses of the slain and killing him who carried it, covered it for his leaders, alone winning for himself a death that knew not defeat.

---

[1] Some islands so called.　　[2] See above, No. 431.
[3] The brother of Aeschylus. He fought at Marathon and Salamis.

742.—ΑΠΟΛΛΩΝΙΔΟΥ

Οὐκέτι Τιμόκλεια τεῶν φάος ὤλεσας ὄσσων
κούρους διοτόκῳ νηδύϊ γειναμένη·
ὄμμασι δ' ἐν πλεόνεσσιν ἀθρεῖς πυριθαλπὲς ὄχημα
ἠελίου, προτέρης οὖσα τελειοτέρη.

743.—ΑΝΤΙΠΑΤΡΟΥ

Εἴκοσιν Ἑρμοκράτεια καὶ ἐννέα τέκνα τεκοῦσα
οὔθ' ἑνὸς οὔτε μιᾶς αὐγασάμην θάνατον.
οὐ γὰρ ἀπωΐστευσεν ἐμοὺς υἷας Ἀπόλλων,
οὐ βαρυπενθήτους Ἄρτεμις εἷλε κόρας·
ἔμπαλι δ' ἁ μὲν ἔλυσεν ἐμὰν ὠδῖνα μολοῦσα,
Φοῖβος δ' εἰς ἥβαν ἄρσενας ἀγάγετο
ἀβλαβέας νούσοισιν. ἴδ' ὡς νίκημι δικαίως
παισὶν καὶ γλώσσῃ σώφρονι Τανταλίδα.

744.—ΔΙΟΓΕΝΟΥΣ

Ἐν Μέμφει λόγος ἐστὶ μαθεῖν ἰδίην ποτὲ μοίρην
Εὔδοξον παρὰ τοῦ καλλίκερω ταύρου·
κοὐδὲν ἔλεξε· πόθεν; βοῒ γὰρ λόγον οὐ πόρε φύτλη,
οὐδὲ λάλον μόσχῳ Ἄπιδι στόμα·
ἀλλὰ παρ' αὐτὸν λέχριος στὰς ἐλιχμήσατο στύλον,
προφανῶς τοῦτο διδάσκων· "Ἀποδύσῃ βιοτὴν
ὅσσον οὔπω." διὸ καί οἱ ταχέως ἦλθε μόρος, δεκάκις
πέντε καὶ τρεῖς εἰσιδόντα ποίας.

745.—ΑΝΤΙΠΑΤΡΟΥ ΣΙΔΩΝΙΟΥ

Ἴβυκε, λῃσταί σε κατέκτανον ἔκ ποτε νηὸς
βάντ' ἐς ἐρημαίην ἄστιβον ἠϊόνα,
ἀλλ' ἐπιβωσάμενον γεράνων νέφος, αἵ τοι ἵκοντο
μάρτυρες ἄλγιστον ὀλλυμένῳ θάνατον·

BOOK VII. EPIGRAMS 742–745

742.—APOLLONIDES
(*Not Sepulchral*)

No longer, Timoclea, hast thou lost the light of thy eyes, now thou hast given birth to twin boys, but thou art now more perfect than thou ever wast, looking with more than two eyes on the burning Chariot of the Sun.

743.—ANTIPATER OF SIDON

I, HERMOCRATEA, bore twenty-nine children and have not seen the death of one, either boy or girl. For far from Apollo having shot down my sons and Artemis my daughters for me to lament, Artemis came to relieve me in childbed and Phoebus brought my sons to man's estate unhurt by sickness. See how I justly surpass Niobe both in my children and in restraint of speech.

744.—DIOGENES LAERTIUS

THEY say that Eudoxus learnt his own fate in Memphis from the bull with beautiful horns. It spoke not, how could it? for nature has not given speech to cattle nor a talkative tongue to the calf Apis; but standing beside him it licked his cloak, evidently telling him this. "You will divest yourself of life." So he died shortly after, having seen fifty-three summers.

745.—ANTIPATER OF SIDON

IBYCUS, the robbers slew thee when from the ship thou didst land on the untrodden desert shore. But first didst thou call on the flock of cranes who came to witness that thou didst die a most cruel

395

οὐδὲ μάτην ἰάχησας, ἐπεὶ ποινῆτις Ἐρινὺς   5
  τῶνδε διὰ κλαγγὴν τίσατο σεῖο φόνον
Σισυφίην κατὰ γαῖαν. ἰὼ φιλοκερδέα φῦλα
  ληϊστέων, τί θεῶν οὐ πεφόβησθε χόλον;
οὐδὲ γὰρ ὁ προπάροιθε κανὼν Αἴγισθος ἀοιδὸν
  ὄμμα μελαμπέπλων ἔκφυγεν Εὐμενίδων.   10

746.—ΠΥΘΑΓΟΡΟΥ

Εἰς τάφον τοῦ Διὸς ἐν Κρήτῃ

Ὧδε μέγας κεῖται Ζὰν ὃν Δία κικλήσκουσιν.

747.—ΛΙΒΑΝΙΟΥ

Ἰουλιανὸς μετὰ Τίγριν ἀγάρροον ἐνθάδε κεῖται,
ἀμφότερον, βασιλεύς τ᾽ ἀγαθὸς κρατερός τ᾽ αἰχμητής.

748.—ΑΝΤΙΠΑΤΡΟΥ ΣΙΔΩΝΙΟΥ

Τίς τόδε μουνόγληνος ἅπαν δωμήσατο Κύκλωψ
  λάϊνον Ἀσσυρίης χῶμα Σεμιράμιος,
ἢ ποῖοι χθονὸς υἷες ἀνυψώσαντο Γίγαντες
  κείμενον ἑπταπόρων ἀγχόθι Πληϊάδων
ἀκλινές, ἀστυφέλικτον, Ἀθῴεος ἶσον ἐρίπνᾳ   5
  φυρηθὲν γαίης εὐρυπέδοιο βάρος;
δᾶμος ἀεὶ μακαριστός, ὃς ἄστεσιν Ἡρακλείης
  οὐρανίων [νεφέων τεῦξεν ἐπ᾽][1] εὐρυάλων.

[1] The words in brackets are added in the MS. by a later hand. They give no sense.

death.   And not in vain didst thou cry out, for
through the calling of the cranes the Erinys avenged
thy death in the land of Corinth.   O ye race of
robbers greedy of gain, why fear ye not the anger of
the gods?   Not even did Aegisthus, who of old slew
the singer, escape the eyes of the dark-robed Furies.

746. PYTHAGORAS

HERE lies great Zan whom they call Zeus.[1]

747.—LIBANIUS

JULIAN [2] lies here on the further bank of the
strong current of Tigris, "a good king and a valiant
warrior." [3]

748.—ANTIPATER OF SIDON

WHAT one-eyed Cyclops built all this vast stone
mound of Assyrian Semiramis, or what giants, sons
of earth, raised it to reach near to the seven Pleiads,
inflexible, unshakable, a mass weighing on the broad
earth like to the peak of Athos?   Ever blessed
people, who to the citizens of Heraclea . . .

---

[1] Supposed to have been written on the tomb of Zeus, in
Crete.
[2] The emperor.   [3] Homer, *Iliad* iii. 279.

BOOK VIII

THE EPIGRAMS OF SAINT GREGORY
THE THEOLOGIAN

I SHOULD personally have preferred to follow the Teubner edition in omitting this book, as it forms no part of Cephalus' Anthology and merely, because all the epigrams are in the form of epitaphs, occupies this place in the Palatine MS. It has, however, been included in the Didot edition, which still remains the standard text of the Anthology,[1] and it is the rule of the Loeb Library to reproduce the standard text. The proper place for this collection of the Epigrams of St. Gregory would be in his very voluminous works.

Gregory of Nazianzus was one of the great triad of Church Fathers of the fourth century (the Τρεῖς Ἱεράρχαι as they are styled in the Orthodox Calendar). The other two, Basil and Chrysostom, were his contemporaries and friends, as will be seen from some of these epigrams. Basil especially had been his friend from his youth up, and Gregory's wife was Basil's sister (see Epigr. 164). Gregory evidently enjoyed making verses, but the epigrams make somewhat tedious reading, as there are so many on the same subject.

---

[1] Other epigrams of St. Gregory's which are found elsewhere in the Palatine MS. have not been included in the Didot edition.

Η

ΕΚ ΤΩΝ ΕΠΙΓΡΑΜΜΑΤΩΝ ΤΟΥ ΑΓΙΟΥ ΓΡΗΓΟΡΙΟΥ ΤΟΥ ΘΕΟΛΟΓΟΥ

1.—᾿Επιτύμβιον εἰς ᾿Ιωάννην καὶ Θεοδόσιον

᾿Ενθάδε τύμβος ἔχει θεοειδέας ἀνέρας ἐσθλούς,
  θεῖον ᾿Ιωάννην, τὸν πάνυ Θευδόσιον,
ὧν ἀρετὴ πολύολβος ἐς οὐρανοῦ ἄντυγας ἦλθε,
  καὶ φωτὸς μετόχους δεῖξεν ἀκηρασίου.

2.—Εἰς τὸν μέγαν Βασίλειον τὸν Καισαρείας ἐπίσκοπον τῆς ἐν Καππαδοκίᾳ

Σῶμα δίχα ψυχῆς ζώειν πάρος ἢ ἐμὲ σεῖο,
  Βασίλιε, Χριστοῦ λάτρι, φίλ᾿, ᾠόμην·
ἀλλ᾿ ἔτλην καὶ ἔμεινα. τί μέλλομεν; οὔ μ᾿ ἀναείρας
  θήσεις ἐς μακάρων σήν τε χοροστασίην;
μή με λίπῃς, μή, τύμβον ἐπόμνυμι· οὔ ποτε σεῖο   5
  λήσομαι, οὐδὲ θέλων. Γρηγορίοιο λόγος.

3.—Εἰς τὸν αὐτὸν Βασίλειον τὸν μέγαν

᾿Ηνίκα Βασιλίοιο θεόφρονος ἥρπασε πνεῦμα
  ἡ Τριὰς ἀσπασίως ἔνθεν ἐπειγομένου,
πᾶσα μὲν οὐρανίη στρατιὴ γήθησεν ἰόντι,
  πᾶσα δὲ Καππαδοκῶν ἐστονάχησε πόλις·
οὐκ οἶον· κόσμος δὲ μέγ᾿ ἴαχεν· "῎Ωλετο κῆρυξ,
  ὤλετο εἰρήνης δεσμὸς ἀριπρεπέος."

BOOK VIII

THE EPIGRAMS OF SAINT GREGORY THE THEOLOGIAN

1.—*For the tomb of the Emperor Theodosius and St. John Chrysostom*

Here the tomb holds the good godlike men, divine Joannes and the most excellent Theodosius, whose rich virtue reached to the vault of heaven, and showed them partakers of the pure light.

2.—*On St. Basil the Great, Bishop of Caesarea in Cappadocia*

Methought, dear Basil, servant of Christ, that a body could sooner live without a soul than myself without thee. But I bore it and remained. Why do we delay? Wilt thou not lift me up on high and set me in the company of thyself and the blessed ones? Desert me not, I supplicate by thy tomb! Never, even if I would, shall I forget thee. It is the word of Gregory.

3.—*On the Same*

When the Trinity carried away the spirit of godly Basil, who gladly hastened hence, all the host of Heaven rejoiced at his going, and not only the whole Cappadocian city[1] groaned, but the world lamented loudly. He is gone, the herald, the bond of glorious peace[2] is gone.

[1] Caesarea.   [2] *i.e.* he who was a bond of peace among men.

4.—Εἰς τὸν αὐτόν

Κόσμος ὅλος μύθοισιν ὑπ' ἀντιπάλοισιν ἀεικῶς
σείεται, ὁ Τριάδος κλῆρος ὁμοσθενέος·
αἰαῖ· Βασιλίου δὲ μεμυκότα χείλεα σιγᾷ.
ἔγρεο· καὶ στήτω σοῖσι λόγοισι σάλος
σαῖς τε θυηπολίῃσι· σὺ γὰρ μόνος ἶσον ἔφηνας   5
καὶ βίοτον μύθῳ καὶ βιότητι λόγον.

5.—Εἰς τὸν αὐτόν

Εἷς θεὸς ὑψιμέδων· ἕνα δ' ἄξιον ἀρχιερῆα
ἡμετέρη γενεὴ εἶδέ σε, Βασίλιε,
ἄγγελον ἀτρεκίης ἐριηχέα, ὄμμα φαεινὸν
Χριστιανοῖς, ψυχῆς κάλλεσι λαμπόμενον,
Πόντου Καππαδοκῶν τε μέγα κλέος· εἰσέτι καὶ νῦν,   5
λίσσομ', ὑπὲρ κόσμου ἵστασο δῶρ' ἀνάγων.

6.—Εἰς τὸν αὐτόν

Ἐνθάδε Βασιλίοιο Βασίλιον ἀρχιερῆα
θέντο με Καισαρέες, Γρηγορίοιο φίλον,
ὃν περὶ κῆρι φίλησα· θεὸς δέ οἱ ὄλβια δοίη
ἄλλα τε, καὶ ζωῆς ὡς τάχος ἀντιάσαι
ἡμετέρης· τί δ' ὄνειαρ ἐπὶ χθονὶ δηθύνοντα   5
τήκεσθ', οὐρανίης μνωόμενον φιλίης;

7.—Εἰς τὸν αὐτόν

Τυτθὸν ἔτι πνείεσκες ἐπὶ χθονί, πάντα δὲ Χριστῷ
δῶκας ἄγων, ψυχήν, σῶμα, λόγον, παλάμας,
Βασίλιε, Χριστοῖο μέγα κλέος, ἕρμ' ἱερήων,
ἕρμα πολυσχίστου νῦν πλέον ἀτρεκίης.

4.—*On the Same*

THE whole world, the inheritance of the co-equal Trinity, is shaken in unseemly wise by strife of words. Alas, the lips of Basil are closed and silent. Awake, and by thy words and by thy ministry make the tossing to cease; for thou alone didst exhibit a life equal to thy words and words equal to thy life.

5.—*On the Same*

THERE is one God who ruleth on high, and our age saw but one worthy high-priest, thee, Basil, the deep-voiced messenger of truth, the Christians' bright eye, shining with the beauty of the soul, the great glory of Pontus and Cappadocia. Continue, I implore thee, to stand offering up thy gifts for the world.

6.—*On the Same*

HERE the Caesareans laid me their high-priest, Basil the son of Basil, the friend of Gregory, whom I loved with all my heart. May God grant him all blessings, and especially to attain right soon to this life that is mine. What profiteth it to linger on earth and waste away, longing for a celestial friendship?

7.—*On the Same*

A LITTLE time didst thou still breath on earth, but gavest all thou hadst to Christ, thy soul, thy body, thy speech, thy hands, Basil, the great glory of Christ, the bulwark of the priestly order, and now even more the bulwark of the truth so rent by schism.

8.—Εἰς τὸν αὐτόν

Ω μύθοι, ὦ ξυνὸς φιλίης δόμος, ὦ φίλ᾽ Ἀθῆναι,
  ὦ θείου βιότου τηλόθε συνθεσίαι,
ἴστε τόδ᾽, ὡς Βασίλειος ἐς οὐρανόν, ὡς ποθέεσκεν,
  Γρηγόριος δ᾽ ἐπὶ γῆς χείλεσι δεσμὰ φέρων.

9.—Εἰς τὸν αὐτόν

Καισαρέων μέγ᾽ ἄεισμα, φαάντατε ὦ Βασίλειε,
  βροντὴ σεῖο λόγος, ἀστεροπὴ δὲ βίος·
ἀλλὰ καὶ ὡς ἕδρην ἱερὴν λίπες· ἤθελεν οὕτω
  Χριστός, ὅπως μίξῃ σ᾽ ὡς τάχος οὐρανίοις.

10.—Εἰς τὸν αὐτόν

Βένθεα πάντ᾽ ἐδάης τὰ πνεύματος, ὅσσα τ᾽ ἔασι
  τῆς χθονίης σοφίης· ἔμπνοον ἱρὸν ἔης.

10в.—Εἰς τὸν αὐτόν

Ὀκτάετες λαοῖο θεόφρονος ἡνία τείνας,
  τοῦτο μόνον τῶν σῶν, ὦ Βασίλει᾽, ὀλίγον.

11.—Εἰς τὸν αὐτόν

Χαίροις, ὦ Βασίλειε, καὶ εἰ λίπες ἡμέας, ἔμπης·
  Γρηγορίου τόδε σοι γράμμ᾽ ἐπιτυμβίδιον,
μῦθος ὅδ᾽ ὃν φιλέεσκες· ἔχοις χερός, ὦ Βασίλειε,
  τῆς φιλίης καὶ σοὶ δῶρον ἀπευκτότατον.
Γρηγόριος, Βασίλειε, τεῇ κόνι τήνδ᾽ ἀνέθηκα   5
  τῶν ἐπιγραμματίων, θεῖε, δυωδεκάδα.

8.—*On the Same*

O CONVERSE, O friendship's common home, O dear Athens, O distant covenant we made to lead the divine life, know that Basil, as he desired, is in Heaven, but Gregory on earth, his lips chained.

9.—*On the Same*

O MOST glorious Basil, the great vaunt of Caesarea, thy word was thunder and thy life lightning. But none the less thou hast left thy holy seat; for such was the will of Christ that he might join thee early to the heavenly ones.

10.—*On the Same*

THOU knewest all the depths of the spirit and all that pertains to earthly wisdom. Thou wast a living temple.

10B.—*On the Same*

FOR but eight years didst thou hold the reins of the pious people, and this was all pertaining to thee that was little.

11.—*On the Same*

HAIL, Basil, yea even though thou hast left us. This is Gregory's epitaph for thee, this is the voice thou didst love. Take from the hand that was dear to thee the gift though it be right grievous to give. Gregory dedicates to thee, divine Basil, this dozen of epigrams.

12.—Εἰς τὸν ἑαυτοῦ πατέρα

Ἔνθ' ἑκατονταέτης, ζωῆς βροτέης καθύπερθε,
πνεύματι καὶ θώκῳ τεσσαρακονταέτης,
μείλιχος, ἡδυεπής, λαμπρὸς Τριάδος ὑποφήτης,
νήδυμον ὕπνον ἔχω, Γρηγορίοιο δέμας·
ψυχὴ δὲ πτερόεσσα λάχεν θεόν. ἀλλ' ἱερῆες   5
ἁζόμενοι κείνου καὶ τάφον ἀμφέπετε.

13.—Εἰς τὸν αὐτόν

Ἔκ με πικρῆς ἐκάλεσσε θεὸς μέγας ἀγριελαίης,
ποίμνης <δ'> ἡγεμόνα θῆκε τὸν οὐδ' οἴων
ἔσχατον· ἐκ πλευρῆς δὲ θεόφρονος ὄλβον ἔνειμεν·
γῆρας <δ'> ἐς λιπαρὸν ἱκόμεθ' ἀμφότεροι.
ἱρὸς ἐμῶν τεκέων ἀγανώτατος· εἰ δὲ τελευτὴν   5
ἔτλην Γρηγόριος, οὐ μέγα· θνητὸς ἔην.

14.—Εἰς τὸν αὐτόν

Εἴ τις ὅρους καθύπερθεν ἁγνῆς ὀπὸς ἔπλετο μύστης
Μωσῆς, καὶ μεγάλου Γρηγορίοιο νόος,
ὅν ποτε τηλόθ' ἐόντα χάρις μέγαν ἀρχιερῆα
θήκατο· νῦν δ' ἱερῆς ἐγγὺς ἔχει Τριάδος.

15.—Εἰς τὸν αὐτόν

Αὐτὸς νηὸν ἔρεψα θεῷ, καὶ δῶχ' ἱερῆα
Γρηγόριον καθαρῇ λαμπόμενον Τριάδι,
ἄγγελον ἀτρεκίης ἐριηχέα, ποιμένα λαῶν,
ἠΐθεον σοφίης ἀμφοτέρης πρύτανιν.

406

12.—*On his own Father*

HERE I sleep the sweet sleep, the body of Gregory, the mild sweet-spoken glorious interpreter of the Trinity. I lived to a hundred years, more than the span of man's life, and for forty years lived in the spirit and occupied the episcopal throne. But my winged soul is with God.—Ye priests, care reverently for his tomb too.

13.—*On the Same*

GREAT God called me from the bitter wild-olive,[1] and made me, who was not even the last of the sheep, the shepherd of the flock. From my devout rib[2] he gave me wealth of children, and both of us reached a prosperous old age. The mildest of my sons is a priest. If I Gregory suffered death, it is no marvel; I was mortal.

14.—*On the Same*

IF there was one Moses privileged on the mountain to hear the pure voice, there was also the mind of great Gregory, whom once God's grace called from afar and made a great high-priest. Now he dwells near the Holy Trinity

15.—*On the Same*

I BOTH built a temple to God and gave him a priest, Gregory illumined by the pure Trinity, the sonorous messenger of truth, the shepherd of the people, a youth excelling in holy and profane learning.

[1] *cp.* Rom. xi. 17.   [2] *i.e.* wife.

16.—Εἰς τὸν αὐτόν

Τέκνον ἐμόν, τὰ μὲν ἄλλα πατρὸς καὶ φέρτερος εἴης,
    τὴν δ' ἀγανοφροσύνην ἄξιος (οὔ τι πλέον
εὔξασθαι θέμις ἐστί)· καὶ ἐς βαθὺ γῆρας ἵκοιο,
    τοίου κηδεμόνος, ὦ μάκαρ, ἀντιάσας.

17.—Εἰς τὸν αὐτόν

Οὐκ ὄϊς, εἶτ' ὀΐων προφερέστατος· αὐτὰρ ἔπειτα
    ποιμήν, εἶτα πατήρ, καὶ νομέων νομέας,
θνητοὺς ἀθάνατόν τε θεὸν μέγαν εἰς ἓν ἀγείρων,
    κεῖμαι Γρηγόριος Γρηγορίου γενέτης.
ὄλβιος, εὐγήρως, εὔπαις θάνον, ἀρχιερῆος
    ἀρχιερεύς τε πατήρ, Γρηγόριος· τί πλέον;

18.—Εἰς τὸν αὐτόν

Οὔτι μὲν ἐς πολύκαρπον ἀλωὴν ὄρθριος ἦλθον,
    ἔμπα δὲ τῶν προτέρων πλείονα μισθὸν ἔχω
Γρηγόριος, ποιμήν τε καλὸς καὶ πλείονα ποίμνην
    Χριστῷ ἀναθρέψας ἤθεσι μειλιχίοις.

19.—Εἰς τὸν αὐτόν

Οὐχ ὁσίης ῥίζης μὲν ἐγὼ θάλος, εὐαγέος δὲ
    συζυγίης κεφαλὴ καὶ τεκέων τριάδος·
ποίμνης ἡγεμόνευσα ὁμόφρονος· ἔνθεν ἀπῆλθον
    πλήρης καὶ χθονίων κουρανίων ἐτέων.

20.—Εἰς τὸν αὐτόν

Γρηγόριος, τὸ δὲ θαῦμα, χάριν καὶ πνεύματος αἴγλην
    ἔνθεν ἀειρόμενος ῥίψ' ἐπὶ παιδὶ φίλῳ.

---

[1] i.e. Bishop.   [2] By the Eucharist.   [3] cp. I. Cor. xi. 3.

16.—*On the Same*

MAYEST thou, my son, excel thy father in other things and in gentleness be worthy of him (we may not pray for more); and mayest thou reach a ripe old age, blessed man, whose lot it was to have such a guardian.

17.—*On the Same*

No sheep, then the first of the sheep and next their shepherd, then their father and the shepherd of the shepherds,[1] gathering in one mortals and the immortal God,[2] I lie here, Gregory the father of Gregory. Happy I died in hale old age, blessed in my offspring, I Gregory the high-priest and father of a high-priest. What more could I desire?

18.—*On the Same*

I, GREGORY, came not early to the vineyard, but yet I have higher wage than those who came before me. I was a good shepherd and reared for Christ a greater flock by my gentle usage.

19.—*On the Same*

I AM the scion of no holy root, but the head[3] of a pious wife and of three children. I ruled over a flock united in spirit, from which I departed full of earthly and heavenly years.[4]

20.—*On the Same*

GREGORY, (marvellous it was) as he was taken up, cast on his dear son grace and the light of the Spirit.

[4] Years passed in the priesthood and previously.

409

GREEK ANTHOLOGY

21.—Εἰς τὸν αὐτόν

Τυτθὴ μάργαρος ἐστίν, ἀτὰρ λιθάκεσσιν ἀνάσσει,
   τυτθὴ καὶ Βηθλέμ, ἔμπα δὲ χριστοφόρος·
ὡς δ' ὀλίγην μὲν ἐγὼ ποίμνην λάχον, ἀλλὰ φερίστηι
   Γρηγόριος, τὴν σύ, παῖ φίλε, λίσσομ', ἄγοις.

22.—Εἰς τὸν αὐτόν

Ποιμενίην σύριγγα τεαῖς ἐν χερσὶν ἔθηκα
   Γρηγόριος· σὺ δέ μοι τέκνον ἐπισταμένως
σημαίνειν· ζωῆς δὲ θύρας πετάσειας ἅπασιν,
   ἐς δὲ τάφον πατέρος ὥριος ἀντιάσαις.

23.—Εἰς τὸν αὐτόν

Στράψε μὲν οἷς τὸ πάροιθεν ἐν οὔρεϊ Χριστὸς ἀμείφθη,
   στράψε δὲ Γρηγορίου τοῦ καθαροῖο νόῳ,
τῆμος ὅτ' εἰδώλων ἔφυγε ζόφον· ὡς δ' ἐκαθάρθη,
   ἧσι θυηπολίαις λαὸν ὃν εἰσέτ' ἄγει.

24.—Εἰς τὴν μητέρα ἐκ τοῦ θυσιαστηρίου προσληφθεῖσαν

Παντός σοι μύθοιο καὶ ἔργματος ἧεν ἄριστον
   ἦμαρ κυριακόν. πένθεῑ πένθος ἅπαν,
μῆτερ ἐμή, τίουσα, μόναις ὑπόεικες ἑορταῖς.
   εὐφροσύνης, ἀχέων ἵστορα νηὸν ἔχεις·
χῶρος ἅπας δάκρυσι τεοῖς σφρηγίζετο, μῆτερ·
   μούνῳ δὲ σταυρῷ πήγνυτο καὶ δάκρυα.

25.—Εἰς τὴν αὐτὴν μητέρα Νόνναν

Οὔποτε σεῖο τράπεζα θυηδόχος ἔδρακε νῶτα,
   οὐδὲ διὰ στομάτων ἦλθε βέβηλον ἔπος·
οὐδὲ γέλως μαλακῇσιν ἐφίζανε, μύστι, παρειαῖς.
   σιγήσω κρυφίους σεῖο, μάκαιρα, πόνους.
καὶ τὰ μὲν ἔνδοθι τοῖα, τὰ δ' ἔκτοθι πᾶσι πέφανται·
   τοὔνεκα καὶ θείῳ σῶμ' ἀπέλειπες ἕδει.

21.—*On the Same*

SMALL is the pearl, but the queen of jewels; small is Bethlehem, but yet the mother of Christ; so a little flock was mine, Gregory's, but of the best; and I pray, my dear son, that thou mayest lead it.

22.—*On the Same*

I, GREGORY, put into thy hands my shepherd's pipe. Rule over the flock skilfully my son. Open the gates of life to all, and ripe in years share thy father's tomb.

23.—*On the Same*

CHRIST shone in the eyes of those before whom he was transfigured on the mountain and he shone in the mind of pure Gregory when he escaped the darkness of idolatry.   But since he was purified, he leads his people ever by his priestly ministrations.

24.—*On his Mother who was taken to God from the Altar*

THE Lord's day was the crown of all thy words and deeds, my mother.   Honouring as thou didst all mourning by mourning, thou didst yield thee to rejoicing but on holy days.   The temple was the witness of thy joy and grief alike : all the place was sanctified by thy tears, and by the cross alone those tears were stayed.

25.—*On the Same*

THE sacrificial table never saw thy back, nor did a profane word ever pass thy lips, nor did laughter ever sit, O God's initiated, on thy soft cheeks.   I will say naught of thy secret troubles, O blessed woman.   Such wast thou within, and what thou wast outwardly was manifest to all.   Therefore didst thou take leave of thy body in the house of God.

26.—Εἰς τὴν αὐτήν

Πῶς ἐλύθη Νόννης καλὰ γούνατα; πῶς δὲ μέμυκεν
    χείλεα; πῶς ὄσσων οὐ προχέει λιβάδας;
ἄλλοι δ' αὖ βοόωσι παρ' ἠρίον· ἡ δὲ τράπεζα
    οὐκέτ' ἔχει καρποὺς τῆς μεγάλης παλάμης·
χῶρος δ' ἐστὶν ἔρημος ἁγνοῦ ποδός, οἱ δ' ἱερῆες
    οὐκέτ' ἐπὶ τρομερὴν κρατὶ βαλοῦσι χέρα.
χῆραι δ' ὀρφανικοί τε, τί ῥέζετε; παρθενίη δὲ
    καὶ γάμος εὐζυγέων, κέρσατ' ἄπο πλοκάμους,

    *   *   *   *   *   *

τοῖσιν ἀγαλλομένη κρατὸς φέρε πάντα χαμᾶζε,
    τῆμος ὅτ' ἐν νηῷ ῥικνὸν ἀφῆκε δέμας.

27.—Εἰς τὴν αὐτήν

Σάρρα σοφὴ τίουσα φίλον πόσιν· ἀλλὰ σύ, μῆτερ,
    πρῶτα Χριστιανόν, εἶθ' ἱερῆα μέγαν,
σὸν πόσιν ἐσθλὸν ἔθηκας ἀπόπροθι φωτὸς ἐόντα.
    Ἄννα, σὺ δ' υἷα φίλον καὶ τέκες εὐξαμένη,
καὶ νηῷ μιν ἔδωκας ἁγνὸν θεράποντα Σαμουήλ·
    ἡ δ' ἑτέρη κόλποις Χριστὸν ἔδεκτο μέγαν·
Νόννα δ' ἀμφοτέρων ἔλαχε κλέος· ὑστάτιον δὲ
    νηῷ λισσομένη πάρθετο σῶμα φίλον.

28.—Εἰς τὴν αὐτήν

Ἐμπεδόκλεις, σὲ μὲν αὐτίκ' ἐτώσια φυσιόωντα
    καὶ βροτὸν Αἰτναίοιο πυρὸς κρητῆρες ἔδειξαν·
Νόννα δ' οὐ κρητῆρας ἐσήλατο, πρὸς δὲ τραπέζῃ
    τῇδέ ποτ' εὐχομένη καθαρὸν θύος ἔνθεν ἀέρθη,
καὶ νῦν θηλυτέρῃσι μεταπρέπει εὐσεβέεσσι,
    Σουσάννῃ, Μαριάμ τε καὶ Ἄνναις, ἕρμα γυναικῶν.

26.—*On the Same*

How are Nonna's goodly knees relaxed, how are her lips closed, why sheds she not fountains from her eyes? Others cry aloud by her tomb, and the holy table no longer bears the gifts of her generous hands. The place misses her holy foot, and the priests no longer shall lay their trembling hands upon her head. Widows and orphans! what will ye do? Virgins and well mated couples! shear your hair . . . glorying in which she let fall on the ground all that was on her head, then when in the temple she quitted her wrinkled body.

27.—*On the Same*

SARAH was wise, honouring her dear husband, but thou, mother, didst make thy good husband, once far from the light, first a Christian and then a bishop. Thou Anna[1] didst both bear the dear son for whom thou didst pray and gavest thy Samuel to be a holy servant in the temple; but the second Anna[2] took to her bosom the great Christ. Nonna shared the fame of both, and at the end, praying in the church, she laid aside there her body.

28.—*On the Same*

EMPEDOCLES, the fiery crater of Etna received thee, a mortal puffed up with vanity. Nonna leapt into no crater, but praying by this table was taken up thence a pure victim, and now, one of the guardians of her sex, shares the glory of the pious women, Susanna, Mary and the two Annas.

[1] *i.e.* Hannah.   [2] Luke ii. 36.

29.—Εἰς τὴν αὐτήν

Ἥρακλες, Ἐμπεδότιμε, Τροφώνιε, εἴξατε μύθων,
καὶ σύ γ' Ἀρισταίου κενεαυχέος ὀφρὺς ἄπιστε·
ὑμεῖς μὲν θνητοὶ καὶ οὐ μάκαρες παθέεσσι·
θυμῷ δ' ἄρρενι Νόννα βίου τμήξασα κέλευθον,
Χριστοφόρος, σταυροῖο λάτρις, κόσμοιο περίφρων,   5
ἦλατ' ἐπουρανίην εἰς ἄντυγα ὡς ποθέεσκεν,
    τρίσμακαρ ἐν νηῷ σῶμ' ἀποδυσαμένη.

30.—Εἰς τὴν αὐτήν

Γρηγόριον βοόωσα παρ' ἀνθοκόμοισιν ἀλωαῖς
ἤντεο, μῆτερ ἐμή, ξείνης ἄπο νισσομένοισι,
χεῖρας δ' ἀμπετάσασα φίλας τεκέεσσι φίλοισι,
Γρηγόριον βοόωσα· τὸ δ' ἔζεεν αἷμα τεκούσης
ἀμφοτέροις ἐπὶ παισί, μάλιστα δὲ θρέμματι θηλῆς·
τοὔνεκα καὶ σὲ τόσοις ἐπιγράμμασι, μῆτερ, ἔτισα.

31.—Εἰς τὴν αὐτήν

Ἄλλη μὲν κλεινή τις ἐνοικιδίοισι πόνοισιν,
    ἄλλη δ' ἐκ χαρίτων ἠδὲ σαοφροσύνης,
ἄλλη δ' εὐσεβίης ἔργοις καὶ σαρκὸς ἀνίαις,
    δάκρυσιν, εὐχωλαῖς, χερσὶ πενητοκόμοις·
Νόννα δ' ἐν πάντεσσιν ἀοίδιμος· εἰ δὲ τελευτὴν
    τοῦτο θέμις καλέειν, κάτθανεν εὐχομένη.

32.—Εἰς τὴν αὐτήν

Τέκνον ἐμῆς θηλῆς, ἱερὸν θάλος, ὡς ἐπόθησα,
    οἴχομαι εἰς ζωήν, Γρηγόρι', οὐρανίην·

---

[1] A curious choice of names. Empedotimus was an

29.—*On the Same*

YIELD up your place in story, Heracles, Empedotimus, Trophonius and thou unbelieving pride of vainglorious Aristaeus.[1] Ye were mortal and not blessed in your affections; but Nonna the bearer of Christ, the servant of the cross, the despiser of the world, after travelling the path of life with virile spirit, leapt to the vault of heaven, even as she desired, thrice blessed in having put off the vesture of her body in the temple.

30.—*On the Same*

CALLING on Gregory, mother, thou didst meet us by the flowery fields on our return from a strange country, and didst reach out thy arms to thy dear children, calling ever on Gregory. The blood of the mother boiled for both her sons, but mostly for him whom she had suckled. Therefore have I honoured thee, mother, in so many epigrams.

31.—*On the Same*

ONE woman is famed for her domestic labours, another for grace and chastity, another for her pious deeds and the pains she inflicts on her body, her tears, her prayers, and her charity; but Nonna is renowned for everything, and, if we may call this death, she died while praying.

32.—*On the Same*

CHILD of my paps, holy sprout, Gregory, I go, as I longed, to the heavenly life. Much didst thou toil

obscure Pythagorean Philosopher, Trophonius the builder of the Delphian temple, and Aristaeus a Cyrenaean seer.

καὶ γὰρ πόλλ᾽ ἐμόγησας ἐμὸν κομέων πατέρος τε
γῆρας, ἃ καὶ Χριστοῦ βίβλος ἔχει μεγάλη·
ἀλλά, φίλος, τοκέεσσιν ἐφέσπεο, καί σε τάχιστα   5
δεξόμεθ᾽ ἡμετέροις φάεσι προφρονέως.

33.—Εἰς τὴν αὐτήν

Ψυχὴ μὲν πτερόεσσα πρὸς οὐρανὸν ἤλυθε Νόννης,
σῶμα δ᾽ ἄρ᾽ ἐκ νηοῦ Μάρτυσι παρθέμεθα.
Μάρτυρες, ἀλλ᾽ ὑπόδεχθε θύος μέγα, τὴν πολύμοχθον
σάρκα καὶ ὑμετέροις αἵμασιν ἑσπομένην,
αἵμασιν ὑμετέροισιν, ἐπεὶ ψυχῶν ὀλετῆρος   5
δηναιοῖσι πόνοις κάρτος ἔπαυσε μέγα.

34.—Εἰς τὴν αὐτήν

Οὐ μόσχων θυσίην σκιοειδέα, οὐδὲ χιμάρρων,
οὐδὲ πρωτοτόκων Νόνν᾽ ἀνέθηκε θεῷ·
ταῦτα νόμος προτέροισιν, ὅτ᾽ εἰκόνες· ἡ δ᾽ ἄρ᾽ ἑαυτὴν
δῶκεν ὅλην βιότῳ, μάνθανε, καὶ θανάτῳ.

35.—Εἰς τὴν αὐτήν

Εὐχομένη βοόωσα παρ᾽ ἁγνοτάτῃσι τραπέζαις
Νόννα λύθη. φωνὴ δ᾽ ἐδόθη καὶ χείλεα καλὰ
γηραλέης. τί τὸ θαῦμα; θεὸς θέλεν ὑμνήτειραν
γλῶσσαν ἐπ᾽ εὐφήμοισι λόγοις κληῗδα βαλέσθαι·
καὶ νῦν οὐρανόθεν μέγ᾽ ἐπεύχεται ἡμερίοισιν.   5

36.—Εἰς τὴν αὐτήν

Εὐχωλαῖς καὶ πόντον ἐκοίμισε Νόννα θεουδὴς
οἷς τεκέεσσι φίλοισι, καὶ ἐκ περάτων συνάγειρεν
ἀντολίης δύσιός τε, μέγα κλέος, οὐ δοκέοντας,
μητρὸς ἔρως· νοῦσόν τε πικρὴν ἀποέργαθεν ἀνδρός·
λισσομένη, τὸ δὲ θαῦμα, λίπεν βίον ἔνδοθι νηοῦ.   5

to tend my own and thy father's old age, and all this is written in the great book of Christ. But follow thy parents, dear, and we shall soon receive thee gladly to our splendour.

33.—*On the Same*

THE winged soul of Nonna went to heaven, and from the temple we bore her body to lay it beside the martyrs. Receive, ye martyrs, this great victim, her suffering flesh that follows your blood—your blood I say, for by her long labours she broke the mighty strength of the destroyer of souls.

34.—*On the Same*

No shadowy[1] sacrifice of calves or goats or first-born did Nonna offer to God. This the Law enjoined on men of old, when there were yet types, but learn that she sacrificed her whole self by her life and by her death.

35.—*On the Same*

NONNA was released as she was calling aloud in prayer by the most holy table; there the voice and the lovely lips of the aged woman were arrested. Why marvel thereat? God willed to put the lock on her hymning tongue as it was in the act of uttering words of happy omen, and now from heaven she prays aloud for mortals.

36.—*On the Same*

GOD-LIKE Nonna stilled the sea by her prayers for her dear sons, and their mother's love gathered them from the extremes of east and west, when they thought not to return—a great glory to her. And by her prayers she dispelled her husband's grave illness, and (what a marvel!) she ended her life in the church.

[1] Which is "a shadow of things to come." (Col. ii. 17).

37.—Εἰς τὴν αὐτήν

Πολλάκις ἔκ με νόσων τε καὶ ἀργαλέων ὀρυμαγδῶν,
σεισμῶν τε κρυερῶν, καὶ ἄγρια κυμαίνοντος
οἴδματος ἐξεσάωσας, ἐπεὶ θεὸν ἵλαον εἶχες·
ἀλλὰ σάω καὶ νῦν με, πάτερ, μεγάλῃσι λιτῇσι,
καὶ σύ, τεκοῦσα, μάκαιρα ἐν εὐχωλῇσι θανοῦσα.   5

38.—Εἰς τὴν αὐτήν

Νόνναν ἐπουρανίοισιν ἀγαλλομένην φαέεσσι,
καὶ ῥίζης ἱερῆς πτόρθον ἀειθαλέα,
Γρηγορίου ἱερῆος ὁμόζυγα, καὶ πραπίδεσσιν
εὐαγέων τεκέων μητέρα, τύμβος ἔχω.

39.—Εἰς τὴν αὐτήν

Εὐχαί τε στοναχαί τε φίλαι καὶ νύκτες ἄϋπνοι,
καὶ νηοῖο πέδον δάκρυσι δευόμενον,
σοί, Νόννα ζαθέη, τοίην βιότοιο τελευτὴν
ὤπασαν, ἐν νηῷ ψῆφον ἑλεῖν θανάτου.

40.—Εἰς τὴν αὐτήν

Μούνη σοὶ φωνὴ περιλείπετο, Νόννα φαεινή,
πάνθ' ἄμυδις ληνοῖς ἐνθεμένη μεγάλοις,
ἐκ καθαρῆς κραδίης ἁγνὸν θύος· ἀλλ' ἄρα καὶ τὴν
ὑστατίην νηῷ λεῖπες ἀειρομένη.

41.—Εἰς τὴν αὐτήν

Οὐδὲ θάνεν νηοῖο θυώδεος ἔκτοθι Νόννα,
φωνὴν δὲ προτέρην ἥρπασε Χριστὸς ἄναξ
λισσομένης· πόθεεν γὰρ ἐν εὐχωλῇσι τελέσσαι
τόνδε βίον πάσης ἁγνότερον θυσίης.

37.—*On the Same*

OFTEN from disease and grave disturbance, and dreadful earthquake, and the wild tossing of the waves hast thou saved me, as God inclined his ear to thee. But save me now, father, by thy prayers of might, and thou, mother, blessed in that thou didst die while praying.

38.—*On the Same*

I AM the tomb which holds Nonna glorying in celestial splendour, the evergreen sapling of a holy root, the wife of the priest Gregory and mother of pious children.

39.—*On the Same*

THY prayers and the groans thou didst love, and sleepless nights, and the floor of the church bedewed with tears procured for thee, divine Nonna, such an end—to receive the doom of death in church.

40.—*On the Same*

ONLY thy voice was left to thee, shining Nonna, who didst cast all that was thine together into the great wine-vats,[1] a pure offering from a pure heart; but at the end when thou wast taken thou didst leave that too in the church.

41.—*On the Same*

NONNA did not even die outside the incense-breathing church, but Christ took her voice first as she was praying. For she desired to finish in prayer this life purer than any sacrifice.

[1] *i.e.* churches. The word was so interpreted in the heading to Ps. viii.

42.—Εἰς τὴν αὐτήν

Νόνν' ἱερή, σὺ δὲ πάντα θεῷ βίον ἀντείνασα
    ὑστάτιον ψυχὴν δῶκας ἁγνὴν θυσίην·
τῇδε γὰρ εὐχομένη ζωὴν λίπες· ἡ δὲ τράπεζα,
    μῆτερ ἐμή, τῷ σῷ δῶκε κλέος θανάτῳ.

43.—Εἰς τὴν αὐτήν

Τῆσδε πατὴρ μὲν ἐμὸς λάτρις μέγας ἦε τραπέζης,
    μήτηρ δ' εὐχομένη πὰρ ποσὶ λῆξε βίου,
Γρηγόριος Νόννα τε μεγακλέες· εὔχομ' ἄνακτι
    τοίαν ἐμοὶ ζωὴν καὶ τέλος ἀντιάσαι.

44.—Εἰς τὴν αὐτήν

" Πολλά, τράπεζα φίλη, Νόννης καὶ δάκρυ' ἐδέξω·
    δέχνυσο καὶ ψυχήν, τὴν πυμάτην θυσίην."
εἶπε καὶ ἐκ μελέων κέαρ ἔπτατο· ἐν δ' ἄρα μοῦνον,
    παῖδ' ἐπόθει, τεκέων τὸν ἔτι λειπόμενον.

45.—Εἰς τὴν αὐτήν

Ἔνθα ποτ' εὐχομένης τόσσον νόος ἔπτατο Νόννης,
    μέσφ' ὅτε καὶ ψυχὴ ἔσπετ' ἀειρομένῳ·
εὐχομένης δὲ νέκυς ἱερῇ παρέκειτο τραπέζῃ.
    γράψατ' ἐπερχομένοις θαῦμα τόδ', εὐσεβέες.

46.—Εἰς τὴν αὐτήν

Τίς θάνεν ὡς θάνε Νόννα, παρ' εὐαγέεσσι τραπέζαις,
    τῶν ἱερῶν σανίδων χερσὶν ἐφαπτομένη;
τίς λῦσεν εὐχομένης Νόννης τύπον; ὡς ἐπὶ δηρὸν
    ἤθελεν ἔνθα μένειν καὶ νέκυς εὐσεβέων.

42.—*On the Same*

HOLY Nonna, thou who hadst offered all thy life to God, didst give him thy soul at the end as a pure sacrifice.   For here thou didst depart this life in prayer, and the altar gave glory, my mother, to thy death.

43.—*On the Same*

MY father was the distinguished servant of this table, and my mother died in prayer at its feet.— Gregory and Nonna of good fame.   I pray to the King that such a life and death may be mine.

44.—*On the Same*

" MANY of Nonna's tears, dear table, didst thou receive ; receive now her soul, her last sacrifice," so spake she, and her soul flew from her limbs.   One thing alone did she lack, her son, her still surviving child.

45.—*On the Same*

HERE the mind of Nonna in her prayers flew so often on high that at length her soul too followed it as it mounted.   She fell a corpse even as she prayed at the foot of the holy table.   Write this marvel, O holy men, for generations to come.

46.—*On the Same*

WHO died as Nonna died by the pure table, touching with her hands the holy planks ?   Who dissolved the form of Nonna as she was praying ?   For she wished to tarry long here, pious even when she was a corpse.

47.—Εἰς τὴν αὐτήν

Ἔνθα ποτ' εὐχομένῃ Νόννῃ θεὸς εἶπεν ἄνωθεν·
  "Ἔρχεο." ἡ δ' ἐλύθη σώματος ἀσπασίως,
χειρῶν ἀμφοτέρων τῇ μὲν κατέχουσα τράπεζαν,
  τῇ δ' ἔτι λισσομένῃ· "Ἵλαθι, Χριστὲ ἄναξ."

48.—Εἰς τὴν αὐτήν

Ῥίζης εὐσεβέος γενόμην καὶ σὰρξ ἱερῆος,
  καὶ μήτηρ· Χριστῷ σῶμα, βίον, δάκρυα,
πάντ' ἐκένωσα φέρουσα· τὸ δ' ἔσχατον, ἔνθεν ἀέρθην
  νηῷ γηραλέον Νόννα λιποῦσα δέμας.

49.—Εἰς τὴν αὐτήν

Πίστις Ἐνὼχ μετέθηκε καὶ Ἠλίαν, ἐν δὲ γυναιξὶ
  μητέρ' ἐμὴν πρώτην· οἶδε τράπεζα τόδε,
ἔνθεν ἀναιμάκτοισιν ὁμοῦ θυέεσσιν ἀέρθη
  εἰσέτι λισσομένη σώματι Νόννα φίλη.

50.—Εἰς τὴν αὐτήν

Οὐ νόσος, οὐδέ σε γῆρας ὁμοίϊον, οὔ σέ γ' ἀνίη,
  καίπερ γηραλέην, μῆτερ ἐμή, δάμασεν·
ἀλλ' ἄτρωτος, ἄκαμπτος ἁγνοῖς ὑπὸ ποσσὶ τραπέζης,
  εὐχομένη Χριστῷ, Νόνν', ἀπέδωκας ὄπα.

51.—Εἰς τὴν αὐτήν

Δῶκε θεῷ θυσίην Ἀβραὰμ πάϊν, ὡς δὲ θύγατρα
  κλεινὸς Ἰεφθάε, ἀμφότεροι μεγάλην·
μῆτερ ἐμή, σὺ δ' ἔδωκας ἁγνὸν βίον, ὑστάτιον δὲ
  ψυχήν, εὐχωλῆς, Νόννα, φίλον σφάγιον.

47.—*On the Same*

HERE once God said from on high to Nonna as she was praying "Come," and gladly she was released from her body, holding the table with one hand and with the other praying "Lord Christ, have mercy upon us."

48.—*On the Same*

SPRINGING from a pious root I was the flesh [1] of and the mother of a priest.   To Christ I brought my body, my life, my tears, emptying out my all; and last of all here in the church I Nonna was taken up, leaving my aged body.

49.—*On the Same*

FAITH translated Enoch and Elias, but among women my mother first of all; the table knows this, whence dear Nonna still praying in the body was taken up together with the bloodless Sacrifice.

50.—*On the Same*

NEITHER sickness nor age, the common lot of all, nor grief subdued thee, my mother, old though thou wast, but unwounded, unbent, at the holy feet of the altar, in the act of praying, thou didst render up thy voice to Christ.

51.—*On the Same*

ABRAHAM gave his son a sacrifice to God, and renowned Jephtha his daughter, a great sacrifice in each case, but thou, my mother, didst give thy holy life and finally thy soul, the dear victim of thy prayer.

[1] *i.e.* wife.

52.—Εἰς τὴν αὐτήν

Σάρρα φίλη, πῶς τὸν σὸν Ἰσαὰκ λίπες, ἢ ποθέουσα
    τῶν Ἀβραὰμ κόλπων ὡς τάχος ἀντιάσαι,
Νόννα, Γρηγορίοιο θεόφρονος; ἢ μέγα θαῦμα
    μηδὲ θανεῖν νηῶν ἔκτοθι καὶ θυέων.

52β.—Εἰς τὴν αὐτήν

Μάρτυρες, ἱλήκοιτε· μόγοις γε μὲν οὔτι χερείων
    Νόννα φίλη, κρυπτῷ κἀμφαδίῳ πολέμῳ·
τοὔνεκα καὶ τοίης κύρσεν βιότοιο τελευτῆς,
    εὐχῆς καὶ ζωῆς ἐν τέλος εὑραμένη.

53.—Εἰς τὴν αὐτήν

Ἡ Τριὰς ἣν ποθέεσκες, ὁμὸν σέλας, ἔν τε σέβασμα,
    ἐκ νηοῦ μεγάλου σε πρὸς οὐρανὸν ἥρπασε, Νόννα,
εὐχομένην· ζωῆς δὲ τέλος καθαρώτερον εὗρες.
    οὔποτε χείλεα μίξας ἀνάγνοις χείλεσιν ἁγνά,
οὐδ᾽ ἀθέῳ παλάμῃ καθαρὰν χέρα μέχρις ἐδωδῆς,
    μῆτερ ἐμή· μισθὸς δὲ λιπεῖν βίον ἐν θυέεσσιν.

54.—Εἰς τὴν αὐτήν

Ἄγγελος αἰγλήεις σὲ φαάντατος ἥρπασε, Νόννα,
    ἔνθα ποτ᾽ εὐχομένην, καθαρὴν μελέεσσι νόῳ τε·
καὶ τὸ μὲν ἥρπασε σεῖο, τὸ δ᾽ ἐνθάδε κάλλιπε νηῷ.

55.—Εἰς τὴν αὐτήν

Νηὸς ὅδ᾽ (οὐ γὰρ ὅλην Νόνναν θέμις ἦεν ἐρύξαι),
    ψυχῆς οἰχομένης, μοῦνον ἐπέσχε δέμας,
ὡς πάλιν ἐγρομένη καθαρώτερον ἔνθεν ἀερθῇ,
    σώματι τῷ μογερῷ δόξαν ἐφεσσομένη.

52.—*On the Same*

DEAR Sarah, how didst thou leave thy Isaac? Was it, Nonna, that thou didst desire to come as quickly as might be to the bosom of Abraham, of pious Gregory?[1] Verily a great marvel was it that thou didst not even die outside the temple and the incense.

52B.—*On the Same*

FAVOUR us, ye martyrs! Dear Nonna was not inferior to you in the pains she suffered in secret and open war. Therefore she met with such an end, finishing at once her prayer and her life.

53.—*On the Same*

THE Trinity for which thou didst long, one light and one majesty, carried thee off, Nonna, from the great church to heaven, and a purer end was thine than the common one. Never, my mother, didst thou join thy pure lips to impure ones, nor thy clean hand to a godless one so far as to join in meals with the heathen. Thou wast rewarded by dying at the place of sacrifice.

54.—*On the Same*

AN angel of dazzling lightness carried thee off, Nonna, whilst thou wert praying here, pure in body and spirit. Part of thee he carried off and part he left in the temple.

55.—*On the Same*

THIS temple (it was not allowed to keep the whole of Nonna) only retained her body when her soul departed, so that awaking again she may be taken up on high more purely, her suffering body clothed in glory.

[1] By Sarah he means Nonna, by Abraham his father, by Isaac himself.

56.—Εἰς τὴν αὐτήν

Ἄλλοις μὲν Νόννης τις ἁγνῶν ἐσθλοῖσιν ἐρίζοι,
εὐχωλῆς δὲ μέτροισιν ἐριζέμεν οὐ θέμις ἐστίν·
τέκμαρ καὶ βιότοιο τέλος λιτῇσι λυθέντος.

57.—Εἰς τὴν αὐτήν

Ὦ στοναχῶν δακρύων τε καὶ ἐννυχίων μελεδώνων·
ὦ Νόννης ζαθέης τετρυμένα γυῖα πόνοισι·
ποῦ ποτ’ ἔην, νηὸς μόχθων λῦσε γῆρας ἄκαμπτον.

58.—Εἰς τὴν αὐτήν

α. Νόννῃ Φιλτατίου. β. Καὶ ποῦ θάνε; α. Τῷδ’
            ἐνὶ νηῷ.
   β. Καὶ πῶς; α. Εὐχομένη. β. Πηνίκα; α. Γηραλέη.
β. Ὦ καλοῦ βιότοιο καὶ εὐαγέος θανάτοιο.

59.—Εἰς τὴν αὐτήν

Ἅρματι μὲν πυρόεντι πρὸς οὐρανὸν Ἠλίας ἦλθεν·
Νόνναν δ’ εὐχομένην πνεῦμ’ ὑπέδεκτο μέγα.

60.—Εἰς τὴν αὐτήν

Ἐνθάδε Νόννα φίλη κοιμήσατο τὸν βαθὺν ὕπνον,
ἵλαος ἑσπομένη ᾧ πόσι Γρηγορίῳ.

61. <Εἰς τὴν αὐτήν>

Τάρβος ὁμοῦ καὶ χάρμα· πρὸς οὐρανὸν ἔνθεν ἀέρθη
εὐχῆς ἐκ μεσάτης Νόννα λιποῦσα βίον.

56.—*On the Same*

ANOTHER of the saints might vie with the other good works of Nonna; let it be allowed to none to vie with the extent of her prayers. The end of her life which came while she was praying testifies to this.

57.—*On the Same*

O GROANS and tears and cares of the night, O limbs of holy Nonna worn with toil! Her unbent old-age was released from trouble by that temple in which she was.

58.—*On the Same*

A. "NONNA the daughter of Philtatius." *B.* "And where died she?" *A.* "In this church." *B.* "And how?" *A.* "Praying." *B.* "When?" *A.* "In old age." *B.* "O excellent life and pious death!"

59.—*On the Same*

ELIAS went to heaven in a fiery chariot, and the Great Spirit took to Itself Nonna while she was praying.

60.—*On the Same*

HERE dear Nonna fell into the deep sleep, following gladly her husband Gregory.

61.—*On the Same*

TERROR and joy together! Hence in the middle of her prayers Nonna quitted this life and was taken up to heaven.

GREEK ANTHOLOGY

62. <Εἰς τὴν αὐτήν>

Εὐχῆς καὶ βιότου Νόννῃ τέλος· ἡ δὲ τράπεζα
μάρτυς ἀφ' ἧς ἤρθη ἄπνοος ἐξαπίνης.

63.—Εἰς τὴν αὐτήν

Νόννης ἠρίον εἰμὶ σαόφρονος, ἥ ῥα πύλῃσιν
ἔχριμψ' οὐρανίαις, πρὶν βιότοιο λυθῇ.

64. <Εἰς τὴν αὐτήν>

Δακρύετε θνητούς, θνητῶν γένος· εἰ δέ τις οὕτως
ὡς Νόνν' εὐχομένη κάτθανεν, οὐ δακρύω.

65.—Εἰς τὴν αὐτήν

Νόννης ἀζόμενος ἁγνὸν βίον, ἄζεο μᾶλλον
καὶ τέλος· ἐν νηῷ κάτθανεν εὐχομένη.

66. <Εἰς τὴν αὐτήν>

Ἔνθα ποτ' εὐχομένη πρηνὴς θάνε Νόννα φαεινή·
νῦν δ' ἄρ' ἐν εὐσεβέων λίσσεται ἱσταμένη.

67.—Εἰς τὴν αὐτήν

Στήλη σοὶ θανάτου μελιηδέος ἥδε τράπεζα,
Νόννα, παρ' ᾗ λύθης εὐχομένη πύματα.

67Β. <Εἰς τὴν αὐτήν>

Μικρὸν ἔτι ψυχῆς ἦν τὸ πνέον· ἀλλ' ἄρα καὶ τὸ
Νόνν' ἀπέδωκε θεῷ ἔνθα ποτ' εὐχομένη.

62.—*On the Same*

THERE was one end to Nonna's life and prayer. The table from which she was of a sudden taken lifeless testifies to it.

63.—*On the Same*

I AM the tomb of chaste Nonna, who approached the gates of Heaven even while yet alive.

64.—*On the Same*

YE mortals, weep for mortals, but for one who, like Nonna, died in prayer, I weep not.

65.—*On the Same*

REVERING Nonna's pure life, revere even more her death. She died in the church while praying.

66.—*On the Same*

HERE bright Nonna while praying fell prone in death, but now she stands and prays in the home of the blest.

67.—*On the Same*

THIS table is the monument of thy sweet death, Nonna, the table by which, while praying thy last, thou didst die.

67B.—*On the Same*

ONLY a little breath had her soul left, but that Nonna, praying here, rendered up to God.

68.—Εἰς τὴν αὐτήν

Πέμψατε ἐκ νηοῦ θεοειδέα Νόνναν ἅπαντες,
πρέσβειραν μεγάλην πέμψατ᾿ ἀειρομένην.

69. <Εἰς τὴν αὐτήν>

Ἔκ με θεὸς καθαροῖο πρὸς οὐρανὸν ἥρπασε νηοῦ
Νόνναν, ἐπειγομένην οὐρανίοις πελάσαι.

70.—Εἰς τὴν αὐτήν

Νόνν᾿ ἀπανισταμένη νηοῦ μεγάλου τόδ᾿ ἔειπε·
"Τῶν πολλῶν καμάτων μείζονα μισθὸν ἔχω."

71. <Εἰς τὴν αὐτήν>

Νόννα φίλης εὐχῆς ἱερήιον ἐνθάδε κεῖται·
Νόννα ποτ᾿ εὐχομένη τῇδ᾿ ἐλύθη βιότου.

72.—Εἰς τὴν αὐτήν

Ἔνθα ποτ᾿ εὐχομένης ψυχὴ δέμας ἔλλιπε Νόννης·
ἔνθεν ἀνηέρθη Νόννα λιποῦσα δέμας.

73.—Εἰς τὴν αὐτήν

Ἐκ νηοῦ μεγάλοιο θύος μέγα Νόνν᾿ ἀπανέστη·
νηῷ Νόνν᾿ ἐλύθη· χαίρετε, εὐσεβέες.

74. <Εἰς τὴν αὐτήν>

Ἥδε τράπεζα θεῷ θεοειδέα Νόνναν ἔπεμψεν.

68.—*On the Same*

Escort divine Nonna from the church, all ye people, escort the grand old woman raised on high.

69.—*On the Same*

God from his pure temple took to heaven Nonna eager to join the heavenly ones.

70.—*On the Same*

Nonna rising from the great church said "I have a reward greater than all my many labours."

71.—*On the Same*

Here lies Nonna, victim of a pure prayer. Here Nonna while praying was released from life.

72.—*On the Same*

Here Nonna's soul left her body while she was praying. Hence Nonna leaving her body was taken up.

73.—*On the Same*

Nonna rose, a great sacrifice, from the great church. In the church Nonna died. Rejoice all ye pious.

74.—*On the Same*

This altar sent God-like Nonna to God.

75.—Εὐχὴ παρὰ τῶν γονέων εἰς τὸν μέγαν Γρηγόριον

Εἴη σοὶ βίος ἐσθλὸς ἐπ' εὐλογίῃσιν ἁπάσαις
ὁσσάτιαι τοκέων υἱέσι γηροκόμοις·
καὶ κούφης βιότοιο τυχεῖν ὁσίης τε τελευτῆς,
οἵην ἡμετέρῳ γήραϊ δῶκεν ἄναξ,
ἠϊθέων λογίων τὸ μέγα κράτος, ἠδ' ἱερήων,   5
καὶ πολιῆς σκίπων, Γρηγόρι', ἡμετέρης.

76.—Παρὰ τῶν γονέων

'Ασπάσιοι χθόνα τήνδε φίλαις ὑπὸ χείρεσι παιδὸς
ἐσσάμεθ' εὐσεβέος Γρηγορίου τοκέες·
ὃς καὶ γῆρας ἔθηκεν ἑοῖς μόχθοισιν ἐλαφρὸν
ἡμέτερον, καὶ νῦν ἀμφιέπει θυσίαις.
ἄμπνεε γηροκόμων καμάτων, μέγα φέρτατε παίδων   5
Γρηγόρι', εὐαγέας Μάρτυσι παρθέμενος
σοὺς τοκέας· μισθὸς δὲ μέγαν πατέρ' ἵλαον εἶναι,
πνευματικῶν τε τυχεῖν εὐσεβέων τεκέων.

77.—Εἰς τὸν πάντων αὐτῶν τάφον

Λᾶας ὁ μὲν γενέτην τε καὶ υἱέα κυδήεντας
κεύθω Γρηγορίους, εἷς λίθος ἶσα φάη,
ἀμφοτέρους ἱερῆας· ὁ δ' εὐπατέρειαν ἐδέγμην
Νόνναν σὺν μεγάλῳ υἱέϊ Καισαρίῳ.
τὼς ἐδάσαντο τάφους τε καὶ υἱέας· ἡ δὲ πορείη,   5
πάντες ἄνω· ζωῆς εἷς πόθος οὐρανίης.

78.—Τίς πρῶτος καὶ τίς μετέπειτα ἀπῆρε

Πρῶτος Καισάριος ξυνὸν ἄχος· αὐτὰρ ἔπειτα
Γοργόνιον, μετέπειτα πατὴρ φίλος· οὐ μετὰ δηρὸν
μήτηρ. ὦ λυπρὴ παλάμη καὶ γράμματα λυπρὰ
Γρηγορίου· γράψω καὶ ἐμὸν μόρον ὑστατίου περ.

432

75.—*Prayer of his Parents for Gregory the Great*

GREGORY, great champion of the learned youth and of the priesthood, staff of our grey years, may thy life be happy and enjoy all the blessings which fall to sons who tend their parents' old age and mayst thou meet with an easy and holy end, even as the Lord gave to our many years.

76.—*Similar*

BY the dear hands of our son, the pious Gregory, we are clothed in this welcome earth. He it was also who lightened our old age by his toil, and now tends us with sacrifices. Gregory, best of sons, repose from thy labour of tending our old age, now that thou hast laid thy pious parents beside the martyrs. Thy reward is to be thyself a great and kind father and to have pious spiritual children.

77.—*On the tomb of all of them*

ONE stone encloses the renowned Gregories, father and son, two equal lights, both of them priests, the other received noble Nonna with her great son Caesarius. So they separated their tombs and sons, but the journey of all is on high; one desire of eternal life fills all.

78.—*Who first and who last departed this life*

FIRST died Caesarius, a grief to all, next Gorgonion, then their beloved father and not long after their mother. O mournful hand and mournful writing of Gregory! But I will write my own death also, although I am the last to die.

79.—Εἰς ἑαυτόν

Πρῶτα μὲν εὐξαμένη με θεὸς πόρε μητρὶ φαεινῇ·
  δεύτερον, ἐκ μητρὸς δῶρον ἔδεκτο φίλον·
τὸ τρίτον αὖ, θνήσκοντά μ᾽ ἁγνὴ ἐσάωσε τράπεζα·
  τέτρατον, ἀμφήκη μῦθον ἔδωκε Λόγος·
πέμπτον, Παρθενίη με φίλοις προσπτύξατ᾽ ὀνείροις·   5
  ἕκτον, Βασιλίῳ σύμπνοα ἱρὰ φέρον·
ἕβδομον, ἐκ βυθίων με φερέσβιος ἥρπασε κόλπων·
  ὄγδοον εὖ νούσοις ἐξεκάθηρα χέρας·
εἴνατον ὁπλοτέρῃ Τριάδ᾽ ἤγαγον, ὦ ἄνα, Ῥώμῃ·
  βέβλημαι δέκατον λάεσιν ἠδὲ φίλοις.   10

80.—Εἰς ἑαυτόν

Ἑλλὰς ἐμή, νεότης τε φίλη, καὶ ὅσσα πεπάσμην,
  καὶ δέμας, ὡς Χριστῷ εἴξατε προφρονέως.
εἰ δ᾽ ἱερῆα φίλον με θεῷ θέτο μητέρος εὐχὴ
  καὶ πατρὸς παλάμη, τίς φθόνος; ἀλλά, μάκαρ,
σοῖς με, Χριστέ, χοροῖσι δέχου, καὶ κῦδος ὀπάζοις   5
  υἱέι Γρηγορίου σῷ λάτρι Γρηγορίῳ.

81.—Ἐπὶ τῷ ἰδίῳ τάφῳ

Γρηγορίου Νόννης τε φίλον τέκος ἐνθάδε κεῖται
  τῆς ἱερῆς Τριάδος Γρηγόριος θεράπων,
καὶ σοφίῃ σοφίης δεδραγμένος, ἠίθεός τε
  οἷον πλοῦτον ἔχων ἐλπίδ᾽ ἐπουρανίην.

82.—Εἰς ἑαυτόν

Τυτθὸν ἔτι ζώεσκες ἐπὶ χθονί, πάντα δὲ Χριστῷ
  δῶκας ἑκών, σὺν τοῖς καὶ πτερόεντα λόγον·
νῦν δ᾽ ἱερῆα μέγαν σε καὶ οὐρανίοιο χορείης
  οὐρανὸς ἐντὸς ἔχει, κύδιμε Γρηγόριε.

79.—*On Himself*

FIRSTLY God gave me to my glorious mother in answer to her prayers; secondly, He received me a welcome gift from her; thirdly, the holy table saved me from death: fourthly, the Word gave me two-edged speech;[1] fifthly, Virginity enfolded me in her dear dreams; sixthly, I entered the priesthood in union with Basil; seventhly, my father saved me from the deep; eighthly, I cleansed well my hands by disease (*sic*); ninthly, I brought the doctrine of the Trinity, O my Lord, to New Rome;[2] tenthly, I was smitten by stones and by friends (*sic*).

80.—*On Himself*

MY Greece, my dear youth, my possessions, my body, how gladly ye yielded to Christ! If my mother's vow and my father's hand made me a priest acceptable to God, why grudge me this? Blessed Christ receive me in thy choirs and give glory to thy servant Gregory son of Gregory.

81.—*On his own Tomb*

HERE lies Gregory, the dear child of Gregory and Nonna, the servant of the Holy Trinity, who grasped wisdom by wisdom and as a youth had no riches but the hope of heaven.

82.—*On Himself*

A SHORT time didst thou dwell on earth, but didst freely give all to Christ, the winged word too. But now, glorious Gregory, heaven holds thee a high priest in the celestial choir.

---

[1] *i.e.* sacred and profane.   [2] Constantinople.

83.—Εἰς ἑαυτόν

Ἔκ με βρέφους ἐκάλεσσε θεὸς νυχίοισιν ὀνείροις·
   ἤλυθον ἐς σοφίης πείρατα, σάρκα λόγῳ
ἥγνισα καὶ κραδίην· κόσμου φλόγα γυμνὸς ἀλύξας,
   ἔστην σὺν Ἀαρὼν Γρηγορίῳ γενέτῃ.

84.—Εἰς ἑαυτόν

Πατρὸς ἐγὼ ζαθέοιο καὶ οὔνομα καὶ θρόνον ἔσχον,
   καὶ τάφον· ἀλλά, φίλος, μνώεο Γρηγορίου,
Γρηγορίου, τὸν μητρὶ θεόσδοτον ὤπασε Χριστὸς
   φάσμασιν ἐννυχίοις, δῶκε δ' ἔρον σοφίης.

85.—Εἰς Καισάριον τὸν ἑαυτοῦ ἀδελφόν

Σχέτλιός ἐστιν ὁ τύμβος. ἔγωγε μὲν οὔποτ' ἐώλπειν
   ὥς ῥα κατακρύψει τοὺς πυμάτους προτέρους
αὐτὰρ ὁ Καισάριον, ἐρικυδέα υἷα τοκήων,
   τῶν προτέρων πρότερον δέξατο· ποία δίκη;

85β.—Εἰς τὸν αὐτόν

Οὐκ ἔσθ' ὁ τύμβος αἴτιος· μὴ λοιδόρει.
φθόνου τόδ' ἐστὶν ἔργον· πῶς δ' ἤνεγκεν ἂν
νέον γερόντων εἰσορῶν σοφώτερον;

86.—Εἰς τὸν αὐτόν

Γρηγόριε, θνητῶν μὲν ὑπείροχον ἔλλαχες υἷα
   κάλλεϊ καὶ σοφίῃ, καὶ βασιλῆϊ φίλον·
κρείσσονα δ' οὐκέτι πάμπαν ἀπηλεγέος θανάτοιο.
   ἦ μὴν ὠιόμην· ἀλλὰ τί φησι τάφος;
"Τέτλαθι· Καισάριος μὲν ἀπέφθιτο· ἀλλὰ μέγιστον
   υἱέος εὖχος ἔχεις, υἱέος ἀντὶ φίλου."

83.—*On Himself*

GOD called me by dreams of the night from my childhood: I reached the limits of wisdom, I sanctified my flesh and heart by reason. Naked I escaped from the fire of the world and stood with Aaron my father Gregory.

84.—*On Himself*

MINE were the name, the throne, and the tomb of my holy father; but, friend, remember Gregory, whom Christ granted,[1] a gift from God, in visions of the night to his mother, and to whom He gave the love of wisdom.

85.—*On Caesarius his Brother*

THE tomb is wicked. Never did I believe that it would cover the last first. But it received Caesarius, his parents' distinguished son, before his elders. What justice!

85B.—*On the Same*

IT is not the tomb's fault. Rebuke it not. This is the work of envy. How could envy have supported seeing a young man wiser than the old.

86.—*On the Same*

GREGORY, thou hadst a son, most excellent among mortals in beauty and wisdom and beloved by the Emperor; yet not stronger than ruthless death. I deemed it might be so indeed; but what saith the tomb? "Bear it. Caesarius is dead, but instead of your dear son you have great glory of his memory."

[1] *i.e.* promised.

437

87.—Εἰς τοὺς γονεῖς τοῦ μεγάλου Γρηγορίου καὶ
Καισαρίου

Ὥριοι εἰς τάφον ἦμεν, ὅτ᾽ ἐνθάδε τοῦτον ἔθηκαν
   λᾶαν ἐφ᾽ ἡμετέρῳ γήραϊ λαοτόμοι·
ἀλλ᾽ ἡμῖν μὲν ἔθηκαν· ἔχει δέ μιν οὐ κατὰ κόσμον
   Καισάριος, τεκέων ἡμετέρων πύματος.
ἔτλημεν πανάποτμα, τέκος, τέκος· ἀλλὰ τάχιστα
   δέξαι ἐς ὑμέτερον τύμβον ἐπειγομένους.

88.—Εἰς τὸν αὐτὸν Καισάριον

Τόνδε λίθον τοκέες μὲν ἑὸν τάφον ἐστήσαντο,
   ἐλπόμενοι ζωῆς μοῖραν ἔχειν ὀλίγην·
Καισαρίῳ δ᾽ υἱῆϊ πικρὴν χάριν οὐκ ἐθέλοντες
   δῶκαν, ἐπεὶ πρότερος τοῦδε λύθη βιότου.

89.—Εἰς τὸν αὐτόν

Γῆρας ἐμὸν δήθυνεν ἐπὶ χθονί· ἀντὶ δὲ πατρὸς
   λᾶαν ἔχεις, τεκέων φίλτατε, Καισάριε.
τίς νόμος; οἵα δίκη; θνητῶν ἄνα, πῶς τόδ᾽ ἔνευσας;
   ὦ μακροῦ βιότου, ὦ ταχέος θανάτου.

90.—Εἰς τὸν αὐτόν

Οὐκ ἄγαμ᾽, οὐκ ἄγαμαι δῶρον τόδε· τύμβον ἐδέξω
   μοῦνον ἀφ᾽ ἡμετέρων, Καισάριε, κτεάνων,
γηραλέων τοκέων πικρὸν λίθον· ὁ φθόνος οὕτως
   ἤθελεν. ὦ ζωῆς πήμασι μακροτέρης.
438

87.—*On the Parents of Gregory and Caesarius*

WE were ripe for the tomb, when the stone-cutters laid this stone here for our old age. But they laid it for us, and Caesarius, the last of our children, occupies it, not as was meet. My child, my child, we have suffered the greatest of misfortunes, but as soon as may be receive in thy tomb us who hasten to depart.

88.—*On Caesarius*

THIS stone was erected to be their own sepulchre by the parents who expected that they had but a small portion of life over ; but against their will they did a sad favour to their son Caesarius, since he departed this life before them.

89.—*On the Same*

MY old age lingered long on earth, and thou dearest of sons, Caesarius, occupiest the stone tomb in thy father's place. What law is this, what justice ? Lord of mortals, how didst thou consent thereto ?   O long life, O early death !

90.—*On the Same*

I DO not esteem, I do not esteem this gift.   Of all my possessions, Caesarius, thou hast got but a tomb, the melancholy stone tomb of thy old parents.   Thus did envy will.   O for our life rendered longer by sorrows !

91.—Εἰς τὸν αὐτόν

Πᾶσαν ὅση σοφίη λεπτῆς φρενὸς ἐν μερόπεσσιν
    ἀμφὶ γεωμετρίην καὶ θέσιν οὐρανίων,
καὶ λογικῆς τέχνης τὰ παλαίσματα, γραμματικήν τε
    ἠδ᾽ ἰητορίην, ῥητορικῆς τε μένος,
Καισάριος πτερόωντι νόῳ μοῦνος καταμάρψας,
    αἰαῖ· πᾶσιν ὅμως νῦν κόνις ἐστ᾽ ὀλίγη.

92.—Εἰς τὸν αὐτόν

Πάντα κασιγνήτοισιν ἑοῖς λίπες· ἀντὶ δὲ πάντων
    τύμβον ἔχεις ὀλίγον, κύδιμε Καισάριε·
ἡ δὲ γεωμετρίη τε, καὶ ἀστέρες ὧν θέσιν ἔγνως,
    ἤ τ᾽ ἰητορίη οὐδὲν ἄκος θανάτου.

93.—Εἰς τὸν αὐτόν

Κάλλιμον ἐκ πατρίης σὲ μεγακλέα τηλόθ᾽ ἐόντα,
    ἄκρα φέροντα πάσης, Καισάριε, σοφίης,
πέμψαντες βασιλῆϊ τὸν ἔξοχον ἰητήρων,
    φεῦ, κόνιν ἐκ Βιθυνῶν δεξάμεθ᾽ αὖ σε πέδου.

94.—Εἰς τὸν αὐτόν

Σεισμῶν μὲν κρυερῶν ἔφυγες στονόεσσαν ἀπειλήν,
    ἡνίκα Νικαίης ἄστυ μίγη δαπέδῳ·
νούσῳ δ᾽ ἀργαλέῃ ζωὴν λίπες. ὦ νεότητος
    σώφρονος, ὦ σοφίης, κάλλιμε Καισάριε.

95.—Εἰς τὸν αὐτόν

Γρηγορίου Νόννης τε θεουδέος υἷα φέριστον
    τύμβος ὅδ᾽ εὐγενέτην Καισάριον κατέχω,
ἔξοχον ἐν λογίοισιν, ὑπείροχον ἐν βασιλῆοις,
    ἀστεροπὴν γαίης πείρασι λαμπομένην.

440

91.—*On the Same*

CAESARIUS, who alone by his winged mind grasped the whole wisdom of man's subtle thought concerning geometry and the position of the heavenly bodies, and also the falls of the art of Logic, and Grammar too and Medicine and powerful Rhetoric, is now, alas! like all the rest, a handful of dust.

92.—*On the Same*

THOU didst leave all to thy brothers, noble Caesarius, and in place of all thou hast a little tomb. Geometry and the Stars whose positions thou knewest, and Medicine were no cure for death.

93.—*On the Same*

BEAUTIFUL Caesarius, widely famous, who hadst attained to the height of all wisdom, we sent thee, the first of physicians from thy country to the King, but received only thy ashes back from the Bithynian land.

94.—*On the Same*

THOU escapedst the roaring menace of the cruel earthquake when Nicaea was levelled with the ground, and didst perish by painful disease. O for thy chaste youth, and thy wisdom, lovely Caesarius!

95.—*On the Same*

This tomb holds noble Caesarius, the best son of Gregory and divine Nonna. He was excellent among the learned and of highest station at Court, flashing like lightning to the ends of the earth.

96.—Εἰς τὸν αὐτόι

Καισαρίου φθιμένοιο κατήφησαν βασιλῆος
   αὐλαί, Καππαδόκαι δ᾽ ἤμυσαν ἐξαπίνης·
καὶ καλὸν εἴ τι λέλειπτο μετ᾽ ἀνθρώποισιν ὄλωλεν,
   οἱ δὲ λόγοι σιγῆς ἀμφεβάλοντο νέφος.

97.—Εἰς τὸν αὐτόν

Εἴ τινα δένδρον ἔθηκε γόος, καὶ εἴ τινα πέτρην,
   εἴ τις καὶ πηγὴ ῥεῦσεν ὀδυρομένη,
πέτραι καὶ ποταμοὶ καὶ δένδρεα λυπρὰ πέλοισθε,
   πάντες Καισαρίῳ γείτονες ἠδὲ φίλοι·
Καισάριος πάντεσσι τετιμένος, εὖχος ἀνάκτων,
   (αἰαῖ τῶν ἀχέων) ἤλυθεν εἰς ἀΐδην.

98.—Εἰς τὸν αὐτόν

Χεὶρ τάδε Γρηγορίοιο· κάσιν ποθέων τὸν ἄριστον,
   κηρύσσω θνητοῖς τόνδε βίον στυγέειν.
Καισαρίῳ τίς κάλλος ὁμοίϊος; ἢ τίς ἀπάντων
   τόσσος ἐὼν τόσσης εἷλε κλέος σοφίης;
οὔτις ἐπιχθονίων· ἀλλ᾽ ἔπτατο ἐκ βιότοιο
   ὡς ῥόδον ἐξ ἀνθέων, ὡς δρόσος ἐκ πετάλων.

99.—Εἰς τὸν αὐτόν

Γείτονες εὐμενέοιτε καὶ ἐν κόλποισι δέχοισθε,
   Μάρτυρες, ὑμετέροις αἷμα τὸ Γρηγορίου,
Γρηγορίου Νόννης τε μεγακλέος, εὐσεβίη τε
   καὶ τύμβοις ἱεροῖς εἰς ἓν ἀγειρομένους.

96.—*On the Same*

When Caesarius died the Emperor's court was dejected and all Cappadocia bent her head straightway. If aught of good was left among men, it is gone, and learning is clouded in silence.

97.—*On the Same*

If mourning made any one into a tree or a stone, if any spring ever flowed as the result of lament,[1] all Caesarius' friends and neighbours should be stones, rivers and mournful trees. Caesarius, honoured by all, the vaunt of princes (alas for our grief!) is gone to Hades.

98.—*On the Same*

This is the hand of Gregory. Regretting my best of brothers, I proclaim to mortals to hate this life. Who was like Caesarius in beauty, or who was so great and so celebrated for wisdom? None among mortals; but he took wing from life, like a rose from the flowers, like dew from the leaves.

99.—*On the Same*

Ye neighbour martyrs, be kind and receive in your bosom the blood [2] of Gregory, of Gregory and famous Nonna, gathered together by their piety in this holy tomb.

---

[1] The allusions are to Niobe, to the daughters of Phaethon and to Byblis.　　[2] Presumably the children.

100.—Εἰς τὸν αὐτὸν καὶ εἰς Φιλάγριον

Κλῦθι, Ἀλεξάνδρεια· Φιλάγριος ὤλεσε μορφὴν
  τῆς λογικῆς ψυχῆς οὔτι χερειοτέρην,
Καισάριον δὲ νέον φθόνος ἥρπασεν· οὔποτε τοῖα
  πέμψεις εὐίπποις ἄνθεα Καππαδόκαις.

101.—Εἰς Γοργόνιον τὴν ἑαυτοῦ ἀδελφήν

Γρηγορίου Νόννης τε φίλον τέκος ἐνθάδε κεῖμαι
  Γοργόνιον, ζωῆς μύστις ἐπουρανίης.

102.—Εἰς Γοργόνιον

Οὐδὲν Γοργόνιον γαίῃ λίπεν, ὀστέα μοῦνα·
  πάντα δ᾽ ἔθηκεν ἄνω, Μάρτυρες ἀθλοφόροι.

103.—Εἰς τὴν αὐτὴν καὶ εἰς Ἀλύπιον τὸν αὐτῆς ἄνδρα

Κτῆσιν ἐὴν σάρκας τε καὶ ὀστέα πάντ᾽ ἀναθεῖσα
  Γοργόνιον Χριστῷ, μοῦνον ἀφῆκε πόσιν·
οὐ μὰν οὐδὲ πόσιν δηρὸν χρόνον· ἀλλ᾽ ἄρα καὶ τὸν
  ἥρπασεν ἐξαπίνης κύδιμον Ἀλύπιον.
ὄλβιε ὀλβίστης ἀλόχου πόσι· τοῖς ῥα λοετροῖς   5
  λύματ᾽ ἀπωσάμενοι ζῆτε παλιγγενέες.

104.—Ἐπιτάφιον εἰς Μαρτινιανόν

Εἴ τις Τάνταλός ἐστιν ἐν ὕδασιν αὖος ἀπίστοις,
  εἴ τις ὑπὲρ κεφαλῆς πέτρος ἀεὶ φοβέων,
δαπτόμενόν τ᾽ ὄρνισιν ἀγήραον ἧπαρ ἀλιτροῦ,
  καὶ πυρόεις ποταμός, καὶ ζόφος ἀθάνατος,
ταρτάρεοί τε μυχοὶ καὶ δαίμονες ἀγριόθυμοι,   5
  ἄλλαι τε φθιμένων τίσιες εἰν ἀΐδι·
ὅστις Μαρτινιανὸν ἀγακλέα δηλήσαιτο
  τύμβον ἀνοχλίζων, δείματα πάντα φέροι.

444

100.—*On the Same and Philagrius*

LISTEN, Alexandria, Philagrius has lost his beauty, a beauty not inferior to his rational soul, and envy hath carried off Caesarius yet in his youth. Never again shalt thou send such flowers to Cappadocia, the land of beautiful horses.

101.—*On his Sister Gorgonion*

HERE I lie Gorgonion the dear child of Gregory and Nonna, a partaker in the mysteries of life eternal.

102.—*On the Same*

YE triumphant martyrs, Gorgonion left naught but her bones on earth. She dedicated all on high.

103.—*On the Same and her Husband Alypius*

GORGONION having dedicated to Christ her possessions, her flesh, her bones, and everything, left her husband alone, yet not for long, but Christ carried off suddenly glorious Alypius too. Happy husband of a most happy wife, ye live born again, having washed off all filth in the baptismal bath.

104.—*On Martinianus*

IF there be any Tantalus dry-throated in the deceitful waters, if any rock above his head ever frightening him, if any imperishable liver of a sinner that is a feast for birds, if there be a fiery river and eternal darkness and depths of Tartarus and savage demons, and other punishments of the dead in Hades, may whoever injures renowned Martinianus by disturbing his tomb, suffer every terror.

105.—Κατὰ τυμβωρύχου

Οὔρεά σοι καὶ πόντος, ἀτάσθαλε, καὶ πεδίοισι
τέρπῃ πυροφόροις τετραπόδων τ᾽ ἀγέλαις·
καὶ χρυσοῖο τάλαντα καὶ ἄργυρος, εὐγενέες τε
λᾶες καὶ σηρῶν νήματα λεπταλέα,
πάντα βίος ζωοῖσι· λίθοι δ᾽ ὀλίγοι τε φίλοι τε   5
τοῖς φθιμένοις. σὺ δέ μοι κἀνθάδε χεῖρα φέρεις,
οὐδὲ σὸν αἰδόμενος, τλῆμον, τάφον, ὅν τις ὀλέσσει
ἄλλος σοῖσι νόμοις, χερσὶ δικαιοτέραις.

106.—Εἰς Μαρτινιανόν

Ἡνίκα Μαρτινιανὸς ἔδυ χθόνα, μητέρα πάντων,
πᾶσα μὲν Αὐσονίων ἐστονάχησε πόλις·
πᾶσα δὲ Σικανίη τε, καὶ εὐρέα πείρατα γαίης
κείρατ᾽, ἀπ᾽ ἀνθρώπων οἰχομένης Θέμιδος.
ἡμεῖς δ᾽ ἀντί νυ σεῖο τάφον μέγαν ἀμφιέποντες,   5
αἰὲν ἐπερχομένοις δώσομεν ὥς τι σέβας.

107.—Εἰς τὸν αὐτόν

Οἱ Χριστὸν φορέοντες ἀκούσατε, οἵ τε θέμιστας
εἰδότες ἡμερίων καὶ φθιμένων ὁσίην·
πάντα λιπών, βασιλῆα, πάτρην, γένος, εὖχος
ὑπάρχων,
αἰαῖ, πᾶσιν ὁμῶς νῦν κόνις εἰμ᾽ ὀλίγη,
Μαρτινιανὸς πᾶσι τετιμένος· ἀλλ᾽ ἐπὶ τύμβῳ   5
βάλλειν ἡμετέρῳ δάκρυα, μὴ παλάμας.

105.—*Against the Violator of a Tomb* [1]

IMPIOUS man, thou hast the sea and the mountains and rejoicest in possession of fields rich in corn and herds of cattle, yea and talents of gold and silver and precious stones and the silk-worm's delicate threads. To the living everything is valuable, but to the dead only their little but beloved grave-stones ; and thou layest hold of them too, not even reverencing thine own tomb, which some other will destroy after thy example, but with juster hands.

106.—*On Martinianus*

WHEN Martinianus went under Earth the mother of all, every city in Italy groaned and all Sicily and the broad boundaries of the land shore the head, for Themis had departed from among mortals. But we, tending on thy great tomb instead of thee, will hand it on an object of reverence to future generations.

107.—*On the Same*

LISTEN, ye who bear Christ, and ye who know the laws of living men and the respect due to the dead. Leaving all, King, country, family, I Martinianus, honoured by all, the pride of Prefects, am now, alas, like all mankind, but a handful of dust. But on my tomb shed tears and lay not hands on it.

---

[1] As all the epitaphs on Martinianus imply that his tomb was in danger of violation, this one is probably likewise meant for him.

GREEK ANTHOLOGY

108.—Εἰς τὸν αὐτόν

Μουσοπόλον, ῥητῆρα, δικασπόλον, ἄκρον ἄπαντα,
τύμβος ὅδ᾽ εὐγενέτην Μαρτινιανὸν ἔχω,
ναύμαχον ἐν πελάγεσσιν, ἀρήιον ἐν πεδίοισιν·
ἀλλ᾽ ἀποτῆλε τάφου, πρίν τι κακὸν παθέειν.

109.—Εἰς τὸν αὐτόν

Μὴ πόλεμον φθιμένοισιν—ἅλις ζώοντες, ἀλιτροί—
μὴ πόλεμον φθιμένοις· Μαρτινιανὸς ἐγὼ
ταῦτα πάσιν ζώοις ἐπιτέλλομαι. οὐ θέμις ἐστὶν
τῶν ὀλίγων φθονέειν τοῖς φθιμένοισι λίθων.

110.—Εἰς τὸν αὐτόν

Ὦ Θέμι, τῆς πολλοῖσιν ἐγὼ νώμησα τάλαντα
ὦ φοβεραὶ ψυχῶν μάστιγες οὐχ ὁσίων·
οὗτος ἐμοῖσι λίθοισι φέρει στονόεντα σίδηρον·
οὗτος ἐμοί. φεῦ, φεῦ· ποῦ δὲ λίθος Σισύφου;

111.—Εἰς τὸν αὐτόν

Ὄλβιος, εὐγήρως, ἄνοσος θάνον, ἐν βασιλῆος
πρῶτα φέρων, ἱερῆς ἄκρον ἔχων σοφίης·
εἴ τινα Μαρτινιανὸν ἀκούετε· ἀλλ᾽ ἀπὸ τύμβου,
μηδὲ φέρειν ἐπ᾽ ἐμοὶ δυσμενέας παλάμας.

112.—Εἰς τὸν αὐτόν

Χάζεο, χάζεο τῆλε· κακὸν τὸν ἄεθλον ἐγείρεις,
λᾶας ἀνοχλίζων καὶ τάφον ἡμέτερον·
χάζεο· Μαρτινιανὸς ἐγώ, καὶ ζῶσιν ὄνειαρ
καὶ νέκυς οὐκ ὀλίγον ἐνθάδε κάρτος ἔχω.

108.—*On the Same*

THIS tomb holds noble Martinianus, an orator, a judge, excelling in everything, a brave warrior at sea, valiant on land. But keep far from his tomb, lest thou suffer some evil.[1]

109.—*On the Same*

WAR not with the dead (the living are enough for you, ye evil-doers), war not with the dead. This I enjoin on all men. It is not right to grudge the dead their little stones.

110.—*On the Same*

O THEMIS, in whose scales I weighed justice for many, O dread scourgers of impious souls! This man attacks my grave-stones with wretched iron, this man dares do this to me! Alas! Alas! where is Sisyphus' rock?[2]

111.—*On the Same*

BLESSED, in ripe old age, without disease I died. Heard ye never of Martinianus of high rank in the palace, supreme in sacred wisdom? But away from my tomb and lay not hostile hands on me.

112.—*On the Same*

AWAY, far away! It is an evil exploit ye attempt, heaving up the stones of my tomb. Away! I am Martinianus. The living I benefited and here dead I have no little power.

[1] He is addressing the man who contemplates violating the tomb. [2] See Homer, *Odyss.* xi. 593.

449

113.—Εἰς τὸν αὐτόν

Καππαδοκῶν μέγ' ἄεισμα, φαάντατε Μαρτινιανέ,
σεῖο, βροτῶν γενεή, καὶ τάφον αἰδόμεθα·
ὅς ποτ' ἔης βασιλῆος ἐν ἕρκεσι κάρτος ὑπάρχων,
δουρὶ δὲ Σικανίην κτήσαο καὶ Λιβύην.

114.—Εἰς τὸν αὐτόν

Ὄμνυμεν ἀθανάτοιο θεοῦ κράτος ὑψιμέδοντος,
καὶ ψυχὰς νεκύων, κύδιμε, σήν τε κόνιν,
μήποτε, Μαρτινιανέ, τεοῖς ἐπὶ χεῖρας ἐνέγκαι
στήλῃ καὶ τύμβῳ· οὐδὲ γὰρ οὐδ' ἱεροῖς.

115.—Εἰς τὸν αὐτόν

Ῥώμη καὶ βασιλῆες ἐμοὶ καὶ πείρατα γαίης
στῆλαι Μαρτινιανῷ, τὰς χρόνος οὐ δαμάσει·
ἀλλ' ἔμπης ὀλίγῳ περιδείδια, μή τι πάθῃσι,
τῷδε τάφῳ· πολλῶν οὐχ ὅσιαι παλάμαι.

116.—Εἰς τὸν αὐτόν

Μαρτινιανοῦ σῆμα μεγακλέος, εἴ τιν' ἀκούεις
Καππαδοκῶν Ῥώμης πρόθρονον εὐγενέων,
παντοίαις ἀρετῇσι κεκασμένον, ἀλλὰ κόνιν περ
ἁζόμενοι στήλην καὶ τάφον ἀμφιέπειν.

117.—Εἰς τὸν αὐτόν

Οὔποτ' ἐγὼ φθιμένοισιν ἐπέχραον, οὐδ' ἀπὸ τύμβων
ἔργον ἔγειρα, δίκην ὄμνυμι καὶ φθιμένους·
τοὔνεκα μηδ' ἐπ' ἐμοῖσι φέρειν λάεσσι σίδηρον·
εἰ δὲ φέροις, τὴν σὴν ἐς κεφαλὴν πεσέτω.
Μαρτινιανὸς ἐγὼ τάδε λίσσομαι· εἴ τις ἐμεῖο   5
κύδεός ἐστι χάρις, τύμβος ἀεὶ μενέτω.

113.—*On the Same*

Most distinguished Martinianus, great vaunt of Cappadocia, we mortals reverence thy tomb too, who wert once in the King's citadel, strong among Prefects, and didst conquer Sicily and Libya by thy arms.

114.—*On the Same*

We swear, famous Martinianus, by the power of eternal God who ruleth on high and by the souls of the dead and thy dust, that we will never lay hands on thy monument and tomb. We never indeed lay hands on holy things.

115.—*On the Same*

Rome[1] and my princes and the limits of the earth are the monuments of Martinianus which time shall not destroy. But yet I fear lest this little tomb may meet with some evil. Many have impious hands.

116.—*On the Same*

The tomb of renowned Martinianus. Heard ye never of the president of the noble Cappadocians in Rome, adorned with every virtue? But reverence even his dust and tend his monument and tomb.

117.—*On the Same*

I never insulted the dead or used tomb-stones for building, I swear by justice and the dead. Therefore bring no more iron to attack my stones, or if thou dost, let it fall on thy own head. It is I, Martinianus, who request this. If there be any gratitude for my glory, let my tomb remain for ever.

[1] *i.e.* Constantinople, here and below.

GREEK ANTHOLOGY

118.—Εἰς Λιβίαν τὴν γαμετὴν Ἀμφιλόχοι

Εἷς δόμος, ἀλλ' ὑπένερθε τάφος, καθύπερθε δὲ σηκός·
τύμβος δειμαμένοις, σηκὸς ἀεθλοφόροις·
καί ῥ' οἱ μὲν γλυκερὴν ἤδη κόνιν ἀμφεβάλοντο
ὡς σὺ μάκαιρα δάμαρ Ἀμφιλόχου, Λιβίη,
κάλλιμέ θ' υἱήων, Εὐφήμιε· τούσδ' ὑπόδεχθε,   5
μάρτυρες ἀτρεκίης, τοὺς ἔτι λειπομένους.

119.—Εἰς τὴν αὐτήν

Ὤφελες, ὦ Λιβία, ζώειν τεκέεσσι φίλοισιν·
ὤφελες ἄχρι πύλης γήραος ἐμπελάσαι·
νῦν δέ σε μοῖρ' ἐδάμασσεν ἀώριον, εἰσέτι καλήν,
εἰσέτι κουριδίοις ἄνθεσι λαμπομένην.
αἰαῖ· Ἀμφίλοχος δὲ τεὸς πόσις ἀντὶ δάμαρτος   5
ἐσθλῆς καὶ πινυτῆς τλήμονα τύμβον ἔχει.

120.—Εἰς τὴν αὐτὴν Λιβίαν

Αἰαῖ· καὶ Λιβίαν κατέχει κόνις. οὔποτ' ἔγωγε
ὠϊσάμην θνητὴν ἔμμεναι, εἰσορόων
εἶδος, μειλιχίην τε σαοφροσύνην τε γυναικός,
τοῖς φῦλον πασέων καίνυτο θηλυτέρων·
τοὔνεκα καὶ τοίῳ σε τάφῳ κύζηνε θανοῦσαν   5
σῶν τε τριὰς τεκέων καὶ πόσις Ἀμφίλοχος.

121.—Εἰς Εὐφήμιον καὶ Ἀμφίλοχον αὐταδέλφους

Ἦν δυὰς ἦν ἱερή, ψυχὴ μία, σώματα δισσά,
πάντα κασιγνήτω, αἷμα, κλέος, σοφίην,
υἱέες Ἀμφιλόχου, Εὐφήμιος Ἀμφίλοχός τε,
πᾶσιν Καππαδόκαις ἀστέρες ἐκφανέες.
δεινὸν δ' ἀμφοτέρους φθόνος ἔδρακε· τὸν μὲν ἄμερσε   5
ζωῆς, τὸν δ' ἔλιπεν ἥμισυν Ἀμφίλοχον.

118.—*On Livia, the Wife of Amphilochus*

THE building is one, but beneath is a tomb, above a chapel, the tomb for the builders, the chapel for the triumphant martyrs. And some of the builders have already put on sweet dust, like thee, Livia, blessed wife of Amphilochus, and thee, Euphemius loveliest of her sons. But, ye martyrs of truth, receive those who still survive.[1]

119.—*On the Same*

THOU shouldest have lived for thy dear children, Livia, thou shouldest have reached the gate of old age, but now Fate has overcome thee before thy time, still beautiful, still shining with the flower of youth. Alas! thy husband Amphilochus in place of a good and wise wife has but a wretched tomb.

120.—*On the Same*

ALAS! the earth holds Livia too. Never could I believe her to be mortal, when I looked on her beauty, her sweetness, her chastity, in all of which she surpassed the rest of her sex. Therefore on thy death thou hast been honoured by such a tomb at the hands of thy three children and thy husband Amphilochus.

121.—*On the Brothers Euphemius and Amphilochus*

IT was a holy pair, one soul in two bodies, brothers in everything, blood, fame, wisdom, the sons of Amphilochus, Euphemius and Amphilochus, conspicuous in the eyes of all Cappadocia. But Envy cast a terrible glance on both and depriving one of life, left Amphilochus, but half himself, behind.

---

[1] *i.e.* may they be buried in the same blessed place.

453

122.—Εἰς Εὐφήμιον

Ῥήτωρ ἐν ῥητῆρσιν, ἀοιδοπόλος δ' ἐν ἀοιδοῖς,
   κῦδος ἑῆς πάτρης, κῦδος ἑῶν τοκέων,
ἄρτι γενειάσκων Εὐφήμιος, ἄρτι δ' ἔρωτας
   ἐς θαλάμους καλέων, ὤλετο· φεῦ παθέων·
ἀντὶ δὲ παρθενικῆς τύμβον λάχεν, ἠδ' ὑμεναίων
   ἤματα νυμφιδίων ἦμαρ ἐπῆλθε γόων.

123.—Εἰς τὸν αὐτόν

Εἰκοσέτης πᾶσαν Εὐφήμιος, ὡς μίαν οὔτις,
   Ἑλλάδα κ' Αὐσονίην μοῦσαν ἐφιπτάμενος,
στράπτων ἀγλαΐῃ τε καὶ ἤθεσιν ἦλθ' ὑπὸ γαῖαν.
   αἰαῖ· τῶν ἀγαθῶν ὡς μόρος ὠκύτερος.

124.—Εἰς τὸν αὐτόν

Χρυσείης γενεῆς Εὐφήμιος ἦν ἔτι τυτθὸν
   λείψανον, εὐγενέτης ἤθεα καὶ πραπίδας,
μείλιχος, ἡδυεπής, εἶδος Χαρίτεσσιν ὁμοῖος·
   τοὔνεκα καὶ θνητοῖς οὐκ ἐπὶ δὴν ἐμίγη.

125.—Εἰς τὸν αὐτόν

Στράψε μέγ' ἀνθρώποις Εὐφήμιος, ἀλλ' ἐπὶ τυτθόν·
   καὶ γὰρ καὶ στεροπῆς οὐ μακρόν ἐστι σέλας·
στράψεν ὁμοῦ σοφίῃ τε καὶ εἴδεϊ καὶ πραπίδεσσιν·
   τὰ πρὶν Καππαδόκαις ἦν κλέα, νῦν δὲ γόος.

126.—Εἰς τὸν αὐτόν

Τίς; τίνος;—Ἀμφιλόχου Εὐφήμιος ἐνθάδε κεῖται,
   οὗτος ὁ Καππαδόκαις πᾶσι διὰ στόματος·
οὗτος ὃν αἱ Χάριτες Μούσαις δόσαν· οἱ δ' ὑμέναιοι
   ἀμφὶ θύρας· ἦλθεν δ' ὁ φθόνος ὠκύτερος.

122.—*On Euphemius*

EUPHEMIUS, an orator among orators, a poet among poets, the glory of his country, the glory of his parents, is dead, but just bearded, but just beginning to call the loves to his chamber. Alas for the misfortune! Instead of a virgin bride he possesses a tomb, and the day of wailing overtook the days of the bridal song.

123.—*On the Same*

EUPHEMIUS, but twenty years old, gathering the honey of both the Greek and Latin muse, as none else gathered that of either, in all the splendour of his beauty and virtue, is gone under earth. Alas, how swift is the death of the good!

124.—*On the Same*

EUPHEMIUS was a little relic of the golden age, noble alike in character and intellect, gentle, sweet of speech, beautiful as the Graces. Therefore he dwelt not long among mortals.

125.—*On the Same*

EUPHEMIUS shone bright among men, but for a brief season; for the flash of the lightning too is not long. He shone alike in learning, beauty and intellect. His qualities were once the glory and are now the lament of Cappadocia.

126.—*On the Same*

WHO, and whose son? Euphemius the son of Amphilochus lies here, he who was the talk of all Cappadocia, he whom the Graces gave to the Muses. The chanters of the bridal song were at his gate, but Envy came quicker than they.

127.—Εἰς τὸν αὐτόν

Ἔρνος ἀμώμητον, Μουσῶν τέκος, εἶαρ ἑταίρων,
καὶ χρύσεον Χαρίτων πλέγμα ἰοστεφέων,
ᾤχετο ἐκ μερόπων Εὐφήμιος· οὐδ᾽ ἔτ᾽ ἀνίσχεν,
αἰαῖ, σοῖς θαλάμοις πυρσὸς ὃν ἧψεν Ἔρως.

128.—Εἰς τὸν αὐτόν

Αἱ Χάριτες Μούσαισι· "Τί ῥέξομεν; οὐκέτ᾽ ἄγαλμα
χειρῶν ἡμετέρων Εὐφήμιος ἐν μερόπεσσιν."
χαὶ Μοῦσαι Χαρίτεσσιν· "'Επεὶ φθόνος ἐστὶν ἀλιτρός,
τόσσον ἔχοι· ἡμῖν δὲ τόδ᾽ ὅρκιον ἔμπεδον ἔστω,
μηκέτ᾽ ἀναστῆσαι τοῖον μερόπεσσιν ἄγαλμα."   5

129.—Εἰς τὸν αὐτόν

Κρῆναι καὶ ποταμοὶ καὶ ἄλσεα, καὶ λαλαγεῦντες
ὄρνιθες λιγυροὶ καλὸν ἐπ᾽ ἀκρεμόνων,
αὖραί τε μαλακὸν συρίγμασι κῶμα φέρουσαι,
καὶ κῆποι Χαρίτων εἰς ἓν ἀγειρομένων,
κλαύσατε. ὦ χαρίεσσ᾽ Εὐφημιάς· ὥς σε θανὼν περ   5
Εὐφήμιος κλεινὴν θῆκατ᾽ ἐπωνυμίην.

130.—Εἰς τὸν αὐτόν

Κάλλιμος ἠϊθέων Εὐφήμιος, εἴποτ᾽ ἔην γε·
κάλλιμος ἐν χώροις χῶρος ὅδ᾽ ἠλύσιος·
τοὔνεκεν εἰς ἓν ἄγερθεν· ἐπεὶ ζωὴν μὲν ἔλειψεν,
οὔνομα δ᾽ ἐν χώρῳ κάλλιπεν ἠγαθέῳ.

131.—Εἰς Ἀμφίλοχον

Ἦλθε κ᾽ Ἀμφιλόχοιο φίλον δέμας ἐς μέγα σῆμα,
ψυχὴ δ᾽ ἐς μακάρων ᾤχετ᾽ ἀποπταμένη.

127.—*On the Same*

EUPHEMIUS the faultless blossom, the son of the Muses, the spring of his comrades, the golden chaplet of the violet-crowned Graces, is gone from amongst men, and woe is me, the torch that love lit shone not on thy bridal chamber.

128.—*On the Same*

THE Graces to the Muses: "What shall we do? Euphemius the statue moulded by our hands is no longer among the living." And the Muses to the Graces: "Since Envy is so wicked, let her have this much, but let us swear a sure oath, never again to raise such a statue among men."

129.—*On the Same*

SPRINGS, rivers and groves, and singing birds that twitter sweetly on the branches, and breezes whose whistling brings soft sleep, and gardens of the linked Graces, weep. O charming Euphemias,[1] how Euphemius though dead has made thy name famous.

130.—*On the Same*

EUPHEMIUS was the most beautiful among the young men, if ever indeed there was such a one, and this Elysian place is most beautiful among places. Therefore were they united. He lost his life, but left his name to a lovely spot.

131.—*On Amphilochus*

AMPHILOCHUS' dear body has come too to the great tomb, but his soul flew away to the place of the

---

[1] The place where he was buried was called so.

πηοῖς πάντα πέπασσο, μακάρτατε· βίβλον ἐῴξας
πᾶσαν ὅση θνητῶν, κεἴ τις ἐπουρανίη.
γηραλέος φιλίην ὑπέδυς χθόνα· τέκνα λέλοιπας   5
κρείσσονα καὶ τοκέων· τὸ πλέον οὐ μερόπων.

132.—Εἰς τὸν αὐτόν

Ἄσμενος ἦ τε δάμαρτι καὶ υἱέι πάρθετο σῶμα
Ἀμφίλοχος, λιπαροῦ γήραος ἀντιάσας,
ὄλβιος, εὐγενέτης, μύθων κράτος, ἄλκαρ ἁπάντων,
πηῶν, εὐσεβέων, εὐγενέων, λογίων,
καὶ μύθοιο δοτὴρ περιώσιος. ἠνιδ᾽ ἑταίρων   5
σῶν ἑνός, ὦ φιλότης, γράμμ᾽ ἐπιτυμβίδιον.

133.—Εἰς τὸν αὐτόν

Ὦ μάκαρ᾽, ὦ ξυνὸν πενίης ἄκος, ὦ πτερόεντες
μῦθοι, καὶ πηγὴ πᾶσιν ἀρυομένη,
ἄσθματι πάντα λίπες πυμάτῳ· τὸ δ᾽ ἅμ᾽ ἕσπετο μοῦνον
ἔνθεν ἀειρομένῳ κῦδος ἀεὶ θαλέθον.
Γρηγόριος τάδ᾽ ἔγραψα, λόγῳ λόγον ὃν παρὰ σεῖο   5
Ἀμφίλοχ᾽, ἐξεδάην ἀντιχαριζόμενος.

134.—Εἰς τὸν αὐτόν

Ἀμφίλοχος τέθνηκεν· ἀπώλετο εἴ τι λέλειπτο
καλὸν ἐν ἀνθρώποις, ῥητορικῆς τε μένος,
καὶ Χάριτες Μούσαισι μεμιγμέναι· ἔξοχα δ᾽ αὖ σε
ἡ Διοκαισαρέων μύρατο πάτρα φίλη.

135.—Εἰς τὸν αὐτόν

Τυτθὸν μὲν πτολίεθρον, ἀτὰρ πολὺν ἀνέρα δῶκα
βήμασιν ἰθυδίκοις ἡ Διοκαισαρέων,
Ἀμφίλοχον· φθιμένῳ δὲ συνέφθιτο καὶ πυρόεσσα
ῥήτρη, καὶ πάτρης εὖχος ἀριστοτόκου.

blest. All thy possessions were thy kinsmen's, blessed among men.   Thou didst leave no book human or divine unopened.   In old age thou didst descend beneath the kind earth.   Thou hast left children even better than their parents.   More is not for mortals.

132.—*On the Same*

AMPHILOCHUS in ripe old age gladly went to lie beside his wife and son.   Happy he was, and noble, powerful of speech, the support of all—his relatives, the pious, the noble, the learned—lavish of excellent discourse.   Lo, my friend, the epitaph written by one of thy comrades.

133.—*On the Same*

O BLESSED man, O universal healer of poverty, O winged words, O fountain from which all drew, with thy last breath thou didst leave all that was thine, and alone thy eternal good fame followed thee when thou wast taken.   Gregory wrote this repaying thee by words for the skill of speech he learnt from thee.

134.—*On the Same*

AMPHILOCHUS is dead: if aught good were left among men it is gone, the force of eloquence is gone, the Muses mingled with the Graces and above all did thy dear native city Diocaesarea mourn for thee.

135.—*On the Same*

I, DIOCAESAREA, am a small town, but gave a great man, Amphilochus, to the Courts of Law.   With him perished the fire of oratory and the boast of his native city which his birth ennobled.

136.—Εἰς τὸν αὐτόν

Τὸν ῥήτρην πυρόεσσαν ἐπ' ἀντιπάλοισι φέροντα,
τὸν μέλιτος γλυκίω ἤθεα καὶ πραπίδας
Ἀμφίλοχον κατέχω τυτθὴ κόνις, ἔκτοθι πάτρης,
υἱέα Φιλτατίου Γοργονίας τε μέγαν.

137.—Εἰς τὸν αὐτόν

Ῥητῆρες, φθέγγοισθε· μεμυκότα χείλεα σιγῇ
Ἀμφιλόχου μεγάλου τύμβος ὅδ' ἀμφὶς ἔχω.

138.—Εἰς τὸν αὐτόν

Ἠρίον Ἀμφιλόχοιο μελίφρονος, ὅς ποτε ῥήτρῃ
πάντας Καππαδόκας καίνυτο καὶ πραπίσιν.

139.—Εἰς Νικομήδην

Οἴχεαι, ὦ Νικόμηδες, ἐμὸν κλέος· ἡ δὲ συνωρὶς
σῶν καθαρὴ τεκέων πῶς βίον ἐξανύσει;
τίς δὲ τέλος νηῷ περικάλλεΐ χεὶρ ἐπιθήσει;
τίς δὲ θεῷ πέμψει φρὴν τελέην θυσίην,
σεῖο, μάκαρ, μιχθέντος ἐπουρανίοισι τάχιστα;   5
ὦ γενεὴ τλήμων, οἷα πάθες, μερόπων.

140.—Εἰς τὸν αὐτόν

Δέρκεο καὶ τύμβον Νικομήδεος, εἴ τιν' ἀκούεις,
ὃς νηὸν Χριστῷ δειμάμενος μεγάλῳ,
αὐτὸν μὲν πρώτιστον, ἔπειτα δὲ τὴν περίβωτον
δῶκεν ἁγνὴν θυσίην παρθενίην τεκέων,
φέρτερον οὐδὲν ἔχων, ἱερεύς, γενέτης τε φέριστος.   5
τοὔνεκα καὶ μεγάλῃ ὦκα μίγη Τριάδι.

136.—*On the Same*

A LITTLE dust covers far from his native place Amphilochus the great son of Philtatius and Gorgonia, armed ever with fiery speech against his adversaries, but of a disposition and mind sweeter than honey.

137.—*On the Same*

SPEAK now, ye orators. This tomb contains the lips now closed of great Amphilochus.

138.—*On the Same*

THIS is the tomb of sweet-souled Amphilochus, who surpassed all Cappadocians in eloquence and intellect.

139.—*On Nicomedes*

THOU art gone, Nicomedes, my glory, and how shall the pure pair, thy children, pass their life? What hand shall finish the lovely church, and what mind shall render a perfect sacrifice to God, now that thou, blessed man, hast early joined the heavenly ones? O wretched race of mortals, what a misfortune is yours!

140.—*On the Same*

LOOK on the tomb of Nicomedes, if thou hast ever heard of him, who having built a temple to Great Christ, gave himself first and then the renowned virginity of his children a pure sacrifice to God, having no better to offer, the best of priests and fathers. Therefore he soon was united with the Great Trinity.

141.—Εἰς τὸν αὐτόν

Ὕστατος ἐς βίον ἦλθες ἀοίδιμον, ἀλλὰ τάχιστα
  ἔνθεν ἀνηέρθης· τίς τάδ' ἔνευσε δίκη;
Χριστὸς ἄναξ, Νικόμηδες, ὅπως σέο λαὸν ἄνωθεν
  ἰθύνοις τεκέων σὺν ἱερῇ δυάδι.

142.—Εἰς Καρτέριον ἑταῖρον τοῦ μεγάλου Γρηγορίου

Πῇ με λιπὼν πολύμοχθον ἐπὶ χθονί, φίλταθ' ἑταίρων,
  ἤλυθες ἀρπαλέως, κύδιμε Καρτέριε;
πῇ ποτ' ἔβης νεότητος ἐμῆς οἰήϊα νωμῶν,
  ἦμος ἐπ' ἀλλοδαπῆς μῦθον ἐμετρεόμην,
ὃς βιότῳ μ' ἔζησας ἀσαρκέϊ; ἦ ῥ' ἐτεόν σοι   5
  Χριστὸς ἄναξ πάντων φίλτερος, ὃν νῦν ἔχεις.

143.—Εἰς τὸν αὐτόν

Ἀστεροπὴ Χριστοῖο μεγακλέος, ἕρκος ἄριστον
  ἠϊθέων, ζωῆς ἡνίοχ' ἡμετέρης,
μνώεο Γρηγορίοιο, τὸν ἔπλασας ἤθεσι κεδνοῖς,
  ἣν ὅτε ἦν, ἀρετῆς κοίρανε Καρτέριε.

144.—Εἰς τὸν αὐτόν

Ὦ πηγαὶ δακρύων, ὦ γούνατα, ὦ θυέεσιν
  ἁγνοτάτοις παλάμαι Χριστὸν ἀρεσσάμεναι
Καρτερίου· πῶς λῆξεν ὁμῶς πάντεσσι βροτοῖσιν;
  ἤθελεν ὑμνοπόλον κεῖθι χοροστασίη.

145.—Εἰς τὸν αὐτόν

Ἥρπασας, ὦ Νικόμηδες, ἐμὸν κέαρ· ἥρπασας ὦκα
  Καρτέριον, τῆς σῆς σύζυγον εὐσεβίης.

141.—*On the Same*

LATE didst thou come to glorious life, but early wert thou taken thence. What justice so decreed? It was Christ the Lord, Nicomedes, so that from heaven thou mightest rule thy people together with the holy pair, thy children.

142.—*To Carterius, the comrade of Gregory the Great*

DEAREST of comrades, noble Carterius, how hast thou suddenly departed, leaving me full of cares on earth? How hast thou departed, thou who didst direct the rudder of my youth, when in a strange land I was composing verse, thou who wert the cause of my spiritual life. Of a surety Christ the Lord, who now is thine, is dearer to thee than all.

143.—*On the Same*

LIGHTNING of glorious Christ, best bulwark of youth, charioteer of my youth, remember Gregory whom thou didst mould in moral excellence once on a time, Carterius, lord of virtue.

144.—*On the Same*

O FOUNTS of tears, O knees, O hands of Carterius, that appeased Christ by most pure sacrifices. How like all mortals has he ceased to be? The choir there in heaven required a hymner.

145.—*On the Same*

THOU hast torn from me my heart, Nicomedes, thou hast carried off too soon Carterius, the partner of thy piety.

146.—Εἰς τὸν αὐτόν

Ὦ Ξώλων ζαθέων ἱερὸν πέδον, οἷον ἔρεισμα
σταυροφόρων κόλποις Καρτέριον κατέχεις.

147.—Εἰς Βάσσον τινὰ παρὰ λῃστῶν ἀποκτανθέντα

Βάσσε φίλος, Χριστῷ μεμελημένος ἔξοχον ἄλλων,
τῆλε τεῆς πάτρης λῃστορι χειρὶ δαμάσθης,
οὐδέ σε τύμβος ἔχει πατρώϊος· ἀλλὰ καὶ ἔμπης
πᾶσιν Καππαδόκεσσι μέγ' οὔνομα σεῖο λέλειπται,
καὶ στῆλαι παγίων μέγ' ἀμείνονες, αἷς ἐνιγράφθης·   5
Γρηγορίου τόδε σοι μνημήϊον, ὃν φιλέεσκες.

148.—Εἰς τὸν αὐτόν

Ὡς Ἀβραὰμ κόλποισι τεθεὶς ὑποδέχνυσο, Βάσσε,
σὸν τέκος ἀτρεκέως πνεύματι Καρτέριον·
αὐτὰρ ἐγών, εἰ καί σε τάφος σὺν πατρὶ καλύπτοι,
οὔποτ' ἀφ' ὑμετέρης στήσομ' ὁμοζυγίης.

149.—Εἰς Φιλτάτιον

Ἠίθεον μεγάλοιο μέγαν κοσμήτορα λαοῦ
χθὼν ἱερὴ κεύθω Φιλτατίοιο δέμας.

150.—Εἰς Εὐσέβειαν καὶ Βασίλισσαν

Εὐσέβιον, Βασίλισσα, μεγακλέες, ἐνθάδε κεῖνται,
Ξώλων ἠγαθέων θρέμματα χριστοφόρα,
καὶ Νόννης ζαθέης ἱερὸν δέμας. ὅστις ἀμείβεις
τούσδε τάφους, ψυχῶν μνώεο τῶν μεγάλων.

146.—*On the Same*

O HOLY soil of divine Xola, how strong a support of the Christians was Carterius whom thou holdest in thy bosom.

147.—*On Bassus who was slain by Robbers*

DEAR Bassus, the special darling of Christ, far from thy home thou hast fallen by the robber's hand; nor dost thou even rest in the tomb of thy fathers. But yet great is the name thou hast left in all Cappadocia. The columns[1] in which thy name is written are far better than solid ones. This is the memorial made for thee by Gregory whom thou lovedst.

148.—*On the Same*

RECEIVE, Bassus, as one lying in Abraham's bosom, Carterius, truly thy spiritual child. But I, though the tomb holds thee and thy father, will never desert your fellowship.

149.—*On Philtatius*

THIS holy earth covers the body of Philtatius, a youth who was the great ruler of a great people.

150.—*On Eusebia and Basilissa*

HERE lie the most noble Eusebia and Basilissa, Christian nurslings of lovely Xola, and also Nonna's holy body. Thou who passest these tombs, remember the great souls.

---

[1] The minds of men.

151.—Εἰς Ἑλλάδιον καὶ Εὐλάλιον αὐταδέλφους

Αἰεί σοι νόος ἦεν ἐς οὐρανόν, οὐδ᾽ ἐπὶ γαίης
  ἤρειδες χθαμαλῆς ἴχνιον οὐδ᾽ ὀλίγον·
τοὔνεκεν ὡς τάχος ἦλθες ἀπὸ χθονός· Εὐλάλιος δὲ
  σὴν κόνιν ἀμφιέπει σὸς κάσις, Ἑλλάδιε.

152.—Εἰς Ἑλλάδιον

Τὸν νεαρόν, Χριστῷ δὲ μέγαν, πολιόν τε νόημα,
  χῶρος ὅδ᾽ ἀθλοφόρων Ἑλλάδιον κατέχω·
οὐ νέμεσις· κείνοις γὰρ ὁμοίϊον ἄλγος ἀνέτλη,
  σβεννὺς ἀντιπάλου τοῦ φθονεροῖο μόθον.

153.—Εἰς τὸν αὐτόι

Μικρὸν μὲν πνείεσκες ἐπὶ χθονὶ σαρκὸς ἀνάγκη,
  πλείονα δὲ ζωῆς ὑψόθι μοῖραν ἔχεις,
Ἑλλάδιε, Χριστοῖο μέγα κλέος· εἰ δὲ τάχιστα
  δεσμῶν ἐξελύθης, τοῦτο γέρας καμάτων.

154.—Εἰς Γεώργιον

Καὶ σὺ Γεωργίοιο φίλον δέμας, ἐνθάδε κεῖσαι,
  ὃς πολλὰς Χριστῷ πέμψας ἁγνὰς θυσίας·
σὺν δὲ κασιγνήτῃ σῶμα, φρένας, ἡ Βασίλισσα
  ξυνὸν ἔχει μεγάλη καὶ τάφον ὡς βίοτον.

155.—Εἰς Εὐπράξιον

Χώρης τῆσδ᾽ ἱερῆς Εὐπράξιον ἀρχιερῆα
  ἠδ᾽ Ἀριανζαίη χθὼν μεγάλη κατέχω,
Γρηγορίοιο φίλον καὶ ἥλικα, καὶ συνοδίτην·
  τοὔνεκα καὶ τύμβου γείτονος ἠντίασεν.

151.—*On the Brothers Helladius and Eulalius*

THY mind was ever in heaven, nor didst thou set foot at all on this low earth.   Therefore very early hast thou gone from earth, and Eulalius thy brother tends thy dust, Helladius.

152.—*On Helladius*

THIS burial place of the martyrs holds Helladius young in years, but great in Christ and grey in thought.   This is no profanation, for he suffered pains like theirs, extinguishing the attack of his envious adversary.

153.—*On the Same*

FOR a little season by the necessity of the flesh thou didst breathe on earth, but above a greater share of love is thine, Helladius, great glory of Christ.   If thou wast early released from thy bonds, this was the reward of thy labours.

154.—*On George*

AND thou dost lie here also, dear body of George, who didst render many pure sacrifices to Christ, and Basilissa the great, thy sister in body and spirit shares thy tomb as she shared thy life.

155.—*On Eupraxius*

THIS great land of Arianza contains the body of Eupraxius, high priest of the holy country, the friend and contemporary and fellow-traveller of Gregory. Therefore he lies buried near at hand.

156.—Εἰς Ναυκράτιον τὸν ἀδελφὸν τοῦ μεγάλου Βασιλείοι

Ἰχθυβόλον ποτ' ἔλυε λίνον βυθίης ἀπὸ πέτρης
  Ναυκράτιος, δίναις ἐν ποταμοῦ βρυχίαις·
καὶ τὸ μὲν οὐκ ἀνέλυσεν· ὁ δ' ἔσχετο· πῶς ἁλιῆα
  εἴρυσεν ἀνθ' ἁλίης δίκτυον, εἰπέ, λόγε,
Ναυκράτιον, καθαροῖο βίου νόμον, ὥσπερ ἔϊσκω,   5
  καὶ χάριν ἐλθέμεναι καὶ μόρον ἐξ ὑδάτων.

157.—Εἰς τὸν αὐτόν

Ναυκράτιος στροφάλιγγι θάνε φθονεροῦ ποταμοῖο,
  δεσμοῖσιν βυθίης ἄρκυος ἐνσχόμενος·
ὣς κε μάθῃς σύ, θνητέ, τὰ παίγνια τοῦδε βίοιο,
  ἔνθεν ἀνηέρθη πῶλος ὅδ' ἄκρα θέων.

158.—Εἰς τὸν αὐτόν

Ναυκράτιος πλεκτοῖο λίνου δεσμοῖσιν ἐλυσθείς,
  δεσμῶν τοῦδε βίου ἐξ ἁλίης ἐλύθη.

159.—Εἰς Μαξέντιον

Αἵματος εὐγενέος γενόμην, βασιλῆος ἐν αὐλαῖς
  ἔστην, ὀφρὺν ἄειρα κενόφρονα. πάντα κεδάσσας,
Χριστὸς ἐπεί με κάλεσσε, βίου πολλαῖσιν ἀταρποῖς
  ἴχνος ἔρεισα πόθοιο τινάγμασιν, ἄχρις ἀνεῦρον
τὴν σταθερήν· Χριστῷ τῆξα δέμας ἄλγεσι πολλοῖς·   5
  καὶ νῦν κοῦφος ἄνω Μαξέντιος ἔνθεν ἀνέπτην.

160.—Εἰς τὸν αὐτὸν Μαξέντιον

Πάλλετ' ἐμοὶ κραδίη, Μαξέντιε, σεῖο γράφουσα
  οὔνομα, ὃς στυφελὴν ἦλθες ὁδὸν βιότου,
ἄμβροτον, αἰπήεσσαν, ἀτερπέα· σεῖο, φέριστε,
  ἄτρομος οὐδὲ τάφῳ χριστιανὸς πελάει.

156.—*On Naucratius, the Brother of Basil the Great*

NAUCRATIUS was once freeing his fishing-net from a
sunken rock in the roaring eddies of the river.[1] The
net he did not free, but was caught himself. Tell
me, O Word, how the net landed the fisherman
Naucratius, an example of pure life, instead of fish.
As I conjecture, both grace and death came to him
from the water.

157.—*On the Same*

NAUCRATIUS died in the eddy of the envious river,
entangled in the toils of his sunken net, so that,
mortal, thou mayst know the tricks of this life, from
which this fleet-footed colt was removed.

158.—*On the Same*

NAUCRATIUS, caught in the fetters of his net, was
released from the fetters of this life by fishing.

159.—*On Maxentius*

I, MAXENTIUS, was born of noble blood; I stood in
the Emperor's Court, I was puffed up by vainglory.
But when Christ called me, throwing all to the
winds, I walked, stimulated by love for him, in many
ways of life, until I found the steadfast one. I
wasted my body for Christ by many hardships, and
now flew up lightly from here.

160.—*On the Same*

MY heart trembles as it writes thy name, Maxen-
tius, who didst traverse a hard road of life, a lonely
road, and steep and dismal. No Christian, O best of
men, approaches even thy tomb without trembling.

[1] The river Iris, as Gregory of Nyssa tells us. He was
fishing to provide food for his aged parents.

161.—Εἰς Ἐμμελίαν τὴν μητέρα τοῦ ἁγίου Βασιλείου

Ἐμμέλιον τέθνηκε· τίς ἔφρασεν; ἢ γε τοσούτων
  καὶ τοίων τεκέων δῶκε φάος βιότῳ,
υἱέας ἠδὲ θύγατρας ὁμόζυγας ἀζυγέας τε·
  εὔπαις καὶ πολύπαις ἤδε μόνη μερόπων.
τρεῖς μὲν τῆσδ᾽ ἱερῆες ἀγακλέες, ἡ δ᾽ ἱερῆος
  σύζυγος· οἱ δὲ πέλας ὡς στρατὸς εὐαγέων.

162.—Εἰς τὴν αὐτὴν Ἐμμελίαν

Θάμβος ἔχεν μ᾽ ὁρόωντα τόσον γόνον Ἐμμελίοιο
  καὶ τοῖον, μεγάλης νηδύος ὄλβον ὅλον·
ὡς δ᾽ αὐτὴν φρασάμην Χριστοῦ κτέαρ, εὐσεβὲς αἷμα,
  Ἐμμέλιον, τόδ᾽ ἔφην· "Οὐ μέγα· ῥίζα τόση."
τοῦτό σοι εὐσεβίης ἱερὸν γέρας, ὦ παναρίστη,
  τιμὴ σῶν τεκέων, οἷς πόθον εἶχες ἕνα.

163.—Εἰς Μακρίναν τὴν ἀδελφὴν τοῦ μεγάλου Βασιλείου

Παρθένον αἰγλήεσσαν ἔχω κόνις, εἴ τιν᾽ ἀκούεις
  Μακρίναν, Ἐμμελίου πρωτότοκον μεγάλης·
ἢ πάντων ἀνδρῶν λάθεν ὄμματα· νῦν δ᾽ ἐνὶ πάντων
  γλώσσῃ καὶ πάντων φέρτερον εὖχος ἔχει.

164.—Εἰς Θεοσέβιον ἀδελφὴν Βασιλείου

Καὶ σὺ Θεοσέβιον, κλεινῆς τέκος Ἐμμελίοιο,
  Γρηγορίου μεγάλου σύζυγε ἀτρεκέως,
ἐνθάδε τὴν ἱερὴν ὑπέδυς χθόνα, ἕρμα γυναικῶν
  εὐσεβέων· βιότου δ᾽ ὥριος ἐξελύθης.

161.—*On Emmelia, the Mother of St. Basil*

EMMELIA is dead; who would have thought it, she who gave to life the light of so many and such children, sons and daughters married and unmarried? She alone among mortals had both good children and many. Three of her sons were illustrious priests, and one daughter the wife of a priest, and the rest like an army of saints.

162.—*On the Same*

I MARVELLED when I looked on the great and goodly family of Emmelia, all the wealth of her mighty womb; but when I considered how she was Christ's cherished possession of pious blood I said this: " No marvel! The root is so great." This is the holy recompense of thy piety, thou best of women, the honour of thy children, with whom thou hadst one desire.

163.—*On Macrina, the Sister of St. Basil*

THE earth holds the glorious virgin Macrina, if ye ever heard her name, the first-born child of great Emmelia. She let herself be seen by no man, but is now on the tongues of all, and has glory greater than any.

164.—*On Theosebia, the Sister of St. Basil*

AND thou, Theosebia, child of noble Emmelia, and in very truth spouse of great Gregory, liest here in holy soil, thou stay of pious women. Ripe in years didst thou depart this life.

165.—Εἰς Γρηγόριον τῆς μητρὸς ἀδελφόν

Γρηγόριον μήτρως, ἱερεὺς μέγας, ἐνθάδ᾽ ἔθηκε
Γρηγόριος, καθαροῖς Μάρτυσι παρθέμενος,
ἠΐθεον, θαλέθοντα, νεόχνοον· αἱ δὲ πάροιθεν
τῆς γηροτροφίης ἐλπίδες ἤδε κόνις.

166.—Πρὸς τοὺς ἐν μαρτυρίοις τρυφῶντας

Εἰ φίλον ὀρχησταῖς ἀθλήματα, καὶ φίλον ἔστω
θρύψις ἀεθλοφόροις· ταῦτα γὰρ ἀντίθετα.
εἰ δ᾽ οὐκ ὀρχησταῖς ἀθλήματα, οὐδὲ ἀθληταῖς
ἡ θρύψις, πῶς σὺ Μάρτυσι δῶρα φέρεις
ἄργυρον, οἶνον, βρῶσιν, ἐρεύγματα; ἦ ῥα δίκαιος   5
ὃς πληροῖ θυλάκους, ἂν ἀδικώτατος ᾖ;

167.—Εἰς τοὺς αὐτούς

Μάρτυρες, εἴπατε ἄμμιν ἀληθῶς, εἰ φίλον ὑμῖν
αἱ σύνοδοι; τί μὲν οὖν ἤδιον; ἀντὶ τίνος;
τῆς ἀρετῆς· πολλοὶ γὰρ ἀμείνους ὧδε γένοιντ᾽ ἄν,
εἰ τιμῷτ᾽ ἀρετή. τοῦτο μὲν εὖ λέγετε.
ἡ δὲ μέθη, τό τε γαστρὸς ὑπάρχειν τοὺς θεραπευτὰς   5
ἄλλοις· ἀθλοφόρων ἔκλυσις ἀλλοτρία.

168.—Εἰς τοὺς αὐτούς

Μὴ ψεύδεσθ᾽ ὅτι γαστρὸς ἐπαινέται εἰσὶν ἀθληταί·
λαιμῶν οἵδε νόμοι, ὦ ᾽γαθοί, ὑμετέρων·
μάρτυσι δ᾽ εἰς τιμὴν ἓν ἐπίσταμαι· ὕβριν ἐλαύνειν
ψυχῆς καὶ δαπανᾶν δάκρυσι τὴν πιμελήν.

165.—*On Gregory, his Mother's Brother*

GREGORY the high priest, laid here his nephew Gregory, yet in the first bloom of youth, entrusting him to the pure martyrs. His former hopes of being tended by him in his old age are here turned to dust.

166.—*On those who feast luxuriously in the Churches of the Martyrs* [1]

IF the pains of martyrdom are dear to dancers, then let luxury be dear to the martyrs, for these two things are opposite. But if neither these pains are dear to dancers, nor luxury to the martyrs, how is it thou bringest as gifts to the martyrs, silver, wine, food, belching? Is he who fills that bag his body just, even if he be most unjust?

167.—*On the Same*

"TELL me, martyrs, truly, if ye love the meetings?" "What could be dearer to us?" "For the sake of what?" "Virtue, for if virtue were honoured, many men would become better." "Ye are right in this, but drunkenness and enslavement to the belly is for others. Dissipation is alien to the martyrs."

168.—*On the Same*

ASSERT not falsely that martyrs are commenders of the belly. This is the law of your gullets, good people. But I know one way of honouring the martyrs, to drive away wantonness from the soul, and decrease thy fatness by weeping.

---

[1] These meetings had of course a religious character to celebrate the festivals of the martyrs. What Gregory complains of is that festivals degenerated into festivities.

169.—Εἰς τοὺς αὐτούς

Μαρτύρομ', ἀθλοφόροι καὶ μάρτυρες· ὕβριν ἔθηκαν
  τιμὰς ὑμετέρας οἱ φιλογαστορίδαι.
οὐ ζητεῖτε τράπεζαν εὔπνοον, οὐδὲ μαγείρους·
  οἱ δ' ἐρυγὰς παρέχουσ' ἀντ' ἀρετῆς τὸ γέρας.

170.—Εἰς τοὺς αὐτοὺς καὶ κατὰ τυμβωρύχων

Τρισθανέες, πρῶτον μὲν ἐμίξατε σώματ' ἀνάγνων
  ἀθλοφόροις, τύμβοι δὲ θυηπόλον ἀμφὶς ἔχουσι·
δεύτερον αὖτε τάφους τοὺς μὲν διεπέρσατ' ἀθέσμως,
  αὐτοὶ σήματ' ἔχοντες ὁμοία· τοὺς δ' ἀπέδοσθε,
πολλάκι καὶ τρὶς ἕκαστον· ὁ δὲ τρίτον, ἱεροσυλεῖς   5
  μάρτυρας οὓς φιλέεις· Σοδομίτιδες ἤξατε πηγαί.

171.—Εἰς τοὺς αὐτοὺς καὶ κατὰ τυμβωρύχων

Παῖδες Χριστιανῶν τόδ' ἀκούσατε· οὐδὲν ὁ τύμβος·
  πῶς οὖν ὑμετέρους χώννυτ' ἀριπρεπέας;
ἀλλ' ἔστιν καὶ πᾶσι γέρας τόδε, μηδὲ τάφοισιν
  βάλλειν ἀλλοτρίοις δυσμενέας παλάμας.
εἰ δ' ὅτι μὴ νέκυς οἶδε τὰ ἐνθάδε, τοῦτ' ἀδίκαστον,   5
  πείθομαι, ἢν σὺ φέρῃς πατρὸς ὕβριν φθιμένου.

172.—Εἰς τοὺς αὐτοὺς καὶ κατὰ τυμβωρύχων

Τυμβολέται, γάστρωνες, ἐρευγόβιοι, πλατύνωτοι,
  μέχρι τίνος τύμβοις Μάρτυρας ἀλλοτρίοις
τιμᾶτ', εὐσεβέοντες ἃ μὴ θέμις; ἴσχετε λαιμούς,
  καὶ τότε πιστεύσω Μάρτυσιν ἦρα φέρειν.

169.—*On the Same*

I TESTIFY, ye martyrs. The belly-lovers have made your worship into wantonness. Ye desire no sweet-smelling table, nor cooks. But they honour you with belching rather than righteousness.

170.—*On the Same, and on Violators of Tombs*

THRICE worthy of death, first ye laid beside the martyrs the bodies of impure men, and their tombs contain the bodies of pagan priests. Secondly, ye wickedly destroyed some tombs, ye who have tombs like unto them; and others ye sold, often each tomb thrice. In the third place, ye are guilty of sacrilege to those martyrs whom ye love. Come, ye fiery founts of Sodom!

171.—*On the Same*

HEARKEN to this, ye sons of Christians. The tomb is nothing. Why, then, do ye make your tombs magnificent? But this reverence is due to all, not to lay hostile hands on the tombs of others. But if this should escape punishment, because the corpse does not feel what is done to it here, I agree, if thou canst put up with an outrage done to thy dead father.

172.—*On the Same*

DESTROYERS of tombs, gluttons who live but for belching, broad-backed, how long shall ye continue to honour the martyrs by the spoils of the tombs of others, with impious piety? Contain your greed, and then I will believe ye bring what is acceptable to the martyrs.

173.—Πρὸς τοὺς ἀπὸ τῶν ἐκ τάφων λίθων ναοὺς
οἰκοδομοῦντας

Τιμὴ Μάρτυσίν ἐστιν ἀεὶ θνήσκειν βιότητι,
  αἵματος οὐρανίου μνωομένους μεγάλου,
τύμβοι δὲ φθιμένοις· ὃς βήματα δ᾽ ἡμῖν ἐγείρει
  ἀλλοτρίοισι λίθοις, μηδὲ τάφοιο τύχοι.

174.—Πρὸς τοὺς ἐν μαρτυρίοις τρυφῶντας

Μάρτυρες, αἷμα θεῷ μεγάλην ἐσπείσατε λοιβήν,
  καὶ μέντοι θεόθεν ἄξια δῶρ᾽ ἔχετε,
βήμαθ᾽, ὕμνους, λαούς, εὐχῶν σέβας. ἀλλ᾽ ἀπὸ
  τύμβων
φεύγετε, νεκροκόμοι, Μάρτυσι πειθόμενοι.

175.—Πρὸς τοὺς αὐτούς

Δαίμοσιν εἰλαπίναζον, ὅσοις τὸ πάροιθε μεμήλει
  δαίμοσιν ἦρα φέρειν, οὐ καθαρὰς θαλίας·
τούτου Χριστιανοὶ λύσιν εὕρομεν, ἀθλοφόροισι
  στησάμεθ᾽ ἡμετέροις πνευματικὰς συνόδους.
νῦν δέ τι τάρβος ἔχει με· ἀκούσατε οἱ φιλόκωμοι·
  πρὸς τοὺς δαιμονικοὺς αὐτομολεῖτε τύπους.

176.—Κατὰ τυμβωρύχων

Μηκέτι πηκτὸν ἄροτρον ἀνὴρ ἐπὶ γαῖαν ἐλαύνοι,
  μὴ πέλαγος πλώοι, μὴ δόρυ θοῦρον ἔχοι·
ἀλλὰ φέρων σκαπάνην τε καὶ ἄγριον ἐν φρεσὶ θυμόν,
  ἐς τύμβους πατέρων χρυσὸν ἴοι ποθέων·
ὁππότε καὶ τοῦτόν τις ἐμὸν περικαλλέα τύμβον
  σκάψεν ἀτασθαλέων εἵνεκα κερδοσύνης.

173.—*To those who build Churches out of Stones taken from Tombs*

IT is paying honour to the martyrs always to die to life, remembering the great heavenly blood; but tombs are an honour to the dead. Let him who erects shrines to us out of the stones belonging to others lack himself a tomb.

174.—*On those who feast in Martyrs' Churches*

MARTYRS, ye poured your blood a great libation to God, and from God ye have fitting reward, shrines, hymns, congregations, the honour of prayers. But ye worshippers of the dead, do as the martyrs bid you, and keep away from tombs.

175.—*On the Same*

IN honour of the demons those who wished formerly to gain the favour of the demons celebrated impure banquets. This we Christians abolished, and instituted spiritual meetings for our martyrs. But now I am in some dread. List to me, ye revellers: ye desert us for the rites of devils.

176.—*On Violators of Tombs*

(*The remaining Epigrams are all on the same Subject*)

LET no man any longer drive a sturdy plough into the land; let him not sail the sea, nor bear a threatening spear, but with pickaxe and savage heart go to seek gold in the tombs of his fathers, now that some wicked man has dug up, for the sake of gain, this beautiful tomb of mine.

177.—Ἄλλο

Ἑπτὰ βίοιο πέλει τάδε θαύματα· τεῖχος, ἄγαλμα,
    κῆποι, πυραμίδες, νηός, ἄγαλμα, τάφος·
ὄγδοον ἔσκον ἔγωγε πελώριος ἐνθάδε τύμβος,
    ὑψιπαγής, σκοπέλων τῶνδ᾽ ἀποτῆλε θέων·
πρῶτος δ᾽ ἐν φθιμένοισιν ἀοίδιμος, ἔργον ἄπληστον   5
    τῆς σῆς, ἀνδροφόνε, μαινομένης παλάμης.

178.—Ἄλλο

Ἦν ὅτε ἦν ἀτίνακτος ἐγὼ τάφος οὔρεος ἄκρην
    πουλὺς ὑπερτέλλων τηλεφανὴς σκόπελος·
νῦν δέ με θὴρ ἐτίναξεν ἐφέστιος εἵνεκα χρυσοῦ·
    ὧδε δ᾽ ἐτινάχθην γείτονος ἐν παλάμαις.

179.—Κατὰ τυμβωρύχων

Τὸν τύμβοιο τόσου λῃστορα, ὃν πέρι πάντη
    λάων τετραπέδων ἀμφιθέει στέφανος,
ἄξιον αὐτίκ᾽ ἔην, αὐτῷ ἐνὶ σήματι θέντας
    αὖθις ἐπικλεῖσαι χάσματα δυσσεβέϊ.

180.—Κατὰ τυμβωρύχων

Ἔργον ἀλιτρὸν ὄπωπα, κεχηνότα τύμβον, ὁδεύων·
    χρυσοῦ ταῦτα πέλει ἔργματα τοῦ δολίου·
εἰ μὲν χρυσὸν ἔχεις, εὗρες κακόν· εἰ δ᾽ ἄρα κεινὸς
    ἔνθεν ἔβης, κενεὴν μήσαο δυσσεβίην.

181.—Εἰς τοὺς αὐτούς

Ὁσσάτιον παράμειψα βροτῶν βίον· οὐδ᾽ ἄρ᾽ ἔμελλον
    ἐκφυγέειν παλάμας γείτονος οὐλομένας,
ὅς με καὶ αἰπὺν ἐόντα χαμαὶ βάλε νηλέϊ θυμῷ,
    οὔτε θεὸν δείσας, οὔθ᾽ ὁσίην φθιμένων.

ᵇ (1) The wall of Babylon, (2) The statue of Zeus at

177

THESE are the seven wonders of the world: a wall, a statue, gardens, pyramids, a temple, another statue, a tomb.[1] The eighth was I, this vast tomb rising high above these rocks; and among the dead I am most celebrated, owing to the greed of thy furious hand, murderer.

178

I WAS once an undisturbed tomb, like a rock rising high above the mountain summit, and conspicuous from afar; but now a beast of my own house has destroyed me for the sake of gold, and thus I was demolished by the hands of my neighbour.

179

FOR the spoiler of so fine a tomb, with a cornice of squared stones all round it, it were a fitting fate to put him in the tomb, and close on the impious wretch the gaps he made.

180

As I journeyed I saw an impious thing, a gaping tomb. This is the work of deceitful gold. If thou didst find gold, thou hast acquired an evil, but if thou wentest away empty thou hast got thee empty impiety.

181

How long did I outlive the life of man! Yet it was not my fate to escape the destructive hands of my neighbour, who relentlessly cast me down, high as I was, fearing neither God nor the respect due to the dead.

Olympia, (3) the hanging gardens of Babylon, (4) the pyramids, (5) the temple of Diana at Ephesus, (6) the Colossus of Rhodes, (7) the Mausoleum.

182.—Εἰς τοὺς αὐτούς

Τὸν τύμβων κακοεργὸν ἀλάστορα φεύγετε πάντες·
  ἠνίδ' ὅσην σκοπιὴν ῥήξατο ῥηϊδίως·
οὐ μὲν ῥηϊδίως ἐρρήξατο· ἀλλ' ἀποτῆλε
  χάζεσθε· φθιμένους ὧδ' ἂν ἀρεσσάμεθα.

183.—Εἰς τοὺς αὐτούς

Αἰαῖ ὥς τι κακὸν προτιόσσομαι ἐγγύθεν ἤδη
  τοῖσί τε τυμβορύχοις, τοῖς τε περικτιόσιν,
σήματος ὑψιθέοντος ὀλωλότος· ἀλλὰ τὸν ἐχθρὸν
  οἶδε δίκη· δακρύειν δ' ἡμέτερον φθιμένους.

184.—Εἰς τοὺς αὐτούς

Μαυσωλοῦ τάφος ἐστὶ πελώριος, ἀλλὰ Κάρεσσι
  τίμιος· οὔτις ἐκεῖ τυμβολέτις παλάμη·
Καππαδόκεσσιν ἔγωγε μέγ' ἔξοχος, ἀλλὰ δέδορκας
  οἷα πάθον· στήλῃ γράψατε νεκροφόνον.

185.—Εἰς τοὺς αὐτούς

Τοῖχος ἐνὶ προπόδεσσι καὶ ὄρθιος· ἔνθεν ἔπειτα
  ὕπτιος, ἐκ λαγόνων εἰς ἓν ἀγειρομένων
τύμβος ἔην, καθύπερθε λόφου λόφος· ἀλλὰ τί ταῦτα;
  οὐδὲν χρυσοφίλαις οἵ μ' ἐτίναξαν ὅλον.

186.—Εἰς τοὺς αὐτούς

Νεκρῶν νεκρὰ πέλοι καὶ μνήματα· ὃς δ' ἀνεγείρει
  τύμβον ἀριπρεπέα τῇ κόνι, τοῖα πάθοι·
οὐ γὰρ ἂν οὗτος ἀνὴρ τὸν ἐμὸν τάφον ἐξαλάπαξεν,
  εἰ μὴ χρυσὸν ἔχειν ἤλπετο ἐκ νεκύων.

182

Avoid, all men, the wicked profaner of tombs. Lo! what a high tower has he broken down with ease; surely he has not easily broken it down; but retire far from him, and thus shall we please the dead.

183

Woe is me! I foresee some evil about to befall the profaners of tombs and the neighbours, now the lofty tomb has been destroyed. But Justice knows the enemy, and it is ours but to weep for the dead.

184

The tomb of Mausolus is vast, but the Carians honour it; there are no desecrating hands there. I was chief among the Cappadocians, but you see what I have suffered. Write on the stele the name of the murderer of the dead.

185

The lower courses of the tomb were perpendicular, but above this it was composed of four inclined flanks meeting in one. It was like a hill surmounting a hill. But what use was all this? It was nothing to the gold-seekers who demolished it entirely.

186

Let the monuments of the dead be dead too, and let him who erects a magnificent tomb to the dust meet with this fate. For that man would never have pillaged my tomb if he had not expected to get gold from the dead.

GREEK ANTHOLOGY

187.—Εἰς τοὺς αὐτούς

Τίς τίνος;   Οὐκ ἐρέει στήλη· πρὸ γὰρ ὤλετο τύμβου
    Τίς χρόνος;   Ἀρχαίης σῆμα τόδ᾽ ἐργασίης.
Τίς δέ σ᾽ ἐνήρατο; εἰπέ· φόνος τόδε. Χεῖρες ἀλιτραὶ
    γείτονος. Ὡς τί λάβῃ;   Χρυσόν.   Ἔχοι σκοτίην

188.—Εἰς τοὺς αὐτούς

Ὅστις ἐμὸν παρὰ σῆμα φέρεις πόδα, ἴσθι με ταῦτα
    τοῦ νεοκληρονόμου χερσὶ παθόντ᾽ ἀδίκως·
οὐ γὰρ ἔχον χρυσόν τε καὶ ἄργυρον, ἀλλ᾽ ἐδοκήθην,
    κάλλεϊ μαρμαίρων τοσσατίων λαγόνων.

189.—Εἰς τοὺς αὐτούς

Στῆθι πέλας, καὶ κλαῦσον ἰδὼν τόδε σῆμα θανόντος,
    εἴποτ᾽ ἔην, νῦν αὖτε τάφον δηλήμονος ἀνδρός·
σῆμα πέλω μὴ τύμβον ἐγείρειε βροτὸς ἄλλος.
    τί πλέον, εἰ παλάμαισι φιλοχρύσοισιν ὀλεῖται;

190.—Εἰς τοὺς αὐτούς

Αἰὼν καὶ κληῖδες ἀμειδήτου θανάτοιο,
    καὶ λήθη, σκοτίης βένθεα, καὶ νέκυες,
πῶς ἔτλη τύμβον τις ἐμὸν ἔπι χεῖρας ἐνεγκεῖν;
    πῶς ἔτλη; φθιμένων κήδεται οὐδ᾽ ὁσίη;

191.—Εἰς τοὺς αὐτούς

Τέτρωμαι πληγῇσιν ἀεικελίῃσιν ὁ τύμβος
    τέτρωμ᾽, ὥς τις ἀνὴρ ἐν δαΐ λευγαλέῃ.
ταῦτα φίλα θνητοῖσι; τὸ δ᾽ αἴτιον ὡς ἀθέμιστον·
    τὸν νέκυν οἷον ἔχων, χρυσὸν ἀποξέομαι.

482

187

" Who and whose son ? " " The slab will not tell you, for it perished before the tomb." " What is the date ? " " This is a tomb of old workmanship." " And who slew thee, for this is murder ? " " The criminal hands of my neighbour." " To get what ? " " Gold." " May he dwell in darkness."

188

Let whoever passes by my tomb be aware that I was injuriously treated by the new heir. I contained no gold and silver, but I looked as if I did so, glistening as I was with the beauty of so many faces.

189

Stand hard by and weep as ye look on this tomb of some dead man, if ever he existed, but which is now the tomb of an evil-doer. I am a monument proclaiming that none else should erect a tomb ; for what does it serve, if it is to perish by hands greedy of gold ?

190

Ages eternal, and locked portals of solemn death, and river of forgetfulness, and abysses of darkness, and ye dead, how did any man dare to lay hands on my tomb ? How did he dare ? Does not even religion protect the dead ?

191

I, the tomb, am wounded by shameful blows ; I am wounded like a man in the fierce battle. Is this what pleases mortals ? And how lawless the motive ! I contain but a corpse, and am stripped of my gold.

192.—Εἰς τοὺς αὐτούς

Πρός σε θεοῦ ξενίου λιτάζομαι, ὅστις ἀμείβεις
    τύμβον ἐμόν, φράζειν· "Τοῖα πάθοις ὁ δράσας."
οὐκ οἶδ' ὅντινα τύμβος ἔχει νέκυν· ἀλλ' ἐρέω γε
    δάκρυ' ἐπισπένδων· "Τοῖα πάθοις ὁ δράσας."

193.—Εἰς τοὺς αὐτούς

Πάντα λιπών, γαίης τε μυχοὺς καὶ πείρατα πόντου,
    ἦλθες ἔχειν ποθέων χρυσὸν ἐμοῦ νέκυος.
νεκρὸν ἔχω καὶ μῆνιν ὀλωλότος· ἤν τις ἐπέλθῃ,
    ταῦτ' εἰ λείζῃ, δώσομεν ἀσπασίως.

194.—Εἰς τοὺς αὐτούς

Εἴ σοι χρυσὸν ἔδωκα μόνῳ μόνος, οὐκ ἐφύλασσες
    τοῦθ' ὅπερ εἰλήφεις; ἢ κακὸς ἦσθ' ἂν ἄγαν.
εἰ δὲ τάφον σκάπτεις, τὴν αἰδέσιμον παραθήκην,
    καὶ τόδ' ἐπὶ χρυσῷ, ἄξιος, εἰπέ, τινος;

195.—Εἰς τοὺς αὐτούς

Τοὺς ζῶντας κατόρυσσε· τί γὰρ νεκροὺς κατορύσ-
        σεις;
ἄξιοί εἰσι τάφων, οἳ σὲ ζῆν εἴασαν οὕτω,
    τὸν τῶν οἰχομένων ὑβριστὴν καὶ φιλόχρυσον.

196.—Εἰς τοὺς αὐτούς

Καὶ σύ, τάλαν, παλάμῃσι τεαῖς ἢ μύστιν ἐδωδὴν
    δέξῃ θαρσαλέως, ἢ θεὸν ἀγκαλέσεις
χείρεσιν αἷς διόρυξας ἐμὸν τάφον; ἢ ῥα δίκαιοι
    οὐδὲν ἔχουσι πλέον, εἰ σὺ τάλαντα φύγοις.

192

" I beseech thee, who passest by my tomb, by that God who protects strangers to say, ' May the like befall thee who did it.' " " I know not who lies in the tomb, but shedding on it a tear I will say, ' May the like befall thee who did it.' "

193

Neglecting all else, the bowels of the earth and the uttermost seas, thou comest lusting to get gold from my corpse. I hold but a corpse and the wrath of the dead. If anyone attack me to rob me of these things I will give him them gladly.

194

If I had given thee gold without the cognisance of any, wouldest thou not have kept for me what thou didst receive? Otherwise thou wouldst have been very wicked. But if thou diggest up a tomb, a solemn trust, and this for the sake of gold, say of what art thou worthy?

195

Bury the living, for why dost thou bury the dead? They are worthy of burial, who thus allowed thee to live, insulter of the departed and luster after gold.

196

Wretch, shalt thou take boldly in thy hands the mystic food, or invoke God with those hands which broke into my tomb? The just, indeed, have no profit if thou dost escape the scales of Justice.

197.—Εἰς τοὺς αὐτούς

Φησὶ Δίκη· "Τίς πίστις, ὅτ᾿ ὤλεσας ὃν λαγόνεσσι
σῆσιν ἔδωκα, νέκυν, γαῖα φίλη, φθίμενον;"
"Οὐ γαίη μ᾿ ἐτίναξεν· ἀτάσθαλος ὤλεσεν ἀνήρ,
καὶ φιλοκερδείης εἵνεκα.   τοῦτον ἔχε."

198.—Εἰς τοὺς αὐτούς

Πρόσθε τάδ᾿ ἦεν ἄσυλα· θεός, νέκυς. ἀλλὰ θεὸς μὲν
ἵλαος· εἰ δὲ νέκυς, ὄψεθ᾿ ὁ τυμβολέτης.

199.—Εἰς τοὺς αὐτούς

Ἦ ῥά σε δινήσουσιν Ἐρινύες· αὐτὰρ ἔγωγε
κλαύσομ᾿ ἀποφθιμένους, κλαύσομ᾿ ἄγος παλάμης.

200.—Εἰς τοὺς αὐτούς

Λήξατε, τυμβοχόοι, ναὶ λήξατε βένθεσι γαίης
κεύθειν τοὺς φθιμένους· εἴξατε τυμβολέταις.
νεκρῶν καὶ τάδε γ᾿ ἐστὶ σοφίσματα, ὡς φιλόχρυσον
εὕρωσιν παλάμην, σήματα τοῖα χέειν.

201.—Εἰς τοὺς αὐτούς

Τίς σ᾿ ἀνέηκεν, ἄπληστε, τόσον κακὸν ἀντὶ τόσοιο
κέρδεος ἀλλάξαι, μηδὲ παρεσταότος;

202.—Εἰς τοὺς αὐτούς

Στῆλαι καὶ τύμβοι, μέγα χαίρετε, σήματα νεκρῶν·
οὐκέτι κηρύξω μνήμασι τοὺς φθιμένους,
ἡνίκα τὸν περίφαντον ἐμὸν τάφον ὤλεσε γείτων.
Γαῖα φίλη, σὺ δέ μοι δέχνυσο τοὺς φθιμένους.

197

QUOTH Justice, "What faith is there, since thou, dear earth, hast destroyed him whom I entrusted to thy womb?" "It was not the earth that disturbed me; a wicked man destroyed me, and for the sake of gain. Lay hold on him."

198

FORMERLY these two were inviolate, God and the dead. God is merciful, but the destroyer of tombs will see if the dead is or not.

199

THE Furies shall torture thee, but I will weep for the dead and for the guilt of thy hand.

200

CEASE, ye builders of tombs; yea, cease to hide the dead in the depths of the earth. Give way before the destroyers of tombs. This is a device[1] of the dead to erect such tombs in order that they may meet with a hand that lusts for gold.

201

WHO prompted thee, insatiable man, to exchange such a crime for such a gain, and that gain non-existent?

202

FAREWELL ye gravestones and tombs, the monuments of the dead! I will no longer proclaim the names of the dead on their tombs now that my neighbour has destroyed my handsome tomb. Dear Earth, I pray thee to receive the dead.

[1] The sense is obscure.

487

203.—Πρὸς τοὺς αὐτούς

Στῆλαι, καὶ πλακόεντες ἐν οὔρεσιν, ἔργα γιγάντων,
  τύμβοι, καὶ φθιμένων ἄφθιτε μνημοσύνη,
σεισμὸς πάντα βράσειεν, ἐμοῖς νεκύεσσιν ἀρήγων,
  οἷς ἔπι χεὶρ ὀλοὴ ἦλθε σιδηροφόρος.

204.—Πρὸς τοὺς αὐτούς

Ἡνίκα τὸν περίβωτον ἐπ᾽ οὔρεος, ἄγριε Τιτάν,
  τύμβον ἀνερρήξω, πῶς ἔσιδες νέκυας,
ὡς δ᾽ ἔσιδες, πῶς χεῖρες ἐπ᾽ ὀστέα; ἦ τάχα κέν σε
  τῇ σχέθον, εἰ θέμις ἦν τοῖσδ᾽ ἕνα τύμβον ἔχειν.

205.—Πρὸς τοὺς αὐτούς

Σήματα, καὶ σποδιή, καὶ ὀστέα, οἵ τε πάρεδροι
  δαίμονες, οἳ φθιμένου ναίετε τόνδε λόφον,
τόνδ᾽ ἀλιτρὸν τίννυσθε, ὃς ὑμέας ἐξαλάπαξεν.
  τῶν δὲ περικτιόνων δάκρυον ὕμμιν ὅσον.

206.—Κατὰ τυμβωρύχων

Τύμβοι, καὶ σκοπιαί, καὶ οὔρεα, καὶ παροδῖται,
  κλαύσατε τύμβον ἐμόν, κλαύσατε τυμβολέτην·
ἠχὼ δ᾽ ἐκ σκοπέλων πυματηγόρος ἀντιαχείτω
  τῶνδε περικτιόνων· " Κλαύσατε τυμβολέτην."

207.—Εἰς τοὺς αὐτούς

Κτείνετε, ληΐζεσθε, κακοὶ κακοκερδέες ἄνδρες·
  οὔτις ἐπισχήσει τὴν φιλοχρημοσυνην.
εἰ τάδ᾽ ἔτλης, κακοεργέ, κακόφρονος εἵνεκα χρυσοῦ,
  πᾶσι τεὴν ἐπέχειν ἁρπαλέην παλάμην.

203

YE gravestones and broad tombs in the hills, the work of giants, and thou eternal memory of the departed, may an earthquake shake you all to pieces, coming to the aid of my dead, whom the destructive hand, armed with the pick, attacks.

204

WHEN, savage Titan, thou didst break into the famous tomb on the hill, how didst thou dare to look on the dead, and, looking on them, how to touch the bones? Verily they would have caught thee and kept thee there, if it were permitted to thee to share their tomb.

205

TOMBS, and dust, and bones, and attendant spirits who dwell in this mound, take vengeance on the wicked man who pillaged you. How the neighbours weep for you '

206

TOMBS, and summits, and hills, and passers by, weep for my tomb and weep for its destroyer. And may echo, that repeats the last words, cry from these neighbouring hills, "Weep for the destroyer."

207

SLAY and plunder, ye evil men, lovers of filthy lucre; none will check your love of money. If thou hadst the courage to do this for the sake of evil-counselling gold, venture to lay thy rapacious hand on all things.

208.—Εἰς τοὺς αὐτούς

Οὗτος ἔπερσεν ἐμὸν φίλιον τάφον ἐλπίδι κούφῃ,
   ὃν μοῦνον κτεάνων ἔνθεν ἀπῆλθον ἔχων·
καὶ τοῦτόν τις ἀλιτρὸς ἑαῖς παλάμαις ὀλέσειεν,
   ἐκ δ᾽ ὀλέσας τύμβου τῆλε βάλοι πατέρων.

209.—Εἰς τοὺς αὐτούς

Τίς τὸν ἐμὸν διέπερσε φίλον τάφον, οὔρεος ἄκρης
   τῆσδ᾽ ἀναειρόμενον ἠλίκον ὀσσατίης;
χρυσὸς ἔθηξε μάχαιραν ἐπ᾽ ἀνδράσι· χρυσὸς ἄπ-
      ληστον
   κύμασι χειμερίοις ὤλεσε ναυσιβάτην·
κἀμὲ χρυσὸς ἔπερσε μέγαν περικαλλέα τύμβον   5
   ἐλπισθείς· χρυσοῦ δεύτερα πάντ᾽ ἀδίκοις.

210.—Εἰς τοὺς αὐτούς

Πολλάκι ναυηγοῖο δέμας κατέχωσεν ὁδίτης
   κύμασι πλαζόμενον, πολλάκι θηρολέτου·
ἤδη καὶ πολέμῳ τις ὃν ὤλεσεν· ἀλλ᾽ ἐμὲ γείτων
   χωσθέντ᾽ ἀλλοτρίαις χερσὶν ἔπερσε τάφον.

211.—Εἰς τοὺς αὐτούς

Ὦ χρυσοῦ δολίοιο, πόσον κακὸν ἔπλεο θνητοῖς·
   ζῶσιν καὶ φθιμένοις χεῖρα φέρεις ἀδικῶν·
οἷς γὰρ ἐμὸν τύμβον τε καὶ ὀστέα δῶκα φυλάσσειν,
   τῶνδ᾽ ὕπο ταῖς μιαραῖς ἐξολόμην παλάμαις.

212.—Εἰς τοὺς αὐτούς

Πάντ᾽ ἔθανεν νεκύεσσι. τι παίζομεν; οὔτις ἔτ᾽ αἰδὼς
   ἐκ ζώντων φθιμένοις· δέρκεο τόνδε τάφον,
ὅν γ᾽ ἐλπὶς χρυσοῖο διώλεσε, τόσσον ἐόντα
   θαῦμα παρερχομένοις, θαῦμα περικτίοσιν.

208

THIS man, in vain hope, pillaged my dear tomb, the only one of my possessions I carried away with me. Let some other sinner's hands destroy him in turn, and afterwards cast him afar from the tombs of his fathers.

209

WHO pillaged my dear tomb that rose so high above this mighty mountain summit? It is gold that sharpens the sword against the life of man, and gold makes the greedy navigator to perish in the wintry seas. I, too, this great and beautiful tomb, was pillaged in the hope of gold. All other things are second to gold in the eyes of the wicked.

210

MANY a traveller has buried the body of a ship-wrecked man found tossing on the waves, and many a one the body of a man slain by beasts. Often has an enemy buried him whom he slew in war, but my neighbour has pillaged this tomb not the work of his own hands.

211

O DECEITFUL gold, what an evil thou art for man! Thou raisest the hand of the wicked against both dead and living. For I perished by the accursed hands of those into whose care I bequeathed my tomb and bones.

212

ALL is dead for the dead. Why do we trifle? There is no shame left among the living for the dead. Look at this tomb, that was such a wonder to travellers and the neighbours, destroyed for the hope of gold.

213.—Εἰς τοὺς αὐτούς

Λίσσομαι· ἤν γε θάνω, ποταμῷ δέμας ἠὲ κύνεσσιν
ῥίψατε, ἠὲ πυρὶ δάψατε παντοφάγῳ·
λώϊον ἢ παλάμῃσι φιλοχρύσοισιν ὀλέσθαι.
δείδια, τόνδε τάφον τοῖα παθόνθ᾽ ὁρόων.

214.—Ἄλλο

Δήποτε Κῦρος ἄναξ βασιλήϊον ὡς ἀνέῳξεν
τύμβον ἐπὶ χρυσῷ, γράμμα τόδ᾽ εὗρε μόνον·
"Οἴγειν ἀπλήστοιο τάφους χερός." ὡς δὲ σὺ τόσσον
σῆμα τόδ᾽ οὐχ ὁσίαις οἶξας, ἄνερ, παλάμαις.

215.—Εἰς τοὺς αὐτούς

Ὃς κακὸς οὐ φθιμένοισι, τάχ᾽ ἂν φθιμένοισιν ἀρήγοι·
ὃς δ᾽ οὐδὲ φθιμένοις, οὔποτ᾽ ἂν οὐ φθιμένοις.
ὡς δὲ σὺ τοῖς φθιμένοισιν ἐπεὶ τάφον ἐξαλάπαξας,
οὔποτ᾽ ἂν οὐ φθιμένοις χεῖρα φέροις ὁσίην.

216.—Πρὸς τοὺς αὐτούς

Μαρτύρομ᾽· οὐδὲν ἔχω· πτωχὸς νέκυς ἐνθάδε κεῖμαι·
μή με τεαῖς ἀτίσῃς τυμβοφόνοις παλάμαις.
οὐδὲ γὰρ οὗτος ἔχεν χρυσὸν τάφος, ἀλλ᾽ ἐδαΐχθη·
πάντα φιλοχρύσοις ἔμβατα· φεῦγε Δίκη.

217.—Πρὸς τοὺς αὐτούς

Οἱ τύμβοι "Φθιμένοισιν ἀρήξατε" εἶπον ἅπαντες,
ἡνίχ᾽ ὁ λυσσήεις τόνδ᾽ ἐτίνασσε τάφον.
οἱ νέκυες τύμβοισι· "Τί ῥέξομεν; αὖθις ἀέρθη
ὡς ἐπὶ βουκτασίῃ γαῖαν ἀφεῖσα Δίκη."

213

I beseech ye, if I die, throw my body into a river or to the dogs, or consume it in the all-devouring fire. That is better than to perish by hands greedy of gold. I am in dread as I look on this tomb which has met with this fate.

214

King Cyrus once, when he opened a royal tomb for the sake of gold, found only this inscription: "To open tombs is the work of an insatiable hand." So hast thou opened this great tomb with impious hands (and in vain).

215

He who is evil to the living might, perhaps, help the dead, but who helps not the dead would never help the living. So thou, since thou hast plundered the tomb of the dead, wouldst never reach out a pious hand to the living.

216

I aver I have nothing; it is a poor corpse that lies here. Do me no injury with thy tomb-slaying hands. This tomb next me never had any gold in it, but yet it was plundered. All is accessible to gold-seekers. Fly from hence, Justice.

217

The tombs all cried " Help the dead !" when the furious spoiler was breaking up this tomb. The dead cry to the tombs, "What shall we do ? Justice has left the earth and flown up to heaven again, even as she did at the first slaying of oxen."

218.—Ὁμοίως

Ἦλυθεν εἰς Ἀΐδην τις· ὁ δ' ἔπτατο· ἄλλος ὄλεσσε
θῆρας· ὁ δὲ πλεκτὸν υἱέϊ τεῦξε δόμον·
τούτων οὗτος ἀνὴρ οὐ δεύτερον ἔργον ἔρεξεν,
τόνδε τάφον ῥήξας χείρεσιν οὐχ ὁσίαις.

219.—Πρὸς τοὺς αὐτούς

Εἰ τόσον ἔργον ἔγειρας ὀλωλότι, οὐ μέγα θαῦμα·
εἰ δὲ τόσον διέπερσας, ἀοίδιμος ἐσσομένοισιν·
καί σέ τις ἐν μεγάλοισιν ἀριθμήσει κακοεργοῖς,
τύμβον ἀναρρήξανθ', ὃν καὶ τρομέουσι φονῆες.

220.—Πρὸς τοὺς αὐτούς

Χρυσὸς μὲν Ῥοδίοισιν ἐπέκλυσε· σοὶ δ' ἀπὸ τύμβων
χρυσὸν φέρει σίδηρος, ὃς κακὸν φέρει·
ὄρυσσ' ὄρυσσε πάντας· ἦ τάχ' ἄν σέ τις
τύμβος κ' ἐξολέσειε πεσών, νεκύεσσι δ' ἀρήγοι.

221.—Εἰς τοὺς αὐτούς

Τύμβος ἔην· νῦν δ' εἰμὶ λίθων χύσις, οὐκέτι τύμβος.
ταῦτα φιλοχρύσοις εὔαδε· ποία δίκη.

222.—Ἄλλο

Αἰαῖ καὶ τέφρη γενόμην, καὶ χεῖρας ἀλιτρῶν
οὐκ ἔφυγον· χρυσοῦ τίπτε χερειότερον;

---

¹ It is not known to whom he alludes.
² In audacity.

218

ONE (Orpheus) descended to Hades, a second (Daedalus) flew, another (Heracles) slew beasts, another made a woven house for his son.[1] Not second[2] to those was the work of the man who broke down this tomb with his unholy hands.

219

IF thou didst erect such a structure to the dead it is naught to marvel at, but if thou didst destroy so great a work posterity shall celebrate thee, and thou shalt be reckoned among the great criminals in having broken down a tomb that made its very murderers tremble.

220

IT once rained gold on Rhodes,[3] and the iron that brings evil brings gold to thee from tombs. Dig them all up; perhaps some tomb will fall on thee and help the dead.

221

I WAS a tomb, but I am now a heap of stones no longer a tomb. Such was the pleasure of the violators. What justice is this!

222

ALAS! I was burnt to ashes and escaped not the hand of the wicked. What is worse than gold?

[3] Pindar's words (*Ol.* vii, 34) that Zeus " rained gold " on Rhodes were at least generally understood literally, whether he meant them to be so understood or not.

223.—Πρὸς τοὺς αὐτούς

Ἄζομαι ἀνδρομέης γενεῆς ὕπερ, εἴ σε τις ἔτλη,
τύμβε, χαμαὶ βαλέειν οὐχ ὁσίαις παλάμαις.

224.—Πρὸς τοὺς αὐτούς

Τύμβος ἐγώ, σκοπιή τις ἀπ᾽ οὔρεος· ἀλλά με χεῖρες
θῆκαν ἴσον δαπέδῳ· τίς τάδ᾽ ἄνωξε νόμος;

225.—Εἰς τοὺς αὐτούς

Οὗτος ἐμὸς δόμος ἦεν ὀλωλότος· ἀλλὰ σίδηρος
ἦλθ᾽ ἐπ᾽ ἐμῷ τύμβῳ· σὸν δόμον ἄλλος ἔχοι.

226.—Εἰς τοὺς αὐτούς

Τὴν σκαπάνην ἐπ᾽ ἄρουραν, ἐμῷ δ᾽ ἐπὶ σήματι
    βάλλειν
δάκρυα, μὴ παλάμας· ἥδε δίκη φθιμένων.

227.—Εἰς τοὺς αὐτούς

Τὴν σκαπάνην ἐπ᾽ ἄρουραν· ἐμοῦ δ᾽ ἀποχάζεο
    τύμβου,
χάζεο· οὐδὲν ἔχω πλὴν ζακότων νεκύων.

228.—Εἰς τοὺς αὐτούς

Εἴ σ᾽, ἄπληστε, τάφων δηλήμονα τοῖον ἐώλπειν,
πάσσαλος ἂν τῇδε καὶ τροχὸς ἐκρέματο.

229.—Εἰς τοὺς αὐτούς

Τίπτε μ᾽ ἀνοχλίζεις κενεὸν τάφον; ὀστέα μοῦνα
κεύθω καὶ σποδιὴν τοῖσιν ἐπερχομένοις.

223

I AM ashamed for the race of men if one ventured, O tomb, to cast thee down with unholy hands.

224

I WAS a tomb, a watch-tower on the mountain, but the hands of man laid me level with the ground. What law enjoined this?

225

THIS was my home after death, but iron attacked my tomb. May another possess thy home!

226

USE the mattock for husbandry, but on my tomb shed tears and lay no violent hands. That is justice to the dead.

227

USE the mattock for husbandry, but retire from my tomb. It contains naught but the wrathful dead.

228

IF I had known, thou man of greed, that thou wert such a destroyer of tombs, a stake and a wheel had hung here.

229

WHY dost thou disturb me, an empty tomb? I contain nothing for those who attack me but bones and dust.

230.—Εἰς τοὺς αὐτούς

Τύμβος ἐγώ, τύμβων πανυπέρτατος· ἀλλ' ἐμὲ ᾦξεν,
ὥς τινα τῶν πολλῶν, ἀνδροφόνος παλάμη·
ἀνδροφόνος παλάμη με διώλεσε· λήξατε τύμβων,
θνητοί, καὶ κτερέων.   δεῦτ' ἐπὶ νεκρά, κύνες·
δεῦτ' ἐπὶ νεκρά, κύνες.   χρυσοῦ διφήτορες ἄνδρες
ἤδη καὶ νεκύων χρυσολογοῦσι κόνιν.

231.—Εἰς τοὺς αὐτούς

Ἄλλος τύμβον ἔγειρε, σὺ δ' ὤλεσας· ἄλλος ἐγείροι
σὸν τάφον, εὖγε θέμις· ἄλλος ἔραζε βάλοι.

232.—Εἰς τοὺς αὐτούς

Ἤδη καὶ νεκύεσσιν ἐπέχραον οἱ φιλόχρυσοι·
φεύγετε ἐκ τύμβων, εἰ σθένος, οἱ φθίμενοι.

233.—Εἰς τοὺς αὐτούς

Τίπτε μ' ἀνοχλίζεις; νεκύων ἀμενηνὰ κάρηνα
μοῦνα φέρω· τύμβων ὀστέα πλοῦτος ἅπας.

234.—Εἰς τοὺς αὐτούς

Δαίμονας, οἵ με ἔχουσιν, ἀλεύεο· οὔτι γὰρ ἄλλο
τύμβος ἔχω· τύμβων ὀστέα πλοῦτος ἅπας.

235.—Εἰς τοὺς αὐτούς

Εἰ χρυσοῦ δόμος ἦεν ὅλος τάφος, ὦ φιλόχρυσε,
οὔποτ' ἔδει τοίην χεῖρα φέρειν φθιμένοις.

230

I am a tomb surpassing all other tombs in height, but murderous hands opened me as if I had been one of the many. Murderous hands destroyed me. Cease from building tombs and celebrating funerals, ye mortals. Come to the bodies, ye dogs! Come to the bodies, ye dogs! Seekers after gold gather gold now from the dust of the dead too.

231

Another man erected the tomb, and thou didst destroy it. Let another erect thy tomb, if Heaven permits it, and another lay it low.

232

Now the gold-seekers attack the dead, too. Fly from your tombs, ye dead, if ye have the strength.

233

Why dost thou heave up my stones? I contain naught but the feeble dead. The tomb's sole riches are bones.

234

Avoid the wrath of the spirits who haunt me, for I contain nothing else; the tomb's sole riches are bones.

235

If the whole tomb were built of gold, never, ye gold hunters, should ye thus have laid hands on the dead.

236.—Εἰς τοὺς αὐτούς

Λήθη καὶ σιγὴ νεκύων γέρας· ὃς δ' ἀλάπαξεν,
οὗτος ἐμὸν πολλοῖς θῆκεν ἄεισμα τάφον.

237.—Ὁμοίως

Πάντ' ἔχετε ζώοντες· ἐμοὶ δ' ὀλίγοι τε φίλοι τε
λᾶες τῷ φθιμένῳ· φείδεο τοῦ νέκυος.

238.—Πρὸς τοὺς αὐτούς

Οὐ χρυσοῦ δόμος εἰμί· τί τέμνομαι; αὐτὸς ἔγωγε
τύμβος, ὃν ὀχλίζεις· πλοῦτος ἐμοῦ νέκυες.

239.—Ὁμοίως

Τύμβος ἐγὼ κλέος ἦα περικτιόνων ἀνθρώπων·
νῦν δ' εἰμὶ στήλη χειρὸς ἀλιτροτάτης.

240.—Εἰς τοὺς αὐτούς

Εἰ λίην φιλόχρυσον ἔχεις κέαρ, ἄλλον ὀρύσσειν
χρυσόν· ἐμοὶ δ' οὐδὲν πλὴν φθιμένων κτερέων.

241.—Ὁμοίως

Μὴ δείξῃς μερόπεσσι γυμνὸν νέκυν, ἤ σε γυμνώσει
ἄλλος· ὁ δὲ χρυσὸς πολλάκις ἐστὶν ὄναρ.

242.—Εἰς τοὺς αὐτούς

Οὐχ ἅλις ἦε βροτοῖσι βροτοὺς ἐπὶ χεῖρας ἰάλλειν,
ἀλλὰ καὶ ἐκ νεκύων σπεύδετε χρυσὸν ἔχειν;

236

FORGETFULNESS and silence are the privileges of the dead.   But he who despoiled me has made my tomb a theme of song for many.

237

YE have all ye wish, ye living, but I, the dead, only my few dear stones.   Spare the dead.

238

I AM not a house of gold.   Why am I broken?   The tomb thou hackest to pieces is but a tomb.   All my wealth consists of corpses.

239

THIS tomb was the glory of the neighbouring peoples, but is now the monument of a most wicked hand.

240

IF thy hand lust too much for gold, dig up other gold.   I contain nothing but the remains of the dead.

241

SHOW not to men the naked corpse, or another shall strip thee.   Often gold is but a dream.

242

WAS it not enough for men to lay hands on men, but from the dead, too, ye strive to get gold?

243.—Ὁμοίως

Ὑμετέροις τύμβοισιν ἀρήξατε, οἱ τόδ᾽ ὁρῶντες
σῆμα δαϊχθὲν ὅσον. λεύσατε τυμβολέτην.

244.—Εἰς τοὺς αὐτούς

Τίς με τὸν ἐξ αἰῶνος ἀκινήτοισι λίθοισι
κευθόμενον θνητοῖς δεῖξε πένητα νέκυν;

245.—Ὁμοίως

Τίπτε τάφον διέκερσας ἐμόν, τάλαν ; ὡς διακέρσαι
σοί γε θεὸς βιοτήν, ὦ φιλόχρυσον ἄγος.

246.—Εἰς τοὺς αὐτούς

Μῦθος Τάρταρος ἦεν, ἐπεὶ τάφον οὐκ ἂν ἔῳξεν
οὗτος ἀνήρ· οἴμοι, ὡς βραδύπους σύ, Δίκη.

247.—Ὁμοίως

Ὡς βραδύπους σύ, Δίκη, καὶ Τάρταρος οὐκέτι δεινός·
οὐ γὰρ ἂν οὗτος ἀνὴρ τόνδ᾽ ἀνέῳξε τάφον.

248.—Εἰς τοὺς αὐτούς

Ὤμοσα τοὺς φθιμένους, καὶ ὤμοσα Τάρταρον αὐτόν,
μήποτε τυμβολέταις εὐμενὲς ὄμμα φέρειν.

249.—Ὁμοίως

Οὔρεα καὶ πρῶνες τὸν ἐμὸν τάφον ὥς τιν᾽ ἑταῖρον
κλαύσατε· πᾶς δὲ πέσοι τῷ σφε τεμόντι λίθος.

243

COME to the help of your tomb, ye who see this great tomb laid waste. Stone the despoiler.

244

WHO exhibited me to men, the poor corpse hidden for ages by undisturbed stones?

245

WHY hast thou, wretch, despoiled my tomb? So may God despoil thy life, accursed hunter after gold!

246

TARTARUS is, then, a myth, or this man would never have opened this tomb. Alas! Justice, how slow are thy feet!

247

How slow-footed art thou, Justice, and Tartarus is no longer a terror. Or else this man had not opened the tomb.

248

I SWORE by the dead, and by Tartarus itself, never to look with kind eyes on despoilers of tombs.

249

MOUNTAINS and hills, weep for my tomb as for a friend. Let every stone fall on him who broke into it.

250.—Εἰς τοὺς αὐτούς

Πλούσιός εἰμι πένης· τύμβῳ πολύς, ἔνδον ἄχρυσος·
ἴσθι καθυβρίζων νεκρὸν ἀσυλότατον.

251.—Ὁμοίως

Κἂν στῆς πυθμένος ἄχρις ἐμοὺς κευθμῶνας ὀρύσσων,
μόχθος σοὶ τὸ πέρας ὀστέα μοῦνον ἔχει.

252.—Εἰς τοὺς αὐτούς

Τέμνετε, τέμνετε ὧδε· πολύχρυσος γὰρ ὁ τύμβος
τοῖς ποθέουσι λίθους· τἆλλα δὲ πάντα κόνις.

253.—Ὁμοίως

Γαῖα φίλη, μὴ σοῖσι θανόνθ᾽ ὑποδέχνυσο κόλποις
τὸν τυμβωρυχίης κέρδεσι τερπόμενον.

254.—Ὁμοίως

Ὑβριστὴς ἐπ᾽ ἔμ᾽ ἦλθε τὸν οὐ ζώοντα σίδηρος·
καὶ χρυσὸν ποθέων εὗρε πένητα νέκυν.

250

I am a rich poor man, rich in my tomb, but within lacking gold. Know that thou insultest a corpse that hath no booty at all for thee.

251

Even if thou stayest digging up my recesses from the bottom, the end of all thy labour will be to find but bones.

252

Break, break here; the tomb is rich in gold to them who seek stones. Otherwise it hath but dust.

253

Dear Earth, receive not in thy bosom, when dead, the man who rejoices in gain gotten from breaking into tombs.

254

The profaning steel attacked me, the dead, and seeking for gold, found but a needy corpse.

INDEXES

GENERAL INDEX

The references, unless otherwise stated, are to Book VII

epit. = epitaph

509

GENERAL INDEX

GENERAL INDEX

Eresus in Lesbos, 407
Erichthonius, son of Hephaestus and father of Procne, 210
Erinna (v. Index of Authors), epit. on, 11–13; verses on a book of her poems, 713
Erinys, 188, 377, 745, VIII. 199
Eudoxus of Cnidus, astronomer, 4th century B.C., epit. on, 744
Eumolpus, mythical founder of Eleusinian mysteries, 615
Euphorion, father of Aeschylus, 39
Euripides, epit. on, 43–51
Eurotas, river in Laconia, 723
Eurymedon (battle of the, B.C. 466), epit. on fallen, 258
Eurypyle, flame of Anacreon, 27, 31
Euxine Sea, 510, 613

Gadara in Coelesyria, 417–419
Galen, 559
Gauls, 492
Gela in Sicily, 508
Gelas, river near above, 40
Gerania, mountain N of Isthmus of Corinth, 492
Germanicus, nephew of Tiberius, epit. on, 391
Glauce, Corinthian princess, 354
Gorgias, epit. on, 134

Haedi, setting of, dangerous for navigation, 272, 502, 640
Hebrus, river in Thrace, 542
Hector, epit. on, 137–140, 151, 152
Hecuba, 99
Helen of Troy, 218
Hellespont, 639
Hera, 773; marriage goddess, 188; temple of, at Paros, 351
Heraclea (uncertain which town of the name), 748
Heracles, VIII. 29, 218
Heraclides Ponticus, pupil of Plato and Aristotle, epit. on, 114
Heraclitus of Ephesus, epit. on, 79, 127, 128, 479
Heraclitus of Halicarnassus, elegiac poet, epit. on, 80
Hermes, infernal, 408, 545
Hero, v. Leander
Hesiod, epit. on, 52–55
Hipparchia, wife of the Cynic Crates, epit on ,413

Hippocrates, 559, 588; epit on, 135
Hipponax, iambic poet, 6th century B.C., epit. on, 405, 408, 536
Homer, 213; epit. on, 1–7
Hyades, setting of, unfavourable to navigation, 653
Hymenaeus, 188, 407, 547, 568, 653, 712
Hypatius, general under Justinian, 591, 592

Ialysus in Rhodes, 716
Ibycus, lyric poet, 6th century B.C., epit. on, 714, 745
Icaria, island, 499, 651, 699
Icos, small island near Scyros, 2
Idomeneus, Cretan leader in the *Iliad*, epit. on, 322
Ino, 303
Io (turned into a heifer by Hera), 169
Ionian Sea, 498, 624
Ios, Homer's tomb at, 1, 2
Issus, battle of, epit. on the fallen, 246

Julian, the emperor, epit. on, 747
Justinian, 592

Keys of Cyprus, small islands, 738

Lacydes, Peripatetic philosopher, epit. on, 105
Laertes, father of Ulysses, epit. on, 225
Lais, the famous courtesan, 222; epit. on, 218–220
Laodice, daughter of Priam, 564
Larissa, in Thessaly, 327, 528
Leander and Hero, epit. on, 666
Leonidas, King of Sparta, epit. on, 243, 344A, 437
Leonidas of Tarentum (v. Index of Authors), his epit on himself, 715
Lesbos, 501
Lethe, 498
Linus, mythical musician, epit. on, 616
Locri, in Italy, 718
Locris, Hesiod buried in, 55
Lycambes, daughters of, reviled by Archilochus, 69, 70, 71; epit. on, 351, 352

511

GENERAL INDEX

GENERAL INDEX

INDEX OF AUTHORS INCLUDED IN THIS VOLUME

M = Wreath of Meleager
Ph = Wreath of Philippus
Ag = Cycle of Agathias

(For explanation of these terms, v. Introduction to vol. 1. page v.)

INDEX OF AUTHORS

INDEX OF AUTHORS